CAMBRIDGE LIBRAR'

Books of enduring scho

Music

The systematic academic study of music gave rise to works of description, analysis and criticism, by composers and performers, philosophers and anthropologists, historians and teachers, and by a new kind of scholar - the musicologist. This series makes available a range of significant works encompassing all aspects of the developing discipline.

Singing for Schools and Congregations

John Curwen (1816–80), minister and music educationist, is remembered for his promotion in Britain of the tonic sol-fa system of teaching singing. He had an innate understanding of the social value of music in education, and it was in response to being asked in 1841 to recommend the best way of teaching music in Sunday schools that he developed Norwich schoolteacher Sarah Glover's system from her *Scheme for Rendering Psalmody Congregational* (1835). He would spend the rest of his life refining it. Not to be confused with John Hullah's 'fixed doh' system, Curwen's method spread rapidly and by the 1860s over 180,000 people in Britain were learning tonic sol-fa. First published in 1843 and reissued here in its revised and expanded edition of 1848, this thorough textbook sets out Curwen's method, complete with a wide range of exercises for class practice.

Singing for Schools and Congregations

A Grammar of Vocal Music,
with a Course of Lessons and Exercises
Founded on the Tonic Solfa Method,
and a Full Introduction
to the Art of Singing at Sight
from the Old Notation

JOHN CURWEN

CAMBRIDGE
UNIVERSITY PRESS

CAMBRIDGE
UNIVERSITY PRESS

University Printing House, Cambridge, CB2 8BS, United Kingdom

Published in the United States of America by Cambridge University Press, New York

Cambridge University Press is part of the University of Cambridge.
It furthers the University's mission by disseminating knowledge in the pursuit of
education, learning and research at the highest international levels of excellence.

www.cambridge.org
Information on this title: www.cambridge.org/9781108065191

© in this compilation Cambridge University Press 2013

This edition first published 1848
This digitally printed version 2013

ISBN 978-1-108-06519-1 Paperback

Singing for Schools and Congregations.

A

GRAMMAR OF VOCAL MUSIC,

WITH A COURSE OF LESSONS AND EXERCISES

FOUNDED ON

The Tonic Solfa Method,

AND A FULL INTRODUCTION TO

THE ART OF SINGING AT SIGHT

FROM THE

OLD NOTATION,

AND CONNECTED WITH "SCHOOL SONGS, SACRED, MORAL, AND DESCRIPTIVE," 3D.;
LARGE EDITION 6D.; "SCHOOL MUSIC," CONTAINING TUNES TO THE ABOVE, IN THREE PARTS, 1s.
AND "CHILDREN'S SCHOOL MUSIC," IN TWO PARTS, 4D.;
WHERE THE EXERCISES ARE GIVEN IN THE OLD NOTATION.

Edited by

JOHN CURWEN.

SECOND EDITION:

REWRITTEN AND GREATLY ENLARGED.

LONDON:

T. WARD AND CO. PATERNOSTER ROW.

PRICE HALF-A-CROWN.

SCHOOL MODULATOR.

f^1
m^1

r^1

d^1
te
$f'i$—
lah
ne
'soh
——tu_1
fah
me

ray

doh
t_1
$f'i_1$—
l_1

s_1
——tu_2
f_1
m_1

r_1

d_1

PROXIMATE MEASUREMENT
OF THE
COMMON MODE,
OR PERFECT SCALE.

DOH¹
..
..
..
..
TE
..t
..
....fi
..
..
..
..
..
LAH
..
..
..
..
....ne
..
SOH
..
..
..
....tu
..
..
..
FAH
..
..
..
ME
..
..
..
..
....nu
..
..
RAY
..r
..
..
..
..
....ni
..
..
DOH
See p. 40, 49, 64.

GREAT TONE 9 deg. SMALL TONE 8 deg. TONULE 5 deg. GREAT TONE 9 deg. SMALL TONE 8 deg. GREAT TONE 9 deg. TONULE 5 deg.

Places of the "accidentals." The lower position of TE and RAY (p. 40) is marked by the grave accent.

COMPLETE MODULATOR.

$\eth^1$	f^1	
t	m^1	l
ℓ	r^1	s
$\flat$	d^1	f
	t	m
$\int$ —		
u	l	r
	ne	
r	s	d
		— t_1
$\eth$	f	
t_1	m	l_1
		nu
ℓ_1	r	s_1
ni		
$\flat_1$	d	f_1
	t_1	m_1
$\int_1$ —		
u_1	l_1	r_1
r_1	s_1	d_1
		t_2
$\eth_1$	f_1	
t_2	m_1	l_2
ℓ_2	r_1	s_2
$\flat_2$	d_1	f_2

Table of Contents.

N.B. References are given to other parts of the book when the subject is further illustrated or developed. "See q." refers to the "questions and tests of progress" at the end of each "Stage."

Index to the Tunes and Songs.

b

N.B.—See Indexes to Songs and Tunes in "School Songs," and "School Music," but not in Solfa Exercises, p. 146 and 152.

Introduction.

PURPOSE AND ORIGIN OF THIS WORK.

The title, "Singing for Schools and Congregations," briefly describes the purpose of this work, and marks the boundary of its sphere. Although, by virtue of simple and truthful notation, it is enabled to carry pupils much further into the mysteries of musical science than is usual in elementary books, it does not profess to be a guide to the highest refinements of the theatre, the concert hall, or the drawing room. Its mission is to aid in making music a familiar, useful, and beloved companion among the people. It would enter their schools of childhood, and endear, by the charms of music, cheerful and holy sentiments. It would visit their homes, when labour is done, and awake the happy fire-side harmony. It would enable " all the people," in the house of God, to unite in the song of joy and praise, and show that what God has enjoined as a duty, is truly within the power of all to perform. The following statement of the editor's personal connection with this subject, quoted chiefly from a lecture delivered to the teachers of the Home and Colonial School Society, (July 8th, 1846), will illustrate his aim and account for his earnestness.

My own connexion with the system has arisen in this wise. I am one who is deeply interested in the education of children. About eight years ago, I became anxious to teach a number of them, then under my charge, to sing, chiefly with the design of making them love the Sunday school. Having no natural advantages of ear or voice, I sought help. I learnt a few tunes, and with the assistance of a friend, taught them to the children. We had 200 children for two hours twice a week. By dint of loud singing, we carried the voices of the children with us, and taught them many tunes. We endeavoured, most strenuously, also, to give them a knowledge of crotchets and quavers, and flats and sharps, and clefs, hoping thereby to give some permanence to the fruits of our labour; but this was in vain. We succeeded, however, in producing most delightful results for the time, although they extended not beyond the particular tunes which we had taught with extreme labour. I remember a husbandman telling me that, before the singing-school was established, he was constantly grieved by hearing little children, as they wandered along the lanes and by the hedge-rows, disputing, quarrelling, and swearing, but now he heard, instead, nothing but sweet singing of hymns, of which they seemed never to be tired.

For myself, all this while, I could neither pitch a well-known tune properly, nor by any means ' make out' from the notes the plainest psalm-tune which I had not heard before. To obtain that moderate ability was the height of my musical ambition. I therefore sought a private teacher who, with the help of a piano, drummed much *practice* into me, but no independent *power*. I could *run* in the ' go-cart,' but I could not take a step alone. I remember being often told that I did not mark correctly the ' half-tones' (between the 3rd and 4th, and 7th and 8th) of the scale, and I thought, if those same ' half tones' were but marked plainly on the music before me, how gladly and earnestly I would strive to mark them with my voice. But, as it was, I was continually afraid of these ' half-tones.' I knew that they were on the staff before me somewhere, but I could not see them. They lay concealed, but dangerous to tread upon, like a snake in the grass.

No sooner had I, with great pains, taught my ear an interval, than I found, frequently, the very next example of what *seemed* the same, to be quite a different thing by *half a tone!* I longed for some plan by which these puzzling deceivers might be *named* and *detected* with equal facility in all their shifting abodes on the staff.

Some time after this, Mrs. Read, of Hackney, kindly lent me the book describing Miss Glover's system. ("Scheme for rendering Psalmody Congregational"—London, Hamilton.) 'Well,' said I, after a cursory glance, 'if the old notation is puzzling, I am sure this is more puzzling far,' and I laid the book aside. But having occasion again to teach children, I thought proper to give it a more careful perusal, and was persuaded to study the science of music itself in the best works I could obtain, especially those of Dr. Callcott and Mr. Graham. I soon found that the old methods of teaching had deceived me with the shell of knowledge instead of giving me its kernel. The *thing*, music, I perceived to be very different from its names and signs. I found it much more simple and easy in itself, and incomparably more beautiful than the mere explanation of the signs of the old notation, with which elementary books are commonly filled. I had easily mastered them all, and had also studied a 'first book' on harmony, but I seemed to have known nothing of music till then. I now saw that Miss Glover's plan was to teach, first, the simple and beautiful *thing*, MUSIC, and to delay the introduction to the ordinary antiquated mode of writing it, until the pupil had obtained a mastery of the thing itself. Her method was, beyond all controversy, more deeply established on the principles of the science than any other; and, by giving it a fair trial on myself, and on a little child who lived in the same house, I became convinced that it was also the most simple of all—the most easy to teach, and the most easy to learn. The methods of teaching which are truest to the nature of the thing taught, and the least artificial, are always the most successful. In the course of a fortnight, I found myself, *mirabile dictu!* actually at the height of my previous ambition, being able to 'make out' a psalm tune from the notes, and to pitch it myself!! It was the untying of the tongue—the opening of a new world of pleasure. A visit to the school under Miss Glover's patronage at Norwich confirmed my impressions. As I ascended the stairs, the sound of the infants' voices was like that of a musical box for softness, sweetness, and accuracy of tone. I heard there, canons in four, six, and eight parts; and after an hour's singing, I found that the little voices had not flattened at the end of a long tune, by so much as half a tone.

About that time (the autumn of 1841) I was called to attend a meeting of ministers, Sunday school teachers, and the friends of Sunday schools, connected with various denominations, at Hull. Much was said on the present state of Congregational Psalmody, and on the importance of introducing some *simple method* to the churches, which should enable all to sing, with *ease* and *propriety*, the praises of God as their hearts should bid them. I was there commissioned, and in some degree pledged, in connection with another gentleman, to give attention to this subject. I regarded the object as a worthy and a sacred one, and, as opportunities were given, did not scruple to bestow upon it much earnest study and thoughtful practice. This meeting suggested a series of Lessons on Singing, which were published in a periodical in the year 1842. The cessation, for a season, from higher duties, gave leisure for testing the method and promoting its use more fully—first, by teaching two classes, one of adults, the other of children, and making records and observations of each day's progress—next, by explaining the plan and learning the opinions of intelligent men in various parts of the country—and lastly, by preparing (in the spring of 1843,) the first edition of "Singing for Schools and Congregations." After six years more of experience in bible classes, schools, and congregations—aided by correspondence with some of the most philosophical musicians, and by intercourse with intelligent educationalists, as well as by many criticisms both friendly and adverse, another edition, rewritten and greatly enlarged, is presented to the public. May it be the means of rendering yet more popular, and yet more widely known, the excellent Method to which I have referred. I am quite willing that you should think me in earnest; for I believe that this method, which we owe to a lady's invention and skill, is destined to make the delightful art of music both commonly understood and easily practised—to aid the joy of thousands, and to cause our psalmody to be once more the voice of the people.

INFLUENCE OF MUSIC AND POETRY IN EDUCATION.

"Most persons say, that the only purpose of music is to amuse; but this is a profane, an unholy language. To look on music as mere amusement cannot be justified. Music which has no other aim, must neither be considered of value, nor worthy of reverence." (Plato, as quoted in Dr. Mainzer's "Music and Education.") Thus spake the ancient sage; and his opinion is shared by those who are striving to spread music among the people in the present day. The music, for which we contend, is linked with poetry, and employed to carry to the heart some cheerful sentiment, some lofty thought, or some ennobling emotion. The importance, to education, of music thus understood, cannot well be overrated. It occupies ground, in some degree peculiar to itself—ground which it is very important to occupy rightly in these times. Some advantages it brings to physical, and many, when rightly studied, to intellectual education; but it displays its chief power on the field of æsthetics, morals, and religion. In æsthetic education it unites with the art of drawing, and the study of the finest models of literature, to develope the love of whatsoever is orderly, suitable, harmonious, beautiful, and sublime. This is a branch of education which the defenders of truth cannot, in these days, well afford to neglect. In moral education it joins with poetry, to *win the attention* of youth, by the innocent beguilement of their united charms, to truths and duties too often not otherwise attractive. By the same means it *delays* the attention on these truths, and, moreover, secures for them the irresistible power which belongs to *constant reiteration*. It possesses also that mighty sympathetic influence, which the simple *expression of feelings* carries with it to the heart of a child, whose interest has been gained. We beguile him to utter, in the voice of pleasant song, the language of some good emotion or some noble sentiment, and, almost insensibly, he is won to join in the feelings he finds so pleasant to express. This is a power which is felt by us all, and which is greater than many arguments to the child. That which the teacher's moral *lesson* has explained and enforced, the moral *song* shall impress on the memory and endear to the heart. In a similar manner do music and poetry contribute their aid in directly religious education. They impress more deeply truths already taught; they give a language to the faith, and hope, and love, and joy, of youthful piety; they elevate the mind; and help to raise the heart to God. None but the heartless or the unwise can doubt the power for good or evil which poetry and music are constantly exerting on education, or fail to see the importance of earnest study and watchful care, that this power may be well applied. Further illustrations of this power, and the mode of its application, may be found in the following notes.

In PHYSICAL EDUCATION the careful recitation of poetry, which is essential where Vocal Music is rightly taught, occupies a place by no means unimportant. It promotes the right use of the organs of voice, and helps to improve the enunciation. Its measured rhythm gives time for a clear and distinct delivery of syllables, and favours the acquirement of a more telling and effective elocution. (See p. 108.) The power of easy, correct, and agreeable speaking is a most important and delightful accomplishment for the poor as well as the rich.

Singing, as well as the useful practice of reading aloud, promotes a healthy action of the lungs and of the muscles of the chest, most important in a country where consumption lurks for its prey. It is ascertained by statistics that the professions of Public Singer and of Public Speaker are more favourable to long life than any other. Music is well known to possess a direct, though unexplained, influence on the human nerves. It soothes the weary or the excited frame. It promotes the health by recreating the mind. And not the least of its educating advantages is this, that it oftentimes preoccupies and redeems hours of leisure, which might otherwise have become hours of idleness or sin. Mr. Hickson states that the love of song has proved, among the German people, a very powerful antagonist to the drinking customs which formerly prevailed. How good for body and mind is the song round the cottage hearth, when the hours of labour are over! God has made our cheapest pleasures to be our best and purest.

In INTELLECTUAL EDUCATION, Music, studied on the method described in this book, will bear no unworthy part. It will cultivate the habit of Attention and the powers of Perception and Imitation, and it will teach, by example, "how to Observe" in Musical Phenomena, and how to Reason upon them. Every subject should be so taught as to improve the pupil's thinking powers, and music gives better scope than is usually supposed for such an exercise.

The habit of learning poetry, which must always accompany the *extended* and *varied* use of vocal music, has a direct tendency, especially where there is an able master, to promote a correct knowledge and a good usage of words—most important helps to Intellectual Education. One who was both a poet and a philosopher, defined poetry to be—"the best thoughts in the fittest words." It may be easily noticed that nearly all children speak well who have been in the constant habit of repeating poetry with any degree of propriety.

The same practice, when properly directed, helps to refine the imagination, and to train it to useful purposes. That noble power has its humbler offices in common life which are of utmost value. It teaches us, when rightly cultivated, to *associate* good thoughts and kindly feelings with the ordinary incidents of every day. It makes "the best of everything." It has been said to "oil the wheels of life's chariot on this jolty road." It gladdens, by associations of contentment and love, even the poor man's board with truest festive joy. It adorns his cottage home with hues of peace and happiness. It makes "the dear familiar face" grow, to us all, more beautiful with age. It throws on all things the glow of a cheerful affectionate mind. What teacher will not find even his own mind elevated and refined while he traces, with his children, the imagery, brightening with every word, of the lines (School Songs, 160) beginning,

"Triumphal arch, that fill'st the sky
When storms prepare to part;"

or "pictures" that beautiful image of childhood's piety—(School Songs, 22)—a gentle lovely morning star, bathed in the light of heavenly favour—

"A star of early dawn, and bright,
Shining within thy sacred light."

Who would not rejoice to have the mind of his child filled with such "poetry of life" as the following lines (School Songs, 119) express!

"My home, my own dear home,
It is a happy place,
Where smiles of love are brightening
Each dear familiar face;
Where parents' arms enfold me,
In fond embraces pressed,
And daily, nightly blessings
Upon the household rest.

Our morning salutations,
How gladsomely they sound,
And kind "good nights," at evening,
Like curtains close us round."

Who will not bless the imagination of the poet, which has endeared to us the "poor man's garden," (School Songs, 152), and made us love to repeat with sympathetic gladness:

"Ah! yes, the poor man's garden;
It is great joy to me,
This little precious piece of ground,
Before his door to see.

*   *   *   *   *   *   *

And here comes the old grandmother,
When her day's work is done;
And here they bring the sickly babe,
To cheer it in the sun.

And here on sabbath evenings,
Until the stars are out,
With a little one in either hand,
He walketh all about.

For though his garden plot is small,
Him doth it satisfy;
There is no inch of all his ground,
That does not fill his eye.

Yes! in the poor man's garden grow
Far more than herbs and flowers,
Kind thoughts, contentment, peace of mind,
And joy for weary hours."

Who would speak lightly of little songs, full of "the sunshine of the heart," like those which open with the following verses!

"Butter-cups and daisies,
Oh, the pretty flowers,
Coming ere the spring time,
To tell of sunny hours."
SCHOOL SONGS, 154.

"The flowers are blooming everywhere,
O'er every hill and dell,
And oh! how beautiful they are!
How sweetly too they smell!"
SCHOOL SONGS, 159.

"Behold a little baby boy!
A happy babe is he;
His face, how bright! his heart, how light!
His throne, his mother's knee!"
SCHOOL SONGS, 124.

IN MORAL AND RELIGIOUS EDUCATION, we find the beauty of the poem linked with the charm of the music, winning a welcome for the constant reiteration of true and holy sentiments, and making them the sweetest stores of memory for use in future years. *Kindness to animals,* the infant imbibes from the spirit of his pretty songs, " I like little pussy," (132) or, " I'll never hurt my little dog," (131.) The elder child feels the power of the same sentiment, while he yields to the enchantment of that song, (School Songs, 157)

> " The dew was falling fast;
> The stars began to blink;
> I heard a voice which said,
> ' Drink, pretty creature, drink,' " &c.

or while he listens to that beautiful rebuke, (School Songs, 128)

> " Turn, turn, thy hasty foot aside,
> Nor crush that helpless worm;
> The frame thy wayward looks deride,
> None but our God could form."

Sentiments of *sympathy and compassion* are excited by such songs as (School Song, 127), " I am a poor little beggar: my mother is dead,' or Sch. Song, 135.

> " Oh ! say what is that thing called light,
> Which I must ne'er enjoy?
> What are the blessings of the sight?
> Oh ! tell a poor blind boy !"

The inspiring language of *decision and diligence* is learnt in the songs, " Try again," (144). "Begone, dull sloth," (166). " Work while you work, and play while you play," (143); and in that which has for its chorus, " Never fail, sir, to strike while the iron is hot," (145). *Christian boldness* and a *noble patriotism* inflame the soul while we tune our spirits, with our voices, to the songs,

> " We won't give up the Bible,
> God's holy book of truth;
> The blessed staff of hoary age,
> The guide of early youth."
>   SCHOOL SONGS, 149.

> " Our fathers were high-minded men,
> Who firmly kept the faith,
> To freedom and to conscience true,
> In danger and in death."
>   SCHOOL SONGS, 151.

> " My English Home ! My English Home !
> O'er land and sea let others roam;
> I bless my God, who placed my birth,
> On this most favoured spot of earth."
>   SCHOOL SONGS, 147;

or to that hymn (it should be the nation's anthem) which closes with the following verse:—

> " And not this land alone,
> But be thy mercies known
> From shore to shore.

> Lord, make the nations see
> That men should brothers be,
> And form one family,
> The wide world o'er."
>   SCHOOL SONGS, 148.

Then there are songs which will invite our little ones forth to behold and *love the works of God.* " I am very glad the spring is come," (155), or :—

> " 'Tis summer bright ! 'Tis summer bright ! how
>   beautiful it looks !
> There's sunshine on the old grey hills, and
>   sunshine on the brooks."
>   SCHOOL SONGS, 158;

or that beautiful song :—

> " God might have bade the earth bring forth
>   Enough for great and small,
>   The oak tree and the cedar tree,
>   Without a flower at all."
>   SCHOOL SONGS, 117;

or that song of musical rhythm and most inspiring thoughts, which throws a spell even on childhood's ear, as it tells of the " spacious firmament" and " spangled heavens."

> " What though, in solemn silence, all
>   Move round this dark terrestrial ball?
>   What though, no *real* voice nor sound,
>   Amid their radiant orbs be found?
>   In reason's ear they all rejoice,
>   And utter forth a glorious voice;
>   For ever singing as they shine,
>   ' The hand that made us is divine.' "
>   SCHOOL SONGS, 84.

Bible narratives, with their interwoven lessons, are fixed on the memory and heart by such songs as, " Good David, whose psalms have so often been sung," (51); or that vivid picture of a child's emotion :—

> " When little Samuel woke,
>   And heard his Maker's voice,
>   At every word he spoke,
>   How much did he rejoice !
> O, blessed, happy child, to find
> The God of heaven so near and kind !"
>   SCHOOL SONGS, 34;

or that solemn and wondrously touching description :—

> " Lo ! at noon, 'tis sudden night !
>   Darkness covers all the sky !
>   Rocks are rending at the sight !
>   Children, can you tell me why !
> What can all these wonders be?
> Jesus dies on Calvary."
>   SCHOOL SONGS, 58.

The *sense of responsibility* is made familiar to the mind, by —

> " God entrusts to all,
> Talents few or many,
> None so young and small,
> That they have not any."
> SCHOOL SONGS, 92.

The essence of gospel truth is printed on the memory by these condensed and touching lines, which tell us why it was that

> " Jesus, who lived above the sky,
> Came down to be a man and die:"—

> " He knew how wicked man had been,
> He knew that God *must* punish sin;
> So, out of pity, Jesus said,
> He'd bear the punishment instead."
> SCHOOL SONGS, 16.

The *emotions of childhood's piety* find expression and sweet relief in the hymns—" Now that my journey's just begun," (64); or, " Lord, teach a little child to pray," (28); or, " What is there, Lord, a child can do ?" (76.) *Heaven* is presented in vivid pictures, which are most delightful to children, for they have not become so earthly as we. That vision attracts them which has been used in the triumph of simple faith by many a christian infant on his dying bed—

> " Around the throne of God in heaven,
> Thousands of children stand,

> Children whose sins are all forgiven,
> A holy, happy band—
> Singing, Glory, glory, glory."
> SCHOOL SONGS, 2;

or they listen to the song—

> " Oh! happy land! Oh! happy land!
> Where saints and angels dwell ;"
> SCHOOL SONGS, 25;

till they feel this earth, with all its pleasures to them, to be indeed " a desert" in comparison, and delight to think themselves " little pilgrims" to a better world. Even children love this hymn.

> " I am but a stranger here;
> Heaven is my home!
> Earth is a desert drear;
> Heaven is my home!
> Dangers and sorrows stand
> Round me on every hand,
> Heaven is my fatherland,
> Heaven is my home !"
> SCHOOL SONGS, 55.

Imagine all these beautiful songs heightened in effect by the varied delights of music, whose accents are wont to *linger* on the ear, and to invite the frequent and willing repetition. Imagine these impressions made in the fresh and happy days of childhood; and then consider how great must be the power and the blessing of Music and Poetry rightly used in Education !

THE REAL HINDRANCES TO THE UNIVERSAL KNOWLEDGE AND FAMILIAR USE OF
VOCAL MUSIC.—THE OLD NOTATION.—METHODS OF TEACHING.

The physical organs and aptitudes of ear and voice required for vocal music are still very generally regarded as peculiar endowments, rare gifts, possessed only by a few; whereas, in truth, they are the very same as those used for speaking and hearing, the common inheritance of mankind. Every child, not born deaf or dumb, is born with the organs which may be taught to sing as well as to speak. It is by the teaching of example that the child attains the power of speech, but the same opportunities are seldom given to develop the faculty of song. When this teaching has been neglected till advanced age, the vocal organs become less flexible and less obedient to the will, and the art of singing increasingly difficult to commence. But even in these unfortunate cases we have seen enough to prove that Patience, effort of Mind, and a good Method, will awaken to creditable use the neglected faculty. There is, doubtless, a great difference in the physical constitution of individuals, which gives to some a much greater nervous susceptibility and consequent delicacy of ear and voice than others; but all mankind are endowed by the Creator with that glorious faculty of song, which he has made it our duty to improve for his praise.

There is therefore no deficiency of natural voice or ear to account for the common neglect of music, nor is there any general lack of interest or unwillingness to learn among the people, for music is beautiful and attractive to all; nor can any difficulty in the nature of music itself be pleaded, for considered as an art it is certainly more easy than reading, writing, or drawing, and as a science it is most simple in its elements, however rich and varied in its combinations. The one great hindrance to the popular and easy use of music, is to be found in the *complex* and *heterogeneous* system of *notation* by which it is commonly presented to the eye. This notation crowds so many unnecessary difficulties on to the threshold of the science as to discourage the majority of learners, and fails so entirely to render obvious and prominent its leading principles, as to conceal the real simplicity of music and veil the wondrous beauties of its inner temple. The best authorities are agreed in this opinion. A writer in the Quarterly Musical Magazine (1824), quoted by Miss Glover, says distinctly: "Any one who sets himself seriously to consider the present complex system of musical notation, easy as it may appear to those who have gradually mastered its difficulties, must, independent of all historical information, be convinced that its basis was laid in the infancy of musical science, at a time when the attainments of musicians bore no proportion to those of the present day. So many characters have been from time to time added, to keep pace with the improvements of different ages, that Guido himself, were he now to arise from his grave, would not recognise what is usually set down as his handy-work. The world will not much longer agree to be trammelled with the arbitrary characters of a barbarous age, bearing no analogy with the things they are employed to represent." Dr. Burney, also, in his History of Music, (vol. ii, 97,) speaks of a more perfect notation as a thing to be desired. He says, "Guido declares that he writes merely for the Church, where the pure diatonic genus was first used. Transposed keys, however, from c natural major and A natural minor, which are only imagined to change their pitch, when represented by other sounds in the same relation to the key note, and all the accidentals to which modern modulation is subject, should be provided for. To do this in a clear, simple, and practicable manner, would require great meditation. It has frequently been attempted by men of science, as well as by practical musicians, who, though they have obviated former inconveniences, and supplied a few of the defects which have been complained of, have generated others that have been found far more difficult to vanquish, so that *the business still remains to be done.*"

The Philosopher tells us that the symbolic signs, as well as the technical terms, of any science should be based on its most important truths, putting them forward as helps to thought and memory—that each sign should have one distinct meaning, lest the learner's attention should be distracted from the path itself, which he travels by the difficulty of interpreting his guides—and that every mark or term should have a direct reference to some truth or fact of the science itself, and should not be merely the corrective or completion of some other mark or term, lest the learner be condemned to wander in the mazes of notation and nomenclature instead of roaming the fresh fields of truth and knowledge. It is easy to see that any technical notation which is deficient in

c

these respects must become a clog to progress and not a facility, and that, to those who have not yet explored the science to which it relates, it must be like a clouded glass instead of a telescope of power to direct the eye and to promote the clear analysis of truth. In every point the Old Notation of Music is most deficient.

Every one knows the advantage we possess in the beautiful notation of Number which the Arabians have given us. It proceeds on one simple uniform principle, is easily recognised and easily combined; while the Old Roman numerals adopt various and heterogeneous contrivances for denoting numbers, expressing some by the direct symbol, others by a multiplication of symbols, and others again by a curious sort of subtraction and addition of symbols. The Old Notation of Music is of kindred structure with the latter. Heterogeneous and indirect, it exhibits the pitch of notes partly by the inaccurate *pictorial* appearance of the staff, and partly by the *symbols* of flat and sharp; it shows the length of notes sometimes by one symbol and sometimes by another, without any direct relation to the regular recurring accents, which are the only true measurers of time; and, instead of making obvious and prominent, the simple and beautiful relationships of key, on which the whole framework of music rests, it shrouds them in mystery, and keeps them in constant subserviency to the incomparably less important indications of pitch. See pp. 132, 136, 138, 141, 152. Now, let the reader think, what would become of Arithmetic if we were compelled to work all our sums by help (!) of the Old Roman numerals? Would it not be made, like music, the possession of the few to whom lengthened practice has given a facility, which is the fruit more of instinct than reason, instead of being, as now it is, the common attainment of the people? What would be said of the signs of Algebra if "plus" were sometimes represented by a cross, and sometimes by a round O—that same round O, moreover, being occasionally used for "minus"? and yet this is just the position of "sharp," "flat," and "natural" in the Old Notation!

But it is chiefly the good *teacher*—more anxious to teach things than words or signs—who experiences the difficulties of the Old Notation, and he feels them to a degree which the mere amateur or the professional singer cannot appreciate.

Those who have studied much the art of teaching will readily acknowledge how very important it is, both for facility of communication on the part of the teacher, and for quickness of apprehension on the part of the scholar, to have one distinct and appropriate term for each fact in the science which is taught. Nor will they fail to recall how often an ill-defined or double-meaning word has seriously retarded or painfully misdirected the progress of a pupil. But an imperfect Notation has brought with it an imperfect system of technical terms. The teacher who examines the ordinary Nomenclature of music will find it to be such a jumble of unfixed, equivocal, and barbarous words as almost to defy any useful selection, and he will be glad of any means of teaching the facts of music, apart, for awhile, from its ordinary misguiding terms.

The teacher moreover finds it important to remove every *unnecessary* difficulty out of his pupil's path; for, while he would encourage the strenuous exercise of mind in seeking a clear comprehension of truth after truth, he is anxious that whatever difficulty his pupil has to encounter shall be a difficulty of the thing itself which is taught, and not of its mere signs and terms. But, alas, the pupil cannot take a single step in the practice of music, without plunging into a needless jungle of sharps and flats and clefs and variable scales. The understanding is at once overburdened and confused. Instead of one thing at a time, the very first piece of notation he uses requires him to know many things at once.

The good teacher is also anxious to found his methods of teaching as directly as possible on the nature of the thing taught. "The husbandman," says Dr. Bryce, in his admirable Introduction, addressed to teachers, "is guided in his operations by the nature of the seed he is to sow. Even a carpenter varies his mode of putting a nail into a piece of wood, according to the form, size, and material of the nail. But in Education this obvious dictate of common sense is too often neglected. Let us endeavour to rescue Music from the consequences of that neglect, as Pestalozzie has rescued Arithmetic. In order to do this, we must bear in mind that the *nature and essence of music* is the Relation which all other notes in a tune have to the tonic or key note. So long as this *relation* remains the same, it matters not what the notes are *in themselves;* the tune is unchanged. Every one knows that we may have the very same melody and harmony in a very high or in a very low key, or in any intermediate one. It is this relation of the other notes to the key note, therefore, that constitutes music. It follows that this relation is THE VERY FIRST THING to which the learner's attention ought to be directed, instead of making them spend months, sometimes years, in the laborious and fruitless attempt to acquire what perhaps no human ear ever perfectly attained—an accurate perception of the absolute pitch of each note independently and by itself." But the Old Notation gives "pitch" the forward place and makes "key" a mystery. Neither by the shape of a note, nor by its position on the staff, can we tell at once its relation to the *key.* That is left to be found out. But its place in *pitch* is made plain as possible! As a consequence of this, most elementary books confine the majority of their exercises within the meagre limits of one key.

Again, let us apply the same rule of the true teacher to, what is called, the Practice of Interval, which aims to give the Ear a command over the Voice, so as to produce any note which may be indicated. It is manifest that this must be done by first establishing in the Ear a clear individualised perception of the given note, and then practising until the voice can produce at bidding a sound, which shall have the peculiar musical character and mental effect thus recognised. Now the most recognisable quality of notes—that effect on the mind by which they are most easily distinguished one from the other—does not arise from their absolute pitch, for the *same* sound, when it is the *fifth* above the key note, will leave a very different feeling on the mind from that which it produced, in another tune, where it was the *fourth*. See note, p. 19. Nor does it arise from their distance above or below the preceding note or the absolute interval, for the *same* interval which produces a given effect when its notes hold a certain relation to the key, will produce a very different effect, in another tune, where its notes hold a different relation to the key. See notes, p. 29, 97. Thus the perfect fourth formed by the Dominant and the Tonic above (SOH DOH') has a very different character from that which is formed by the Leading Note and the Mediant above (TE₁ ME), and is much easier to sing;—and the fifth produced by the Tonic with the Dominant (DOH SOH), is totally different in its effect from that produced by the Submediant with the Mediant above (LAH₁ ME), and very much easier to sing. That quality of a note then by which we most easily "individualize" it, so as to know it again, or to reproduce it with the voice, arises from its relation to the system of notes, called a key, which has been previously established in the ear. But this principle of key-relationship, so essential for the practice of "Interval," is the very thing which is rendered the least obvious in the Old Notation. Hence we find most elementary books filled up with the most dry, tedious, unmusical, and unprofitable exercises on Thirds, Fourths, Fifths, &c., in which, to make confusion more confused, the major and minor intervals are mixed up together!

Thus is the teacher hindered at every turn, and singing made almost a hopeless thing, by the stereotype faults of the Old Notation. And yet it cannot be entirely laid aside. It must be taught. For the works of all the great Masters are printed in it. We must give our pupils access to them. Then let it be laid aside only for a time, until, by some simpler means, the real nature of music itself is understood, just as, in Pestalozzian schools, the notation and the figures of arithmetic lie untouched, till the pupil has obtained some clear ideas of Number itself, and is able to perform some of its simpler operations, intelligently, by the help of the Bead-Frame or the Box of various Objects. It will be all the better if the notation thus used as the simplest possible introduction in our first acquaintance with music, should prove itself so facile a guide in the rest of our journey, and so useful an interpreter in the higher departments of musical science, as never to be entirely laid aside. A most skilful invention is the Old Notation for the times in which it was framed; it is full, moreover, of ingenious contrivances for amending its own defects; but let us not, as many do, treat those defects as virtues. It is only by exposing them that we can vindicate that simplicity and beauty in Music which its notation so unworthily represents. It may be long before another Notation is perfected, which serves the purpose of Instrumental music better. Instruments themselves, as well as the Methods of teaching them, must be wonderfully altered, and more nearly conformed to truth and science before that time. But let not the Human Voice, "the most perfect of all instruments," remain in shackles with the rest. Let us welcome for it any notation, which, combining simplicity with scientific truthfulness, will enable us to unravel the intricacies of the old one, and carry us forward on a well-lighted path to the knowledge and enjoyments of music.

The following account of various methods of teaching music will be useful to the student, and will illustrate several of the topics mentioned above.

For some of the earlier of the following statements the editor is indebted to the kindness of Mr. Graham of Edinburgh.

Nearly forty years ago the principles of Pestalozzi's general method of instruction were applied to music and taught in several Swiss schools. The system of musical instruction in these schools was drawn up by Pfeiffer and Nägeli of Zurich, and published in 1809. The principles of this new method consisted "in laying well the foundations of the science and of the art—in giving, at the commencement, a little at a time—in well separating and simplifying the elements—in rendering them familiar one by one—advancing constantly, though by insensible degrees—and in building little by little the science, as the practice is well established in the mind."

In 1817, Pierre Galin, professor of mathematics in the Lyceum at Bordeaux, opened a class for teaching music by what he called "the method of the meloplast." This meloplast was a board with ruled lines and without notes. By means of *two* wands M. Galin pointed out two places for notes, at once; and the pupils, divided into two classes, and following these indications, thus sang in two parts. He also taught his pupils *a current musical hand,* in which, from dictation, they could write down any melody without the aid of ruled music paper.

In 1822, M. Jeu de Berneval, then a professor of music in Paris, "modified Galin's method, and introduced, among other improvements, what he calls the monogamic signs." These are certain *shapes* given to the heads of notes, in his earlier exercises, by which their place in the key may be distinguished. Thus, the Tonic (DOH) is represented by a square head, open for a minim, filled for a crotchet—any note which may be the Dominant (SOH) of the key in which it occurs is distinguished by a square standing on one of its angles —the Mediant (ME) is round like the ordinary crotchet or minim—the Subdominant (FAH) is triangular with its point downwards—the Leading note (TE) is also triangular, but with its point upwards—the Supertonic (RAY) has a crescent shape—and the Submediant (LAH) a diamond form. Those who have studied the real qualities of notes as described pages 19, 20, 28, 39, will perceive with what ingenuity and propriety some of these shapes have been selected. "The Monogamic Method," says M. Jeu, "is distinguished from all others by several characteristics. The first that will strike you is that, instead of beginning, as other methods generally do, by the study of the [absolute] *intervals,* our system commences with the *properties* of sounds. • • • There are only seven sounds. Each of those sounds differs from all the rest in its manner of affecting the ear: therein consists its *property.* There are consequently only *seven* properties to study, and we in nowise trouble ourselves with the [absolute] intervals whose number of major and minor combinations are interminable. The properties of the sounds are to the ear what those of colour are to the eye. • • • There is but one Gamut or Scale, for all are constructed after the same model. Our knowledge of one applies to all the rest. Once acquainted with the properties of the Tonic, the Mediant, the Dominant, the Leading note, &c., you know all the scales, since, however burthened such scales may be with sharps and flats, the same *seven* properties are therein reproduced at corresponding degrees of pitch. Music contains no more, and change the name as you

please, the fact remains the same. • • • I cannot but repeat that the Gamut contains only seven properties; however disguised by various names, we can never meet with anything but Tonics, Dominants, &c.; and again, no matter what be the Interval, major or minor dispersed or close, that may lead us from one note to another, we have still but a *known* property to reproduce. Thus, instead of having to become acquainted with two hundred different intervals, our labour is reduced to the study of seven properties, which are easily impressed on the ear."

M. Jeu reminds us that, in Education, theory and practice "should ever go hand in hand. Without theory practice gropes along blindfold, and loses time first by committing errors and then in correcting them. Again, if theory be not supported by a display of effects, the result is not more satisfactory: the pupil is lost in a maze of vain systems." In the ordinary methods of teaching, however, "the theoretical developments of the art, so conducive to its practical performance," are necessarily laid aside in the first stages (where they would be most useful) on account of the difficulties of notation, and "after six months application the pupil is mortified to perceive that, when *alone,* or without the assistance of an instrument, he is not able to make out the most simple tune, and still less to *write* his own ideas or such Melodies as he may hear or remember."

"Three difficulties," he says, "are generally presented simultaneously to the learner, *reading, intonation,* (or the art of striking the notes correctly) and *time* or measure." In the Monogamic System, as in our own, each difficulty is met separately before they are met combined. The causes of hesitation and fatigue are removed, and these advantages arise from "each note being in its appearance as distinct from the rest as if its name were written in full, and the respective forms being such as to convey to the eye a recollection of those essential *properties* which must ever be present to the mind."

The principle of Relationship to the Tonic or Tonality (the "Common Mode") he describes thus: "By Tonality is meant the assemblage of all the properties of the Gamut. It is Tonality which enables us not to confound one note with any other, and which causes us to appreciate the functions performed by every note individually. Tonality is that attractive power which causes all the notes, while gravitating [moving with concentric tendency and] with more or less energy round one principal sound, to solve themselves finally into that one, namely, the TONIC." "Tonality," he says, "must be our support and the property of sounds our clew. The Tonic must constantly resound in our ear as well as the Dominant. Without the Tonic no Dominant can exist. Without the Tonic and Dominant you have no

Tonality. The more you advance, the more you will feel convinced that, *unknown to himself*, the merest routine music-reader clings to Tonality. What he does while actuated by instinct only, let us do according to the dictates of judgment, and our performance will be at the same time more rapid and more correct."

The English edition of M. Jeu's work was published by him as Professor to the Royal Academy of Music. It is entitled "Music Simplified," (price £1. 10s.) and, although strangely wandering in the latter part into that bad method of solfaing which makes the solfa syllables represent sounds of absolute pitch and not the relation of notes to the key, is full of ingenious explanations, and is most valuable. The students of this work are deeply indebted to it for suggesting the principle on which the subject of "Interval" (as it is commonly called), or the correct Modulation of notes, is here developed. In the first edition M. Jeu's principles occupied only a single chapter, but, in this edition, three full sections are given to them. They form the ground-work of the elementary part of the book, and extend their influence through the whole. The principle of "individualizing" each note of the scale, and each accidental, is indeed carried out much more fully than in M. Jeu's own work. For much experience in teaching both children and adults has shown the editor the great importance, especially in this instance, of making sound Philosophy accompany careful Practice.

The labours of W. E. Hickson, Esq., should next be acknowledged. His "First Lessons on Singing and the Notation of Music," though not sufficiently using the relationship of key, were written with the happiest educational talent. His selection of school melodies and hymn tunes was just made to catch the popular taste and to improve it. These, with his very felicitous adaptations of words to popular airs, produced an impression in favour of Music on the English mind, more widely spread and more deeply felt than any other. His society for the promotion of vocal music" had commenced by declaring a fair and open competition for all methods, when its progress was interrupted by the sudden tide of fashion which set in with the Government Singing Book.

M. Bosquillon Wilhem, who was appointed, under Louis Phillippe, "Inspector General of Singing" for all the Public Schools of Paris, employed, in teaching his pupils, what he called "l'indicateur vocal." This *Vocal Indicator* had been, it seems, employed in the sixteenth century by Sebald Hayden, in whose very rare book M. Wilhem said he found the method which he adopted. It is thus described:—"On a board are drawn horizontal lines in imitation of those on ruled music paper. Upon one of these lines,

Wilhem, in teaching, places a clef, and when he or one of the monitors touches a line or a space with the end of a wand, the pupils represent to themselves a note at the point touched by the wand, and immediately give the name and the sound of that note as if it had been drawn on the board. By changing from one line or space to another, all the intervals are brought out, and the whole class is exercised in reading and singing without having any piece of music before their eyes. It is curious to hear the voices of the children follow in unison the gestures of their master, who thus runs over all the parts of the board." In order that the pupils, when out of the class room, may exercise themselves, M. Wilhem shows them that they always carry about with them a "vocal indicator;" for when the *hand* is open, the five fingers placed parallel, imitate the five lines of a musical staff. This is what he denominates the "musical hand." It is only a revival of the old Guidonian hand of the eleventh century.

This method of M. Wilhem's was adapted to English use by John Hullah, Esq., a gentleman known before as the composer of an opera, and whose excellent voice, good talents, and good disposition seem to be highly appreciated by all parties. It is generally understood that he was aided in this work by Dr. Kay (now Dr. Shuttleworth), whose private indefatigable efforts and generous sacrifices in the cause of Education cannot be too gratefully acknowledged by all parties. The book thus produced was ushered into public notice with all the eclat which was naturally attached to the first attempt of a great government in the art of education. Mr. Hickson, in the Westminster Review for January, 1842, thus gives his opinion of the Government plan:— " The art of teaching does not lie so much in the methods employed, as in the ability to correct the mistakes of a pupil when they occur, and explain at the moment how they are to be avoided. This art Mr. Hullah eminently possesses, and be is therefore deservedly popular with his classes. No person who wished to improve himself in the knowledge of written music, if gifted with sufficient perseverance to go through a very dry course of exercises, could fail to profit by joining Mr. Hullah's class. At the same time we would caution him against the method developed in Mr. Hullah's book, as one which will necessarily fail in the hands of ordinary teachers, and which is about as ill adapted to the instruction of children as any method yet devised." To the same opinion of the book our own previous examination had promptly and decisively led us. Those who have studied the nature of music and the principles of teaching as applied to it, and have noticed what advances had already been made towards the emancipation of the art, as indicated above, will regret that M. Wilhem should have taken the pains to build so elaborate a system upon unsound foundations.

Its most obvious and disastrous fault is the adoption of the French method of solfaing, which makes the syllables DO, RE, MI, &c., nothing but substitutes for the letters C, D, E, &c., and uses them to represent *fixed* sounds, instead of the English method which makes them synonymous with the technical terms Tonic, Supertonic, Mediant, &c., and thus establishes a connection with the science of harmony, and renders prominent the relationships of key. It is sufficiently unfortunate for us that the common Notation commits this great error of preferring Pitch to Key—but, to have forced upon us also a system of note-naming, which, instead of guiding us through the mystery, plays as much at cross purposes with music as the Old Notation itself—this is unfortunate indeed. "But," it is asked, "is there not an advantage in learning to recognise the sounds of absolute pitch? For the mere purpose of pitching the key note of a tune, it is, no doubt, useful to remember the absolute pitch of each note in the Standard Scale. See p. 29. But this knowledge of pitch "is not *essential*," (we use the words of Dr. Bryce) "either to the perception of melody and harmony, or to their execution, and it may be acquired with far greater ease after the mind has learnt to feel the relation of the notes of the scale to one another," which *is* essential both for melody and harmony—both for perception and execution. *But are we not, by that means, able to attach to each place on the staff the idea of its own proper sound, and so as to read at sight any music placed before us?*" To which we answer;—Suppose each degree on the staff *had* its own proper sound of a certain pitch—and you could strike that sound at will, with the mechanical accuracy of an instrument—would it not puzzle you to find that same sound, out of your own throat, sometimes producing one effect on the mind, and sometimes another, (mournful as LAH, piercing as TE, desolate as FAH, &c.) according to the relationships of key that were thrown around it, and to discover that you had learnt to recognise and remember notes by one of the least important properties that attach to them? For it is position in key, and not place in pitch, that gives a musical sound its most noticeable quality, and chiefly contributes to its mental effect; and would it not be better to strive a note with a foreknowledge of its mental effect than merely with a foreknowledge of its pitch? In truth, however, each degree of the staff has *not* a note proper to itself; but is used, in turn, to represent *three* perfectly distinct notes—the flat, the natural, and the sharp, one of them about a whole tone from the other! How clear and definite this "idea of pitch" which you would attach to each

place on the staff! How much it will help you to an accurate and expressive modulation!

The students of Mr. Hullah's book do not, however, find themselves in this predicament at first. They pass through half his exercises, really attaching the idea of a distinct sound to each distinct place on the staff; for they are singing, all this while, only in one key—the key of C. Notice the effect of this. Directly they enter a new key, they have to unlearn the idea of pitch, which they had laboured through half their toilsome course to attach to one or more of the lines or spaces, according to the number of flats or sharps in the signature; and they have to establish a new and perfectly distinct association with each of those lines or spaces. It is of no avail to reply that the difference is only that of half a tone, for no one, after making the experiment, can assert that F SHARP, when played or sung *in connection with* the key of G, has any resemblance to F NATURAL when taken in connection with the key of C. Thus each new key brings with it a new perplexity, and there are twelve of them, whereas in music itself one key is *quite* as natural and easy as the other! Is not this *making* difficulties for the pupil instead of removing them? But Mr. Hullah's pupils have done something else in the first half of their course. They have learnt to *associate* with each syllable, though it may be unconsciously to themselves, that peculiar mental effect, of which we have spoken, which may be considered apart from pitch, and which arises from the position the note holds in a key. All this, which would be most valuable if he changed his DOH with the key note, and so retained for each syllable its peculiar mental effect, has also to be unlearnt or confused. Mr. Hullah's FAH has sometimes the effect of a Subdominant, sometimes that of a Leading note, and sometimes that of a Tonic—and yet how totally different is each one from the others! How much better is the old English method of solfaing, according to which FAH might, indeed, sometimes represent one pitch of sound, and sometimes another, but would always stand for the same distinguishable quality or mental effect, which is the rememberable thing in a note. This principle of mental association, which is so important in all education, is abused even in connection with the favourite theory of teaching by absolute interval. For instance; through about thirty lessons the pupil labours to associate the syllables DOH ME with the accurate intonation of a *Major* Third, and then discovers, to his dismay, that he will have to sing them, in half of the twelve keys, as a *Minor* Third! *But is it not easier to solfa upon this plan than on that which moves DOH with the key note?* Yes, easier to solfa *wrong*, for you have no *fixed* mental association to guide you. It is true that you have a more direct and easy correspondence with the *faults* of the Old *Notation;* but we hold a direct and simple relation to the *truths* of music itself, and we always find that practice the most satisfactory, and therefore the easiest, in which intelligence bears us company. Your easy road leads to perplexity. Our apparently more difficult path brings us sooner to the end, and gives us a better view of the country by the way. Of course our "moveable DOH" is no difficulty whatever in the Solfa Notation. We simply mention its pitch in the signature. And even when applied to the Old Notation, on the plan described in the second appendix to this work, all difficulty vanishes; the *relative* positions of the syllables on the staff are really learnt as quickly as their *absolute* and unchanging places on the other plan, and, when once learnt, they apply to all keys alike.

The other prominent defect of this method, which, like the preceding one, it has in common with many other methods, is the development of "intonation" by means of "absolute interval," beginning with Seconds, Thirds, Fourths, &c., instead of using the principles of "key relationship," and beginning with those notes whose Consonance with the Tonic is most easily recognised. It is obvious that the voice will be most correctly tuned by studying first those intervals which the ear can most easily and with the greatest certainty recognise. Such are the perfect concords —the Octave, the Fifth, and the Third from the key note. The frame-work of the scale being thus firmly put together, the other notes can be easily attached. But to begin tuning the voice by means of the worst of the discords—the Second —is preposterous indeed, and it appears still more so when you consider that, in scientific accuracy, no two seconds of the scale are precisely alike, and besides that two are "semitones," three of the whole tones are much larger than the other two. The first second below the key note (TE), and the first second above it (RAY), lead to the most difficult notes of all the scale. See pp. 39, 40. What a strange standard of accuracy is this, to guide the pupil in his first efforts to attain perfect tune! We need not wonder at the harshness and untunableness of voice which commonly results from this system.

Mr. Hickson, in the review above mentioned, has the following admirable remarks on these subjects. "We attach comparatively little importance to exercises of fourths, or sevenths, or any other intervals; they may be learnt by ear as well as nursery songs, *and are so learnt in large classes;* but the difficulty is in remembering, when fourths, thirds, sixths, and sevenths are grouped promiscuously together, what is the precise sound belonging to each; and to learn this without the incessant practice of professional singers, which makes it an affair, not of mind, but of habit, an appeal must be made to the

understanding, and the pupil must be taught to mark *the quality of the sounds characteristic of the different intervals.*

"We have already shown that the art of reading music at sight depends upon the ability to recognise, at a glance, the intervals of the scale, in whatever key they may be written; that is to say, to distinguish at once, not which is A or B, but which is the key note—which is the third, fifth, seventh, &c. It will therefore at once be seen that Forde, by adopting Rousseau's rule for using the solfeggio syllables as names for the intervals, converts them into a most profitable exercise; an exercise which compels the pupil to study the intervals at every bar he sings, and to give up guessing. A teacher, upon this method, listening to his pupil, knows at once, by the syllable the pupil chooses, whether he recognises the interval of the scale to which the note belongs, or is taking no trouble about it. If in the key of D the pupil sing 'RE' for D, instead of 'DO,' the teacher would at once perceive that his pupil did not understand the key in which he was singing.

"Observe, now, the confusion and perplexity created by the opposite method of Wilhem. By incessantly singing the solfeggio syllables to the finger exercise, in which the intervals of the scale correspond with their natural order in the key of C, the pupil learns to associate (rightly enough) certain sounds with those syllables, but no sooner has this been done than the pupil is told, when in another key, to use the same syllables in singing *other* sounds; so that the association of ideas established in the first instance becomes a source of the greatest embarrassment in the second.

"We think it must be obvious from the preceding, that the solfeggio syllables *thus employed* tend to mislead the pupil rather than to assist him in learning the art of sight-singing. It is using words, as a lawyer would say, in the sense of a *suggestio falsi.*"

Dr. Mainzer adopted the same false method of solfaing. He also employed, in his large classes, the Piano, an "imperfect" and "tempered" instrument, to guide and form the Human Voice, which is naturally a "perfect" instrument not needing "temperament"! There was little of system in his method, but much of generous enthusiasm. His "Choruses," so simple and yet so effective, show how well he understands how to wield large masses of voice; and his recent work, "Music and Education," is full of learning, genius, and poetry.

The Rev. R. J. Bryce, L.L.D., Principal of the Belfast Academy, well known and distinguished as an Educationalist, published in 1845, "A Rational Introduction to Music"—the word Rational "merely indicating that the object of the work is to explain Reasons as well as to make known

Facts." "The teacher must remember," he says, "that the great secret of success is to call in the understanding to the assistance of the ear at every step." "The Principal and Masters of the Belfast Academy had tried the system of Wilhem and found it to fail. They gave every consideration to that of Mainzer, and saw no reason to expect better results. It appears that no pupils derive much improvement from either, except those who are gifted with a naturally good ear, and who, therefore, would improve under any system; and even these make scarcely any progress towards the art of singing at sight." Dr. Bryce perceived clearly that Interval must be measured from the key note. "If we attempt," he says, " to teach a class by directing their attention to the absolute pitch of the notes, those who have a good ear will *unconsciously* pick up some idea of the *relative* pitch, and will thus derive some advantage *in spite of the system*. Those whose ear is less perfect will receive no benefit at all; except, perhaps, a little more relish for music, in consequence of hearing it so much and so attentively. Such is the system of Wilhem, and such are its results. If, on the contrary, we direct the attention of the class to the *relative* pitch of the notes, and make them sing an interval—1, 5, (DOH SOH) for example—*in as great a variety of keys as the compass of their voices will allow*, those who have only a tolerable ear will easily and rapidly form an accurate general idea of the relation between the Key Note and the Fifth in all scales whatever, and will be able to sing the fifth to any note that may be given them. Two, three, or four lessons will suffice to give a general idea of the character and effect of the other notes; after which a large proportion of the class will be able to make out for themselves any easy tune without ever hearing it sung or played, while those whose ear is not so good, will be able to *follow* with a degree of accuracy and confidence not attainable by any other mode of teaching." Dr. Bryce lays aside the Old Notation for the first nine lessons and the first sixty-three exercises. He uses the figures 1, 2, 3, &c. ("one" standing for the key note and so on), to represent notes to the eye, but employs the solfa syllables, as we do, for the vocal exercises. He adopts, what we are constrained to regard as, the wrong method of developing interval, and the wrong view of the "minor scale." But the work is distinguished by great accuracy, by science, and by teaching skill. We earnestly hope that, in a future edition, Dr. Bryce will be encouraged to develope his principles more fully in their bearings on the science of music. See p. 100. A friendly criticism, in his preface, and kind notice of the former edition of the present work, led to a correspondence, from which, as well as from a diligent reperusal of Dr. Bryce's own book, the editor has very greatly profited;

d

and he takes pleasure in thus acknowledging his obligation.

The Rev. J. J. Waite, to whose devout and generous labours in the revival of Psalmody reference has been made at pp. 114, 115 of this work, produces very excellent practical results in his large congregational classes, without much either of theory or system, by leading his pupils in the simplest way to measure interval from the key note. He uses the figures, in his vocal exercises, on the plan which Dr. Bryce learnt, he says, from Mr. James Gall, jun. of Edinburgh, and which we have known to be used by several organists in teaching their choirs. This use of the seven figures has, at first sight, an advantage over the seven syllables, inasmuch as the figures have not *to be learnt*, and this is not an unimportant matter in such classes as Mr. Waite has to instruct. But it should be remembered, first, that in seven minutes a pupil may learn the seven syllables by rote, perfectly, both backwards and forwards; secondly, that the figures, especially *six* and *seven*, are not so pleasant to the ear as the syllables; thirdly, that the "accidentals" are much better represented by individual names, as TU, FI, NE, &c., than by the awkward sounds "four*sharp*," " seven*flat*," "five*sharp*," &c.; fourthly, that, by using the figures in this way we are deprived of the advantage of using them in the manner described p. 22—an exercise very important as a test of mere musical attainment, before the pupil attempts singing the tune to words, at which stage he should be perfect in the music, and be able to give his attention to the artistic " expression" of the poetry—and fifthly, we should remember that it is not alone the measured distance from the key note, above or below, which gives a note its characteristic sound, but its relation also to the other notes of the key. Something of its peculiar complexion and mental effect is contributed to each note by each of the others which has been heard before it. See notes, p. 19, 28. We have therefore preferred the system of distinct names.

Mr. Waite does not, like Miss Glover and Dr. Bryce, lay aside the Old Notation for a time, but he *accompanies it*, through nearly the whole of his course, with the figure notation as an interpreter. This constantly tempts the pupils to sing from the figures rather than from the notes above, as they find the figures easier. Should they not be taught (as in our second appendix) how to apply the figures *for themselves?* This shows at once the facility which the learner derives from a figure or letter notation on the principle of key relationship, and the danger of unfitting the child to walk alone by too long a use of the go-cart. We can, however, heartily recommend Mr. Waite's method, especially when the pupil has received the above warning, as a very effective Pioneer in the glorious Reformation of Psalmody.

The "Sequential System of Musical Notation," invented in 1843, by Arthur Wallbridge, Esq., and since that time greatly improved, well deserves study. "The striking characteristics of the Sequential reform," says Mr. W., "may be described in a few words—as, firstly, the reduction of the present artificially-constructed four-and-twenty major and minor keys to the one natural scale of seven sounds, denoted by *some certain seven numerals* selected from the *twelve* numerals which signify the twelve sounds of the Chromatic Scale; and, secondly, the reduction of the present various and perplexing *times* to the only two natural kinds, double and triple. The absurd flat and sharp signatures of the Old Notation—the meaningless leger lines—the arbitrary clefs, are altogether swept away, and no difficulties are presented to the student of the Sequential System except those really inherent in music itself." Mr. Wallbridge uses a staff of three lines, and places the Key Note uniformly in the space below the first line, whatever its pitch may be. In tunes which range below the key note, (Plagal tunes, from SOH₁ to SOH) he adds, at a short distance, another staff of three lines, or part of it, and by not using a line between the two staves, but by making the degree next below DOH, which was in the space below the upper staff, to be TE in the space above the lower staff, he secures a uniform position on both staves for each note of the scale. Thus FAH is always on the second line, TE on the highest space, DOH on the lowest, &c. This is very ingenious. It retains a pictorial representation of interval. It is imperfectly pictorial, of course, not showing the "semitones," but its uniform representation of key greatly atones for this fault.

If, in addition to this, Mr. Wallbridge had used the common letters C, D, E, F, &c., to give the pitch of DOH in the signature, and the common notes on his staff, taking the crotchet for his "standard aliquot," (see p. 136) and a thin bar for the medium accent, his notation would be more popular and equally useful. The figures, into which he changes the heads of his notes, and which are intended to indicate pitch *symbolically* by reference to his "sequences" of fixed semitones, (untrue in nature and science, and taken from "tempered" instruments) cannot make his notation easier to play from than Miss Glover's. "Transition" is still a difficulty, and the Sequential, like the Old Notation, is obliged to mix the symbolic with the pictorial principle in showing the "accidentals." We must still prefer our symbolic notation connected, in the mind's eye, with the *perfect* pictorial scale of the Modulator, showing *time*, moreover, *pictorially* by measurement along the page, and used as an introduction and interpreter to the Old Notation, which cannot for many years be overthrown.

We have dwelt thus largely on these topics because we are not among those who suppose the world is to be taught to sing upon any one method. We have been scrupulously, severely anxious to provide for our friends *the best* method; but, as we shall not convince every one that this has been done, we have also sought, by fully exposing to the public the principles on which all methods must depend for success, and by friendly criticism, to necessitate the improvement of other methods. And if, by this means, we should even raise other methods to excel and supplant our own, we shall be thankful that the world is advantaged.

THE ADVANTAGES OF MISS GLOVER'S SYSTEM.

Miss Glover's method had been in practical operation for ten years before the Government Singing Book was published; and, if it had been a little more popular in its cast, and the Old Notation had not so successfully concealed the real nature of music, by its blinding mist of signs and symbols, as to disqualify the public mind for judging a true system, it must have been very generally adopted long ago. Miss Glover states her claims ingenuously. In reference to the quotation from Dr. Burney given above, she says:—"Men of science who are practical musicians, so seldom, if ever, possess in the same degree as myself, leisure for meditation, combined with opportunities for making experiments with children of the efficacy of new plans, that I hope I may be excused for having ventured, notwithstanding the limited extent of my musical science, to supply as far as I can, a deficiency which Dr. Burney acknowledges." "I hope that a new notation may not only provide a remedy for the defects of the old, but add the following advantages:—define *Rhythm* more clearly, characterize each

Interval of the key, mark the *Scale*, express the relationship (generally) existing between keys where " *Modulation*" [transition] occurs, render Transposition perfectly easy, and furnish a set of syllables favourable to good *Intonation.* The tendency of such a notation is, I think, to lead the pupils to sing *better in tune* and *sooner at sight*, and to imbibe *more correct notions* of the Theory of Music. A convenient circumstance attending the notation here proposed is, that it admits of being printed in common type. The principal objection I anticipate to its use is that the quantity of music already published in the usual notation by points, will be unintelligible to the student acquainted only with the new. * * * The new notation, however, may easily and usefully be applied *as an introduction* to the pointed notation; and in such a manner as to divest that of much of its seeming irrationality. I am persuaded that on the whole, *a more rapid progress* would be made by pupils thus instructed, than by those who are obliged to encounter the defects of the pointed notation *at the commencement;* while those who require no more knowledge than would qualify them for skill in Psalmody, might easily be supplied with a collection of tunes printed in the solfa notation, ample enough for all the purposes of social and congregational worship." See "A Manual of the Norwich Solfa System, or a Scheme for rendering Psalmody Congregational," published by Hamilton and Adams.

The TEACHING ADVANTAGES of Miss Glover's plan are obvious. (1) By laying aside the Old Notation, at the commencement, it prevents a thousand misconceptions, inaccuracies, and discouragements which are so commonly entertained. The teacher knows how much depends on our first impressions of an art being correct and true. (2) It seeks as its first object, to elucidate the simple and beautiful facts of music itself, and makes them throw light upon notation, instead of letting notation throw mystery upon them. (3) It teaches "one thing at a time," and that perfectly. It, first, engages the learner's attention to the *tuning* of voice and ear, by means of the vocal pattern, (p. 2) which he must observe and imitate, and in connection with a perfect pictorial scale (the " musical ladder," or modulator, p. 5), which presents to his eye the exact positions and the distinctive names of notes. This " tuning" is founded on the leading and most marked intervals of the scale. It, next, developes Interval more fully, giving an individualized conception of each note in the scale. Then, gradually, it introduces into the exercises and explains in the lessons the difficulties of accent, " time," transition, chromatic notes, &c., one by one : all this time employing a letter-notation (taken from the Modulator already fixed in the mind's eye of the pupil) which is so simple and so direct and clear in its bearings on the facts of music, that it can scarcely be said to occupy any time in learning or to distract any attention towards itself. And, lastly, or *at any earlier stage* of progress if necessary, it gives an introduction to the familiar and masterly use of the Old Notation.

The pretensions and advantages of the solfa *notation* may be summed up thus :—

ITS PRETENSIONS are—1. To assist in giving to young children an acquaintance with the elements of music, upon scientific principles, long before they are of an age to grapple with the difficulties of the old notation. 2. To facilitate the efforts of those who wish to read the old notation with ease and accuracy: for to learn the use of this notation is one of the quickest ways of becoming truly master of the other. 3. To answer all the purposes of a *notation for congregational psalmody*, or for *school use*, with the following advantages; (1) that it is more scientific in its structure, (2) that it may be more easily learnt, and (3) *more cheaply printed* than the other.

ITS ADVANTAGES are—1. The signs and terms employed are few and simple, and each one *directly* expressive of some musical truth. 2. By the use of the "modulator," the ear and the voice of the pupil may be trained to a considerable extent before he is troubled with terms and signs at all. He is thus, in accordance with an important principle of education, made thoroughly conscious of the thing signified before the sign is shown him. 3. The *pictorial* representation of the intervals on the modulator, *to which the whole notation bears reference*, is *accurate* and *invariable*. A marked distinction is shown between the tones and "half" tones, and neither the names of the intervals nor their *relative* positions change with the change of the key. 4. By adopting the scientific usage of the solfa syllables there is formed a PERFECT AND UNCHANGING LANGUAGE OF INTERVAL. This, by means of the power of association, becomes a very great facility to the learner.

The following notes contain an answer to two very common objections, and an account of our first visit to Miss Glover's school, with the impressions which her method then produced.

The reader will now be prepared to answer such objections as the following. " But, does not the staff in the Old Notation give to the pupil a *picture* of interval, and must not that be much more easy to sing from than your merely *symbolic* letters ?" Yes, undoubtedly, if it gave a *correct* picture of interval, and pictured that interval, *according to its true nature*, in key-relationship. The sequential notation does the latter, but no staff of lines and spaces can perfectly picture the "semitones:" they will still require some diagram, like the modulator, to explain the nature of a key. *Correct symbols* associated in the mind with a perfect pictorial scale, and that so strongly that the symbols themselves seem to rise or fall, as we sing them, to their proper places in the imagined scale, must be incomparably better than an *inaccurate* and *misleading* pictorial staff. Again, however, it is objected—" Why teach a new notation if you must come back again to the old? Why take the trouble of teaching two ?" First, because there is really *no* trouble in teaching the solfa notation. We have seen children in an infant school use it before they had learnt to read. It was, to them, simply the letters of their Modulator "written down." Secondly, because the Old Notation presents such difficulties to the learner as to make it impossible to teach music, in any short time, by its means alone. Thirdly, because the use of some such new notation is the quickest and most perfect means of gaining a real

command of the old. The maze of flats and sharps and keys and clefs, which, if the pupil had entered it at the first, would have taken him a long time to pierce, and might have proved to him, as it does to thousands, an effectual barrier to progress, he can now easily *see through*, having the light of *knowledge* to guide him. He has already gained a command of interval—a correct practical knowledge of measure and accent—an insight into the first principles of melody, and of harmony—a taste for the finer beauties of music—and a practised voice. In all this he will find that there is nothing to *unlearn*, but rather that everything is learnt except the use of a few marks and signs, which one evening's study will make plain to him. Moreover, when he *has* added to his previous acquirements the knowledge of the "old notation," he will use it with an intelligence and pleasurable insight which the ordinary methods of musical instruction do not give, and which, by means of the Old Notation alone, it would take him more than twice as long, with the study of difficult books, to obtain. The pupil, in studying the Old Notation, will find himself in the position of one who is tracing the map of a country *already visited*. He excuses the rough and inaccurate outlines for the sake of the delightful and familiar regions of which they remind him.

VISIT TO MISS GLOVER'S SCHOOL.—This is an infant school at Norwich. It does not differ in its general aspect and arrangement from other infant schools. The daily employments of the children, their average age, and their appearance, correspond with what may be seen in most schools of a similar kind. But in one thing they are remarkably distinguished from all other schools that we have ever seen:—these little children conduct their *Singing Exercises* with so much facility and delight, and, at the same time, with such accuracy both of time and tune, as to fill with astonishment all who hear them. Our readers will readily believe that this must be the case, when we tell them that, in the course of our visit, we heard the children sing canons in four, six, and even in eight parts, with great precision and beauty of execution. This was done from notes, without any instrument to lead them, and only in one case did the voices flatten, and in that case only by half a tone. To those who have been accustomed to the singing of young children, this will appear indeed astonishing; but we shall astonish them still more when we say, that the training which has produced such results does not occupy more than two hours in the week! A length of time not greater than is given to singing exercises in every infant school in the land! Whence then arises the difference? From this cause—that, while in other schools, the time is loosely spent without plan or design, and consequently without progression, in Miss Glover's school the time is husbanded by a carefully arranged method. But this is not sufficient to explain all: it is necessary to add, that the method itself contains *more of true science*, and *less of technicality*, than any other method now taught in England.

We will first describe the system as we saw it in operation, and then examine briefly its principles.

As we entered the room, the soft and regulated tone, and the sweet blending of the voices, such as take not the ear by force, but steal on the senses as by some magic spell, assured us that music; real music, with all its subduing power, dwelt there.

On the gallery were seated all the younger children, with heads erect, and shoulders back, singing, (with the solfa syllables) and as they sung, eagerly looking towards an upright board which stood at a little distance from the foot of the gallery. On this board were printed one above the other, the initial letters of the solfa syllables, showing much shorter distances between ME and FA, and between TE and DO, (the third and fourth and seventh and eighth *of the scale*, for in this method, DO is always the key note) than between the other notes. This *Musical Ladder*, as it is styled, corresponds with what we have called the Modulator. By the side of the "Ladder" stood a little monitor with a wand in her hand. She was pointing to the notes as the children sang

them. The very movement of her wand was musical. She also held in charge with her other hand, a little infant, the youngest of the school, who could scarcely stand, but who nevertheless could sing. The children are taught to sing in this way, looking at the exact intervals as depicted on the Musical Ladder, until they enter the higher class of the school. This may be in the course of six months, or in a much shorter time. We did not observe any distinct classification for the singing lessons; they are taken as part of the ordinary routine of the school. The children are thus rendered perfectly familiar with *an accurate pictorial representation of interval*: indeed they must carry a musical ladder in their mind's eye wherever they go, and by the correct association of mind thus established, they are well prepared for the next stage in their advancement.

This we had an opportunity of examining in another part of the room, where stood a class of twenty—the elder children in the school—having in their left hands the "Solfa Tune Book," and in the right, short wands for the purpose of beating time.

The tune books were supported on a small instrument in the shape of a cross, with the longest bar extending beyond the book to the right hand. Upon this projecting part of the "book-holder," as soon as the tune began, the loud beats of the measure were pretty sharply struck, while the soft beats were indicated by gentle touches of the wand on their left arm.

Miss Glover, the lady from whose invention and zealous patronage all these results have sprung, and whose christian solicitude for the better interests of the children thus taught we have been thankful to witness, with a courtesy which we cannot too gratefully acknowledge, kindly exhibited to us every part of the method. The plan of procedure was in this wise;—supposing them about to sing the 14th canon, which is in eight parts, the teacher steps into the middle of the circle and announces "fourteenth canon." Immediately all find the place. "Eight leaders." Immediately eight children hold up their wands, dividing the class into equal portions, so that each child may know which leader she is to follow. The chord of the key note is then struck on a glass harmonicon, which is placed in the room for the purpose, and the canon begins. When the first division has sung the first measure, the monitor of the next division, giving a glance at those under her, which means, "follow me," takes up the strain—beating time upon the book-holder and her arm. The rest of the division marked the time by *touching*, with their wands, the accent marks in their books. Thus round the class the growing harmony proceeds, until it swells out in the fullest chorus. Turning round we observed that the children on the gallery, by the help of a monitor and the musical ladder, were joining in the melody. Several pieces with words were also sung very beautifully; and on the following day Miss Glover very kindly exhibited to us, with a select class, her method of teaching the minor scale, and the manner in which the more advanced children were introduced, by easy steps, to the correct use of the old notation. From a very careful inspection, we felt quite convinced that, considering this method of teaching music as only *introductory* to the use of the common notation, it is the best introduction—the quickest and the most efficient, and, judging by its own merits, it appears to us—simple and easy though it is to a child—amply sufficient for all the purposes of psalmody.

In examining the method itself, two things occurred to us as worthy of special notice. First, the principle of solfaing which is practised. It is entirely distinct from that made use of by Mr. Hullah and Mr. Mainzer. Those gentlemen make the solfa syllables only other names for the fixed notes, C, D, E, F, G, A, B, C^1. This is the common French method. Miss Glover follows the scientific usage of England, which, according to the best authorities, makes DO always the KEY NOTE, whatever that may be. Those who are unaccustomed to this more scientific method of solfaing can scarcely form any estimate of the very great assistance which it offers to the learner. Our readers will readily understand the means by which it does so when they recal so familiar a thing as this;—how common it is with us, when we wish to remember a *tune*, to recal the *words* we are accustomed to sing it to, and the moment we remember the words, that moment occurs to us the tune. Why is this? Because we have

associated the first *syllables* of the verse with the first *intervals* of the tune. The method of solfaing we speak of, is only a more perfect development of the same principle, thus bringing in, with full force, the strongest of our mental powers to aid the pupil's progress.

The other thing observable is this, that the number of singing exercises is very few. They consist of only as many canons as might be printed on two pages of this magazine. But these canons contain all the intervals of the scale, and are learnt with very great accuracy and precision. We were very strongly reminded of Jacotot's principles of teaching. "Learn one thing well, and learn everything else by the help of that." This principle he applied, we understand, to music teaching. It is remarkable that the same plan was employed in the Romish church upwards of eight hundred years ago! The pupil was then first made to learn thoroughly a particular chant, so as to know all its intervals by heart, and was next carried on to learn other chants, referring everything to the preceding lessons. This is evidently the same principle as that which we have recommended so strongly in the "Look-and-say Method of Teaching to Read;" but whether, as applied to music, it is preferable to any other mode of progression, we are at present unable to decide. Miss Glover's success strongly inclines us to think that it is.—*Independent Magazine, May,* 1842.

On the point last mentioned we have now concluded that, although to some extent all good teaching should be conducted on that principle, yet it is better if some philosophical principle of arrangement and development can accompany it, as in this book. For day schools we wish the "Look and Say" plan to be so modified.

THE MODIFICATIONS OF MISS GLOVER'S PLAN ADOPTED IN THIS WORK.

It is due to Miss Glover—the intelligent and noble-minded inventor of this method, to state distinctly the modifications of her plan which have been adopted in this work, and to give sufficient reasons for them. This will be done in the following extracts, from a letter addressed (Dec. 10, 1846), when the last edition was out of print, to one who wished the editor then to lay aside his modifications and to promote the system in its original form.

"I was very anxious that those leading principles of Miss Glover's method, which had been so useful to me, should be popularly known and generally adopted; but my previous experience, as a teacher both of young and old, led me to think that there was no probability that the system in its original form would become so * * * I still think the alterations too important to be relinquished. May I ask your kind attention to a few of them.

1. The substitution of small letters, in the notation, for capitals and small letters mixed. This, besides giving a more even and neat appearance to the music, enables the printer to put a larger quantity into the same space without making it less readable. It thus facilitates *cheapness of production*—an advantage which should not be thrown away or lightly esteemed in these days of competition—especially in an undertaking which we wish to make as accessible as possible

even to the poorest. It also very greatly facilitates—I had almost said *introduces*—the important practice of writing music with freedom, for we can scarcely suppose that children or other pupils would very readily take to the writing of music, when they were compelled to do so chiefly in capital letters; the process indeed would of necessity be much slower than that of writing in the Old Notation.

2. The use of such signs and marks as were more likely, than the original ones, to be found, *in sufficient numbers*, in every printer's "case," or such as might be obtained at small cost from the type founders. The use of the small letters is important here. This also points to cheapness and facility of production. Illustrations of its usefulness have already appeared. In a large private school, the boys have frequently printed pieces of music for their own use at public examinations and on other occasions, in this "Small-letter Solfa Notation." A numerous choir connected with a large place of worship in the north of England printed a considerable number of psalm tunes for their own use. It appears to me that this sort of free trade in music printing is of the utmost importance to those who wish to throw music open to all. In both of the above cases the cause of music would have suffered, had there been any difficulties in the way of home-printing.

3. The plan of measuring time more distinctly to the eye by means of the accent-marks placed at equal distances along the page. This has been recognised by many teachers as one of the first and most obvious advantages of the New Notation. It gives a distinct pictorial notion of time. But its chief importance arises from its enabling me to provide the next facility for the spread of music; I refer to—

4. The introduction of the solfa music paper, and the "solfa black board"—both prepared for our musical short-hand by having the accent marks ready placed at equal distances. The children of our day school would indeed feel themselves in a sad plight if deprived of these facilities. The master frequently—as a treat and reward—writes some new school song upon the black board, in this quick notation, and permits the children to copy it on their music paper. Many of the pieces with which he thus supplies them are taken from expensive and copyright works, which we dare not reprint, and which would be quite beyond the reach of the children of the poor except by such means as these. Miss Matthews, whose time is fully occupied in teaching music, and exclusively on the solfa method, informs me that the music paper was generally welcomed by her pupils, as offering great advantages. For myself, I should be without a considerable collection of beautiful airs, which I have

picked up, in various places and from a great variety of books and persons, if it had not been for this musical short-hand. If we were to return to the original capital letters with accent marks at irregular intervals, we might indeed *write* music, but this musical *short-hand* could not exist.

5. The establishment of a closer relationship with the Old Notation, by retaining the old names of the pitch-notes C, D, E, F, &c., with their sharps and flats, instead of using the new nomenclature of O, Q, V, W, &c. This makes the transition into the Old Notation very much easier to the pupil. It forms a point of connection between the two systems, which is of great use, especially to those who have been accustomed to the older one. I propose to introduce in my new editions some still further condescensions to the Old Notation, which it is in vain for us to attempt to supersede. [This refers to the humbler method of denoting transition. See note, pp. 53, 54.] I think the public generally will esteem these the most useful "modifications" of all.

6. The use of a much more *ample* and *varied* selection of exercises, chiefly copied from the first masters. I cannot conceal from you that, without these, I should have been unable to get on at all. A few canons and a small number of psalm tunes would not have been sufficient to interest those whom I have had to instruct, or rightly to form their taste. My anxiety now is to make a yet larger and more lively and varied selection. [This has been done in the present edition.]

7. A full course of progressive lessons on music itself. This forms the body of the book called "Singing for Schools and Congregations." As a book of instruction on the art, and of information on the science, of music, I have found it extremely useful for teachers, and for advanced classes. It is the result of long study and practice, and so far from being able to lay it aside, I am more than ever convinced of the importance of a yet fuller development of the principles of music, and a yet more careful arrangement of progressive exercises and examinations. [The editor has indeed been led, by the necessity of stereotyping, into a far more laborious and anxious exposition of these topics than he ever anticipated.] Miss Glover's brief "directions for instructing a school," *most admirable as they are*, could not at all supply the place which this book seeks to fill."

The editor is desirous not to deceive the public by allowing them to suppose that these modifications go forth under Miss Glover's full approval; and, at the same time, he is most anxious that to Miss Glover should be given the fullest credit for that admirable genius, patience, and research which have been shown in the construction of her system, and that to her should be yielded the chief praise for whatever success his own work may obtain. In a letter to the editor, dated Oct. 5th, 1846, when the modifications were first proposed, Miss Glover says : " But though you prefer some alterations, yet you keep to the *leading principles* of the Solfa Notation, and my pupils would soon sing from your book and yours from mine." Subsequent letters also implied acquiescence and consent, and showed that, although she would have been more gratified by a stricter adherence to her own method, yet she was pleased that the leading principles were retained, and rejoiced that good was done. This reception of his alterations which, when well considered, will appear truly noble and generous, the editor acknowledges with gratitude and respect. He has rejoiced also to know that his own work, going, as it does, into different circles and opening entirely new fields, instead of hindering the sale of Miss Glover's work, has promoted it, and will continue to do so; for every student by this means made acquainted with the system will naturally turn to the original work, especially when he knows that it can be obtained from its enterprising publishers at the price of one shilling. Miss Glover's method is called " The Norwich Solfa System;" ours, that we may not be mistaken, is called " The Tonic Solfa Method"—the word Tonic referring to the principle of key-relationship which is made so prominent both by Miss Glover and ourselves. Miss Glover's notation is called " *The* Solfa Notation;" ours is distinguished as " The Small-letter Solfa Notation."

OF THE MODULATOR.

The Modulator, or "Pointing Board for teaching tunes" (see back of title-page) is a scale of notes arranged pictorially according to their position in key, and indicated by distinct names called the solfa syllables or else by the initial letters of those syllables. On this scale of notes in key the teacher points to those which he wishes his pupils to sing. His pupils follow the movements of the pointer, which makes thus a constant appeal to " interval," and shows the eye precisely what the voice is doing. This accurate pictorial treatment of interval is found to concentrate attention and to facilitate greatly the early progress of the pupil; whereas the inaccurate pictorial representation of the staff, in the Old Notation, is a constant cause of incertitude and confusion to learners. In connection with the Modulator, the practice of

TEACHING BY PATTERN is of the highest importance. (See p. 2.) The teacher sings, softly and distinctly, a short phrase of the tune to be taught. To this vocal pattern the pupils so listen that they may be able to imitate immediately afterwards. Thus are they at once encouraged by the teacher's example, and stimulated to a *strong mental effort* in endeavouring to bring the ear and the voice to do the mind's bidding. In this effort alone consists the whole work of learning to sing. That method is the best, therefore, which requires the most of it. One hour's training of this kind is far more effective than five spent in singing *with* a leader. The teacher also, not singing with his pupils, is better able to criticise and patiently correct their mistakes. The physical effort too of teaching to sing becomes comparatively small; and thus is removed a very great hindrance to the progress of music in day schools, for the day school teacher has usually quite enough labour for his voice without adding to it the task of *outsinging* (by way of "leading") the discordant voices of some hundred or two of children.

Great advantage also is gained by the adoption of the old " tonic method of solfaing," which allows us to establish a fixed and invariable association of mind between certain syllables and their corresponding intervals. The semitones (tonules), for instance, are *always* between ME FAH and TE DOH, and the pupil is so accustomed to sing those syllables to that interval, that he would find it difficult to sing them wrongly. Thus an interval thoroughly learnt in one tune or key becomes, to the learner, a "pattern" for that same interval occurring in any other tune or key; and soon he is able to leave both the teacher's pattern and the modulator, and read music for himself.

OF THE EXERCISES AND CRITICISMS ON TUNES.

Each exercise, here printed in the solfa letters, has a reference, in its title, to "School Music," (s. M.) in which it may be found printed in the Old Notation, so that the teacher may use which notation he pleases. There is also a reference to "School Songs," (s. s.) in which appropriate words may be found.

The introductory exercises, some of which should be sung at the opening of every lesson, are designed to tune the voice. They are founded on the boldest and most consonant intervals of the scale. These prepare the way for that development of interval which is founded on the recognition of the individual character and peculiar mental effect which belongs to each note of a key. The other difficulties of music are introduced gradually, as they are explained by the accompanying lessons. The proper use of the exercises is described on pages 21, 22.

It accords with the principle of development adopted in this book that the exercises should be nearly all *tunes*. These have been selected largely from the first masters, and are designed to exhibit a sufficient variety of musical style, and to cultivate and refine the taste. Thus, instead of toiling unrewarded through dull exercises on interval, the pupil realizes the fruit of his attainments at every step.

The editor is indebted, for the harmonies accompanying the exercises, to the kindness and well-practised skill of George Hogarth, Esq. The tunes are harmonized for two male voices, or for two trebles and (in School Music) an accompanying bass. It is due to Mr. Hogarth to state that, the tunes having sometimes to be sung in three parts, and sometimes only in two, he was compelled occasionally to sacrifice musical effect in one part for the sake of the other. But the teacher will find these cases few, and he can very easily correct them with a pen. In classes of males exclusively, or of females exclusively, the Air and "Second" should be sung, as in this book. In mixed classes, the higher voices of both sexes may sing one part and the lower voices the other—or the women and children may sustain the air and second while the men sing the bass. In female schools only two parts will be heard, but in those conducted by a male teacher, there will be three parts. See note, p. 89. The practice of singing in two parts only is an excellent training to the ear, for a better appreciation of fuller chords.

The "seconds" part should often be sung alone for practice, all the pupils joining in it. In such cases it should be pitched a third higher. In an infants' school the teacher should take care not to strain the voices of her children. She will often find it necessary to lower the pitch of the key note.

The places of the knots in the STRING PENDULUM (p. 12) are not given with perfect precision, but so as to be most easily made. The metronome figures attached to each tune should not be neglected by the teacher. But, when once

e

he has caught the rate of movement, it is not necessary that he should use the pendulum throughout the tune.

A large and ever-fresh supply of tunes is needed in teaching to sing. This selection of one hundred and eighty may be indefinitely enlarged by the use of the Solfa Music Paper, which may be made into books and interleaved with plain paper for the words. The works of Mr. Hickson, Dr. Mainzer's Choruses, Mr. Callcott's " Child's Own Singing Book," Mrs. Herschell's " Fireside Harmony," the Sunday School Union's " Juvenile Harmonist," " The Singing Book," by Messrs. Turle and Taylor, &c., will yield an ample supply.

The day school teacher should multiply, as much as possible, the number of good Children's Ballads and of true Children's Lyrics, with which to ply the minds of his pupils. Many of the " Original Poems" and " Nursery Rhymes," by Jane Taylor, which we could not purchase permission to reprint, might, by help of the copy books above described, be adapted to the tunes in " School Music." For instance the following :—

" Spring," " Summer," " Autumn," " Winter," " Morning," " Snow," " The way to be happy," " The Sparrows," and " The little ants"—to JESSE.

" The idle boy," and " The shepherd boy"—to LEYBURN, omitting one " repeat."

" The little fisherman"—to MASBURY, with comic expression.

" Never play with fire"—to OLD BASING.

" The lark," " The spring nosegay," and " The little lark"—to CROSSCOMBE.

" The fox and the crow," " The holidays," " The chatterbox," and " Dirty Jim"—to BO-PEEP.

" Turnip tops"—to BAVARIAN.

" The pond," and " The notorious glutton"—to THE BABY, with a comic expression.

" My Mother"—to CLIFTON GROVE—the first part of the tune ; making the last line, " My mother! oh, my mother!"

" The horse"—to CLIFTON GROVE, sung quickly with comic expression.

" The good-natured girls," and " Contented John" —to BLACKSMITH or BABY.

" The baby"—to OLD BASING, omitting the first " repeat."

" Poor donkey's epitaph"—to MASBURY.

" The village green," " The star," and " The little husbandman"—to THE SWALLOW.

" The cow"—to TROUBADOUR or LAUSANNE.

" Good night"—to PASCAL.

" The baby's dance" may be adapted to THE BABY.

" The cut"—to THE RAINY DAY.

" Questions and answers"—to STRAWBERRY GIRL.

" Dutiful Jem"—to BINFIELD HEATH, with the first two lines for a chorus or to the tune given in a note, p. 29 of this book.

" Little birds and cruel boys," and the " Honest ploughman"—to THE BABY, repeating the last line of each verse.

" Romping"—to BLACKSMITH, repeating the last two lines of each verse.

" Some think it a hardship to work for their bread," from " Original Hymns for Sunday Schools"—to JESSE.

Could not the publisher print these forty-two songs in a small separate book, as a companion, in school work, to our " School Songs" and " School Music ?"

The editor has desired throughout this work not only to improve the Understanding and to give Skill to the voice, but also to cultivate the Taste and to encourage right Emotion. With this view great care has been given to the selection of words—that they might be simple and " taking" to a child, and yet not debasing to his taste ; and with this view also the " Hints and Criticisms on Tunes" have been written. It may be easily noticed that every good teacher has, in addition to his ability and accuracy of teaching, an influence of sympathy over his pupils—which he gains by the natural and incidental *expression* of his own feelings in connection with the subject taught—an influence which has its own peculiar province, and which is as important and useful as any other. The editor wished to set a pattern to the teacher, in forming this habit of incidental remark sprung from sympathetic emotion, which is almost our only means of cultivating the feelings and the taste.

OF THE LESSONS TO CHILDREN AND THE TESTS OF PROGRESS.

The skilful teacher will not need the minute directions, for introducing thought to a child's mind, which are given in connection with the grammatical portions of this book.   He will often make better lessons than these, but he is not likely to complain of the room they take.   Many persons, however, into whose hands this book may fall, are altogether ignorant of the difficulty there is in *putting* thoughts transparently before the mind of another, and they would teach very inefficiently without such helps as these.   The editor is not without hope that a more general acquaintance with the art of teaching itself may, to some extent, be promoted by this means.   The teacher of adults may obtain many hints from these lessons to children.   The solitary student too will often see, in them, the points of his condensed "proposition" more fully explained or thrown into some new light.   A thought which the reader does not catch when expressed in one form of words, he will often grasp at once when thrown into another.   With this view the editor has purposely varied his phraseology in the headings of pages, the questions at the end of each "stage," and the table of contents.   A new form of words often compels fresh thought.

The TESTS OF PROGRESS (see p. 16) will often supply, in addition to the questions, new exercises.   The skilful teacher would invent similar ones for himself—for he knows the importance of "taking the soundings," as the sailors would say, at frequent intervals.   Others, it is hoped, will find them very useful; for it is not an easy thing to ask a teacher's question, and without good questions, we cannot teach much.

OF THE GRAMMATICAL PARTS OF THIS WORK.

The work is not divided into lessons, as in the former edition, for it was found that the apportionment which suited one capacity and stature of mind did not suit the other.   The division is therefore by *sections*.   This enables us to maintain a clearer distinction of topics, which is very important in a book which must often be used for reference.   The teacher has before him then, not the lesson, but the materials for a lesson.   Let him, in each lesson hour, occupy part of the time in grammatical explanations, part in exercises, and part in examination and tests of progress.

For everything of choicest value in this department of the work the editor is indebted to the aid and suggestion of friends.   To G. F. Graham, Esq., of Edinburgh, author of the article "Music" in the last edition of the "Encyclopædia Britannica," (reprinted and enlarged as "The Theory and Practice of Musical Composition") a gentleman whose work denotes him to combine, in a remarkable manner, the most extensive learning—a learning confined to no country and no school—with a free unburdened originality of thought, it is a pleasure to acknowledge obligation.   To his correspondence as well as to his work, the editor is indebted for the clear development of MEASURE (p. 6), and for many suggestions on the terminology of music.   To the valuable aid of Dr.

Bryce and Col. Thompson, reference is made on many of the following pages.
For a kind revision of the educational arrangements of the earlier parts of this
book, the editor has to thank his valued friend Mr. Dunning, Principal of the
Home and Colonial Normal School; and for many sound practical suggestions,
especially bearing on the importance of a closer relationship with the Old Notation, he is indebted to a patient examination of this method, and a most skilful
testing of its results conducted by Mr. Gordon, who visited the Plaistow schools
as Inspector for the above-named institution.

It is hoped that the sections on the mental effect of notes will throw an
intelligent interest around the ordinary practice of music, and that those on
Transition will give the key to many of its most magical effects. In some
places, as in the section on "Minor Tunes," and in those on "Chanting" and
"Psalmody," the editor has given space to somewhat lengthened arguments; for
he was aware that his book will have to fight its way as well as to do its work,
and he was anxious that no novelty either in theory or practice should be here
broached, which could not show for itself *high authority, strong reason,* or *careful
and repeated experiment.*

It is hoped that the method of marking EXPRESSION as applied to words,
(p. 14), will be a constant facility to the teacher, and an encouragement in the
exercise of taste.

The exposition of MELODY and the practice of elementary COMPOSITION
should not be neglected even in schools. For developing the constructive and
imaginative faculties and improving the taste, such exercises are highly important. Nageli recommends that they should commence at a much earlier stage
of the pupil's progress. The skilful teacher will easily introduce them as opportunity offers. So also may the exercise of COPYING BY EAR be used as a
pleasing variety and a reward long before the exercises attached to the previous
sections are concluded.

The section on HARMONY is rendered interesting by the combination of the
Philosophic Theories of Dr. Bryce and M. Jeu de Berneval, with the Practical
Rules of Musicians. Counterpoint in two parts may be practised even in schools,
especially where there is a "Tonic Solfa Harmonicon."

The section on CHANTING develops a peculiar treatment of the reciting note,
which promises to deliver the chant from that hurry and gabble by which it is
so often desecrated—to enable a whole congregation to use with one voice this
simplest form of sacred song—and to restore to their proper place, in our
sanctuaries, the inspired psalms of memorial and of praise.

THE INTRODUCTION TO THE OLD NOTATION is given partly in the manner
of oral lessons, and partly in a more condensed form, as the different topics
needed more or less elucidation. In schools, where there is time for a complete
course, it is strongly recommended that the Old Notation should not be introduced till the end of the third stage, certainly not before the close of the
second. This part of the book is so arranged, however, that the teacher may
introduce the Old Notation, unwisely, at the very beginning of the course, if he
pleases. In the lessons on harmony the pupil should be led to "parse" and to
copy the various chords, and to write exercises in both notations.

SINGING FOR SUNDAY SCHOOLS.

If we would produce any wide and permanent result in the revival of psalmody, we must commence among the teachers and children of the sabbath school. There do we cultivate the spirit of love and gratitude—the spirit of "joy in God." There too let us give to that noblest joy its first and sweetest voice. The following hints may be useful:—

1. Give great care that each child be provided with his hymn book, and that the hymns are carefully explained, illustrated, and committed to memory; so that there be no "lining out" of the hymns, a practice which sadly spoils the melody, and painfully disturbs the onward flow of thought and feeling. 2. Teach the tunes to as many as can be gathered into bible classes or special singing meetings—held in the course of the week, according to the tonic solfa method developed in this book. These, on the sabbath day, will easily "lead" the rest. But if you must have the teaching of tunes on the sabbath— 3. Do not desecrate sacred words by using them in the first practice of a tune, but sing "one," "two," "three," according to the number of syllables in each line (see p. 22); and 4. Teach by pattern (see p. 2). Do this patiently, but never sing *with* the children. This is the *quickest* as well as the *best* method. 5. Be careful, if as leader you find it necessary to criticise, on the sabbath, the *singing* of the children, that you also make incidental remarks on the point and beauty of the hymn as your heart shall prompt you, lest the children should suppose that your attention, like theirs too often, is wholly given to the music.

The course of exercises pursued by a week-night singing class, for preparing and supporting the songs of the sabbath school, would include nearly all in this book, the secular tunes being omitted. The teacher could use the Modulator and the "School Course of Exercises," (4d.) and he should accompany the practice with grammatical instruction in music; taking care that every four, three, or two weeks, as the case may require, he and his class are ready to introduce a new hymn and a new tune to the sabbath school to which they belong. Let him persuade all the male teachers to join him in singing the bass from "School Music," and some of the female teachers to sing the "second." A tune thus introduced would be used with profit from the beginning.

SINGING FOR BIBLE CLASSES.

We refer especially to those which are held in the week. Ten minutes or a quarter of an hour, employed in singing exercises, at the opening of each bible class, would tend to keep up the knowledge and the love of psalmody among the young people of a congregation.

The minister or other teacher of the class would use the Modulator and the "School Course of Exercises." The exercises might at first be confined to those which are adapted for the opening and closing hymns of a bible class; such as the following, Ex. 13, 15, 17, 20, 25; and all those tunes in this book which have the metres marked in the title. The teacher should carefully prepare a list of hymns which are suitable for this purpose. If possible, each member of the class should have a copy of this book; they could then, occasionally, study the grammar of music with their teacher, reading proposition by proposition in turn.

SINGING FOR DAY SCHOOLS.

In Day Schools, whether for rich or poor, a complete and thorough course should be pursued. The teacher should use the grammar of music as a means of cultivating the reasoning faculties, and its practice as one of his most powerful agents for developing right moral feeling and good taste. He should make each song, before the tune is taught, the subject of a distinct lesson, or lecture, to the whole school, illustrating and impressing it by explanation and anecdote. It will then be "a thing of power," and he should require it to be learnt by rote. For the vocal exercises, he should require from his pupils a quarter of an hour of strenuous mental application to them *every day*. This will be much more efficient than an hour twice a week. The master should himself teach singing, and be ashamed to put it among the "extras." For *marching tunes*, in which we want more the bold rhythm and pleasant sound of the music than any expressive sentiment, we would recommend the simple solfaing "by heart" and in lively style of the boldest tunes:—such as Ex. 61, 24, 21, 23, 34, 39, 41, 80, 82; and "School Music," 79, 88, 110, 107, 108, 89, 67. If words are required, the words to many of the foregoing will be found suitable, and, by pattern or by the solfa music paper, any new ones can be taught.

In INFANTS' SCHOOLS those tunes should be selected which are distinguished by the bold notes (DOH ME SOH), and by a marked rhythm. The words should always be learnt by rote. We recommend after the first five exercises the following course:—Ex. 15, 16, 13, 21, 24, 30, 31, 34, 41, 42, 23, 44, 50, 86; and "School Music," 79, 88, 12, 117, 108, 29, 89, 18, 22.

The following remarks of Dr. Mainzer, and the lecture to the teachers of the "Home and Colonial School Society," continued from page vii, will be useful to the teacher.

"Besides the physical difficulties of teaching singing after the age of childhood, another not less prejudicial presents itself: and this is, the defective musical education which young ladies have previously received in the tedious and mechanical study of the piano. Instead of learning the poetical part of music and its bearings, the pupils in general pass year after year in the drudgery of seeking mechanical perfection, hardly even acquiring the exterior form, and never looking below the surface for a thought or the connection of ideas. If, in learning music, it is not the object to learn its meaning, to understand and enjoy the deeper sense hidden under the beauty of the form, it is scarcely worth the trouble, and certainly deserves not, as a mere fashion, the sacrifice of so much labour and so many of the most interesting moments and best years of life. Singing is the foundation of all musical education, and ought to precede the study of any instrument. In singing classes, children learn to read at sight, and are made acquainted with the general elements of the art, before their attention is called to the mechanical part of it. Thus prepared, they appreciate and enjoy the study of an instrument, instead of finding it, as is usually the case, tedious and interminable. Years of pianoforte instruction may be spared in following this more rational plan, universally recognised and adopted in Germany with such practical advantage.

"Experience of many years and observation of every day's occurrence, have taught us, that a considerable proportion of the numerous children with whom we have met, could, at first, neither sound a single note, nor distinguish one from another: ALL, without exception, have acquired ear and voice, and some of them have even become superior in both to their apparently more gifted companions; in others the very weak or indifferent voices have, in a short time, become pleasing, strong, clear, and extended. With regard to young persons, *comparatively* less advantages are to be expected than from children. The nerves and muscles have no longer the same elasticity; the voice and ear are less flexible; and the teacher has lost that *creative power*, which he possessed in so high a degree during infancy. Then he could *awaken* musical faculties, *form* an ear, *call forth* a voice, *inspire* a love for music, and break through every obstacle.

"At that period of life, when the voice undergoes a change, boys loose their voice altogether; the notes of a higher pitch disappear one after another, till, by degrees, a new voice presents itself upon a lower octave of the scale in the form of a tenor or a bass. Often an excellent treble is, in the space of a few months, or a few weeks, replaced by a bass of the roughest kind. Although the female voice does not undergo such a remarkable transformation, it nevertheless changes its whole character; a low voice often becomes a high one, and a high voice descends and becomes a contra-alto; a good voice changes into an indifferent one, and vice versa. This depends entirely upon the development of the bodily frame and the state of health, so that no one can say with certainty what the voice of a child will be at a more mature age. * * * It must be evident that, when the voice is thus changing its scale and character, it is no time to *begin* to sing; on the contrary, this is the time *not* to sing, or to do it with great care, avoiding every violent exertion." It is at this period that a voice may be injured or destroyed, but not in childhood, "when every trial is *gain*, every exercise is *strength*."— *From Mainzer's "Music and Education."*

The lecture, above referred to, proceeds to illustrate the application of this method to the different "stages" of intelligence in a large educational establishment.

SINGING FOR BABIES.—"The most that you can do systematically with these dear little tinies, is to 'tune' their voices. The voice should be tuned, like any other instrument, by first setting it right on the bold clear notes of the scale; in other words, by teaching the ear to recognise, and the voice to produce firmly, the chord of the tonic or key note. This once done, the other notes will easily take their places around these. For the tonic (or, in our baby-language, DOH), with its companions the MEDIANT and DOMINANT (ME and SOH), is as the father to a family—as the foundation to a house. All the other notes flock in various relationship and dependence around it. They gain from it their several 'characters.' It starts them in every movement, and they lean upon it at the close. You will, first, get the little ones to listen while you sing one note (DOH), and then to imitate it. When they can accomplish this feat, you may give them a second note (DOH—ME; DOH—ME), which they will listen to and imitate; and afterwards a third (DOH—ME—SOH), which they will treat in the same manner. I have often tuned the voice of an adult by long and patient exercises of this kind. Anything will yield to patience. You may then sing these notes with their replicates, in various little tunes, as given in the earlier 'exercises,' pointing, if you please, upon the 'modulator.' Three minutes, twice a day, is as much time as these exercises will require. Apart from mere system, however, it would be your business to make the babies love singing, by the power of 'sympathy.' Sit on the floor in the midst of them, and 'sing them a pretty song' now and then. Teach them 'by pattern' (I mean, by giving them a few notes, or half a line, at a time, to imitate—not singing with them)—such simple songs as 'Thank you, pretty cow,' or 'I will not hurt my little dog.' Do not be too solicitous about progress. Teach well, and progress will take care of itself. It will make itself known in due time."

In this part of the lecture, Mr. Curwen caused the chord to be sung by the audience, and taught them also to sing a chant from "pattern." The few mistakes which were made afforded a favourable illustration of the efficacy of the method, when patiently repeated. Mr. C. went on to describe the plans to be adopted in

SINGING FOR INFANTS.—"In the Infants' room the 'modulator' comes into use, and seven or ten minutes a-day may be employed in the exercises. The modulator which hangs before you, is a scale of notes as they stand in a 'key,'—that is, with the part tones (semitones) between the third and fourth, and seventh and eighth notes. You see the part-tones here marked by shorter distances. Why it is that the part-tones

are always in these particular places, we do not know. We can only notice it as a *fact*, that a tune would be unpleasant to the ear if it neglected this arrangement of part-tones. And a very important fact it is. Now, by making DOH always represent the key-note, we always secure those part-tones which gave me so much trouble, safely between ME and FAH, and TE and DOH. They are 'named and detected.' And the difficulty would be, after a little practice, to sing them wrong. Each note in the 'key,' and each note that occasionally travels out of the key, has here its own proper name. The names are very simple, but they answer our purpose as well as more learned ones, and enable us to bring some of the most beautiful truths of musical science down to the capacity of children. For instance, if we find in Dr. Callcott or M. Jue de Berneval anything asserted about the musical effect, or any other quality of the DOMINANT (or fifth note of the scale), we can tell the whole of it to our children as true of the note which they call SOH. If our books of science teach any fact or rule concerning the SUBDOMINANT, or the LEADING-NOTE, we can teach our little ones to notice carefully the same things concerning FAH, and LAH, and TE. If they tell us of the 'distinguishing' notes of the dominant, or subdominant keys, we tell the same to our children of TU and FI, in the side columns, and so on. What is true of the one, is quite as true of the other. We do not alter the science, but only substitute more simple and more singable names for these beautifully-related notes.

"The next step of systematic progress with your children, is to give them a notion of the movements of their voices *up* and *down*, to teach them to distinguish the *high* and *low* in sound. Many adults who can sing 'by ear' very well, are yet quite unable to tell whether, in any case, the voice goes up or down; much less can they distinguish *how far* it moves at each change of note. The modulator supplies you with an accurate measure of *interval*—by which we mean the distance of notes, as higher or lower in sound. By the frequent use of the modulator its measurement of interval becomes gradually fixed in the mind's eye. The child carries a modulator with him wherever he goes, and he cannot name a note without remembering its position in the scale. You will therefore teach a selection of the boldest and prettiest among the exercises, by 'pattern,' as before, while you point to the notes on the modulator. Take care not to sing with the children, but sing to them, softly and clearly a 'pattern,' and then listen that you may quickly perceive and patiently correct the mistakes of their imitation. Singing with the children is very hard work for you, and prevents your hearing mistakes. Teaching by pattern, on the other hand, cultivates delightfully in your pupils the memory of the ear and the command of the voice.

"While you are thus practising your children frequently from the modulator (for all arts are best taught by frequent rather than lengthened practice), you will find another process going on. Your children will begin to associate in their minds the syllables they so much use with the fixed intervals which they invariably represent. I have no doubt that you, when trying to remember a tune, have often found yourselves assisted by recalling the words you are accustomed to sing it to. The first syllables of the hymn at once recalled the first notes and intervals of the tune with which they had been so long associated. In the same way the solfa syllables give help to the children; only their assistance is *systematic* and *constant*. In a little while, you will find that any DOH, or key-note, being struck, the mere name of any other note will be enough to remind your children of its sound. That this important power of association may be well established, be careful not to allow your children to sing carelessly from the modulator; that is, without full attention of ear and eye. Practise them often in 'following the pointer,' without the aid of a previous pattern; you leading them from note to note with such intervals as you think they can take."

This last plan Mr. C. illustrated, by asking the teachers who had learned this method to follow his pointing. This they did very skilfully, even when he tried them with a chant, which required "transition," both into the "dominant" and "subdominant" keys. The teachers also sang, at various parts of the lecture, a number of school songs and hymns, in two parts, very beautifully. The words were from "Hymns and Poetry, &c.," and the tunes from the "Exercises."

Mr. C. then illustrated another point of advantage to the teacher, which arises from the tonic principle of solfaing, or the making DOH the key-note. It enables the pupil to recognise a certain quality or musical effect as proper to each note of the key, and so to produce the note with greater accuracy and satisfaction. For instance, he is taught that LAH (the sixth from the key-note), when sung slowly, may be called, for musical effect, the "weeping note." And having once satisfied himself of this by experiment, and made familiar acquaintance with the musical effect of LAH (which the name can only proximately describe), he finds himself striking this note ever afterwards with an intelligence and a pleasure which he never knew before. These "qualities of notes" have been often noticed in books of science, and are beautifully developed in the expensive work of M. Jeu de Barneval; but it is surprising that they have been so little used in elementary instruction. It has been fully proved in this establishment, that the rawest singing

recruits among the teachers who come here for training—that even infants are capable of perceiving these points, and find constant practical assistance from the knowledge of them. The musical effect of several of the notes was made evident to the company by illustration. Mr. C. continued—

"But this step of your systematic and scientific progress should not be unaccompanied by pleasant songs. Let pleasure ever go along with progress in your school exercises. As your children gain singing knowledge and singing power, help them to put it into use, and that will be the best reward of their attention and pains. Let me recommend, that the school-songs used at this period be chiefly of a bold and marked character, and in what is called 'common time' (or the binary measure), which marches with a firm and clear step. And let the words you select be simple, and expressive of the natural feelings of the heart, as they would be developed by the daily occurrences of a child's life. Next let us speak of—

SINGING FOR JUVENILES.—"Here you will begin to use the simple solfa notation and the regular 'book of exercises.' Singing in 'parts' will be introduced. The children will pitch the tunes themselves. Tunes will be written out on the black board, and first solfaed, and then sung *at sight*. The elder children will begin to write the musical short-hand which the solfa notation supplies, and to read with intelligence and ease from the *old* notation. The infants, you notice, will have learnt to sing on this plan much as they learn to speak—by imitation. You have not puzzled them with explanations which would be beyond the reach of their undeveloped faculties. They possess, however, much unconscious learning. They can recognise the more marked qualities of notes; something they know of the length of notes: and the modulator has been silently measuring 'interval' to them for a long time past. So that you will have great advantage now in teaching them, as juveniles, the grammar of music, and entering more fully into the reasons of things, according to the course of instruction laid down in your books. A large variety of school songs, religious, moral, and descriptive, should here be introduced. By means of the black board and the 'solfa music paper' you can give an ever fresh and ample supply—and your singing will become the diffuser of pure and joyous sentiments at school, and the charm of many a home. I often go into our little school at Plaistow with some new tune that I wish to hear. It is soon written—in our musical short-hand—on the black board, and almost as soon sung at sight by the elder children —if not very difficult—and caught up by the rest. And this in a school where not more than ten minutes a-day is spent in teaching to sing. May you often enjoy such pleasure as I feel on these occasions." Mr. C. here tested the musical abilities of the teachers present. He wrote a chant upon the black board, and as he wrote the teachers sang it, and that with perfect accuracy.

SINGING FOR TEACHERS was then referred to. "In teaching young persons to sing who expect to become teachers, the greatest pains should be taken to give each one of them an *independent* power. They should learn to solfa every tune 'by heart,' and be able to point it on the modulator, and the strictest examination and the most searching tests of progress should be applied to each individual. A teacher should know something more of a subject than he has to teach; he should, therefore, study with much application of mind, to the end, if possible, of the book of lessons. It will carry him far into a delightful acquaintance with the exceeding beauties of musical science." Mr. C. then showed briefly how easy a mastery of the old notation becomes, when, by means of a simpler one, a knowledge of music itself had already been gained. "Our simple child's notation takes the place of interpreter to the mysteries of the old one. The teacher should, at least, know so much of the old notation as to be able to 'make out' a tune in it, for the use of his children. This

many of your teachers can now do, and I hope that, in half a year's time, the large majority of those who leave this establishment will be able to do so.

"And now, in parting, dear friends and fellow-teachers, permit me to remind you of the importance of well-directed singing among your other school labours. 'Let me have the making of the people's ballads,' said one in former days, 'and I will make the people's character.' Sentiments often recurring to the mind, and endeared by the charms of music and the sweet associations of childhood, must ever be sentiments of power in the moulding of a people's character. Would you wish to give a child at parting some soothing, kindly companion who should follow him through life, and whisper good thoughts to him in his most unguarded leisure? Then plant in his memory some sweet hymn of love, some cheerful song of joy. It shall, perhaps, remind him of his school, his teacher, and *his* God, when all things else around would lead his thoughts astray. Would you teach your child to delight on earth in the highest employment of heaven? Then tune his voice for the song of praise, and attract him to the house of God."

NOTE ON THE TONIC SOLFA HARMONICON.

Miss Glover strongly recommends the use, in schools, of a little instrument in which the sound is produced by striking, with a hammer, on small plates of glass which are supported, in a row, on two pieces of narrow tape. These "Solfa Harmonicons" are very ingeniously constructed, for playing in all keys, by Mr. R. Warne of Norwich, price £1. 11s. 6d. Similar instruments of an inferior kind are commonly sold, at a low price, as children's toys. But hitherto these instruments have all been constructed on the principle of temperament, and form as inaccurate guides for the voice as the piano. We should like to have a Harmonicon connected with the method pursued in this book, to be called, for the sake of distinguishing it, "The Tonic Solfa Harmonicon," which should be tuned *perfectly* by the "Monochord," according to the true intervals of the scale, and supply all the "accidentals" or occasional notes, and the double notes for RAY and TE. (See p. 40, and note, p. 151.) Thus a row of twenty-eight glasses would be required to give the two octaves from G₁ to G¹. These same glasses, tuned to the key of C with its accompanying notes, would also supply, though not so perfectly, the keys of F and G. Another row of twenty-eight glasses, tuned *perfectly* in the key of A would yield also, though less perfectly, the keys of D and E. These six keys would be amply sufficient for all purposes. Indeed one key *perfectly* tuned, would form a far more valuable model for the voice than twelve keys tuned defectively. For an interval perfectly learnt in one key is easily transferred by the voice to any other. An index to each key might be made by means of a moveable strip of wood, planed so as to have *three* sides, placed above and behind the row of glasses. On this the solfa letters could be placed so as to point out the particular glass which belonged to each note of the three keys. The pupil, in playing, would then simply strike the glass in front of each solfa letter required. Such an instrument would be extremely useful to those who are without a teacher. It would give them a clear and perfect "pattern" at any time, and would never get out of tune. If the makers of the toys above-mentioned would give their attention to this matter they would be able to sell such an instrument (with two rows of glasses, and eight keys) for about £1. With only one row of glasses it would be much less costly.

SINGING FOR CONGREGATIONS.

In connection with the great subject of Congregational Psalmody—the chief end for which this book was written—copious practical directions are given in

f

the fourteenth section. When a christian congregation have engaged themselves, with deep and general earnestness, to revive the blessed "service of song
in the house of the Lord," they will not be content with a brief spasmodic effort.
They will well consider their plans. They will use much personal persuasion
and personal example. They will prepare for a weekly Congregational Practice.
But this will not be enough. The love of psalmody must strike its roots more
deeply and securely still. They will therefore "push" the singing movement,
by strong appeal and with serious views of the end to be reached, into every
family, every school, and every bible class which holds connection with them.
And they will expect to continue such a movement for three winters at least
before they can establish a satisfactory result.

In congregational singing classes the first sections of this book may be used
for the purpose of giving correct elementary notions of the nature of music, and
its introductory exercises should be carefully practised at the opening of all the
earlier meetings. When there is a book of Hymn Tunes printed, like those on
pages 122, 123, &c., it will supply the proper course of exercises for such a class,
and the facility which it will give to the voice of the people is greater and more
delightful than any one can conceive who has made no experiment of the plan.
Long before pupils can be taught to use the Old Notation they will sing correctly
from the new one. But, till such a book is provided, it will be necessary to teach
the appendix to this work after the second or third meeting, and to make it
introductory to some tune book in the Old Notation, like Mr. Waite's "Hallelujah" or the "Psalmist"—the class learning to solfa each tune, to "figure" it,
and then to sing it expressively to well chosen words.

In closing this work, the editor feels deeply thankful that he has been permitted to accomplish his task, and earnestly hopes that it may be found worthy
of usefulness. It is his happiness to reflect that he dwells among a people, who
have always encouraged his efforts in the cause of psalmody, and have heartily
united with him to introduce into the family, the school, and the congregation,
both the *voice* and the *spirit* of praise. To them he dedicates this new fruit of
his labour, produced in the intervals allowed by other and higher employments
in their service.

PLAISTOW, ESSEX, *Sept.* 30, 1848.

FIRST STAGE.

SECTION I.

OF MUSICAL SOUNDS AND THE MANAGEMENT OF THE VOICE.

PROPOSITION 1. A sound of the voice in singing is distinctly held, and continues the same from the beginning to the end. It is thus distinguished from the speaking voice, each sound of which has a change in it called an "inflection." A sound of the singing voice is commonly called A NOTE:

* "Listen to me, children, and notice how I say the word—Charles. 'Charles! where are you? Charles!—Charles!' Listen again—'Charles! is that you!!' I was *calling* to Charles the first time, and the second time I was scolding him. Both times I was *speaking*. Now, suppose I try to call to him or to scold him, or to talk to him, not with a speaking, but with a *singing* voice. How would that sound? Listen—'Charles. Charles' (sung to a high loud note). Now let me call him with the speaking voice, 'Charles! Charles!' Listen once more, 'Charles, is that you?' (sung in a low voice). Now let me scold him with the speaking voice, 'Charles! is that you!!' Can you tell me, what is the difference between the singing voice and the speaking voice? * One of you may try it yourself. * Now another. * Now, tell

me. * Yes, in singing, the sound 'holds on the same,' but in speaking, it changes. We say it bends 'up' or 'down.' A sound, in singing, is called a *note*, but a sound in speaking is called an 'inflection.' With a violin you can get either a 'note' or an 'inflection'—which you please. Press your finger steadily on the upper part of a string while you draw the bow, and that will give you a clear beautiful *note*. Listen. * But if instead of that you move your finger up or down the string, that will give you an 'inflection.' Listen *. What is a 'note'? What is an inflection? Now you see that a note ought to have nothing of the inflection about it—no scraping up or scraping down—as some children sing, but it should be *clear, steady,* and *distinct*."

2. To produce a good note, the singer should be in an easy posture, with his head upright and his shoulders back, so as to allow the muscles of the chest and the larynx to have free movement. His mouth should be moderately open. His tongue should lie down—just touching the roots of the lower teeth; and his lips should have the position of a gentle smile.

Some teachers require a small cork, of the thickness of a little finger, or the little finger itself, to be placed between the back teeth during the earlier exercises. The pupil, who would learn to sing without fatigue, should practice, for a few minutes every day, the taking a full inspiration, and then giving out the air very slowly and steadily. This will give command of the muscles of the chest.

"Children, heads up! shoulders back! but sit easily. That is the way in which you should always sit (or stand) when you sing. Can you feel a little lump in your throats? That is the Larynx —the beautiful little instrument that you play upon when you sing. Some day I may show you a picture of it, and tell you more about it. Always hold up your necks to give it plenty of room, when

---

* Those passages in the earlier sections, in which the language of a teacher with a class of children is assumed, are enclosed in inverted commas; and where, in the course of them, a pause is supposed while something is done, it is marked by an asterisk.

B

you sing. Now, let us all take a deep breath. • Once more. • How it seems to open your chest! You should always have your chest open, in that way, if you want to sing easily. Try again, and while I raise my hand do you draw in your breath, and when I lower my hand again gently do you let out the breath again *very slowly.* • Again. • Now you are ready to sing. Who will give us the first sweet and distinct note? Open your mouth a little; let your tongue lie down; and look good tempered about it, and then sing 'Ah' just as I do. • Let those who are willing to try—'hold up hands,' and I will choose who shall sing first. We will all notice whether he sits properly and whether his chest is open, and whether he gives a clear and steady note. • Now, let another try. Any note will do so that it is a good one • •."

3. The sounds of the voice, in singing, should be delivered PROMPTLY and EASILY. If the voice is given out carelessly, it comes roughly through the throat, and is called GUTTURAL; and if produced in a forced manner, it is driven through the nose, and so becomes NASAL.

"Children, remember that whenever you become *lazy* at singing, we must stop. I have seen lazy children scraping out their notes and spoiling the sweet music of all the rest. (Here the teacher may imitate, or caricature the careless guttural style). But, again, I don't wish you to be *rough* in your singing, as though you were pumping the notes out. (Illustrate). One is as bad as the other. What are you *not to be* in singing?" The teacher will very often have to remind his children of these points.

4. The best way of learning to sing, at first, is to imitate with care the voice of the Teacher, who sings for that purpose one note, or several, while the pupil listens. This is called learning to sing by PATTERN. It requires the most attentive listening on the part of the pupil, and a careful endeavour to reproduce, with his voice, the notes he has heard.

It will be perceived that this practice establishes and refines the memory of the ear, and highly cultivates the command of the voice. A strenuous exercise of *mind* is required. It enables the teacher to detect inaccuracies much better than if he had to sing *with* his pupils, and gives him, in the repetition of the pattern, the simplest and most effectual means of correcting them. The pupil also, instead of being lifted from note to note by the labouring voice of the teacher, learns to go by himself, and attains an independent power of voice.

The teacher will now exercise his pupils, first separately and then together, in singing a note which shall be accurately *the same* as any one which he produces. This will often be a difficult exercise and should be carefully practised.

"The little girls know what a 'pattern' is? Yes, it gives you the shape to make things by, and sometimes you take one thing as a 'pattern' for making another. Now I am going to give you a 'pattern' to make a note by. I will sing a note, and then you shall sing one just like it. Only remember two things—first, that you must always *listen* to the pattern with all your minds; and second, that you must then be very careful to sing *exactly like it.* Listening is the most difficult part. *He that listens best will sing best.* Now, let us try •." (Sings to the syllable AH any easy note, for a pattern.)

5. A note may be LOUD or SOFT. The loudness or softness of the voice is called its FORCE. It is very important to cultivate the habit of using a *medium force* of voice, so that it may be always easy to sing a note or a strain more loudly or more softly than the rest.

This habit is important to comfort and pleasure in singing, and absolutely necessary for expression and refinement. Children should be warned against 'bawling.' It spoils the beauty and accuracy of the voice. We cannot command our voice when it is at its stretch. They should be often reminded that "Loud singing is bad singing."

The exercise will now be to produce a note of *medium force*, and the Teacher will notice that the medium voice of one pupil is very different from that of another, according to the size of the Larynx and the power of the Lungs.

6. Notes may be either LONG or SHORT. The length of notes may be measured by the swinging of a pendulum.

The Teacher should be provided with a piece of string having a small weight of any sort at the end of it—for a pendulum.

Exercise. "Give me a long note • —a short note •. This is my 'pendulum.' See how it swings. What is it? • Could you sing a note just while it swings once, and then stop? Let me do it first. • Now try. • Could you make your note as long as two swings? • —as three? • as four? • "

7. Notes may be either HIGH or LOW. The height or lowness of notes is called their PITCH; and the difference of pitch between one note and another is called the INTERVAL between them.

"I wish you just to tell me what you think is the difference between a *high* note and a *low* note. • It is quite different from *loud* and *soft*. Listen and I will give you a high note ('Ah') • Now— a low note ('Ah') • Again, and do you join me. • Once more. • You see that the high notes go up towards a squeak, and the low notes go down towards a growl. Is this a high or a low note • ? —and this • ? Could you give me a high *soft* note? Hold up your hands—who will try? • I will give you one, and you can all imitate it. • Now a *low* soft note? • Now a *loud* high note? • —a loud *low* note? •

Sing a	high,	long,	and	loud	note.
—	—	—	—	soft	—
—	—	short	and	loud	—
—	—	—	-- -	soft	—
—	low	long	and	loud	—
—	—	—	—	soft	—
—	—-	short	and	loud	—
—	—	—	----	soft	—

What would you say of this note? • —and this? •

"Children, notice this. When a note is high, we say it is 'of a high *pitch*.' If a note is low, we say it is 'of a low *pitch*,' and if it is neither very high nor very low, we might say it is of a middle 'pitch.' What do we say of a low note? &c. &c.

"Now I will divide you into two companies, and I will give you two notes—one of a high pitch, and another of a low pitch. One company shall sing the first note, and the other the second. (The Teacher may try this with the key note and its octave DOH, DOH1—or with any two notes that will accord). Now sing them together. • You see, one is high and the other is low—a long way below the first. They are far apart in pitch. What shall we call the distance between them? It is called an '*interval*.' It was rather a large interval, because the notes were far apart. If we had two notes that were not so far apart in pitch, the distance between them would be a smaller interval. Let us try. (The Teacher gives DOH to one company and ME to the others, who sing the notes first alternately and then together). You understand that an Interval is not the two notes, but the *distance between* the two notes, and you see that this sort of interval is very different from an interval of *time*—a minute, or an hour: and it is different from an interval of *space*—a foot or a yard. It is an interval of *pitch*—the distance up or down between two notes. • Now tell me what a musical interval is not. • Now, tell me what it is. • "

SECTION II.

OF REPLICATES, THE GOVERNING OR KEY NOTE, AND THE COMMON MODE, OR SCALE.

1. Every note has other notes related to it, which are of a different pitch, but yet of such a character as to make them regarded as the same. These notes are called REPLICATES.

"I am going to sing two notes, and I wish you to notice them very carefully. (The teacher here sings to the syllable AH the note B, and its lower replicate, or octave, B1). Do you notice that they are very much alike? I will sing them again. • And yet they are not exactly the same. What is the difference? Yes,—one is higher than the other. When two notes are alike, only that one of them is higher than the other, they are called *Replicates* of one another. What are they called?

"Listen again, and I will give you a note with two replicates—one higher and the other lower. (—Sings to the syllable AH, the note B, B1, and B1).

Which did I sing first—the higher or the lower replicate?

"Now, you shall try. Imitate this pattern. (—Sings some such note as the lower E and its higher replicate to the syllable AH). • Try again and imitate another pattern, (—sings the higher F and its lower replicate). •

"One of you shall sing a low note, and the rest shall sing its higher replicate. • One of you give a high note, and the rest give its lower replicate. •

"Have you ever noticed that a man never sings the same notes as a woman or a child? He always sings the lower replicates."

The Teacher will find much careful practice necessary here. He need not delay proceeding until every pupil is able with ease and certainty to produce the replicate. It is sufficient for the present if he thoroughly understands it, and can produce it. It may be mentioned that the replicate is sometimes called the octave.

2. Experience and common practice have decided that, from any given note to its replicate, only seven notes should ordinarily be used in singing, and that only the replicates of these should be used above or below. The attention of the learner may therefore be confined, chiefly to the study of these seven notes.

There are exceptions to this proposition in cases where notes of transition (the sharp fourth TU, the flat seventh FI, and the sharp fifth NE) or chromatic intervals are introduced. It would not be difficult to shew many a short tune in the course of which (by the help of these variations) at least nine or ten notes are used between the key note and its replicate, or octave. But this is the general rule.

It would be *possible* for the human voice to produce almost any number of sounds between a given note and its replicate, but the number is limited for the sake of distinctness and beauty, and for the better appreciation of the common ear. It is

thought by some that the ancient Greeks were much more refined in their appreciation of sounds than we are, and used a larger number of notes. Many nations have deemed a much smaller number sufficient. The old Scottish tunes use only five—omitting the notes which we call the fourth and the seventh of the scale. Some of our best song-birds—endowed with wonderful delicacy of ear and throat—use a far larger number of notes—between a given note and its replicate—than ordinary human ears can count.

"How many notes are there between two replicates?"

3. In every tune there is one note of a given pitch, which regulates the place of the other six notes which, with their replicates, may be used in a tune. It might be called the GOVERNING NOTE: it is commonly called the KEY NOTE.

THE TONIC is another name given to the governing note.

"What is the chief note of a tune called?"

4. It has been found most agreeable to the ear, that the notes, which may be used between a key note and its upper replicate, should be placed at fixed intervals, in the following order. The key note being called the first, the second note is at a short interval above, which is called a TONE; the third is a TONE higher; the fourth is higher by an interval, which is slightly more than half a tone, and which we call a T O N U L E; the fifth, sixth, and seventh are each a TONE higher, and the replicate of the key note is a T O N U L'E higher than the seventh. This arrangement of notes is called the COMMON MODE, or scale.

Those who wish to study the structure of the *common mode* in connection with the beauties of acoustic and mathematical science, are referred to Dr. Bryce's admirable "Rational Introduction to Music," and to the deeply interesting article "SCALE" in the Penny Cyclopedia.

"Come, children, and I will show you how notes are arranged. But first tell me how many notes you have to attend to?—Yes, seven notes and their replicates. And what is the governing note of a tune called? • Yes,—then let us have seven

pennies to stand for the seven notes, and one more for the upper replicate of the key note. We will call it the eighth. This large penny shall stand for the key note. See now I have placed them.

•   •   ••   •   •   ••
1.   2.   3.4.   5.   6.   7.8.

Do you see that some are nearer together than others? Count from the first—the key note, and tell me which are nearest together. Yes—the third and fourth, and seventh and eighth. The distance (interval) from one note to the next is called *a tone*, except where you have a short distance, and that is called a *tonule*. What is a tone? What is a tonule? What notes are the tonules between? Now, hold up hands—who would like to arrange the pennies for themselves. * Who else will try? * This way of arranging the notes is called the *Common Mode*, and sometimes the common scale. What is it called?

Would you like to hear how it sounds? I will sing it to the syllable AH both up and down. Try to notice the tonule. * Notice again." *Tonule* is suggested by Dr. Bryce instead of *semitone*, which is inaccurate. He objects to our previous word "part-tone," on account of its German structure. See "measurement of the mode," p.,40.

5. The seven notes of the common mode, with some of their replicates are represented on the MODULATOR. The syllable DOH represents the *key note*, RAY the second of the mode, ME the third, FAH the fourth, SOH the fifth, LAH the sixth, and TE the seventh. The replicates are marked by the initial letters of the syllable, the upper replicates having a mark (1) above, and the lower replicates a mark (1 or 2) below, to distinguish them. These syllables are called the SOL-FA SYLLABLES.

The syllable TE is used, instead of the ordinary SI, that it may be distinguished in its initial from SOH.

The names of the notes in the common mode should, now, be learnt by rote both up and down.

" You remember what use we made of the pennies. What did we show by them? Yes—the arrangement of notes in the Common Mode. Where did the tonules come? Now let us make a *mode* on our black board with chalk, and don't you think it will be pleasant for us to have *names* to the notes? Do you say the notes as I write them. The note next above (writing it above) is RAY; the third is ME; the fourth—what distance is the fourth above the third? Yes, a tonule—the fourth is FAH, (and so on, to the upper doh.)

" Now I will sing the mode to you. Shall I run up? or shall I sing it down as the bells ring? We call this, that I have written, a *Modulator.*—I will show you a larger one with the replicates—you see how they are marked.

" I want you to learn the names of the notes by rote both up and down, and let me see to-morrow morning how many can bring me a Modulator written down like this with the part-tones in their right places."

6. The Modulator is used in teaching tunes. The teacher points to the notes, both while he gives the 'pattern,' and while the pupil imitates it. This measures to the eye the exact intervals which the voice is taking. And the constant use of the sol-fa syllables, in connection always with the same intervals, helps the mind to recal those intervals with the greater ease.

MODULATOR.

—

f¹
m¹

r¹

d¹
te

lah

soh

fah
me

ray

doh
t₁

l₁

s₁

f₁
m₁

r₁

d₁

" Children, I wish you to understand the use of the Modulator. When I give you a pattern I shall point to the notes that I sing; so that when my voice goes up, the pointer will go up too—and when my voice goes down, the pointer will go down. You will always see by this which way my voice moves and how far it moves. And when you copy my pattern, I shall point out the notes for you, as you sing them up and down. Don't you think that will be a help to you? How will the pointing help you? After a time I shall expect some of you to point out the tunes as we sing them.

" Let me tell you one thing more about the Modulator; you will soon grow so used to these syllables that you will be able to sing them more easily and more correctly than anything else, and knowing them so well will help you to sing other things.

" Now, I will give you a pattern from the Modulator. Listen well and sing with care." *

The teacher will give some such exercises as these, on DOH, ME, and SOH.

DOH, ME.   ME, DOH.   DOH, ME, SOH.
DOH, SOH, &c. &c.

7. The mode or scale is divisible into similar sets of four notes—each set including two tones crowned by a part-tone. These are called TETRACHORDS. If the replicate of the key note be included (d¹), DOH, RAY, ME, FAH will form the first tetrachord, and SOH, LAH, TE, DOH¹ the second. These are called the *disjunct* tetrachords, because they have no point of junction. The interval FAH, SOH separates them. If the key note is made the highest note of one, and the lowest of the other tetrachord, SOH₁, LAH₁, TE₁, DOH will form the first, and DOH, RAY, ME, FAH the second. These are called the *conjunct* tetrachords, because they are joined in the key note.

The observation of these facts will fix the pupil's attention on the structure of the mode and help him to remember it. The pupil should be practised to point out the tetrachords—to make (or arrange) them, first disjunct and then conjunct, with coins to represent the notes—and when they are arranged to name the notes.

The teacher's singing the tetrachords, to the syllable AH, will help the pupils to distinguish better both the place and sound of the tonules.

There is only one interval of three successive tones :—which is it?

"Now sing DOH after my *pattern* on the Modulator. Now DOH, DOH, DOH. * Now DOH, ME. * Now DOH, DOH, ME, ME. * ME, ME, DOH, DOH. *

"Look and listen again—DOH, ME, SOH. * DOH, DOH, ME, ME, SOH, SOH. * DOH, SOH. * SOH, ME, DOH. * SOH, DOH. *

"Now the replicate DOH, ME, SOH, DOH¹. * DOH¹, SOH, ME, DOH. * DOH, DOH, ME, ME, SOH, SOH, DOH¹, DOH¹. * DOH¹, DOH¹, SOH, SOH, ME, ME, DOH, DOH. *

Let the teacher chose some low note—say D— as the key note or DOH of these exercises. Let him teach them by *pattern* and *pointing*, step by step, from the Modulator, with *utmost patience*. He is *forming the voice* of his pupils, and must not be surprised if some of them are difficult to mould. He need not in these exercises pay attention to measure or accent, but be content with a clear and accurate note.

SECTION III.

OF ACCENT, RHYTHM, AND MEASURE.

1. It may be easily noticed that, at certain distances throughout a tune, the voice is delivered with increased distinctness and force, and closer observation will distinguish three degrees of ACCENT thus produced—the *louder*, the *softer*, and the *medium*.

Accent is produced by the combined use of *distinctness* (or abruptness) and *force*—in their various degrees, and it differs in quality as one or the other element predominates. Is it not thus in elocution also?

"I wish you to listen while I sing a tune, and to notice whether I sing some notes louder than others. * Did you notice that the louder notes come regularly, and the softer notes between them? Let us try part of another tune. · I will sing it to 'one, two, three, four,' and you will tell me which figures were loud and which soft. (The teacher sings parts of several of the earlier exercises to 'one, two, three, &c.,' causing the children to notice the loud and soft notes. Presently he introduces a tune with the medium accent, thus—) Now notice this tune; you will find something different in it. * Were all the loud notes of the same loudness? * No, some were not loud, like the others, and yet they were not soft. They are called *medium* notes. How many kinds of notes have you noticed?" It will not be necessary to trouble children with the word 'accent.'

2. The accents recur in regular order, and at equal distances of time. The distance of time from one of the louder accents to the next is called a MEASURE. The distance of time between *any* accent and the next is called an ALIQUOT, or equal part, of the measure :—it may also be called a PULSE of the voice.

"Let us try and notice these loud and soft sounds of the voice a little more. We will see whether they come regularly. This string 'pendulum' of ours moves *regularly*. You know that one swing always takes the same time as another, even when it does not swing so far. Now, while I sing—do you notice how many swings of the pendulum there are between one lond note and the next (—Sings HART'S to 'one, two, three, four, five, six, seven.') • Yes, two. Was that the case all through the tune? Were there not sometimes three? Let us try again. • There was first a loud note and then a soft note all through the tune: the loudness and softness of the voice came *regularly*.

"The time from one loud note to another is called a *measure*. What is it called? • How many 'swings' were there to a measure in the tune I just sang? • Yes, two.

"Listen again, and tell me how many swings there are to a measure in this tune. (Sings PROSPECT, with the pendulum swinging). • Yes, three. Did they come regularly?

"The time of a 'swing' of the pendulum is called a PULSE. What is a pulse? The first tune had—how many pulses to a measure? • Yes, we may say it was a tune in TWO-PULSE MEASURES. There are many other tunes like it. What measures are they all in? And now, what measures would you say the second tune was in? • Yes, there were three swings, or pulses, to a measure. It is a tune in THREE-PULSE MEASURES." This anticipates some of the following propositions for the sake of convenience in teaching. Children need not be puzzled with the words RHYTHM or ALIQUOT. Use as few technical terms as possible, but let them be well understood.

3. The order in which the accents recur in any tune is called its RHYTHM. There are four kinds of Rhythm, in common use, which are distinguished by the structure of the measures which they severally require.

Much of the delicacy and expressiveness of music depends on Rhythm, or accent. By neglect of this, a properly beautiful tune is often made dull, heavy, and unmeaning, while careful attention to it will give beauty to some of the plainest melodies. Many of our most popular tunes owe their effect almost entirely to Rhythm.

Rhythm forms nearly the sole power of the drum and the tambourine. It makes even the regulated step of the soldier and the dancer akin to music. The philosophy of the origin of Rhythm is treated very beautifully in the appendix to Dr. Bryce's "Rational Introduction to Music." He shows its connection with the "*pulsations*" of the heart.

4. THE BINARY OR TWO-PULSE MEASURE contains two aliquots, one having the louder, and the other the softer accent. The Rhythm may commence on either aliquot, but always closes on the one contrary to that on which it commenced, so as to complete the measure.

This is the boldest of the measures and the one most easily felt or performed. It is by far the best for large masses of voice. It is well adapted to aid in giving majesty to a tune. Try ST. STEPHEN'S or BEDFORD, first in the THREE-PULSE measure (lengthening the accented notes) and then in the TWO-PULSE measure, and you will understand the character of the Binary Rhythm.

Exercises, such as those below, should now be given from the Modulator to illustrate this measure, and to give further practice in the use of the *chord* (DOH, ME, SOH,) and the scale or "common mode." Notice that the pupils should sing the exercises of this section from the Modulator *exclusively*—that the eye may be well accustomed to the relative position of notes.

"Look and listen, Children, while I give you a 'pattern' in two-pulse measures. (Sings four notes). Did you notice which were the louder, and which were the softer notes? I will point while you sing, but perhaps you would like the 'pattern' again. • "

In this way the teacher will proceed through the exercises in this section, with patience and care, attracting attention to the most important points by the pattern, and exhibiting faults for correction in the same way, but never singing with the pupils.

EXERCISES 1, 2, 3, and 4. The teacher will have to learn these by rote (an exercise which in reference to all tunes he will soon find very easy) that he may feel free in pointing on the Modulator. He will first pitch the key note and take his rate of movement, as directed in Section four —then sing the upper line of the exercise with *decision and spirit*, making the accent well and pointing on the Modulator. Next, he will pattern the exercise, two or four notes at a time, listening and correcting faults, till his pupils can follow his pointing accurately and easily. He may then 'accompany' them by singing the lower line (which repeats the key note) while they sustain the upper part; and afterwards, dividing his class into two companies, he may cause the quicker children to sing DOH (or 'toll the bell,' as

8   EXERCISES.

they may call it) while the others take the first part. Let him be very strict in reference to ACCENT, the MEDIUM FORCE OF VOICE, ACCURACY OF NOTE, and prompt, easy, undelayed MOVEMENT. He will easily explain the *two-pulse* notes in the second exercise.

EXERCISES 5, 6, and 7. Only the upper part of these exercises should be taught. The pupil will return to sing the seconds when he has passed through the next section of lessons.

1. EXERCISE.   KEY D.   M. 66.

```
{ | d :m | s :d¹ | d¹ :s | m :d ||
( | d :d | d :d  | d :d  | d :d ||
```

2. EXERCISE.   KEY D.   M. 66.

```
{ | d :— | m :— | s :— | d¹ :— | d¹ :— | s :— | m :— | d :— ||
( | d :d | d :d | d :d | d :d  | d :d  | d :d | d :d | d :d ||
```

3. EXERCISE.   KEY D.   M. 66.

```
{ | d :m | s :m | s :m | d¹ :— | d¹ :s | m :s | s :m | d :— ||
( | d :d | d :d | d :d | d :—  | d :d  | d :d | d :d | d :— ||
```

4. EXERCISE.   KEY D.   M. 66.

```
{ | d :d | m :m | s :s | m :— | d¹ :d¹ | m :m | s :s | d :— ||
( | d :d | d :d | d :d | d :d | d :d   | d :d | d :d | d :— ||
```

5. EXERCISE.   KEY G.   M. 66.

```
{ | d :— | s :— | m :— | d :— | m :— | m :— | d :— ||
( | d :— | d :— | d :— | s₁ :— | s₁ :— | s₁ :— | d :— ||
```

6. EXERCISE.   KEY D.   M. 66.

```
{ | d :r | m :f | s :l | t :d¹ | d¹ :t | l :s | f :m | r :d ||
( | d :t₁ | d :r | m :f | s :l | l :s | f :m | r :d | t₁ :d ||
```

7. EXERCISE.   KEY D.   M. 66.

```
{ :d | r :m | f :s | l :t | d¹ :d¹ | t :l | s :f | m :r | d ||
( :d | t₁ :d | r :m | f :s | l :l | s :f | m :r | d :t₁ | d ||
```

5. THE TRINARY OR THREE-PULSE MEASURE contains three aliquots, one of which has the louder and the others the softer accent. The Rhythm often commences on the softer accent, but it always completes the imperfect measure at the end of the tune.

This measure is well adapted to aid in producing a soft and soothing musical effect. When the tune is simple, it is not unfit for Congregational use; especially if the people have been trained to keep the accent.

EXERCISE 8. The pupils should be taught by pattern, first the lower and next the upper part. They may then sing the parts together. It should be sung boldly and quickly.

EXERCISE 9. Only the upper part should be practised at present. Take care that the softer notes are sung lightly and 'trippingly.' It should be more bold and quick than the last.

8. EXERCISE. KEY D. M. 80.

$$\left\{\begin{array}{l} \text{d :m :s } | \text{s :m :d } | \text{d :---:d } | \text{d :---: } | \text{m :s :d}^1 | \text{d}^1 \text{:s :m} \\ \text{d :d :d } | \text{d :d :d } | \text{d :d :d } | \text{d :---: } | \text{d :d :d } | \text{d :d :d} \end{array}\right.$$

$$\left\{\begin{array}{l} \text{d}^1 \text{:---:d}^1 | \text{d}^1 \text{:---:---} \| \\ \text{d :d :d } | \text{d :---:---} \| \end{array}\right.$$

9. EXERCISE. KEY E. M. 112.

$$\left\{\begin{array}{l} \text{d :r :m } | \text{f :s :l } | \text{t :d}^1 \text{:r}^1 | \text{d}^1 \text{:---: } | \text{d}^1 \text{:t :l } | \text{s :f :m} \\ \text{d :t}_1 \text{:d } | \text{r :m :f } | \text{s :l :t } | \text{d}^1 \text{:---:t } | \text{l :s :f } | \text{m :r :d} \end{array}\right.$$

$$\left\{\begin{array}{l} \text{r :d :t}_1 | \text{d :---:---} \| \\ \text{t}_1 \text{:l}_1 \text{:t}_1 | \text{d :---:---} \| \end{array}\right.$$

6. THE QUATERNARY OR FOUR-PULSE MEASURE, is formed from the Binary Measure by changing every alternate louder accent into one of *medium* force. It contains four aliquots arranged thus,—*loud, soft, medium, soft.* The Rhythm may commence on the softer parts of the measure, but the measure must be completed at the end of the tune.

This measure, when delicately performed, (as it seldom is), gives much elegance to a tune. It is adapted to congregational tunes when the movement is not too slow. Try VESPER—taking care to give the medium accent accurately.

"Now, children, hear me sing a tune in two-pulse measures. (Sings VESPER, or Ex. 10, 11, in the pumping way, each louder accent being of equal force). I think I could improve that—but listen again. * Now, let me sing it better.

* Was not it more light and smooth? What made the difference? * Yes, I made every other loud pulse into a medium pulse. Let us try again * How many pulses were there, then, between one loud pulse and the next? Yes, *four*, so that the tune is in—what kind of measures? *Four-pulse measures.* Now, let us learn a tune in four-pulse measures." Only the upper part of Ex. 10 and 11 should be practised under this section.

10. EXERCISE. KEY G. M. 112.

$$\left\{\begin{array}{l} \text{d :d |d :d } | \text{d :m |s :--- } | \text{s :s |s :s } | \text{s :m |d :---} \| \\ \text{d :s}_1 \text{ |s}_1 \text{:d } | \text{d :m |m :--- } | \text{m :d |d :m } | \text{m :d |d :---} \| \end{array}\right.$$

c

11.   EXERCISE.   KEY F.   M. 80.

```
{ | d :m |m :d | m :s |s :m | s :d¹ |d¹ :s | d¹ :d¹ |d¹ :— |
{ | d :— |— :— | m :— |— :— | s :— |— :— | m :— |— :— |

{ | d¹ :s |m :s | s :m |d :m | m :d |d :d | d :d |d :— ||
{ | m :— |—:— | d :— |— :— | s₁ :— |— :— | d :— |— :— ||
```

7. THE SENARY OR SIX-PULSE MEASURE, is formed from the Trinary Measure by changing every alternate louder accent into a medium accent. It contains six aliquots arranged thus;—*loud, soft, soft, medium, soft, soft.* As with the other measures a tune may commence on the softer parts of the measure, provided the remaining aliquots are found at the end.

This measure is commonly used in connection with quick movements, and is naturally soft, light, and elegant. It is better adapted to secular than to sacred music. Notice PROSPECT when the medium accent is well observed—how much it is improved. Notice also STRAWBERRY GIRL.

Children should be introduced to the Senary measure, as to the Quaternary above, by attract-ing observation and thought to some good illustration. The WINTER SONG will serve the purpose of the teacher. The previous analogy will lead the children to see what the measure should be called. Let Exercise 12 be sung very quickly and lightly—but only the upper part of it under this Section.

12.   EXERCISE.   KEY D.   M. 160.

```
{ :d | r :m :f |s :l :t | d¹ :— :— |— : : :d¹ | t :l :s |f
{ :d | t₁ :d :r |m :f :s | l :— :— |— : :l | s :f :m |r

{ :m :r | d :— :— |— : ||
{ :d :t₁ | d :— :— |— : ||
```

SECTION IV.

OF THE STANDARD SCALE, THE METRONOME, AND THE SMALL-LETTER SOLFA NOTATION.

C¹
B

A

G

F
E

D

C

STANDARD SCALE.

1. A certain note, "about midway between the highest and the lowest that can be perceived by the ear," is fixed on by musicians as the standard of PITCH, and the notes arranged upon it, according to the order of the 'Common Mode,' are called THE STANDARD SCALE. This note is called C. The second note of its scale is called D, the third E, the fourth F, the fifth G, the sixth A, the seventh B, and the replicate C¹ again. A note which is about half a tone higher than any one of these notes is said to be that note *sharpened*, as—"G SHARP." A note about half a tone lower than any one of these notes is said to be that note *flattened*, as—"B FLAT." By a reference to this fixed scale, the pitch of any other key note may be determined.

'The particular pitch assigned to this c, and consequently to the other notes of its scale, is called *Concert Pitch.* The moderns generally fix the sound of c as that which would be caused by 256 vibrations per second of a sonorous body.' Dr. Bryce's "Rational Introduction to Music."

The pupil will already have perceived, from hearing the teacher pitch DOH, or the key note, that it is at a different pitch in different tunes.

It is said that the sharp and flat mean *about* half a tone higher or lower, because the terms are used very indefinitely, sometimes indicating the Tonule (as we call it) of the common mode or scale, which is more than half a tone, and at other times referring to a chromatic interval, and so representing something less than half a tone. Keyed instruments represent neither of these with perfect accuracy.

2. The pitch of the key note is given in the heading or SIGNATURE of a tune, thus, "KEY A," "KEY G," "KEY B FLAT," &c. In pitching a tune it is customary to take the upper c^1, of the standard scale, from a TUNING FORK, to descend to the pitch-note required, and then give its sound to the syllable DOH. DOH thus fixed, establishes the relative position of all the other notes of a tune.

The upper c^1 is used in pitching, because the higher sounds are found to be more distinctly and correctly appreciable by the ear.

"Children, have you noticed that I sometimes take a low sound for DOH, and sometimes a higher one?—a low sound in one tune, and perhaps a higher sound in the next? • How do I know which sound to take for DOH? The book tells me. At the top of every tune there is a letter which stands for a fixed note. I find out the sound of it by means of this tuning fork, and then give the sound to DOH.

"Do you see the tuning fork? (A harmonicon pipe giving the note c^1 will equally answer the purpose for classes). I will show you how to sound it. (He strikes one prong against the table, or pressing both prongs together with his left hand, liberates them suddenly—and then gives the sound either silently by bringing the fork to the ear, or aloud by resting its handle end on the table during the vibrations). Who would like to try? You will all learn to use this instrument. • What is it called? It always gives the same note, which we call c^1. Let us all sound it together. (c^1) again. • It is a fixed sound, and you can always obtain it from the tuning fork. Perhaps, after a time, you will

remember it so well as to be able to sound it at pleasure. Who can sound it from memory now? • Now let us sound its lower replicate. (c) Between these two Cs there is a regular scale of fixed notes. Listen while I sing down the scale. (Sings | c^1 :— | B :A | G :F | E :D | C :—) Could you sing it? I will write it on the black board for you. (Writes as above, at the side of the page). It forms a *fixed modulator.* It is called the *standard scale.* Let us sing down the scale again, while I point. • It will help you to remember these notes if you notice that after the c^1, running down, they make the two words Bag, Fed. Try again. • Now try without looking.

"Suppose the book tells me that the pitch of DOH, in the tune I am going to sing, is the same as D in the standard scale—what should I do to find it? Yes, run down from c^1, swell out the D, and then sound DOH the same as the D. Let us try. • (| c^1 :— | B :A | G :F | E :— | D :— | DOH :—). Suppose I find in the book "KEY G." That means that the pitch of DOH, or the key note, is the same as G in the standard scale. How should I pitch DOH then? &c. &c.

"Sometimes you will find in the book 'KEY B FLAT.' I will teach you what that means, and how to pitch that key when we come to it."

3. The rate at which a tune is to be sung may be indicated by a reference to the swinging of a pendulum, each swing of the pendulum corresponding with an aliquot of the measure. A short pendulum will, then, indicate a quick, and a longer one a slow, rate of movement. There is an instrument, called a METRO-NOME, or time-measurer, the pendulum of which can be lengthened or shortened according to a graduated scale, so as to swing any required number of times in a minute. If the number at which the weight is set, on the graduated scale of the metronome, be given in the signature of a tune, it will indicate to others the rate at which that tune should be sung. Thus, "M. 66," placed at the head of a tune, signifies that while this tune is sung, the metronome should swing at the rate of 66 swings a minute, and that each aliquot of the measure should keep pace with a swing of the metronome.

In the old notation it is common to state what note—crotchet—quaver or minion—corresponds with each swing of the pendulum.

Some such instrument as this should be in every school. If children are not taught early to "keep time" well, their voices will become a hindrance and annoyance to others. Though the instrument need not be always used in the exercises, it should be constantly referred to as a standard, and strict attention should be given to it in the earlier stages. The *rate of movement* should be taken from it as directed in the fifth section.

The larger Metromone, which is kept in motion by clock-work, and 'ticks' to every accent of the measure, cost 30s. and upward—those which strike a bell on the recurrence of each stronger accent being much more expensive. The smaller Metronomes, which simply oscillate without noise, are sold at 8s. and upward. Very much cheaper instruments will no doubt be made for schools when there is a demand. Meantime each teacher and scholar too may make his own *String Pendulum*, which will answer the end very fairly. For this purpose, fasten a penny or some such weight at the end of a piece of string. Then, at four inches and five eighths from the weight, tie a double knot. Hold the string by this knot, and the weight will swing at the rate of 160 swings a minute, and make your pendulum correspond with M. 160. At 6¼ inches tie a single knot; and that length of pendulum will correspond with M. 138. The double knots may mark the distances most used, and the single knots those used occasionally between them. The rest of the pendulum may be constructed to the following table—S standing for single, and D for double knot.

1st D. at 4½ inches from weight = M. 160.
1st S. at 6¼ in. „ = M. 138.
2nd D. at 9¼ in. „ = M. 112.
2nd S. at 1 foot 1¼ in. „ = M. 96.
3rd D. at 1 foot 7½ in. „ = M. 80.
3rd S. at 2 feet 6¼ in. „ = M. 66.
4th D. at 3 feet 10¼ in. „ = M. 50.

A silk tape with the Metronome figures marked at the proper distances would be preferable to the string. A lath of wood might be graduated in a similar manner, with holes punctured for the points of suspension, but it would require different distances according to its own weight.

It is not an easy thing for an unpractised singer to keep *an equal rate of movement* throughout a tune without aid, but he must learn to do it; and we are persuaded that a careful and frequent use of the pendulum is the best means hitherto proposed for the attainment of this power;—but it is customary to recommend the practice of "beating time." To those who may wish to adopt this plan, the diagrams below—explaining the method of "beating time" for the different measures—may be of use. But we are persuaded that to many persons this is no help at all, but only a hindrance. Let us keep in mind that the object to be gained is—first, a *mental perception* of equal movement, the regular recurrence of the pulses, and secondly, a *mental command*, by which the muscles of the larynx are made to obey the conceptions of the mind. Both these may be gained by careful practice, discipline, and effort on the part of the pupil. If a regular movement of the muscles of the arm is easier to him than a regular movement of the muscles of the larynx, then let him use the first as a guide to the second—not otherwise. It is however frequently necessary, when many sing together, that the leader of the band should beat time, either with a wand, or by the movement of his own hands. The SENARY measure may be beaten in the same way as the *binary*.

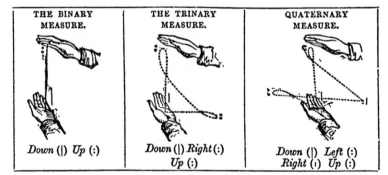

THE BINARY MEASURE.	THE TRINARY MEASURE.	QUATERNARY MEASURE.
Down (|) *Up* (:)	*Down* (|) *Right* (:) *Up* (:)	*Down* (|) *Left* (:) *Right* (ı) *Up* (:)

"You notice this *string pendulum?* I will hold the string near the weight and sing the first exercise, a 'pulse' to every swing. * I was obliged to be quick! Now I will hold the string as far from the weight as possible and sing the same exercise. * How different! If I want to sing quickly where must I hold the string? Where, if I want to sing slowly? You see, I have knots tied on the string at different distances. You shall try them. Sing the first (or any other) exercise, while I swing the pendulum from the first large knot. * Now, sing the same while I hold the string at the second large knot * —at the third * —at the fourth * Now, if you were at a distance, and I wanted to send a message to you to tell you exactly how fast you should sing a tune, what would be my best way of doing it? * Yes, I should say—'keep time with the pendulum, I send, when it is held at such a knot.' That might do; but there is a better instrument than a 'string pendulum.' It is called a *Metronome*, or time-measurer. (The Metronome should be shown.) It has a pendulum so made that the weight can move up and down upon it; and the rod is marked with numbers up and down, which show where you must put the weight if you want

the pendulum to swing 50 times a minute, and how high it must be for the pendulum to swing 100 times a minute, and so on. Now, if you and I had a Metronome, and I want to send a message to say how fast you were to sing, I should say, 'Put the metronome to such a figure;' or I might have written it down like this (writing M. 50, M. 160, &c. on the black board—M. standing for Metronome.) Look into your books. Do you not see every tune marked with some figure of the metronome? Now, if you all had a metronome, you would know from that how fast you were to sing the tunes; but, as you are not rich enough to have one, you may all make string pendulums like mine, and I will tell you what numbers of the metronome each knot corresponds with. Always remember that the higher the number the quicker the tune. Now, let us sing some of our exercises—you pitching the tunes and giving me the rate of movement, from the pendulum."

4. The art of representing musical sounds, by various marks and signs, to the eye, is called NOTATION. The SMALL-LETTER-SOLFA NOTATION, which is used in this book, is founded on the following principles:—

5. NOTATION OF INTERVAL. The notes are represented by the initial letters of the solfa syllables d, r, m, f, s, l, t, the higher replicates having a mark thus d¹, r¹, &c., to distinguish them, and the lower replicates a mark thus t₁, l₁, or, for a second replicate below s₂, f₂, &c. The pupil's previous familiarity with the pictorial representation of interval on the *Modulator*, enables him to recognize at once the relative distances of these notes, and their exact position in reference to the *key note*.

6. NOTATION OF RHYTHM. This mark | shows that the stronger or louder accent follows it. This mark : in the same manner, indicates the softer accent, and this ı the accent of medium force.

7. NOTATION OF THE RELATIVE LENGTH OF NOTES. As the accents recur at equal intervals of time throughout a tune, marking aliquot parts of the measure, the relative length of notes can be clearly indicated by showing what proportion of the measure each note occupies. This is done by first placing the accent marks at equal distances along the page, thus | : | : or thus : | : : | : : | : or thus | : | : &c. and then observing the following rules.

a. A note placed alone immediately after an accent mark is supposed to occupy the time from that accent to the next. Thus | d : d : d | d : d : d | d or thus | d : r ı m : d

b. A stroke — indicates the continuance of the previous note through another aliquot (or pulse), thus | d : d | d : — or thus : d | d : d : d | d : — : — | d : — : d | d : —

c. A dot divides an aliquot into equal parts and shows that the note before it fills half the time from one accent to the next, leaving only half an aliquot to the note or notes which follow, thus | d : d.d | d : d | d : d.d | d : — or | d : m.r | d : s₁ | d : m.r | d : — | l₁ : d | s₁ : m | m.r : d.t₁ | d : —

d. The dot after a mark of continuance shows that the previous note is to be continued through half that alequot, thus | d.r : m.f | m   : d | d   :-.f | m : d

e. A comma signifies that the note before it fills a quarter of the time from one accent to the next. The last note in an aliquot does not require a mark after it, as the proportion left to it is sufficiently evident. Thus, | d   : d.d,d | d   : d or | d   : t₁.d,r | d   : d

f. The dot and comma together show that the note before them fill three-quarters of the time from one accent to the next, thus | d.,r : m.,f | m.,r : d

g. This mark ₍ indicates that the note before it fills one-third of the time from one accent to the next, thus :d | s : l,s,f | m :r | d

h. An aliquot or any part of an aliquot left unfilled indicates a pause of the voice, thus | d : | r : | m : | :t₁ | d :d | r :r | m :— or thus,
          hark!   hark!   hark!   while in- fant voices   sing.
| d : -.f | m : d | d   : .f | m : d

8. NOTATION OF SLURS, REPEATS, AND EXPRESSION.

a. When two or more notes are sung to the same syllable, they are said to be slurred. The slur is indicated by a stroke beneath the notes.

b. In some tunes it is required to repeat certain parts of the strain. The manner in which this is done is indicated by the following signs—

> D. C. abbreviated from the Italian *Da Capo*, means "Return to the beginning."
>
> D. S. abbreviated from *Dal Segno*, means "Return, and sing from the sign."
>
> S. is used for the Sign, and
>
> F. abbreviated from *Fine*, shows where such repetitions *end*.
>
> R. placed over a note shows that a repetition of *words* commences there.

c. Greater "expression" is sometimes given to music by regulating the degree of force with which certain parts of the strain are to be delivered. This is done by means of the following signs placed over the notes—

> *f.* abbreviated from *forte*, signifies *loud.*
>
> *p.* from *piano*, signifies *soft.*
>
> *ff.* *very loud.*
>
> *pp.* *very soft.*

d. Sometimes it is needful to indicate the manner in which that force is to be thrown in. For this purpose the following marks are used—

> <> denotes a *swell*, the voice commencing softly—becoming louder—and then closing softly.
>
> < denotes increasing force.
>
> > denotes diminishing force.
>
> ' or · over a note shows that it should be sung abruptly and with accent.

e. The same piece of music often requires to be sung with different expression, according to the different words with which it may be used. In that case the marks of expression should be placed on the words. It is proposed that—

> CAPITAL LETTERS, in printing, or double lines under the word in writing, should distinguish words to be sung *louder* than others; that
>
> *Italic letters*, in printing, or a single line under the word in writing, should indicate *softness;* that

The acute accent   should denote special abruptness and decision of voice; that

A stroke above the words, in printing, a succession of little strokes over or a stroke through the word in writing, should show a *heavy movement:* the accents being dragged along, and the lighter ones little distinguished from the stronger; and that

The grave accent   placed on the words, which fall to the strong accent of the music, should indicate a *spirited movement,* with marked attention to accent.

A *slower* or *quicker* movement may be expressed by the words *slowly* or *quickly.* The "heavy movement" mentioned above necessarily tends to slacken, as the "spirited movement" does to quicken the pace of the singer.*

9. THE BLACK-BOARD for writing tunes is one which has the marks representing the soft accents painted on it at regular distances—thus,

:   :   :   :   :   :   :   :   :
:   :   :   :   :   :   :   :   :

These form a guide to the hand and eye in writing. A line drawn through them will quickly change them into the stronger or the medium accents as may be desired. The solfa notes can then be inserted with great rapidity, supplying, indeed, a MUSICAL SHORT-HAND. THE SOLFA MUSIC PAPER is similarly arranged, and provided for the same purpose.† A double line should be put at the end of the tune.

10. When two or more "parts" of a tune are to be sung together, brackets are placed at the commencement of the lines, the accent marks and corresponding notes are placed one under the other, and the louder (or stronger) accent marks are extended so as to connect all the parts that move together.

11. DICTATION, as applied to music, is the art of naming musical sounds, in successive announcements, so that they may be written down or sung by others. The manner of making the announcements will be explained by the following examples:—

WELLS would be dictated thus—"loud SOH"—"soft ME"—"the last two slurred"—"soft FAH"—"loud, soft SOH"—"soft upper DOH," &c.

SAMSON thus—"soft DOH"—"loud and half soft ME"—"half soft FAH"— "med. SOH"—"soft ME," &c. One part of it will require this dictation "loud LAH upper DOH slurred"—"soft TE, LAH," &c. Another part will require, "med. SOH"—"soft ME *and* RAY," &c., using the "and" to signify that the larger portion of the aliquot belongs to ME.

The "Solfa Music Paper" has been provided for this purpose. The black board might be used at the same time, by one of the most forward pupils —the master glancing at it to see that the tune is correctly written. No exercises can so thoroughly fix, in the mind of the pupil, the principles of music and the exact use of its symbols, as those of dictating or of writing from dictation. The teacher should require perfect silence during the process of dictation. A whisper must be reckoned the greatest fault. If any one is afraid he has made a mistake or has not heard the "announcement," or wants to cut his pencil, he must not interrupt the whole class for that. He must leave a space and go on. He can correct his manuscript afterwards. The "Dictator" should give each "announcement" distinctly and only once. He should allow a regular interval of six or eight

* See, for example, the note on HARTS, p.23, 30.   † Ward and Co. 1s. a quire.

seconds between each "announcement." In this manner eighteen or twenty copies of many a tune have been made in three or five minutes—each member of the class writing in his own book. By the easy use of this "musical short-hand" the teacher may supply his pupils with any tunes he pleases. The pupils should be taught to make their letters upright.

NOTICE TO THE TEACHER. It is not intended that all which is here gathered together on the subject of "notation" should be taught at once. The whole is introduced here for the sake of more easy reference. But, in practice, these various points will require to be introduced slowly and one by one. The teacher will find that the course of exercises is very carefully graduated in this respect, and he is recommended to introduce each topic of notation, or rhythm, as it arises in the exercises.

After the pitching of tunes and the use of the string-pendulum have been a little practised, the teacher should allow his pupils to sing the exercises from their books, which they have hitherto sung exclusively from the modulator. He may then teach by pattern from the modulator, and afterwards allow the children to sing from the books the seconds of the later exercises which they had omitted before. These should be sung first separately and afterwards with the upper part, the class being divided into two portions for this purpose. The subject of notation may be introduced to children either from the black-board or the " exercise books.' If from the black-board, thus :—

" Let us sing the first exercise from the Modulator. • I should like to write that down on the board. Instead of writing DOH, you would let me put simple d; would you not? • Was d one of the louder or softer notes? • Then I will put this mark before it (| d) to show that it has a strong accent. What note next? Is it loud or soft? • Then I will write it thus (:m)—*soft* ME. Now the others. (| s) *loud* SOH. (:d) soft DOH. But is that the same as the other DOH? • No; it is the higher replicate. Then I will put a mark to show it thus (:d¹) *soft upper* DOH, &c. Now, the second exercises, from the modulator. Each note has two pulses. How shall we write that second *push* of the voice? We will write it thus—(| d :— | m :— &c.) The stroke will mean that you are to continue your voice, &c." Or, with the exercise books, the subject may be thus introduced.

"Open your books. Look at the first exercise, do you see d? That stands for DOH. What would you suppose the m to stand for? • s? • Do you see a mark above the next DOH. What do you think it means? • Do you see a stroke before d? That means that the DOH has a *loud* accent. What do you think the two dots mean? &c. &c. Now let us sing from the book :——" And so with the second exercise when you come to it.

EXAMINATION OF PUPILS ON THE FIRST STAGE.

Every *art* is best taught individually. It is true that there are some advantages, for the singer, in collective teaching. The sympathy of numbers both aids and encourages him. But his *progress* will depend entirely on individual attention, and individual endeavour. In most classes the few make progress and *lead*, while the many—some from timidity, and others from idleness and inattention—hang upon the "leaders," and soon begin to clog their movements. As, however, singing for schools and congregations must be taught in classes, the object of the teacher must be to combine the spirit and sympathy of numbers, with as careful an attention to individual progress as possible. He should also occasionally separate the laggers from the more forward—and, without blaming or discouraging them, cause them to retrace their steps and go by themselves—while the others are advancing freely and rapidly, in a new class. For these purposes the pupil should be led to expect a *rigid personal examination* at the close of each stage, and a division of the class as the result. Several lesson-hours should be devoted to this examination. It might be conducted in a separate room while the rest of the class were practising. In adult classes most of the questions might be announced to the class and the answers given in writing at the time, and they would only require personal examination in connexion with the exercises. The examiner would then decide by the results of the two examinations. A register of each examination should be kept by the teacher, and a memorial of it given to the pupil, either by an entry in his exercise book with the teacher's initals, or by a card of admission to the new class, in some such terms as these—" Admit to the [Second] Singing-class, [Mary Howard] Examined as far as [SECTION iv. 6.] and approved. [August 1st, 1847.] (Signed) [W. G.] Teacher." Where these plans cannot be fully carried out some other scheme for securing individual attention and progress should be devised. The following questions and exercises will assist the teacher.

SECTION I.

1. What is the difference between the sound of the voice in speaking and in singing?

What is a sound of the singing voice called?

2. What is the best posture for the singer, in reference to his head?—his shoulders?—his chest?—his mouth?—his tongue?—his lips?

What is the instrument we sing with? and where is it?

What practice tends to open the chest for singing?

3. In what manner should the voice be delivered? What faults will thus be avoided?

4. What is learning to sing by PATTERN?

What two exercises of mind does it specially require from the pupil?

What other advantages of the practice can you mention?

* Sing a note which is *the same* as any your teacher may sing for a pattern.

5. What do you mean by FORCE of voice?

What force should we cultivate as a general habit? and why should we do so?

What is the effect on our own voices of loud singing (bawling)?

6. How would you measure the LENGTH of notes?

7. What is the height or lowness of notes called?

What name do you give to the *difference* between two notes in height or lowness?

What, then, is an INTERVAL?

There are three things from which a musical interval must be carefully distinguished. What are they?

From what must you distinguish the words *high* and *low*, in music?

5, 6, and 7. How many qualities of notes have you distinguished?

* Sing a note having any combination of *force*, *length*, and *pitch* which the teacher may require.

SECTION II.

1. What do you mean by a *Replicate?*

* Sing the higher replicate to any low note the teacher gives:—the lower replicate to any high note.

What is the difference between a man's voice and that of a woman or child?

2. How many notes may be ordinarily used between a given note and its replicate? and what notes are used above or below these?

By what authority and for what reason is the number thus limited?

3. What is meant by the *key-note* of a tune? and what is its influence?

4. Describe the common order of interval between a key note and its upper replicate. What is this arrangement called?

Where, in the common mode, do the *tonules* occur?

* Arrange eight coins or some other articles according to the " common mode."

5. What does the MODULATOR represent?

What is the name (—the solfa syllable) which stands for the *key-note*?—for the third?—for the fifth? How do you distinguish the replicate?

* Repeat these names of the notes quickly, both up and down.

* Write a modulator—carefully showing the places of the *tonules*.

6. How is the modulator used?

What are its two advantages? What to the eye and understanding? What to the memory?

7. What name is given to any part of the common mode which is found to include two tones, with a tonule above them?

Regarding the common mode as reaching from DOH to *upper* DOH¹, what notes form the tetrachords?

Regarding the mode as extending from *lower* SOH to FAH, what notes form the tetrachords?

How do you distinguish the two couples of tetrachords?

* Arrange eight coins so as to show the disjunct tetrachords, and name the notes.

* Arrange seven coins so as to show the conjunct tetrachords, and name the notes.

* Sing, from the modulator, as the teacher may point, DOH, ME, or SOH.

SECTION III.

1. What is accent?

* Things *to be done* are marked with an asterisk.

How many degrees of accent are distinguished? and what are they called?

2. What may be uniformly observed in reference to the recurrence of accent?

What is a MEASURE?

What is an ALIQUOT?

What is a PULSE?

3. What general name is given to the orderly recurrence of accents?

4. How many aliquot parts (or pulses) does the BINARY MEASURE contain? What are its accents and how may they be arranged?

What is the character of this measure?

• Sing the upper part of exercises 1, 2, 3, 4, 5, 6, 7, (or any of them the teacher chooses,) from the teacher's pointing on the modulator, without mistake and without help.

5. How many aliquots (or pulses) does the TRINARY MEASURE contain, and what is the order of its RHYTHM?

What is the character of this measure?

• Sing, from the teachers's pointing, Ex. 8. and 9.

6. What is the name of the measure which has four pulses? and what is its Rhythm? (or, how are its pulses arranged?)

What is the general effect of this measure?

• Sing, from modulator, Ex. 10, 11.

7. What is the name of the measure which has six pulses? and how are its pulses arranged?

What is the character of this measure?

• Sing Ex, 12. from modulator.

SECTION IV.

1. What note is used as a standard of PITCH?

The note c being used as a key note, (a DOH,) what is the fixed name of its RAY? (D)—of its ME? (E) of its FAH? (F) &c. &c.

What do you mean by any of these notes *sharpened* or *flattened*?

What is the use of this *standard scale of pitch notes*?

2. and 3. What is that part of a tune which informs you of the *key note*, and the *rate of movement* called?

• Pitch Ex. 5. Pitch Ex, 6.

What is a METRONOME? and what may be commonly used in its place?

How would you hold a pendulum so as to make the weight swing quickly? How to make it swing slowly?

What do the figures on the metronome show?

If M 160, placed in the signature of a tune, shows that it is to be sung with very quick pulses, what comparative rate of movement would M 80 indicate?

4. What is NOTATION?

How are the solfa notes written?

5. What is the mark for a *loud* pulse (or accent)? What for a *soft* pulse? What for a *medium* pulse?

6. What is the mark for the continuance of a note through the next pulse (or aliquot)?

• Write Ex. 3, 4, 8, 11, from memory, on slate, "black board," or "solfa music paper."

• Sing the higher or the lower part of any of the Exercises from the book, *pitching* the tune with the aid of a tuning fork or "harmonicon pipe."

SECOND STAGE.

SECTION V.

OF THE CHARACTER OR PROPER MUSICAL EFFECT OF THE MODE-NOTES, ESPECIALLY OF DOH, ME, AND SOH—THE FIRST, THIRD, AND FIFTH OF THE COMMON MODE; WITH DIRECTIONS FOR USING THE EXERCISES.

1. Every note of the common mode produces, by virtue of its relationship to the key note, a certain musical effect peculiar to itself—having relation to certain mental impressions and feelings.

The effect which a given note produces on the mind may be greatly modified by other conditions also;—as, for instance, by *elevation in pitch* giving brilliancy. (We have often noticed the difference between the same tune set in a low and in a high key.)—by "timbre" or *quality of voice*, giving mellowness, sweetness, clearness, &c. (It is this that makes the difference between a note from the flute and the same note from a trumpet or a violin.) —by *rapidity of movement*, and by the various *methods of expression*;—but the effect which the note obtains power to produce, by its relationship to the key note, remains still the most prominent and remarkable.

These "characters" or "properties" of the mode-notes have often been noticed in books of science. Dr. Callcott refers to them in his "Musical Grammar." M. Jeu de Berneval, Professor to the Royal Academy of Music, in his "Music Simplified," illustrates them very ingeniously and beautifully. Dr. Bryce introduces them into his "Rational Introduction." It would seem surprising (did we not know how the Old Notation, with its attempted, but inaccurate, scale of *fixed* sounds, takes up the learner's time, and distracts attention from the real beauties of musical science,) that these interesting facts, so well calculated to aid the pupil, have been so little used in elementary instruction. It is obvious that the moment a pupil can *recognize* a certain musical property in any note he will be able to *produce* that note with the greater accuracy and satisfaction. From extensive experience we have found that infants and persons with untrained voices are able to appreciate these points, and derive constant pleasure and assistance from the knowledge of them. The teacher will find himself well repaid by a most careful attention to this subject.

The subject may be illustrated to the incredulous thus; —Sing or play to them the following notes | F :— | A :F | C¹:— and make them notice the *bold, decisive,* and *rejoicing* character of the last note c¹, then promise them to make the very same sound in pitch give a *forlorn* and *desolate* expression, by simply altering the notes which precede it so as to remind the ear that it is in a different key, and sing | G :— | B :D | C¹:— In the one case you sang | d :— | m :d | s :— In the other | d :— | m :s | f :— Thus c¹ in the first instance was the fifth and in the second the fourth from the key note. It was the same exactly in *pitch*, but different in *relation*, and therefore different in musical character and effect.

If any should be sceptical and say that the effects we speak of result from the sound of the syllables themselves, produce the same effects with other syllables or with the names of the figures one, two, three, &c.

Should they still hesitate to admit the truth announced, saying that these "musical effects" are properties of the particular interval that is taken (a third, a fourth, &c.) irrespective of the relationship of the note to its KEY—then exhibit one of these properties (the *mournful* effect of LAH, for instance) as preceded by every kind of interval. They will then perceive that by whatsoever interval the sixth from the key note is preceded, it still maintains its mournful character.

Why a note's standing at a particular interval from the key note should give it a particular musical effect we do not know. We can only notice the fact, and make use of it in teaching. There must come to us, along with the actual sound itself, some mental *Association* of the Relationship of Interval (indicated by preceding notes) which has been thrown around it. The memory of notes just heard hovers around that which we now hear and gives it its *character*. Quick succession approaches in effect to co-existence, as is familiarly shown in reference to the eye by the Thaumatrope and other optical toys. Thus when once the key is established by the opening notes of the tune—it is still felt to be present, as a mental element, with every single note that follows. In a similar manner the *effect* of a given *colour*—the artist will tell us—is modified by the surrounding ones, or those on which the eye has just rested. This is a deeply interesting subject, and deserves to be well studied and further explored, especially in connection with harmonic combinations and effects.

2. The notes DOH, SOH, and ME, give to the mind an idea of rest and power, (in degrees corresponding with the order in which they are named,) while TE, FAH, LAH, and RAY, (in similar degrees,) suggest the feeling of suspense and dependence. Thus, if after we have heard the principal notes of the key, the voice dwells on the sound TE, the mind is sensible of a desire for something more, but the moment TE is followed by DOH¹ a sense of satisfaction and repose is produced. In the same manner the mind is satisfied when FAH resolves itself in ME, and LAH (though not so decidedly) in SOH. RAY also excites a similar feeling of inconclusiveness, and expectancy, which is resolved by ascending to ME, or, more perfectly, by falling to DOH.

These are the views developed so beautifully by M. Jeu de Berneval.

"Children, I wish you to notice these notes of the modulator so well that you may be able to know one from the other when you hear them. What do I want you to be able to do? * I should like you to call DOH, ME, and SOH, THE STRONG

NOTES. DOH is the strongest, SOH is the next in strength, and ME the next. I think you will understand this better presently when you find that the other notes all lean upon these three strong ones, but even when you sing them alone there is a sound of strength about them. Let us try. (they sing | d :— | m :— | s :— | d¹ :—)

Do you not feel as though you were mounting by firm and solid steps? Try again.   Which are the STRONG NOTES? Which is the strongest?—the next?—the next?

"Now, listen while I sing (pointing to the modulator) | d :— | m :— | s :— | t :— | — :— | d¹ :— Would you have liked me to stop on the TE? No, you were wanting all the time to hear the DOH. Let us try again. • All try. • You see that TE leans up against the DOH. We will call it a LEANING NOTE.

"Would you like to hear another *leaning note?* (points and sings) | d :— | m :— | s :— | f :— | — :— | m :— Which was it? What did it lean on? Now another (taking care to sing in the key which has just been heard) :d | l :— | s Which was that? What did it lean on? It

seems to mount like a rocket, and not to be so anxious to find rest on its *strong note* as FAH was.

"Now let us notice RAY. (Sings and points.) | d :s₁ | m :d | r :— | — :— | m :— | r :— | — :— | d :— Is it a leaning note? What does it lean on? Let us try again.   Perhaps it does not lean so much as the others—but it leans more towards DOH than towards ME.

"Which are the STRONG NOTES, which your voice can rest upon? Which are the LEANING NOTES, which you feel you cannot rest upon? What is the leaning of TE? of FAH? of LAH? of RAY? Once more, notice all these *strong* and *leaning* notes while I sing and point to them on the modulator. | d :— | s :— | m :— | d :— | d :— | r :— | d :d | f :— | m :d | l :— | s :d | t :— | d¹ :— "

3. *a.* DOH, being the governing note, gives a sense of POWER to the hearer, and of SECURITY to the singer, in a greater degree than any other. The singer feels it to be the note to which he can, from any point, most easily return. It is more easy to perceive musical effects than to find words which will sufficiently represent them; but if names must be given this note should be called THE STRONG or *firm* NOTE.

b. SOH has a similar effect to DOH, but is not equal to it in power. It may be distinguished as THE GRAND or *clear* NOTE.

c. ME has a somewhat graver and softer effect than SOH. It may be denominated THE STEADY, or *calm* NOTE.

These musical properties should be introduced to children as they occur in the exercises themselves. Adults also will find the illustration of these points in the tunes which follow. The Teacher may, in passing, sing some of these to his pupils; for DOH, "JESSE," for SOH, "Now steadily, &c.," and for ME the GREGORIAN CHAUNT.

DOH is called, in books of Musical Science, the TONIC, "because," says Dr. Bryce, "it gives the music its tone or character." SOH is called the DOMINANT, and ME, the MEDIANT. See "Rational Introduction to Music," for the probable reasons of these names.

4. When DOH, ME, and SOH predominate in a tune, they contribute to its general character, if the movement be a quick one, great BOLDNESS and DECISION, and, if the movement be a slow one, they give to it DIGNIFIED SOLEMNITY.

The power of any particular note to give a character to the tune will depend on the *frequency* and the *emphasis* with which it is used, and will be modified also by the kind of measure in which it occurs.

The proposition just mentioned may be illustrated by singing, first slowly and then very quickly, the following | d :— | m :d | s :— | s :— | l :m.f | s :— | d :— Children may have this shown to them.

5. SOH forms a more perfect consonance when sounded with DOH than any of the other notes, because it most nearly resembles it in "effect." ME, being less similar to DOH, forms a consonance with it, which is not so "perfect," but more pleasing. DOH, ME, and SOH, sounded together, form the most perfect and delightful union of sounds that is known. When thus used they are called the COMMON CHORD.

See an interesting scientific discussion in Dr. Bryce, p, 78, on the reason of the agreeable effects

produced in harmony. See also the Section HARMONY in this book. These points can be illustrated by the teacher causing his class to sing and lengthen out DOH while he sings first SOH and then ME, causing them to notice which consonance is the pleasanter. The pupils may be divided into two portions, the teacher giving to one the sound of DOH, and to the other that of SOH or ME, to be held together. Then, the class being divided into three companies, the teacher may, in a similar manner, awaken the grand harmony of the COMMON CHORD.

6. The voices of some persons are so formed that they can sing more easily the high notes, and the voices of others produce with greater ease the low notes. In a singing class the higher and lower voices should sit apart; the higher voices ordinarily singing the upper line (or the "air") of a tune, and the lower voices the under line, or the second part. It is advisable however that, in learning each tune, first the "air" and afterwards the "second parts" should be practised by the whole class together. While this is being done, it will usually be an accommodation to the different voices, to pitch the key note for the "air" one tone lower than it is marked, and for the "second" one tone higher. It may afterwards be sung by both voices together in its proper key.

The teacher should take an early opportunity of examining the "compass" of each pupil's voice, and marking upon paper, or on the examination tickets, how high he can sing easily, and how low. Thus, "WILLIAM FLOWER, higher voice, easy compass from C to A¹."

7. Every tune (except the "*minor*" tunes, to be mentioned hereafter, and some few others,) begins on DOH, ME, or SOH. In like manner the accompanying "parts" (adapted to the lower voices) commence, always, on some note of the common chord.

8. When a class is preparing to sing a tune, it is important to establish in the ear a sense of the *key* about to be used. For this purpose, if all begin on the same note, they should strike the *chord* (DOH, ME, SOH, or, if the DOH is A or B, DOH, SOH₁, ME, DOH) immediately that the person appointed has given the key note;—or, if there are several "parts" to be sung together, each company should, at the same moment, strike its own first note.

9. The exercises which follow are designed to give skill in interval and measure, to improve the musical taste, and to yield to the learner at each step the full fruit of his efforts in connecting the music he has learnt with delightful poetry. They are arranged progressively, so that the difficulties of music may be gradually introduced, as the learner gains strength to cope with them. Each exercise should be used in the following manner. First, it should be

a. LEARNT BY PATTERN from the MODULATOR. This will cultivate the ear and voice generally. It will teach the particular tune along with a pictorial representation of its intervals, and will accustom the mind more and more to that beautiful *language of interval*, which by giving a *distinct* and *uniform* syllabic name to each interval of the mode, enables us, by the ever renewed association of the syllable with the sound, to sing with increasing ease and confidence. The "second part" should be learnt in the same manner—as though it were a separate exercise—before it is sung with the "air." The exercise should next be—

b. SOLFAED from the book. This will give scope for a more accurate observance of measure, as indicated by the accent marks, and allow the "parts" of a tune to be sung together. It also strengthens the association between the syllables and their proper intervals. But lest the syllables of a tune should come to be sung by mere "rote"—the pupil having no mental picture of their relative position on the modulator, it will be found advisable to require each exercise to be—

    c. POINTED on the MODULATOR from memory. This will complete the knowledge of the tune, and greatly increase its teaching power. Every pupil should do this in his private practice, and should be ready to do it, at the teacher's call, before the class. But the solfa syllables, though invaluable as the mnemonics and interpreters of interval, and likely to be always useful in learning new tunes, and in studying the difficulties or beauties of particular passages, are only instruments for accomplishing the higher purposes of music. The learner must acquire the power of perceiving the musical "property" of a note, and of producing it, in connection with *any* syllable. With this view, the pupil should not shrink from the mental effort, nor the teacher from the trouble, of having each exercise—

    d. FIGURED, or sung to the words one, two, three, &c., according to the number of syllables in each line of the poetry. Thus " common metre" would be sung 1 | 2 : 3 | 4 : 5 | 6 : 7 | 8 : 1 | 2 : 3 | 4 : 5 | 6 &c., and "sevens" | 1 : 2 | 3 : 4 | 5 : 6 | 7 &c. This will make the perception of the characters and intervals of notes more perfectly mental, and independent of syllabic associations. It will also introduce the use of *slurs*—each utterance corresponding with a syllable of the verse, and not, as before, with every note of the music. As this exercise is difficult, at first—it is an advantage that the words used (1, 2, 3, &c.) require no attention, and that the mind is left free to study the music alone. But the highest atttainment is reached when, the tune itself being perfectly mastered, it is—

    e. SUNG TO SUITABLE WORDS. This exercise should not commence until the words themselves are thoroughly understood, enjoyed, and loved, and then it should be performed with careful regard to EXPRESSION. Thus the pupil is introduced to a new study, most elevating and ennobling to the mind, which he will pursue in sympathetic converse with his teacher.

    It is not necessary that the pupil should thus make the fullest use of one exercise before he passes to the next. It would be better that, at every season of practice, each of the above employments should have place—some new exercise being taught by pattern, a previous one solfaed from books and pointed on the modulator, and an earlier one still "numbered" and sung to words. The teacher should keep a record of progress, both on the book and separately—showing to what extent each exercise has been used. On the book each exercise would be marked with the letters above used in connection with each employment—*a.* indicating that the exercise had only been learnt by pattern—*a. b.* that it had, also, been solfaed from the book, &c. A separate entry might be in this wise—"May 6, Ex. 20. *a.* 19. *b. c.* 18. *d. e.* 13, 14, and 15. *e.*"

    The teacher should make a selection from the exercises according to the kind of class he is teaching.

HARTS. 13, *a.* The teacher requests the pupil, whose turn it is, to pitch A, from the tuning fork. The class strike the chord. The teacher (holding the pendulum by the third double knot, M. 80), sings his "first note" to the swing of the pendulum | s₁ : s₁ | s₁ : s₁ then turning to the modulator) points and patterns the first four notes, which the class imitates—then the next three, and so on. He calls attention, as he proceeds, to the *boldness* of the opening phrase, the *strength* of DOH, the *softness* of ME—to the *clear* and *triumphant* expression of SOH in the third line—and to the *vigour* of the stronger accents in the closing line. The "second" may be taught or not as the teacher thinks better. It is a little altered from that in "School Songs," but not so as to be discordant with it. *b.* The chord or the first notes are taken as directed above, the pendulum consulted by the whole class, as under *a*, and two measures being thus " measured," the tune is entered and sung. *c.* After a day or two members of the class may be called out to point on the modulator, while the rest sing. In a school the elder children may be employed in turn to "pattern" for the younger. *d.* The "first notes" and the rate of movement (from the pendulum) should be taken to the word *one.* | 1 : 1 | 1 : 1, and the tune continued, as before. *e.* The teacher will notice why the hymn should open *with spirit*, and the chorus burst forth in *louder* voice. The second verse requires a very *marked accent.* The fifth verse should be sung *softly*—with *retarded accent ;*—and the last verse should rise, especially in the chorus, to the *loud* and *spirited* expression of thankfulness, confidence, and joy. The books may be marked for expression, as directed in the last section. *Printed* for expression they would appear thus—

1. Let' us with' a glad'some mind
    Praise the Lord for he is kind,
    FOR' HIS MER'CIES SHALL' ENDURE,
    EVER FAITH'FUL, EVER SURE.

2. He' with all'-comMAND'ing MIGHT'
    FILLED' the new'-made WORLD' with light,
        FOR' &c.

5. *He hath with a piteous eye*
    Looked upon our misery,
        For' &c.

GREGORIAN CHANT, 14. *a.* Notice the exquisite *sweetness* of ME, and, *b.* the *unwearying pleasure* with which the consonance (sounding together) DOH, ME, can be listened to. *d.* Sing it to | 1 :— | 2 :3 | 4 :— | 1 :— | 2 :3 | 4 :5 | 6 :— *e.* All the words before the bar are to be sung to the first note, not hurriedly, but with serious and thoughtful expression. The three remaining syllables will take a note each. Then the three syllables before the bar in the second line to the next note, and the rest of the line to the remaining notes of the chant. This will form for children an easy introduction to the art of chanting, but adult classes might chant scripture words, as directed in *School Songs* 39,

41, or 42.   See the section of this book on Chanting.

GLOVER, 15. *a.* Notice the *cheerfulness* of SOH in the first line, then the *leaning* qualities of FAH and LAH, and the *rejoicing boldness* of DOH[1] and SOH at the close. *b.* Attention may be drawn to the great sweetness of the consonance SOH ME, not so firm or enduring as DOH ME, but more sweet. The second is altered like that of HARTS. *d.* The first line has eight, the second seven syllables, and so on. *e.* The second verse should open very softly. The hymn is full of beautiful sentiment, which should be pressed upon the hearts of children.

THE WINTER SONG, 16. *a.* The Teacher will show his pupils how to pitch B FLAT, singing | C[1] :— | B :— | B flat. It is allowable to *pattern* a quick tune like this, very much more slowly than it will afterwards be sung. Notice the *strength* of DOH. *b.* Attention should be drawn to *Senary* or *Six-pulse* Measure. When this measure moves fast it is often more convenient to "beat" it with the hand, or measure it with the pendulum, as though there were only two pulses in the measure, the *loud* and the medium. *d.* The *figuring* may be omitted, because it would be puzzling, with such various lengths of lines. *e.* Tell the pupils to sing *as they feel*, and see what variety of expression they can give to the various actions described. This cheerful, sympathetic song is full of kindly feeling.

LANCASTER, 17. Notice the *Quaternary Measure.* Show how pleasantly the tune rises, in the third line, to the firmness of DOH and thence up into the softer expression of ME, and concluding, in the fourth line, with the clear, bright, and decided enunciation of SOH. If the second is used, the teacher must simply give the sound of the note *tu*, (the "sharp fourth" as it is called,) leaving explanations to some future lesson.

NOW STEADILY, 18. *a.* This should first be patterned and taught to all as a single "part." The teacher will notice the *firmness* of DOH, and the *clear* out-burst of SOH. *b.* The *Trinary Measure* will be noticed. *d.* 11s. *e.* The word "merrily" should ring out clearly and boldly. The class should then be divided into two parts, and directly the first division reaches the note under the asterisk, the second division commences, and each company as it reaches the close begins at the beginning again. The mark D. C. will be explained. The class may afterwards be divided into four companies, and proceed in a similar manner. These "Rounds" are useful in teaching, from their requiring so many leaders.

ENDLESS PRAISES, 19. beautifully exhibits the *strong, grand,* and *steady* characters of DOH, SOH, and ME respectively. Let them be delivered with great clearness and decision. Let there be no hanging notes, and no lagging in the second line.

The third verse should be sung with subdued voice. The other verses are in the spirit of loudest praise. The first verse should be repeated at the close.

PROSPECT, 20. *a.* This tune has a most soft and gentle opening, exhibiting the properties of ME, relieved by those of FAH, and enlivened by SOH. In the fifth line there is a most beautiful *awakening* to brighter and bolder sounds, in which SOH and DOH¹ play their part; and then the music returns to the soft part again. *b.* The signs D.C. and P will be explained and the measure examined. *d.* The use of the *slur* will here be introduced, on the "six" and "eight" of the first line, "two" of the second, &c. The tune would be better in the key of G, or even A, if the higher voices can reach its replicate.

JESSE, 21. The boldness of DOH, contrasted as it is with LAH and RAY, contributes to make this tune so easy and popular. The easily divided aliquots also help the rhythmical effect. The meaning of the dot will be explained. *e.* In using the words, taste will suggest a slight change in the division of the notes occasionally. Thus, "| often : been" is better than "| of : ten been," and "| shepherd : boy" is better than "shep : herd boy," &c. The third and fourth lines of the last verse should be sung with solemnity and with heavy retarded accent.

MOZART, 23. This brilliant tune illustrates well the bold characters of DOH, ME, and SOH. The teacher should take care that, in singing the words, there should be always clear and distinct enunciation. Other words may be found in the works of Mr. Hickson and Mr. Callcott.

---

13. HARTS. 7s. (*School Music* 15, *School Songs*, 19.) KEY A. M. 80.

s₁	:s₁	d	:d	r	:r	m	:—	d	:d	f	:m	d	:m	r	:—
m₁	:s₁	m₁	:m₁	f₁	:t₁	d	:—	d	:l₁	t₁	:d	d	:d	t₁	:—

s	:s	m	:m	f	:f	r	:—	m	:f	s	:f	m	:r	d	:—
m	:m	d	:d	r	:r	t₁	:—	d	:l₁	m₁	:l₁	s₁	:t₁	d	:—

---

14. GREGORIAN CHANT. (S. M. 94., S. S. 99.) KEY G. M. 60.

m	:—	m	:r	m	:—	m	:—	r	:d	r	:r	m	:—
d	:—	d	:t₁	d	:—	d	:—	t₁	:l₁	t₁	:t₁	d	:—

---

15. GLOVER. (S. M. 13., S. S. 18.) KEY F. M. 80.

s	:s	f	:m	s	:s	f	:m	s	:s	l	:s
m	:m	r	:d	m	:m	r	:d	m	:m	f	:m

f	:m	r	:—	s₁	:d	r	:m	f	:s	l	:t
r	:d	t₁	:—	s₁	:d	t₁	:d	r	:m	f	:r

d¹	:d¹	s	:f	m	:r	d	:—
d	:m	m	:r	d	:t₁	d	:—

---

16. THE WINTER SONG. (S. M. 99., S. S. 167.) KEY B flat. M. 160.

:s₁	d :d :d	d :—:d	r :r :r	r :— :r	m :r :d
:s₁	m₁ :m₁ :m₁	m₁ :—:m₁	s₁ :s₁ :s₁	s₁ :— :s₁	s₁ :f₁ :m₁

$\left\{\begin{array}{l}\end{array}\right.$ | d :t₁ :d | r :—:s₁ |s₁ :—:s₁ | d :d :d ｜d :—:d | r :r :r

| m₁ :r₁ :m₁ | s₁ :—:s₁ |s₁ :—:s₁ | m₁ :m₁ :m₁ ｜m₁ :—:m₁ | s₁ :s₁ :s₁

$\left\{\begin{array}{l}\end{array}\right.$ ｜r :—:f | m :f :m ｜r :d :r | d :—:d ｜d :— ‖

｜s₁ :—:s₁ | s₁ :l₁ :s₁ ｜f₁ :m₁ :f₁ | m₁ :—:m₁ ｜m₁ :— ‖

---

17. LANCASTER, C. M. (S. M. 19., S. S. 26.) KEY A. M. 66.

$\left\{\begin{array}{l}\end{array}\right.$:s₁ | d :r ｜m :d | f :m ｜r :r | m :d ｜t₁ :l₁ | s₁ :—｜—:s₁

:m₁ | m₁ :f₁ ｜s₁ :d | r :d ｜t₁ :t₁ | d :l₁ ｜s₁ :tu₂ | s₁ :—｜—:s₁

$\left\{\begin{array}{l}\end{array}\right.$ | l₁ :t₁ ｜d :t₁ | d :r ｜m :m | s :f ｜m :r | d :—｜— ‖

| f₁ :r₁ ｜m₁ :s₁ | s₁ :s₁ ｜s₁ :s₁ | s₁ :l₁ ｜s₁ :t₁ | d :—｜— ‖

---

18. NOW STEADILY. (*A Round for four voices.*) KEY C. M. 160.

$\left\{\begin{array}{l}\end{array}\right.$:d¹ | s :s :s | d¹ :d¹ :d¹ | r¹ :r¹ :r¹ | m¹ :—:m¹ | s¹ :s¹ :s¹

Now | Stead-i- ly | stead-i- ly | let us all | walk, And | mer- ri- ly
Hold | up our heads | high and then | point out the | toe, And | step all to-

$\left\{\begin{array}{l}\end{array}\right.$ | s¹ :f¹ :m¹ | r¹ :d¹ :t | d¹ :—

D. C.

sing or else | so- ber- ly | talk. ‖
ge- ther where- | e- ver- we | go.

---

19. ENDLESS PRAISES. (S. M. 47., S. S. 49.) KEY F. M. 160.

$\left\{\begin{array}{l}\end{array}\right.$ |d :—:— ｜s :—:—|m :—:— ｜d :—:—|r :—:m ｜f :—:m

|d :—:— ｜s :—:—|m :—:— ｜d :—:—|t₁ :—:d ｜r :—:d

$\left\{\begin{array}{l}\end{array}\right.$ |r :—:— ｜—:— :|m :—:r ｜d :—:r|m :—:f ｜s :—:

|d :—:— ｜t₁ :—:|s₁ :—:s₁ ｜s₁ :—:s₁|s₁ :—:s₁ ｜s₁ :—:

$\left\{\begin{array}{l}\end{array}\right.$ |d¹ :r—:— ｜s :—:—|l :—:— ｜r¹ :—:—|d¹ :—:— ｜t :—:—

|m :—:— ｜s :—:—|f :—:— ｜f :—:—|m :—:— ｜r :—:—

$\left\{\begin{array}{l}\end{array}\right.$ |d¹ :—:— ｜—:—:—‖

|m :—:— ｜—:—:—‖

---

20. PROSPECT, C. M. (S. M. 56., S. S. 60, 126.) KEY F. M. 80.

$\left\{\begin{array}{l}\end{array}\right.$ | m :m :m ｜f :—:f | s :f :m ｜r :m :f | s :d :f ｜m :—:r

| d :d :d ｜r :—:r | m :r :d ｜t₁ :d :r | d :m :r ｜d :—:t₁

E

D. C. and F.

```
{ | d :— :— |— :— :s  | s :m :s |d¹ :— :s  | s :m :s |s :—:s
{ | d :— :— |— :— :m  | m :d :m |m :— :m  | m :d :m |m :—:m
```

D. C.

```
{ | l :— :s |f :— :m  | m :— :— |r :— :   ||
{ | f :— :m |r :— :d  | d :— :— |t₁ :— :  ||
```

21. JESSE.   (S. M. 17., S. S. 7. 86.)   KEY B flat. M. 96

```
{ :s₁ | d :d.d |d :d.d  | r :t₁.t₁ |d :d  | m :m.m |f :m.m
{ :m₁ | m₁ :m₁.m₁ |m₁ :m₁.m₁  | f₁ :f₁.f₁ |m₁ :m₁  | s₁ :s₁.s₁ |s₁ :d.d

{ | m :— |r :s₁  | d :d.d |d :d.d  | r.d :t₁.l₁ |s₁ :s₁
{ | t₁ :— |— :s₁.f₁  | m₁ :m₁.m₁ |m₁ :m₁.m₁  | s₁ :s₁.f₁ |m₁ :m₁

{ | l₁ :l₁.l₁ |t₁ :t₁.t₁  | r :— |d  ||
{ | f₁ :f₁.f₁ |r₁ :r₁.r₁  | f₁ :— |m₁  ||
```

22. THE BIRD THAT SOARS. (*A Round for four voices.*) KEY F. M.138

```
{ :d | d :— :r | m :— :f | m :— :r | d :— :m | m :— :f
{    | The | bird | that | soars | on | high- | est | wing, | Builds | on | the
{    | In  | Lark | and  | Night- | in- | gale | we | see, | What | hon- | our

{ | s :— :l | s :— :f | m :— :s | s :l :t | d¹ :— :d¹ | d¹ :—
{ | ground | her | low- | ly | nest; | And | she | that | doth | most | sweet-
{ | hath | Hu- | mil- | i- | ty, | What | hon- | our | hath | Hu- | mil-
```

D. C.

```
{ :t | d¹ :— :d | d :— :d | d :— :d | d :— :s₁ | d :— ||
{    | ly | sing, | Sings | in | the | shade | while | all | things | rest:
{    | i- | ty, | What | hon- | our | hath | Hu- | mil- | i- | ty.
```

23. MOZART.   (S. M. 49., S. S. 77.)   KEY E.   M. 160.

```
{ | m :— :— |f :m :f  | s :— :d¹ |d¹ :— :—  | d :— :— |r :d :r
{ | d :— :— |r :d :r  | m :— :m |m :— :—  | d :— :— |t₁ :l₁ :t₁

{ | m :f :m |r :— :—  | m :— :— |f :m :f  | s :— :d¹ |d¹ :— :—
{ | d :r :d |t₁ :— :—  | d :— :— |r :d :r  | m :— :m |m :— :—

{ | m :— :— |r :d :r  | d :— :— |— : :s  | s :— :f |r :m :f
{ | d :— :— |t₁ :l₁ :t₁  | d :— :— |— : :d  | t₁ :— :t₁ |t₁ :d :r
```

{ | s :— :m ı d :— :s | s :— :f ı r :m :f | s :— :m ı d :— :s
{ | m :— :d ı d :— :d | t₁ :— :t₁ ı t₁ :d :r | m :— :d ı d :— :m

{ | l :— :f ı d¹ :— :l | s :— :m ı d¹ :— :— | s :l :s ı s :f :m
{ | f :— :f ı f :— :f | m :— :d ı d :— :— | m :f :m ı m :r :d

{ | m :— :— ı r :— : | m :— :— ı f :m :f | s :— :d¹ ı d¹ :— :—
{ | d :— :— ı t₁ :— : | d :— :— ı r :d :r | m :— :m ı m :— :—

{ | d :— :— ı r :d :r | m :f :m ı r :— :— | m :— :— ı f :m :f
{ | d :— :— ı t₁ :l₁ :t₁ | d :r :d ı t₁ :— :— | d :— :— ı r :d :r

{ | s :— :d¹ ı d¹ :— :— | m :— :— ı r :d :r | d :— :— ı— :— : ‖
{ | m :— :m ı m :— :— | d :— :— ı t₁ :l₁ :t₁ | d :— :— ı— :— : ‖

24.   THE SWALLOW.   (S. M. 119, S. S. 162.)   KEY C.   M. 80.

{ | s :m.f | s :m.f | s :m¹.r¹ | d¹ :— | s :f¹.m¹ | r¹ :r¹
{ | m :d.r | m :d.r | m :s.f | m :— | m :l.s | f :f

D. C. and F.

{ | s :m¹.r¹ | d¹ :— | s :r¹.d¹ | t :s | s :m¹.r¹ | d¹ :—
{ | m :s.f | m :— | m :f.m | r :f | m :s.f | m :—

D. C.

{ | s :r¹.d¹ | t :s | s :m¹.r¹ | d¹ :— ‖
{ | m :f.m | r :f | m :s.f | m :—

25.   OLD HUNDREDTH, L. M.   (S. M. 74, S. S. 101.)   KEY Bflat. M. 50.

{ | :d | d :t₁ | l₁ :s₁ | d :r | m :m | m :m | r :d | f :m
{ | :m₁ | m₁ :r₁ | d₁ :m₁ | m₁ :f₁.r₁ | d₁ :s₁ | s₁ :s₁ | f₁ :m₁ | r₁ :d₁

{ | r :d | r :m | r :d | l₁ :t₁ | d :s | m :d | r :m | f :r | d ‖
{ | t₂ :m₁ | f₁ :m₁ | s₁ :s₁ | f₁ :r₁ | m₁ :m₁ | s₁ :m₁ | f₁ :m₁ | r₁ :f₁ | m₁ ‖

SECTION VI.

OF THE CHARACTER AND PROPER MUSICAL EFFECT OF THE NOTES FAH AND LAH—THE FOURTH AND THE SIXTH OF THE COMMON MODE.

1. The general character of suspense and expectancy belongs to both FAH and LAH, but more strongly to the former. When FAH is held, at any length, the mind is conscious of an urgent and increasing desire for its solution in ME. But to LAH is allowed a greater independence, and it is not required so soon to find its rest in SOH.

It should be carefully remembered that these "characters," of which we speak, do not reside in the musical sound itself, but in *the association*, with which *the mind* invests each note as it arises—by virtue of its position in relation to *other notes*, just heard, and which still linger on the ear. Those other notes must, therefore, be heard first. In other words, the *key* must be "*established*"—by singing its common chord, or, yet more clearly, by adding also its TE and FAH —before the distinctive character and mental effect of a particular note is felt. The more completely "the ear is filled" with the other notes of the key—especially with those of opposite effect— the more clearly will the "character" of the one to be illustrated be brought out.

Dr. Bryce compares ME and SOH to objects lying at rest on the ground, while LAH is "thrown loose and detached with little indication of return," and FAH is "in the act of alighting." We have often likened FAH to the "sky-rocket," which mounts with an upward aim, but, having reached its height, shines beautifully for a moment, and then softly and elegantly descends. Such comparisons must of necessity be "far-fetched," but let the teacher remember that his pupils cannot form a comparison or judge of one, without minutely *observing* the things compared. Thus the *end* is answered. The pupil observes for himself, and he will presently form a more perfect mental conception of the thing itself, than any description or any language can convey.

The teacher may illustrate these general "properties" of FAH and LAH, by singing from the modulator any little phrases like the following—
KEY G. :d | m :s | f :— | m :d | t₁ :d | l :— | s, or KEY F. :d | m :d | s :m | d¹ :t | l :s | f :m | r &c.

2. If the mental impression produced by FAH and LAH be further sought, it will soon be noticed that they have an effect, especially when sung slowly, which would lead us to denominate FAH as the DESOLATE, or *awe-inspiring* NOTE, and LAH as the WEEPING or *sorrowful* NOTE.

The names thus given help greatly to fix the attention, and many adults as well as children have been very thankful for the aid they give to the mind's command over the voice. We have seen many a class, of both sorts, who could not, at first, strike LAH correctly, but were unable to mistake when told that they must make it a "weeping note." But it should be borne in mind that neither these, nor any other single and ordinary terms of language, can fittingly describe the effect of a note under all its modifications of pitch, force, length, &c. We can only describe proximately, but the effort to do so, or only to *perceive* the proximate truth of the description, kindles thought and feeling. The teacher should first *produce the effect*, and then get *his pupils* to describe their own impressions of it, with as much variety of language as possible. Thus the true conception will be reached. The mind is quicker than our words, and will form the *idea* long before we can express it. Thus it is with some word in a new language which has no perfect synonyme in our own;—much study of dictionary context and "concordance," with many endeavours to express it, at last brings us to *the thought*, and we enter on the luxury of mental translation, which is pleasanter to us than the verbal, but could not have been reached without its aid. Thus may our pupils be taught to study and mentally enjoy the beautiful tunes we lay before them.

LAH is called, in works on musical science, the SUBMEDIANT, and FAH the SUBDOMINANT. Various and conflicting reasons have been *invented* for these curious titles. See Dr. Callcott, Dr. Crotch, and Dr. Bryce.

The character of FAH may be illustrated by such phrases as | d :— | m :s | f :— or the following full of wonder, awe, and mystery from the close of the "Hallelujah Chorus"—(after the key has been thoroughly established) :d | f :d
                                For ever

| :d | f :d | :d | f :d | :d | f :d | :d.d |
| and | ever | For | ever | and | ever | Halle- |

| f :d | :d.d | f :d | :d | f :— | — :— |
| lujah | Halle- | lujah | Hal- le- |

| — :— | f :— | d :— | — :— | — :— | — :— |
| lu- | JAH. |

or, from "I know that my Redeemer liveth"—the touching and worshipful expression of "Re-

deemer" :s | d¹ :— | :m.,r | d :— | :l | f :—.m :f | m :—

LAH might be called "*the beautiful note.*" Its character may be shown by singing the first phrase of the NORWICH CHANT, part of CHORLTON PLACE, or any of the "Minor tunes" in a later part of the work.

3. The effect of these notes is modified by their length of duration, so that they give PATHOS to a tune when sung *slowly,* and a peculiar LIGHTNESS and ELEGANCE when sung *quickly.*

This "lightness" and "elegance" is *akin* to "pathos," the one appealing to the more serious and the other to the more trifling moods of a *feeling* mind. We have often heard persons in a trifling mood, after playing a very expressive and "too touching" melody, repeat it at a very quick rate "to shake off the pathos." Try the exquisite tune called here OAKHILL, or the following well-known phrase of melody | d¹ :— | t.d¹ :r¹.d¹ | t.l :— | f :l | s :— | s.f :m.f | m :— singing them first very slowly and then very quickly. A very common song tune by S. L. Lover —very light and musical—commences on LAH,

introduces it at the close of the third line with much effect, and plays upon it very touchingly with ME in the lines which follow :1 | s :d :d | r :d :d | s :d :d | d :— :l | s :f :m | m :r :d | t₁ :r :r | r :— :l | s :d :d | r :d :d | s :d :d | l :— :s.f | m :f :s | s :l :t | d¹ :d :d | d :— :s | d¹ :t :l | l :m :m | f :m :r | d :— :t₁ | l₁ :t₁ :d | d :r :m | m :l :s | s :— (Repeat the last two lines, and then return to repeat the first four). This tune might be sung by children to *Jane Taylor's* "Dutiful Jem" in "Rhymes for the Nursery."

4. LAH forms a much softer and more pleasant consonance with the key note than FAH. The best consonances with FAH are RAY and LAH, and the best notes to sound with LAH are DOH¹ and FAH. It may be noticed that when the notes of a consonance are in their *closest* position, (as DOH, LAH₁, or FAH LAH,) the proper musical effect of each is sweetly *blended* with that of the other, but when they are more distant (as DOH₁ LAH or FAH₁, LAH,) each produces its own effect with good agreement, but greater *distinctness.*

The teacher will easily illustrate these points to his class (if he introduces them at all) in the manner directed in the last Section, being careful always to "establish the key." It is a good exercise, on the piano forte, to play the *scale* and *chord* of C and strike the consonance c¹, A, (DOH, LAH) de-scribing its effect to yourself in words, and then to play the scale and chord of B flat, followed by the same consonance (now RAY, TE) and ask yourself why the musical effect of the self-same sounds is now so different.

5. The learner should seek in the course of this section of exercises to become independent of the *Pattern* and the *Modulator,* and should be able to sing from the modulator any simple phrases the teacher may point at his own discretion. Such phrases we call VOLUNTARIES. The pupil should also carefully practise to strike the pitch-note C¹ from memory.

The teacher should be careful not to leave the modulator before the relative position of notes is thoroughly fixed in the pupil's mind. Much time may be lost by over haste. If, however, all the previous exercises have been carefully practised, the pupil will, by this time, carry a modulator in his mind, and the notes as he comes to them will seem, in his imagination, to rise or fall to their proper positions in the key.

The practice of pointing "Voluntaries," at the opening of each lesson, is essential to the teacher's good success. For when a tune or an exercise has once been learnt, its intervals are known and *expected.* The remembrance of that particular succession of sounds helps the performer as much as his knowledge of interval. Little mental effort is required. But to follow the unanticipated movements of the pointer requires an immediate and new endeavour of the mind and the voice. The teacher must use his own fancy in pointing voluntaries, only taking care not to introduce too difficult intervals, and not to be content that only half the class should follow him.

At the opening of each lesson the teacher should

now call on one of his pupils to strike c¹ from memory, the others giving an opinion whether he is right, and a final appeal being made to the pitch pipe or tuning fork.

GET UP, &c., 26. *a.* Notice the *desolate* effect of FAH when sung slowly, becoming *urgent* when sung more quickly, and *lively and rousing* when sung very quickly. *d.* may be omitted.

BEDFORD, 27. *a.* Notice the exquisite *pathos* given to this tune by the recurrence of FAH and LAH on the strong accents, the touching voice of LAH at the close of the second line, and the final appeal of FAH. *b.* Let the dissonant FAH at the beginning of the second and fourth lines be held firmly and *melt* into its resting note ME, which follows. Compare the consonances FAH LAH, LAH₁ FAH, DOH LAH, and FAH RAY. Ask which is the *pleasantest?* the most *touching?* the most *mournful?* the most *soft?* &c. This study of the *simple consonances* will greatly increase the pupil's enjoyment of music and encourage him in clear and effective execution. It will also be the best preparative for the higher studies of harmony. If, however, the pupils are not sufficiently advanced to study these points, let the teacher enjoy this luxury himself. It is indeed delightful to listen to the sweet unfoldings of the twin melodies, with their mutual approaches and ever-varying harmonies, especially when such music flows from the voices of our own pupils. *e.* It will be a good exercise of taste for the pupils to find a hymn that will be suitable to a tune of this character.

CHORLTON PLACE, 28. *a.* This most beautiful tune throws into fine relief the touching eloquence of LAH both in its lower and higher replicates. It is thrown into contrast with the softness of ME. After the *repose* of the third line, with its accented SOH and ME, how elegant the *awakening* of FAH and upper LAH in the fourth ! and how *soft* and satisfactory the close ! LAH ME is generally found to be a difficult interval. It is obvious that the *Trinary* measure, in which it is written, contributes largely to the beauty of this tune. *b.* The teacher will "give" to his pupils the sound of FI, (the flat seventh, as it is called,) leaving explanations to a future lesson. The "second" is altered. *d.* Eight syllables in a line. *e.* This hymn was written by a young Christian upon her death-bed, in answer to the question — What think you of another world? The last line of each verse should be sung in the spirit of enkindled fervour, wonder, and desire. " But WHAT' MUST IT BE' TO BE THERE !"

PASCAL, 29. *a.* This beautiful melody of the French Protestants opens with peculiar solemnity, (using the *firmness* of DOH), stirs us with a softer, but not less solemn feeling, in the next line, (dwelling on ME), rises into pathos on RAY and FAH,

and then breaks forth into impassioned expression on the higher LAH. *e.* This hymn, which, from its subject and its pictorial character, is much loved by pious children, should be sung with thoughtful and reverent expression, but not too slowly. If the teacher has accustomed his pupils to use ordinarily a *medium force of voice*, this will not be difficult. Let a fitting musical expression be added to the touching beauty of description and poetry in this hymn, and then may be seen what a hallowed power there dwells in music, rightly used, to aid in producing the most sacred effects on the heart. Verses 1, 3, and 5, should be marked for expression, as directed at pages 14 and 15, thus—

1. Lo', at noon, 'tis sudden night!
   Darkness covers all the sky!
   Rocks' are rend'ing at the sight,
   Children, can you tell me why?
   WHAT' CAN ALL' THESE WON'DERS BE ?
   Jesus dies on Calvary.
   JESUS DIES ON CALVARY.

3. *See the blood is streaming fast*
   From his forehead and his side!
   Hark'! he now hath breathed his last,
   With a mighty groan he died.
   Children, shall I tell you why
   Jesus came from heaven to die ?

4. Come, then, children, come and see;
   Lift your little hands to pray;
   "*Blessed Jesus, pardon me,*
   Help a guilty sinner," say;
   "Since it was for such as I
   THOU DIDST CONDESCEND TO DIE."

On the words " darkness *covers*," " *rending*," " *tender*," " *blood*," " *mighty*," " *wretch*ed," and " *guilty*," the dissonant RAY for the *bass* (see *School Music*) will help the effect if it be delivered in the manner indicated by this mark >. On other words it will be better delivered thus < so as to melt richly into its consonance. The line beginning " cruel hands" should have some tone of indignation thrown into it :—the opening RAY should be delivered thus > .

LAUSANNE, 31. *a.* The teacher will explain and cause his pupils to practise, with great precision, the "lengthened pulse" | m :—.f | See SEC. iv. 7. *d.* Observe the high accented FAH. *e.* The second part of the first verse should not be sung heavily, but in the spirit of joy and gratitude. The last two lines should be sung with loud triumph: " LIFT' YOUR HEADS' YE GOLD'EN GATES. LET' THE LIT'TLE TRAV'LERS IN."

FLOWERS &c., 33. The words of this and " Oh,

be just" are from Mrs. Herschell's "Fireside Harmony," which contains many excellent adaptations.

TROUBADOUR, 34. Shows DOH, ME, and SOH in their liveliest mood, relieved by other notes in the closing lines.

WEIMAR, 35, very obviously and elegantly exhibits LAH and FAH in various positions.

ITALIAN HYMN, 37. This most musical melody, with its fitful rhythmical variations—soft, elegant, and bold, will be greatly enjoyed. Let there be no lagging, and let the opening of the fifth line be struck with unhesitating decision; let each one sing as though the soul of music were in him. Notice how effectively FAH is introduced, also the consonance LAH₁ FAH, and how ME contributes to the soft parts.

THE LITTLE HUSBANDMAN, 38. The rest of the words may be found in "Nursery Rhymes."

FULL MANY, 40. Observe the | f.m :— and | r.d :—

In CARLO, SWEET SPICES, and STEPHENS, let the :s.,f , | r.,m &c., be carefully explained, Sec. iv. 7. *f.* and tastefully sung.

WOODLEIGH, 44. Notice LAH at close. Compare the consonances ME DOH, RAY FAH, and TE RAY.

ST. JAMES', 45. Study this fine psalm tune. Notice how the third line replies to the first, and the fourth to the second. Observe the pathos thrown into it by LAH and FAH. And listen how the dissonances TE FAH resolve themselves respectively into DOH and ME.

LUTHER'S HYMN, 46. The words should be carefully explained. Notice that the vigour and solemnity of this tune, as in the OLD HUNDREDTH, is connected with the predominance of DOH, ME, and SOH on the strong accents, with enough of RAY, FAH, and TE to give it pathos. Its BINARY measure, and the simple but admirable unfolding of the melody, line by line, with its lofty but weighty close, contribute also to make this the most solemn and majestic of tunes.

NORWICH CHANT, 48. This may be patterned, | s :— | d¹ :m¹ | l :— | s :— | l.t :d¹.r¹ | m¹ :r¹ | d¹ :— The Reciting or Declaiming note is repeated according to the requirements of the words, on the principles of chanting developed in a later part of this work. Let the time and accent be carefully kept—as marked—without haste. There will then be no difficulty in taking breath, and the words will be delivered with an emphasis and solemn expression which must help them to reach the heart.

26. GET UP, &c. *(A Round for two voices.)* KEY F. M. 80.

D. C.

	: d		f	: f		: s		m	: m		: s		r	: r		: m		d	:—		
	Get	up	lit-	tle	sis-	ter	the	morn-	ing	is	bright,	
	And th'	birds	are	all	sing-	ing	to	wel-	come	the	light.	

27. BEDFORD, C. M. KEY E. M. 50.

	: s		m	: d		l	: s		f	: m		r	: s		d¹	: t		l	: l		s	: m		f	: s
	: d		d	: d		f	: m		r	: d		t₁	: f		m	: r		d	: d		t₁	: d		r	: m

	l	: s		f	: m		r	: s		d¹	: m		f	: r		d		
	f	: m		r	: d		t₁	: f		m	: d		l₁	: t₁		d		

28. CHORLTON PLACE, 8s. (S. M. 5, S. S. 88.) KEY A. M. 80.

	: d		m	: r	: d		s	: f	: m		r	:—	: s₁		d	: r	: m		l₁	: l₁	: t₁
	: m₁		s₁	: s₁	: d		t₁	: r	: d		t₁	:—	: s₁		s₁	: f₁	: m₁		f₁	: f₁	: r₁

	d	:—	: d		s	: f	: m		m	: r	: d		r	:—	: m		f	: s	: l
	m₁	:—	: d		t₁	: r	: d		t₁	: t₁	: d		t₁	:—	: d.f̠i̠		l₁	: t₁	: d

	m	: m	: r		d	:—	
	d	: d	: t₁		d	:—	

29. PASCAL.   (s. m. 51, s. s. 58, 93.)   KEY G.   M. 80.

```
{ | d  :— :d  | d  :t₁ :d  | r  :m  :r  | d  :— :—  | m  :— :m
{ | s₁ :— :s₁ | s₁ :— :s₁ | l₁ :s₁ :f₁ | m₁ :— :—  | s₁ :— :s₁
```

D. C.
```
{ | m  :r  :m | s  :f  :m | m  :— :r  | r  :— :m | f  :m  :r
{ | s₁ :— :d | m  :r  :d | d  :— :t₁ | t₁ :— :d | r  :d  :t₁
```

```
{ | m  :— :f | s  :— :— | ḷ  :— :l | s  :f  :m | f  :m  :r
{ | d  :— :d | d  :— :— | d  :— :d | d  :t₁ :d | l₁ :s₁ :f₁
```

R
```
{ | m  :— :— | l  :— :l | s  :f  :m | f  :m  :r | d  :— :— ‖
{ | s₁ :— :— | d  :— :d | d  :t₁ :d | l₁ :s₁ :f₁ | m₁ :— :— ‖
```

30. THE SLUGGARD.   (s. m. 82, s. s. 138.)   KEY A.   M. 80.

D. C. and F.
```
{ :d.r  | m  :m  :f.m | m  :r  :m  | d  :r  :t₁ | d  :— :t₁.d
{ :m₁.f₁| s₁ :s₁ :l₁.s₁| s₁ :f₁ :m₁ | m₁ :f₁ :r₁ | m₁ :— :s₁.l₁
```

D. C.
```
{ | r  :r  :d.r | m  :m  :r.m | f  :f  :m.f | l  :s   ‖
{ | t₁ :t₁ :l₁.t₁| d  :d  :t₁.d | r  :r  :d.r | f  :m   ‖
```

31. LAUSANNE.   (s. m. 20, s. s. 36, 129.)   KEY C.   M. 80.

D. C. and F.
```
{ | m :—.f | s :s | ḷ :l | s :—  | d¹:r¹ | m¹:f¹.r¹| d¹:t | d¹:—
{ | d :—.r | m :m | f :f | m :—  | m :f  | s :l.f  | m :r | m :—
```

D. C.
```
{ | f¹:m¹ | r¹:m¹ | f¹:m¹ | r¹:— | f¹:m¹ | r¹:d¹ | t :l  | s :—  ‖
{ | t :d¹ | r¹:d¹ | t :d¹ | s :— | s :s  | s :l  | s :tt₁| s :—  ‖
```

32. OLD BASING. (s. m. 101, s. s. 140, 126, 110, 116.) KEY G. M. 112.

D. C.
```
{ :m | f :m ǀr :d | r.d:r.m ǀd :r.m | f :m ǀr :d | r :— ǀd :d
{ :d | r :d ǀt₁:d | s₁ :f₁ ǀm₁:f₁.s₁| l₁:s₁ ǀf₁:m₁ | f₁:— ǀm₁:m₁.s₁
```

```
{ | d :s ǀs :s | l :s ǀs :s | l :s ǀf :m | m :— ǀr :m.f
{ | d :m ǀm :m | f :m ǀm :m | f :m ǀr :d | d :— ǀt₁:s₁
```

```
{ |s  :—.s |d :—.d |r.d :r.m |d :r.m |f  :m  ır :d  |r  :— ıd      ||
{ |s₁ :—.s₁|s₁:—.s₁|f₁ :f₁  |m₁:f₁.s₁|l₁ :s₁ ıf₁ :m₁ |f₁ :—  ım₁    ||
```

33.   FLOWERS, &c.   (*A Round for three voices.*)   KEY C.   M. 80.

```
{ |d¹ :—  ır¹ :d¹ |t  :—  ıd¹ :—  |m¹ :—  ıf¹ :m¹ |r¹ :—  ım¹ :—
{ |Flowers for your| gar-   den,  | All     freshly| grow-  ing,
```

```
{ |d¹ :—  ıl :f  |s  :—  ıd :—      ||
{ |All    gaily  | blow-  ing.      ||
```

34.   TROUBADOUR.   (S. M. 120, S. S. 115.)   KEY F.   M. 96.

D.C.

```
{ |m :s.m |d  :d  |r  :d.r |m :d  |m :s.m |d: :d  |r  :m.r |d :—
{ |d :m.d |d.s₁ :m₁|f₁ :m₁.f₁|s₁ :m₁ |d :m.d |d.s₁ :m₁|f₁ :s₁.f₁|m₁ :—
```

```
{ |d¹ :t.l |s.m :d |l  :s.f |m :—  |d.r :m |f.s :l |s  :t₁ |d :—  ||
{ |m :s.f |m.d :d |f  :m.r |d :—  |d.t₁ :d.ſ⸍|l₁.s₁ :f₁|m₁ :s₁.f₁|m₁ :— ||
```

35.   WEIMAR.   (S. M. 33, S. S. 14, 43, 123.)   KEY F.   M. 138.

```
{ |:s |l :—:s ıf :—:m |s :—:f ır :—:r |m :—:f ıl :—:s
{ |:m |f :—:m ır :—:d |d :—:d ıt₁ :—:t₁|d :—:d ıt₁ :—:t₁
```

```
{ |m :—:—ı—:—:s |s  :f :m ım :r :d |t₁ :—:r ıf :—:s
{ |d :—:—ı—:—:m |m :r :d ıt₁ :—:d |s₁ :—:t₁ ır :—:m
```

```
{ |l  :s :f ım :—:r |d :—:—ı—:—  ||
{ |f  :m :r ıd :—:t₁|d :—:—ı—:—  ||
```

36.   BO PEEP.   (S. M. 115, S. S. 124.)   KEY B flat.   M. 80.

```
{ |:s₁ |d :—:d ıd :—:d |r :—:r ır :—:r |m :—:s ıs::f :m
{ |:s₁ |m₁:—:m₁ım₁:—:m₁|f₁ :—:f₁ ıf₁ :—:f₁|s₁ :—:d ım :r :d
```

```
{ |m :—:—ır :—:s |s :m :m ım :f :s |f :r :r ır :m :f
{ |d :—:—ıt₁ :—:m |m :d :d ıd :r :m |r :t₁ :t₁ ıt₁ :d :r
```

```
{ |m :—:m ır :d :r |d :—:—ı—:—  ||
{ |d :—:s₁ ıf₁ :m₁:f₁|m₁:—:—ı—:—  ||
    F
```

37.   ITALIAN HYMN, 8.7.   (s. m. 52, s. s. 19.)   KEY F.   m. 80.

```
{| m :f  | r  :r  | m :f  | s :s | f  :m | m  :r    | r  :m.d | d  :t, |
{| d :l, | t, :t, | d :r  | m :m | r  :d | s, :s,   | s, : tu,| s, :—  |

{| m :f  | r  :r  | m :f  | s :s | f  :m | m.r :f.r | d  :m.r | d :—   |
{| d :l, | t, :t, | d :r  | m :m | r  :d | s, :l,.f,| m, :s,.f,| m, :—  |

{| d'.t :l.s | s  :s | f.m :f.s | m :d  | d'.t :l.s | s :s | f.m :f.s | m :—  |
{| m.s :f.m  | m :d  | d  ·t,   | d :d  | m.s :f.m  | m :d | d  :t,   | d :—  |

{| m :f  | r  :r  | m :f  | s :s | f  :m | m.r :f.r | d  :m.r | d :—||
{| d :l, | t, :t, | d :r  | m :m | r  :d | s, :l,.f,| m, :s,.f,| m, :—||
```

38. THE LITTLE HUSBANDMAN. (*Round for three voices.*) KEY F. m. 112.

```
{| m :— :m  | s :— :m  | r :m :f | m :— :   | s :— :d¹ |
      I've  a    heart- y   ap- pe- tite,     And   I

{| d¹ :l :f | m :f :r | d :— :  | d :— :d | m :— :d |
   sound- ly  sleep at  night.    Down I   lie   con-

{| t, :d :r | d :— :  | m :— :m | l :f :r | d :r :t, |
   tent and  say,     "I've been  use- ful  all   the

{| d :— :d | d :— :d | d :— :d | s, :— :s, | d :— :d |
   day."  I'd ra- ther  be  a   plough- boy, than A

                                            D. C.
{| d :— :d | f, :— :f, | s, :— :s, | d :— :  ||
   use- less  lit- tle  gen- tle- man.
```

39. SPRIGHTLINESS.   (s. m. 87, s. s. 143.)   KEY F.   m. 112.

```
{| m  :m.m | m  :d   | r  :t,.t, | d  :s, | m  :m.m | m  :d  |
{| s, :s,.s,| s, :m, | f, :f,.f, | m, :—  | s, :s,.s,| s, :m, |

{| r  :t,.t, | d  :—  | d¹ :t.l | s :m  | f :m.r  | m :—   |
{| f, :f,.f, | m, :—  | m  :s.f | m :d  | r :d.t, | d :—   |

{| d :r.m | f.l  :s.f | m.r :d.t, | d :—  ||
{| d :t,.d| l,.d :t,.l,| s,.f, :m,.f,| m, :— ||
```

40. FULL MANY, &c. (*A Round for three voices.*) KEY G. M. 96.

:s	s	:—	:m	l	:—	:s	s	:—	:f	f.m	:—	:m
Full	many		a	shaft		at	ran-		dom	sent		Finds
And	many		a	word		at	ran-		dom	spoken		May
Oh!	ne-		ver	let		us	light-		ly	fling		A
Oh!	ne-		ver	let		us	haste		to	bring		The

m	:—	:d	f	:—	:m	m	:—	:r	r.d	:—	:d	d	:—	:d
mark		the	arch-		er	lit-		tle	meant,	Finds	mark		the
soothe		or	wound		a	heart		that's	broken,	May	soothe		or
barb		of	woe		to	wound		an-	other,	A	barb		of
cup		of	sor-		row	to		a	Brother,	The	cup		of

D. C.

d	:—	:d	s₁	:—	:s₁	d.d	:—
arch-		er	lit-		tle	meant.	
wound		a	heart		that's	broken.	
woe		to	wound		an-	other.	
sor-		row	to		a	Brother.	

41. CARLO. (S. M. 112, S. S. 131.) KEY A. M. 112.

:s.,f	m	:s	׀d	:m	l₁	:l₁	׀s₁	:d	t₁	:r	׀f	:m	m	:—	׀r	:s.,f
:m.,r	d	:t₁	׀d	:s₁	f₁	:f₁	׀m₁	:m₁	s₁	:t₁	׀r	:d	d	:—	׀t₁	:m.,r

m	:s	׀d	:m	l₁	:l₁	׀s₁	:d	t₁	:r	׀s	:t₁	d	:—	׀
d	:t₁	׀d	:s₁	f₁	:f₁	׀m₁	:m₁	s₁	:f₁	׀m₁	:f₁	m₁	:—	׀

42. SWEET SPICES. (S. M. 30, S. S. 27.) KEY A. M. 80.

:s₁	d	:m	:d	l₁	:s₁	:d	r.,m	:f	:m	r	:—	:m.,f
:m₁	m₁	:s₁	:m₁	f₁	:m₁	:d	t₁.,d	:r	:d	d	:t₁	:d.,r

s	:m	:s	l	:f	:r	d	:d.m	:r.t₁	d	:—	
m	:d	:d	d	:l₁	:l₁	s₁	:s₁	:f₁	m₁	:—	

43. STEPHENS, C. M. (S. M. 59, S. S. 76.) KEY A. M. 50.

:d	s	:m	d	:r.,d	t₁	:d	r	:m	s	:d.,r	m	:r	d	:m
:d	t₁	:d	d	:l₁	s₁	:d	t₁	:s₁	s₁	:l₁	s₁	:t₁	d	:d

f	:r	m	:f	s	:r.,d	t₁	:l₁	s₁	:d.,r	m	:r	d	
l₁	:t₁	d	:l₁	s₁	:f₁.,m₁	r₁	:f₁	s₁	:m₁.,f₁	s₁	:t₁	d	

44.   WOODLEIGH.   (S. M. 84, S. S. 157.)   KEY G orA. M. 80.

$$
\begin{aligned}
&\{\;:s_1 \mid s_1.d \;:d.d \;\mid d \;:t_1.d \mid r.r \;:r.r \;\mid r \;:d.r \mid m.m \;:r.d \;\mid d \;:t_1.d \\
&\{\;:m_1 \mid m_1.m_1 :m_1.m_1 \mid m_1 :r_1.m_1 \mid f_1.f_1 :f_1.f_1 \mid f_1 \;:m_1.f_1 \mid s_1.s_1 :f_1.m_1 \mid m_1 \;:s_1.l_1
\end{aligned}
$$

$$
\begin{aligned}
&\{\; \mid r.t_1 \;:d.l_1 \mid s_1.f :m.r \mid d.d \;:d.d \mid d \;:t_1.d \mid r.r \;:r.r \mid r \;:m.f \\
&\{\; \mid t_1.s_1 :l_1.tu_9 \mid s_1 \;:-.f_1 \mid m_1.m_1 :m_1.m_1 \mid m_1 \;:s_1.l_1 \mid t_1.t_1 :t_1.t_1 \mid t_1 \;:d.r
\end{aligned}
$$

$$
\begin{aligned}
&\{\; \mid s.s \;:m.d \mid l_1 \;:t_1.l_1 \mid s_1.d :m.r \mid d \;\| \\
&\{\; \mid m.d :s_1.m_1 \mid f_1 \;:s_1.f_1 \mid m_1.d :t_1.t_1 \mid d \;\|
\end{aligned}
$$

45.   ST. JAMES, C. M.   KEY B.   M. 50.

$$
\begin{aligned}
&\{\;:s_1 \mid d :r \mid m :d \mid r :f \mid m :m \mid l_1 :t_1 \mid d :l_1 \mid s_1 :r \\
&\{\;:s_1 \mid m_1 :s_1 \mid d :d \mid d :t_1 \mid d :s_1 \mid f_1 :r_1 \mid m_1 :d_1 \mid t_2 :t_1
\end{aligned}
$$

$$
\begin{aligned}
&\{\; \mid m :d \mid f :m \mid l_1 :r \mid t_1 :s_1 \mid d :m \mid f :r \mid d \| \\
&\{\; \mid d :s_1 \mid l_1 :s_1 \mid f_1 :r_1 \mid s_1 :f_1 \mid m_1 :s_1 \mid l_1 :t_1 \mid d \|
\end{aligned}
$$

46.   LUTHER'S HYMN, L. M. P.   (S. M. 75, S. S. 90.)   KEY A.   M. 50.

$$
\begin{aligned}
&\{\;:d \mid d :m \mid r :d \mid r :r \mid m :d \mid m :f \mid s :f.m \mid m :r \\
&\{\;:m_1 \mid m_1 :s_1 \mid f_1 :m_1 \mid l_1 :s_1 \mid m_1 :m_1 \mid s_1 :l_1 \mid s_1 :s_1 \mid s_1 :f_1
\end{aligned}
$$

D. C.
$$
\begin{aligned}
&\{\; \mid d :m \mid f :m \mid r :d \mid t_1 :d \mid r :m \mid d :t_1 \mid d :s_1 \\
&\{\; \mid m_1 :s_1 \mid s_1 :s_1 \mid f_1 :m_1 \mid s_1 :s_1 \mid s_1 :s_1 \mid s_1 :f_1 \mid m_1 :s_1
\end{aligned}
$$

R. ff.
$$
\begin{aligned}
&\{\; \mid d :r \mid m :d \mid m :f \mid s :f.m \mid m :r \mid d \| \\
&\{\; \mid f_1 :f_1 \mid m_1 :m_1 \mid s_1 :l_1 \mid s_1 :s_1 \mid s_1 :f_1 \mid m_1 \|
\end{aligned}
$$

47.   IF HAPPINESS, &c.   (*A Round for four voices.*)   KEY D.   M. 60.

$$
\{\;:s \mid d^1 :d^1 \mid r^1 :r^1 \mid m^1 :m^1 \mid d^1 :\dot{d}^1 \mid l :l \mid t :t \mid d^1 :-\mid-:s
$$
If | hap- pi- ness has | not her seat, And | cen- tre in the | breast,   We

D. C.
$$
\{\; \mid f :f \mid f :f \mid m :s \mid d^1 :s \mid l :f \mid r :s \mid d :-\mid- \|
$$
may be wise or | rich or great, But | ne- ver can be | blest.

48.   NORWICH CHANT.   (S. M. 40, S. S. 40.)   KEY C.   M. 60.

```
{| s   :—    | s   :—    | d¹.,d¹ :m¹ | l   :—    | s   :—.s  | l.t  :d .r
 | Oh        | God,      | Thou art my| God,      | Ear-  ly  | will  ‾‾I‾‾
 | m   :—    | m   :—    | m.,m  :s   | f   :—    | m   :—.m  | f    :m.l

 | m   :r    | d   :—.,s | s.,s  :s.s | s.s   :s  | d¹.d¹ :m¹ | l   :—
 | seek      | thee: Be- | cause thy loving-| kindness is| better  than | life,
 | s   :f    | m   :—.,m | m.,m  :m.m | m.m   :m  | m.m   :s  | f   :—

 | s   :—    | l.t  :d¹.r¹| m¹  :r¹  | d¹  :—.,s | s.s   :s  | d¹  :m¹
 | my        | lips shall | praise   | Thee: Be- | cause thou hast | been  my
 | m   :—    | f    :m.l  | s   :f   | m   :—.,m | m.m   :m  | m   :s

 | l   :—    | s.,s  :s.s | s,s,s  :s| l.t  :d¹.r¹| m¹  :r¹  | d¹  :—      ||
 | help,     | Therefore in the| shadow of Thy| wings will | I    re-   | joice.
 | f   :—    | m.,m  :m.m | m,m,m  :m| f    :m.l  | s   :f   | m   :—      ||
```

EXAMINATION OF PUPILS ON THE SECOND STAGE.

SECTION V.

1. By virtue of what condition does a note obtain its peculiar musical character, and produce a corresponding mental effect?

What other conditions modify the effect of a note?

Do we know, to any extent, why or how it is that the mental effect of a particular note depends more on its position in the key, than on anything in the note itself?

2. Into what two classes may the mode-notes be divided, in reference to the feelings they excite in the mind?

Which are the strong notes?—the leaning notes? What is the leaning of TE, of FAH, &c.?

3. What is the musical effect of DOH, and by what names would you describe it?

* Give illustrations of DOH from the exercises.

* I will sing part of a tune beginning on SOH (or ME) to the figures one, two, three, &c., and you shall tell me which figures were sung to the note DOH.

How would you describe SOH?

* Give illustrations from the exercises.

* I will give you a sound for DOH, and you shall strike its SOH.

* I will "figure" a tune beginning on DOH, and you shall tell me which figures fell upon higher SOH—upon lower SOH.

How would you describe ME?

* Give examples.

* Sing ME to any DOH I give you.

* Tell me which numbers fall on ME when I sing a tune to the figures.

4. What character do DOH, ME, and SOH give to a tune when sung quickly?—when sung slowly?

* Give instances from the exercises.

5. Which of the notes *blends* best with DOH, or forms with it the most "perfect" consonance? Which forms the pleasanter consonance?

What union of notes forms the common chord, or the common chord of the tonic?

6. Which are easier to you—the higher notes or the lower notes? What is the "compass" of your voice? Which "part" in a tune should you ordinarily sing?

7. On what notes do tunes usually begin?

8. What are the different methods of establishing in the ear *a sense of the key* before a tune is begun?

9. Describe the five processes through which each exercise should pass, and especially mention the particular *purposes* and *advantages* of each.

How should each season of practice be occupied?

* Pitch and solfa from the book, without help, any, I may choose, of the exercises you have learnt in this section.

* Choose two-thirds of them, and be prepared to pitch and to "figure" any of these I may fix on.

* Follow my pointing on the modulator—in

any short phrases, which do not take a *skip* except on DOH, ME, and SOH, and which use the other notes only as *passing* notes.

* Point on the modulator, from memory, any which I may select, of five tunes in this section.
* Write the same from memory.

What does a dot placed in the middle of an aliquot mean? SEC. IV. 7. *c*. Show an example.

How do you mark a pause? SEC. IV. 7. *h*. Show an example.

What is a slur?—the mark for a slur?

What characters of notes does HARTS exhibit? With what "expression" should the first verse be sung?—the fifth?

What do you notice in the GREGORIAN CHANT?—in GLOVER?—in NOW STEADILY, &c.? —in ENDLESS PRAISES?

* Describe the tune PROSPECT, especially the qualities of its opening and of the fifth line.

SECTION VI.

1. What is the general character common to FAH and LAH, and how are they distinguished even in this?

Why is it necessary to "establish the key" before we illustrate these "characters" of the mode-notes?

2. What is the mental impression produced by FAH and LAH? and by what names may they be called? What is the advantage of seeking to *name* these characters of notes?

* Give illustrations of FAH.
* I will give you a sound for DOH, and you shall strike its upper FAH—its lower FAH.
* I will "figure" part of a tune and you shall tell me which numbers fall on FAH. (The chord should be given first).
* Give illustrations of LAH.
* Strike the LAH, both above and below, to any DOH that I may give you.
* I will "figure" a tune, and you shall tell me which numbers fall on LAH.

3. How is the effect of FAH and LAH modified by their length of sound?

* Give illustrations of each.

4. Whether does LAH or FAH form the pleasanter consonance with the key note?

What are the best consonances with LAH? —with FAH?

What is the difference of effect between a "close" and a "distant" consonance?

5. What attainment should the pupil reach before he is warranted to lay aside the modulator?

Wherein appears the importance of "Voluntaries?"

* Follow my pointing on the modulator in any "voluntary" including *skips* on DOH, ME, SOH, FAH, LAH, and using RAY and TE only as *passing* notes.
* Strike the pitch-note c¹ from memory.
* Pitch and solfa, from the book, any of the exercises I may choose from those you have learnt in this section.
* Be prepared to "figure," without mistake, at least two-thirds of them.
* Be prepared to point any of the same on the modulator from memory.
* Write from memory any five or six of them.

What is the effect of a change, in the rate of movement, on FAH, as illustrated in the "GET UP, &c."?

What is the spirit of the tune BEDFORD? Select two or three hymns that will suit it.

Have you any remark to make on the consonances illustrated in BEDFORD?

* *Describe* the spirit of the melody of CHORLTON PLACE, and give the proper expression of the last line in each verse.
* Describe the chief points of melodic expression in PASCAL.
* Write out, from memory, the first, third, and fourth verses of "Lo! at noon, &c.," and mark them for expression.

How do you indicate the continuance of a note through half the next pulse or aliquot?

How do you show, in writing, that a note occupies three quarters or a quarter of a pulse?

What points of "expression" do you notice in the hymn beginning, "Who are they, &c."?

Wherein consists the beauty of the ITALIAN HYMN?

* Describe ST. JAMES' and LUTHER'S HYMN.

How should the "declaiming note" of a chant be delivered?

How do you indicate that a note occupies one-third of a pulse or aliquot?

NOTICE TO THE TEACHER. If the OLD NOTATION is taught, it is recommended that it should not be begun until this "stage" has been completed. The teacher may, however, commence at any point, by a proper use of the appendix.

THIRD STAGE.

SECTION VII.

OF THE CHARACTER AND PROPER MUSICAL EFFECT OF THE NOTES RAY AND
TE, THE SECOND AND SEVENTH OF THE COMMON MODE.

1. The note TE, when heard at length, and after "the ear has been filled" with the other notes of the mode, inspires the mind with a feeling of suspense accompanied with a strong desire for its resolution in DOH. The note RAY, when heard in similar circumstances, excites a feeling of suspense almost as strong as TE, but does not so decidedly indicate its resting note. The ear is pleased by its rising to ME, but more fully satisfied by its falling on DOH.

These points should be illustrated as in previous sections. See the GREGORIAN CHANT for RAY resolved in ME. It will be seen that RAY differs from LAH, which indicates less of suspense, and less desire for resolution, but leaves no doubt as to its resting note. The momentary independence of LAH implies no hesitation in this respect, but RAY suggests a continual struggle between its double tendencies — an unwilling independence.

2. The characters of both TE and RAY carry a strong appeal to the mind's emotions, but do nor touch so directly those *softer* and *gentler* feelings which FAH and LAH affect. There is more of hope and energy about them. TE may be called the SENSITIVE or *piercing* note, and RAY the HOPEFUL or *rousing* note.

Though these names are found very useful, it must again be remembered that they but imperfectly and partially describe the real character of the notes, which can only be perceived by individual study of the best examples. When once perceived, however, these "characters" will not be forgotten, even though it be difficult to name them.

The character of RAY preceded by LAH is beautifully shown in the opening of "Angels ever bright and *fair*," thus | s :— | d :— | d¹ :t.l | s :l.r | r :—   Then follows the *soft* appeal of ME, seconded by the *urgency* of FAH, on the words

"Take, O *take* me to thy care," | m :r | f :m | r :d | s :— | — :— which is repeated, and again varied with the introduction of lower TE, thus | f :—.s | m :r.d | t₁ :—.d | d :— and when desire has risen to the intensity almost of despair, it is expressed by the *piercing* voice of the higher TE, thus—"Take, O *take* me to your care" | s :— | — :l | t :d¹ | m :r.d | d :— After several repetitions and variations of the softer "theme," referred to, the whole piece closes with this last piercing appeal. For further illustration the teacher might sing "Battisbill," "Binfield Heath," "Graham," &c.

3. These notes when sung quickly contribute *liveliness* and *piquancy* to the tune in which they are introduced. See SWEET SPICES, THE SWALLOW, FONT-HILL, SONNING, &c.

4. RAY and TE are the only notes of the scale which are not consonant with the key note. The best consonances with RAY are FAH and TE. The best consonances with TE are RAY and SOH.

In works on the science of music, RAY is called the SUPERTONIC and TE the LEADING note. RAY and TE are said to be the most artificial notes of the scale. The writer of the article SCALE, Penny Cyclopædia, states that a note sharper than the present RAY and one flatter than TE would be more *natural*; and Colonel Perronett Thompson, in his "Instructions to my daughter for playing on the Enharmonic Guitar," and in a series of admirable articles from the Westminster Review, reprinted in his "Exercises," very forcibly maintains that these notes are, in fact, *double*, and that any good singer or violinist would naturally produce them at a slightly higher or lower pitch, as might be required to bring them into more perfect consonance with some adjacent note. RAY, for instance, in any near fellowship with FAH and LAH, will be slightly flattened, but to tune well with SOH will remain in its sharpened form. Hence it is found difficult for uncultivated voices to sing these notes correctly. This is especially noticeable on TE in ascending the "common mode" and on RAY in descending. These notes are therefore here placed last in the order of illustration that the pupil may become familiar with the simpler and easier notes of the mode before he advance to any characteristic or difficult use of these.

From Col. Thompson's deeply interesting papers we obtain a proximate statement, in plain figures, of the actual intervals of the common mode;—which we give below, in connection with the technical names of the notes.

The higher positions of TE and RAY are given below, as they are more used;—in the flat positions they are each one degree lower. This measurement is sufficiently accurate to give to the common student a very fair idea of the intervals of the mode. It will be perceived that the TONULES, between ME FAH, and TE DOH, are equal, both measuring five degrees; but that the TONES are of two kinds, the *greater* and the *smaller tone*, one measuring eight degrees and the other nine.

This is the musical scale or mode established in nature—the most pleasing to all ears, and the most accordant with the philosophy of music. This scale, in its exact proportions, is also the most natural and easy for the human voice—that most wonderful of all musical instruments—in any key. The violin too can give accurate *intonation*. But the ordinary piano, organ, and other keyed instruments do not produce this scale of nature and of the voice in exact tune. It may be easily seen that if they were made perfectly correct in one key, some of the notes must of necessity be incorrect, by a degree or two, in all the other keys. They are therefore called "imperfect"

instruments, and, in tuning, they require to be "tempered," or to have their defects so distributed that they shall be as little noticed as possible. Mr. Graham, in his "Theory and Practice of Musical Composition," shows the great injustice, and the great injury to music, which arises from the frequent endeavour to form the voice—a perfect instrument—according to the false intonation of such instruments as these. Col. Thompson says: "It may be hoped the time is approaching when neither singer nor violinist will be tolerant of a tempered instrument. Singers sing to the pianoforte because they have bad ears; and they have bad ears because they sing to the pianoforte."

If we suppose the interval between a key note and its replicate to be divided into *fifty-three degrees*, then the interval from any one note to the next may be indicated, as follows, by the numbers placed between them:

DOH[1], OR THE TONIC.

FIVE DEGREES.

TE, OR THE LEADING NOTE.

NINE DEGREES.

LAH, OR THE SUBMEDIANT.

EIGHT DEGREES.

SOH, OR THE DOMINANT.

NINE DEGREES.

FAH, OR THE SUBDOMINANT.

FIVE DEGREES.

ME, OR THE MEDIANT.

EIGHT DEGREES.

RAY, OR THE SUPERTONIC.

NINE DEGREES.

DOH, OR THE TONIC.

5. It may easily be noticed, that every tune is naturally divisible into parts which correspond with a *line* in poetry. DOH, ME, and SOH, as might be supposed from their character of repose, are the notes most frequently used on the close of a line. Next to them, RAY and TE are used, but FAH and LAH are of too pathetic a character for frequent use in this position. See CHARMOUTH, HOPE, VALLIS VALE, CALLCOTT, &c.

BATTISHILL, 49. After pitching the tune (c¹ being struck from memory) and taking the rate of | movement (to the first note, or to one, two, three, four, &c.) the pupil will be able by this time to sing the simpler tunes at sight, with only occasional help from the Modulator or the Pattern. This tune illustrates the peculiar effect of FAH when used as a closing note. The melody opens with a line of simple beauty; this is answered, in the second line, by a phrase of elegant pathos; the third line at once recalls the mind to the first, but only to display the marked difference of its close, which, instead of giving the repose of ME, mounts direct to the *expectancy* of FAH, which is, as a trumpet note, to prepare and awaken the mind for the bold and touching appeal of pathos in the closing line. The HOPEFUL NOTE is shown in the first line, and the SENSITIVE NOTE, very beautifully, in the last. It is obvious that, in both the hymns to which this tune is adapted, the voice, in the last verse, should be loud and "wax louder and louder," with bold accent, to the expressive close. For the sixty-third hymn this tune is well adapted. It heightens the effect both of its cheerful sweet invitations and of that most touching declaration of wondrous love, with which each invitation is urged.

FAIRFIELD, 50. The replies of line to line in this tune are differently arranged from those in the last. The cheerfulness and piquancy which TE and RAY throw into the higher movement, (unless, indeed, the tune is spoilt by drawling), together with the admirable art with which in its closing half we are reminded of the former movement and prepared to seek repose in its repetition, are interesting to observe. The second is altered from that in the "School Music," but not discordant with it. Notice the consonances.

ST. CLAIR, 51. This tune, sung by a large body of voices, produces a wonderfully grand effect, especially where the genius and spirit of it is felt. None but the least poetical can fail to observe the exquisite elegance which LAH and RAY (followed by the sweet interval SOH ME) give to the opening theme, and the soft reply of the second line which seems almost conclusive, until the theme is revived again with the urgency of TE in the third line, and that gives birth to the lofty, full, and perfect conclusion, which so plainly admits of no reply. Though suitable to the hymns for which it is marked—with occasionally moderated force and retarded accent—this tune could only throw out its full power in connection with a hymn like that which begins—"Come we that love the Lord."

CHARMOUTH, 52. The replies in this tune are not by alternate lines as in BATTISHILL, but the second line gives answer to the first, and the fourth to the third—the spirit of the tune rising in fervour as it proceeds. The pupil cannot help observing how tastefully and effectively the various notes of pathos and emotion are here introduced. By the reply of the second line to the first, the *sequences* (or notes *following* one the other) FAH

RAY and LAH FAH, and the double notes TE and RAY are brought into marked contrast. The second line will be noticed as more serious and elevated than the first, and as preparing the mind for the yet more characteristic and lofty expressions of melody which follow. Such a tune is well suited to the calm proposal of a touching question at the opening of each verse, followed by some high thought or earnest prayer, as in Hymn 52. The proper accents of the Quaternary Measure should be tastefully given, and none who enter into the spirit of the tune will allow it to lag towards the close.

ALL THE SPRINGING, &c., 53. This round from M. Jeu de Berneval is designed to illustrate the dissonance FAH TE (the tritone) in both positions, with its "resolution" into ME, DOH.

CROSSCOMBE, 54. LAH, TE, and RAY successively find their illustration in this tasteful tune so full of varied expression. The teacher will notice the double syllables at the end of some lines, in Song 153, which must be sung to a single note. The last two lines of each verse should be sung with spirit.

SOLOMON, 55. The fall on RAY will require some care. It should be softly and clearly patterned. The second is altered from that in "School Music," but not discordant with it. This touching melody, filled with tenderness, is well adapted to that solemn sweet prayer of a pious child in Hymn 23. Need we remind the teacher of children that every hymn, before it is sung, should be made the subject of a distinct lesson—should be fully explained and urged on the conscience. A careful watch over his own heart the teacher should keep, that his children may learn from sympathy with him how to "sing with the spirit, and with the understanding also."

CALLCOTT, 56. Notice the piercing character of TE thrown into relief by the previous FAH and LAH. Observe how steadily and majestically the melody rises to its bold and lofty close; and mark that the quickening of the movement falls on corresponding syllables in the *related* lines—on the sixth and seventh syllables in the first and third lines, and on the fourth and fifth syllables in the second and fourth lines.

GRAHAM, 57. Study the character of RAY as given in this tune. The second is altered. Let the :m.f be sung lightly.

ELY, 59. The Hymn 22, though very simple and beautiful *to us* in thinking of children, is not so to children themselves without some explanation of the words and some development of the thoughts and images. "A little vessel full of Thee"—will they understand, at first, that that means full of good thoughts and sweet love? "A star of early dawn, &c."—have they ever seen a soft shining star bathed in the loving light of the rising sun? Few would thus understand it.

G

Nevertheless when the meaning is once perceived such imagery is dearly loved even by little children, and it will help them to express their desire to be spiritually minded—and to have the favour of God shining upon their hearts.

HANOVER, 60. It is wonderful to notice how, from so simple a "theme" as the first five notes supply, the genius of Handel could elaborate so many gentle and most tasteful variations in the lines which follow, and, moreover, combine them all into one perfect melody.

VALLIS VALE, 61. Notice the exceedingly soft and gentle opening on ME and LAH, the characters of TE and RAY1, and the lively effect of the quickened movement occasionally thrown in. At the close of the second, fourth, and eighth lines the dissonance DOH RAY melts into TE₁ RAY. For this purpose let the RAY be firmly held, especially on the second pulse.

KETTERING, 62. Notice the piercing and urgent effect of TE in the third line, throwing into relief the last line, with DOH¹ appealing to more firm and trusting, and FAH and LAH to gentler, emotions. This tune well suits the hymn which begins, " Come, my soul, thy suit prepare."

SAMSON, 63. The second is altered. The "responses" of the several members of a melody may sometimes be likened to a conversation, on some subject of common interest, between several persons of different character. Thus, in this case, the first member produces a theme at once bold and of commanding importance, which the second acknowledges with clearness and elegance of expression; but, as though the beauty of the thought had not been recognized by the second with sufficient warmth, the third illustrates and heightens it by a new development full of brilliancy; and the last member, in the most decided manner, and with a full heart, closes the whole subject.

WELLS, 65. Notice, with care, the exceedingly beautiful and tasteful measure | l :-.s :f.m Observe, also, the exquisite and tender response of line to line, the lofty stirring voice of RAY¹ in the conclusion, and the soft close.

THE SKYLARK, 66. Take care to keep the time well, in the complex movements of the two parts, on the closing measure. The note ηĺ indicates transition into the minor of the subdominant key, to be explained hereafter. It is a tonule below RAY.

BINFIELD HEATH, 69. Observe RAY and TE beautifully brought out in the opening lines, and RAY brilliantly at the close;—and notice the gradual but bold, beautiful, and perfect awakening, from lower LAH and FAH to higher DOH ME SOH in the last line.

OAKHILL, 70. Be careful to execute correctly the complex rhythm, which closes the first and commences the second line :—the dissonance SOH LAH will only add piquancy to the consonance SOH TE, into which it is resolved. At the opening of the third line notice the dissonance LAH₁ SOH resolving into LAH₁ FAH. Let the LAH be well held, and the FAH be distinctly sounded. Study, in this tune, the exquisite mingling of the slow and the quick movements—the change of style from the gentler to the bolder expression—the effect of LAH and FAH contrasted with the boldly repeated DOH, and many other points of beauty. The tune has the voice of a soft and fitful reverie. Such a melody must live as long as there are human ears and hearts to feel the power of music.

LIVERPOOL CHANT, 71. Take care that the words are pronounced lightly, but very distinctly —and that the time and accent are well kept as marked. It would be well for the pupil to read the words aloud, with much care in pronunciation, and much effort to appreciate these glorious sentiments of our Saviour's opening ministry. The chant should be solfaed, as written : the varying rhythmical effect of the reciting note will afford an admirable exercise in " keeping time." The teacher should, at first, " beat time" on the table, or use the pendulum. Let him be especially careful that the reciting or " declaiming" note be sung lightly with only the natural accents of the voice as they recur. If these points are well observed there will be no " gabbling" haste—no running of one before the other—no stopping at the end of the reciting note to let the rest overtake you—but the " voice of many people" giving a united and dignified musical expression to incomparable words. The accents are placed in the most natural and easy positions for a singer who keeps the sense in view, so that, after a very little careful practice, the declaiming note will be familiarly and easily executed. How delightful to sing together thus expressively in the very words of the Inspired Book !

49.　　BATTISHILL. 7s.　(s. m. 1, s. s. 10, 63.)　　KEY G.　　M. 50.

$\left\{\begin{array}{l}\text{s :m} \mid \text{r :d} \mid \text{r :m} \mid \text{f :—} \mid \text{l :s} \mid t_1 \text{ :d} \mid \text{m :r} \mid \text{d :—} \|\\ \text{m :d} \mid t_1 \text{ :d} \mid s_1 \text{ :d} \mid l_1 \text{ :—} \mid f_1 \text{ :s}_1 \mid s_1 \text{ :d} \mid \text{d :}t_1 \mid \text{d :—} \|\end{array}\right.$

50. FAIRFIELD. C. M. (s. m. 55, s. s. 62.) KEY D. M. 80.

D. C. and F.

$\left\{\begin{array}{l}\text{:s} \mid d^1 \text{ :s} \mid \text{l :t} \mid d^1 \text{ :}\underline{t.l} \mid \text{s :f} \mid \text{m :}\underline{s.f} \mid \text{m :r} \mid \text{d :— }\text{—: }d^1\\ \text{:}\underline{s.f} \mid \text{m :m} \mid \text{f :r} \mid \text{m :f} \mid \text{m :r} \mid \text{d :r} \mid \text{d :}t_1 \mid \text{d :— —:m}\end{array}\right.$

D. C.

$\left\{\begin{array}{l}\text{t :}d^1 \mid r^1 \text{ :t} \mid d^1 \text{ :}r^1 \mid m^1 \text{ :}d^1 \mid \text{t :}\underline{r^1.d^1} \mid \text{t :l} \mid \text{s :— —}\|\\ \text{r :m} \mid \text{f :r} \mid \text{m :f} \mid \text{s :m} \mid \text{r :r} \mid \text{s :}tu_1 \mid \text{s :— —}\|\end{array}\right.$

51. ST. CLAIR. S.M. (s. m. 65, s. s. 28, 54.) KEY D. M. 66.

$\left\{\begin{array}{l}\text{:}d^1 \mid \text{s :l} \mid \text{r :s} \mid \text{m :s} \mid \text{l :}d^1 \mid \text{t :l} \mid \text{s :s} \mid \text{t :t}\\ \text{:m} \mid \text{m :d} \mid \text{d :}t_1 \mid \text{d :}t_1 \mid \text{d :m} \mid \text{r :}tu_1 \mid \text{s :s} \mid \text{r :r}\end{array}\right.$

$\left\{\begin{array}{l}d^1 \text{ :}d^1 \mid \text{l :}r^1 \mid \text{t :}r^1 \mid m^1 \text{ :}d^1 \mid r^1 \text{ :t} \mid d^1 \|\\ \text{m :m} \mid \text{f :foi} \mid \text{s :s} \mid \text{s :m} \mid \text{f :r} \mid \text{m} \|\end{array}\right.$

52. CHARMOUTH. L.M. (s. m. 62, s. s. 52, 73.) KEY A. M. 50.

$\left\{\begin{array}{l}\text{:m} \mid \text{m :d} \mid \text{f :r} \mid t_1 \text{ :}t_1 \mid \text{d :s} \mid \text{s :m} \mid \text{l :f} \mid \text{r :r} \mid \text{m :d}\\ \text{:}s_1 \mid s_1 \text{ :}s_1 \mid f_1 \text{ :}f_1 \mid s_1 \text{ :}f_1 \mid m_1 \text{:}m_1 \mid m_1 \text{:}s_1 \mid \text{d :d} \mid \text{d :}t_1 \mid \text{d :}m_1\end{array}\right.$

$\left\{\begin{array}{l}\text{f :m} \mid \text{r :d} \mid \text{l :s} \mid \text{f :m} \mid \text{f :s} \mid \text{l :r} \mid \text{d :}t_1 \mid \text{d} \|\\ l_1 \text{ :}s_1 \mid f_1 \text{ :}m_1 \mid f_1 \text{ :}m_1 \mid r_1 \text{ :}s_1 \mid l_1 \text{ :}s_1 \mid f_1 \text{ :}f_1 \mid s_1 \text{ :}\underline{s_1.f_1} \mid m_1 \|\end{array}\right.$

53. ALL THE SPRINGING, &c. (Round for two voices.) KEY F. M. 80.

$\left\{\begin{array}{l}\text{d :r} \mid \text{m :f} \mid \text{f }{\small\leftarrow}\text{— m :} \mid \text{m :f} \mid \text{s :l} \mid \text{t :— }d^1 \text{ :}\\ \text{All the springing} \mid \text{flow- ers,} \mid \text{All the fruitful} \mid \text{show- ers,}\end{array}\right.$

D. C.

$\left\{\begin{array}{l}d^1 \text{ :l} \mid \text{s :f} \mid \underline{\text{f :— m :}} \mid \text{f :r} \mid \text{s :}t_1 \mid \underline{t_1 \text{ :— d :}} \|\\ \text{All the stars a- } \mid \underline{\text{bove,}} \mid \text{Tell us God is} \mid \underline{\text{love.}}\end{array}\right.$

54. CROSSCOMBE. (s. m. 118, s. s. 133, 153, 129.) KEY C. M. 80.

D. C. and F.

$\left\{\begin{array}{l}\text{s :}\underline{s.f} \mid \text{m :}\underline{f.s} \mid \text{l :l} \mid \text{s :—} \mid \underline{\text{l.t}} \text{ :}d^1 \mid \text{t :}\underline{d^1.r^1} \mid m^1 \text{ :}r^1 \mid d^1 \text{ :—}\\ \text{m :}\underline{m.r} \mid \text{d :}\underline{r.m} \mid \text{f :f} \mid \text{m :—} \mid \text{f :m} \mid \text{r :}\underline{m.f} \mid \text{s :f} \mid \text{m :—}\end{array}\right.$

D.C.

```
{ | m¹ :f¹.m¹ | r¹ :d¹.t | d¹ :r¹ | t :s | l.t :d¹ | t :d¹ | d¹.r¹ :m¹.f¹ | r¹ :— ||
{ | s :l.s | f :m.r | m :tu₁ | s :m | f :m | r :m | m.f :s.l | s :— ||
```

55. SOLOMON. C. M.   (s. m. 28, s. s. 23, 128.)   KEY E.   M. 50.

```
{ :d | m :f | s :s | l :l | s :s | l :s | t :d¹ | r :— — :s
{ :d | d :r | m :m | f :f | m :m | f :m | r :d | t₁ :— — :m
```

```
{ | l :l | s :s | f :f | m :r | s :d | m.r :d.t₁ | d :— — ||
{ | f :f | m :m | r :r | d :d | d :d | d.t₁ :d | d :— — ||
```

56. CALLCOTT. L.M.   (s. m. 4, s. s. 35, 96.)   KEY E.   M. 66.

```
{ :d | d :r | m :s | s.f :m.r | m :s | f :m | d¹.t :l.s
{ :d | d :t₁ | d :fi | l₁ :t₁ | d :d | t₁ :d | m.s :f.m
```

```
{ | f :m | r :m | m :f | s :s | f.m :l.s | t :t | d¹ :r¹
{ | r :d | t₁ :d | d :r | m :d.fi | l₁ :r | r :r | d :t₁
```

```
{ | m¹.d¹ :s.l | m :r | d ||
{ | d :d | d :t₁ | d ||
```

57. GRAHAM. 8.7.   (s. m. 14, s. s. 21, 100.)   KEY C.   M. 80.

```
{ | d¹ :r¹ | t :d¹ | r¹ :m¹.f¹ | m¹ :d¹ | r¹ :r¹ | r¹.d¹ :t | l :l | s :—
{ | m :f | r :m | f :s | s :m | t :s | tu₁ :s | s :tu₁ | s :—
```

```
{ | t :l | s :d¹ | r¹ :m¹.f¹ | m¹ :d¹ | t :d¹ | r¹ :m¹ | r¹ :r¹ | d¹ :— ||
{ | r :tu₁ | s.f :m | f :s | s :m | r :m | r :d | d :t₁ | d :— ||
```

58. OH! GIVE THANKS, &c.   (*Round for four voices.*)   KEY A.   M. 96.

```
{ | d :r | m :d | r :t₁ | d :s₁ | m :f | s :m
{ | Oh! give | thanks to the | God of | Hea- ven, | For his | mercy en-
```

```
{ | f :r | m :d | : | : | s₁ :s₁ | s₁ :d
{ | du- reth for | e- ver. | | | Ha- le- | lu- iah!
```

D.C.

```
{ | : | : | s :s | s :m ||
{ | | | Ha- le- | lu- iah! ||
```

59. ELY, L. M. (s. m. 8, s. s. 22, 94, 104.) KEY A. M. 66.

$$
\left\{
\begin{array}{l}
\text{:d} \\
\text{:d}
\end{array}
\right.
\begin{array}{l}
\text{d :r } | \text{m :s} \\
\text{d :t}_1 \, | \text{d :d}
\end{array}
\begin{array}{l}
\text{f :m } | \text{r :m} \\
\text{t}_1 \text{ :d } | \text{s}_1 \text{ :s}_1
\end{array}
\begin{array}{l}
\text{f :m } | \text{r :d} \\
\text{t}_1 \text{ :d } | \text{l}_1 \text{ :l}_1
\end{array}
\begin{array}{l}
\text{t}_1 \text{ :d } | \text{r :s} \\
\text{s}_1 \text{ :d } | \text{t}_1 \text{ :t}_1
\end{array}
$$

$$
\left\{
\begin{array}{l}
\text{f :m } | \text{r :t}_1 \\
\text{t}_1 \text{ :d } | \text{s}_1 \text{ :s}_1
\end{array}
\right.
\begin{array}{l}
\text{d :l}_1 \, | \text{s}_1 \text{ :m} \\
\text{s}_1 \text{ :tu}_2 | \text{s}_1 \text{ :s}_1
\end{array}
\begin{array}{l}
\text{f :m } | \text{r :d} \\
\text{t}_1 \text{ :d } | \text{l}_1 \text{ :l}_1
\end{array}
\begin{array}{l}
\text{m :r } | \text{d} \\
\text{d :t}_1 | \text{d}
\end{array}
\|
$$

60. HANOVER. (s. m. 53, s. s. 44.) KEY B flat. M. 80.

$$
\left\{
\begin{array}{l}
\text{:s}_1 \\
\text{:m}_1
\end{array}
\right.
\begin{array}{l}
\text{d :d :r} \\
\text{m}_1 \text{ :s}_1 \text{ :s}_1
\end{array}
\begin{array}{l}
\text{m :— :s} \\
\text{s}_1 \text{ :— :s}_1
\end{array}
\begin{array}{l}
\text{d :r :t}_1 \\
\text{l}_1 \text{ :l}_1 \text{ :s}_1.\text{f}_1
\end{array}
\begin{array}{l}
\text{d :— :r} \\
\text{m}_1 \text{ :— :s}_1
\end{array}
\begin{array}{l}
\text{m :r :d} \\
\text{s}_1 \text{ :s}_1 \text{ :tu}_2
\end{array}
$$

$$
\left\{
\begin{array}{l}
\text{t}_1 \text{ :— :d} \\
\text{s}_1 \text{ :— :s}_1
\end{array}
\right.
\begin{array}{l}
\text{r :d.t}_1 \text{ :l}_1 \\
\text{s}_1 \text{ :l}_1.\text{s}_1 \text{ :tu}_2
\end{array}
\begin{array}{l}
\text{s}_1 \text{ :— :t}_1 \\
\text{s}_1 \text{ :— :ne}_1
\end{array}
\begin{array}{l}
\text{d :r :m} \\
\text{l}_1 \text{ :l}_1 \text{ :ne}_1
\end{array}
\begin{array}{l}
\text{d :l}_1 \text{ :f} \\
\text{l}_1 \text{ :— :s}_1
\end{array}
$$

$$
\left\{
\begin{array}{l}
\text{m :r :d} \\
\text{s}_1 \text{ :s}_1 \text{ :tu}_2
\end{array}
\right.
\begin{array}{l}
\text{s :— :s}_1 \\
\text{t}_1 \text{ :— :s}_1
\end{array}
\begin{array}{l}
\text{l}_1 \text{ :t}_1 \text{ :d} \\
\text{f}_1 \text{ :f}_1 \text{ :m}_1
\end{array}
\begin{array}{l}
\text{r :s}_1 \text{ :m} \\
\text{f}_1 \text{ :f}_1 \text{ :m}_1
\end{array}
\begin{array}{l}
\text{l}_1 \text{ :r :t}_1 \\
\text{f}_1 \text{ :f}_1 \text{ :r}_1
\end{array}
\begin{array}{l}
\text{d :—} \\
\text{m}_1 \text{:—}
\end{array}
\|
$$

61. VALLIS VALE. (s. m. 70, s. s. 83.) KEY D. M. 80.

D. C.

$$
\left\{
\begin{array}{l}
\text{d :m } | \text{m :f.s} \\
\text{d :d } | \text{d :r.m}
\end{array}
\right.
\begin{array}{l}
\text{l :s } | \text{l :—} \\
\text{f :m } | \text{f :—}
\end{array}
\begin{array}{l}
\text{s :m } | \text{m :r.d} \\
\text{m :d } | \text{d :t}_1.\text{d}
\end{array}
\begin{array}{l}
\text{r :— } | \text{d :—} \\
\text{d :t}_1 \, | \text{d :—}
\end{array}
$$

$$
\left\{
\begin{array}{l}
\text{d}^1 \text{ :d}^1 \text{ | t :l.s} \\
\text{m :m } | \text{s :f.m}
\end{array}
\right.
\begin{array}{l}
\text{l :l } | \text{s :m} \\
\text{f :f } | \text{m :d}
\end{array}
\begin{array}{l}
\text{d}^1 \text{ :d}^1 \text{ | t.d}^1 \text{:r}^1 \\
\text{m :s } | \text{s :s}
\end{array}
\begin{array}{l}
\text{l :l } | \text{s :—} \\
\text{s :tu}_1 | \text{s :—}
\end{array}
$$

$$
\left\{
\begin{array}{l}
\text{d}^1 \text{ :d}^1 \text{ | t :l.s} \\
\text{m :m } | \text{s :f.m}
\end{array}
\right.
\begin{array}{l}
\text{l :l } | \text{s :m} \\
\text{f :f } | \text{m :d}
\end{array}
\begin{array}{l}
\text{f.s :l } | \text{s :f.m} \\
\text{d :d } | \text{d :t}_1.\text{d}
\end{array}
\begin{array}{l}
\text{r :— } | \text{d :—} \\
\text{d :t}_1 \, | \text{d :—}
\end{array}
\|
$$

62. KETTERING. 7s. KEY E. M. 50.

$$
\left\{
\begin{array}{l}
\text{m :d } | \text{s :d} \\
\text{d :d } | \text{t}_1 \text{ :d}
\end{array}
\right.
\begin{array}{l}
\text{r :f } | \text{m :—} \\
\text{d :t}_1 | \text{d :—}
\end{array}
\begin{array}{l}
\text{l :s } | \text{t :d}^1 \\
\text{f :m } | \text{r :d}
\end{array}
\begin{array}{l}
\text{f :m } | \text{r :—} \\
\text{r :d } | \text{t}_1 \text{ :—}
\end{array}
$$

$$
\left\{
\begin{array}{l}
\text{m :d } | \text{s :t} \\
\text{d :d } | \text{m :r}
\end{array}
\right.
\begin{array}{l}
\text{l :t } | \text{s :—} \\
\text{d :r } | \text{t}_1 \text{ :—}
\end{array}
\begin{array}{l}
\text{d}^1 \text{ :l } | \text{f :m} \\
\text{m :d } | \text{r :d}
\end{array}
\begin{array}{l}
\text{f :r } | \text{d :—} \\
\text{l}_1 \text{ :t}_1 | \text{d :—}
\end{array}
\|
$$

63.   SAMSON. L. M.   (S. M. 27, S. S. 16.)   KEY F.   M. 66.

```
{ :d  | m :—.f |s  :m  | l  :t  |d¹ :d¹ | s  :l  |s  :m.,r | d  :r  |m :s
{ :d  | d :—.r |m  :d  | d  :f  |m  :m  | m  :f  |m  :d    | d  :t₁ |d :m

{ |l.d¹ :t.l |s  :m  | f.l :s.f |m :d¹ | t  :—.l |s  :d.r | m  :r  |d    ||
{ |f.l  :s.f |m  :d  | r.f :m.r |d :m  | r  :—.d |t₁ :d   | d  :t₁ |d    ||
```

64.   NORWOOD. 8.7.4   (S. M. 50, S. S. 68.)   KEY E.   M. 80.

```
                                                          D. C.
{ |s  :f  |m  :r  | d  :m.r |d  :t₁ | f  :m  |r  :l  | s  :—.f |s.f :m
{ |m  :r  |d  :t₁ | d  :s₁  |s₁ :s₁ | r  :d  |t₁ :f  | m  :—.r |m.r :d

{ |d¹ :s  |m  :s  | d¹ :s  |m  :s  | d¹ :s  |m.s :d.m | s₁ :t₁ |d  :—  ||
{ |m  :m  |d  :m  | m  :m  |d  :m  | m  :m  |d   :d   | s₁ :f₁ |m₁ :—  ||
```

65.   WELLS. 7s.   (S. M. 69, S. S. 66, 102.)   KEY E.   M. 80.

```
{ |s  :m  :f  | s  :—  :d¹ | r¹ :d¹ :t  | d¹ :—  :—  | l  :d¹ :l
{ |d  :—  :r  | m  :—  :d  | f  :m  :r  | m  :—  :—  | d  :—  :d

{ |s  :—  :m  | s  :f  :m  | r  :—  :—  | s  :m  :f  | s  :—  :d¹
{ |d  :—  :d  | r  :—  :d  | d  :t₁ :—  | d  :—  :r  | m  :—  :d

{ |r¹ :d¹ :t  | d¹ :—  :—  | l  :d¹ :l  | s  :—  :m  | l  :—.s :f.m
{ |f  :m  :r  | m  :—  :—  | d  :—  :d  | d  :—  :d  | f  :—.m :r.d

{ |r  :—  :—  | r¹ :—  :t  | d¹ :—  :s  | m¹ :r¹ :d¹ | d¹ :—  :t
{ |d  :t  :—  | f  :—  :f  | m  :—  :m  | s  :f  :m  | m  :—  :r

{ |d¹ :t  :l  | s  :—  :m  | f  :—  :r  | d  :—  :—  ||
{ |m  :s  :f  | m  :—  :d  | d  :—  :t₁ | d  :—  :—  ||
```

66.   THE SKYLARK. 6s.   (S. M. 83, S. S. 161.)   KEY C.   M. 112.

```
{ |d¹ :—  | t  :l  |s  :f  | m  :—  |d¹ :—  | r¹ :d¹ |t  :l  | s  :—  |d¹ :—
{ |m  :—  | r  :f  |m  :r  | d  :—  |m  :—  | f  :m  |r  :f  | m  :—  |m  :—
```

$$
\begin{array}{l}
\left\{\begin{array}{|l|l|l|l|}
\text{t} :\text{d}^1 \mid \text{r}^1 :\text{m}^1 & \text{f}^1 :\!\!— \mid\!\!— :\text{m}^1 & \text{r}^1 :\text{d}^1 \mid \text{t} :\text{l} & \text{s} :\!\!— \mid :\text{s} \\
\text{r} :\text{m} \mid \text{f} :\text{s} & \text{s} :\!\!— \mid\!\!— :\text{d}^1 & \text{t} :\text{l} \mid \text{s} :tu_1 & \text{s} :\!\!— \mid :\text{m}
\end{array}\right.
\end{array}
$$

$$
\begin{array}{l}
\left\{\begin{array}{|l|l|l|l|}
\text{l} :\text{s} \mid \text{f} :\text{m} & \text{f} :\!\!— \mid\!\!— :\text{f} & \text{s} :\text{f} \mid \text{m} :\text{r} & \text{m} :\!\!— \mid \text{d}^1 :\!\!— \\
\text{f} :\text{m} \mid \text{r} :\eta i & \text{r} :\!\!— \mid\!\!— :\text{r} & \text{m} :\text{r} \mid \text{d} :\text{t}_1 & \text{d} :\!\!— \mid \text{d} :\!\!—
\end{array}\right.
\end{array}
$$

$$
\begin{array}{l}
\left\{\begin{array}{|l|l|l|l|}
\text{r}^1 :\text{m}^1 \mid \text{f}^1 :\text{m}^1 & \text{r}^1 :\text{d}^1 \mid \text{t} :\text{l} & \text{s} :\!\!— \mid \text{t} :\!\!— & \text{d}^1 :\!\!— \\
\text{f} :\text{s} \mid \text{l} :\text{s} & \text{f} :\text{m} \mid \text{r} :\text{d} & \underline{\text{d} :\text{m} \mid \text{s} :\text{f}} & \text{m} :\!\!—
\end{array}\right\|
\end{array}
$$

67. BURNETT. C. M. (S. M. 3, S. S. 8, 43, 156.) KEY B flat. M. 112.

$$
\begin{array}{l}
\left\{\begin{array}{|l|l|l|}
:\text{s}_1 & \text{d} :\!\!— :\text{r} \mid \text{m} :\!\!— :\text{d} & \text{t}_1 :\text{r} :\text{f} \mid \text{m} :\!\!— :\text{d} & \text{l}_1 :\text{r} :\text{d} \mid \text{t}_1 :\text{l}_1 :\text{s}_1 \\
:\text{m}_1 & \text{m}_1 :\!\!— :\text{s}_1 \mid \text{s}_1 :\!\!— :\text{s}_1 & \text{s}_1 :\!\!— :\text{t}_1 \mid \text{d} :\!\!— :\text{s}_1 & \text{f}_1 :\!\!— :\text{l}_1 \mid \text{s}_1 :\!\!— :\text{f}_1
\end{array}\right.
\end{array}
$$

$$
\begin{array}{l}
\left\{\begin{array}{|l|l|l|}
\text{d} :\!\!— :\!\!— \mid : :\text{d} & \text{t}_1 :\!\!-.\text{l}_1 :\text{s}_1 \mid \text{d} :\!\!— :\text{d} & \text{r} :\text{t}_1 :\text{s}_1 \mid \text{d} :\!\!— :\text{d} \\
\text{m}_1 :\!\!— :\!\!— \mid : :\text{s}_1 & \text{s}_1 :\!\!— :\text{s}_1 \mid \text{s}_1 :\!\!— :\text{m}_1 & \text{f}_1 :\!\!— :\text{f}_1 \mid \text{m}_1 :\!\!— :\text{s}_1
\end{array}\right.
\end{array}
$$

$$
\begin{array}{l}
\left\{\begin{array}{|l|l|}
\text{l}_1 :\text{r} :\text{d} \mid \text{t}_1 :\!\!-.\text{l}_1 :\text{s}_1 & \text{d} :\!\!— :\!\!— \mid : \\
\text{f}_1 :\!\!— :\text{l}_1 \mid \text{s}_1 :\!\!— :\text{f}_1 & \text{m}_1 :\!\!— :\!\!— \mid :
\end{array}\right\|
\end{array}
$$

68. (*A Round for two or four voices.*) KEY G. M. 80.

d : r	m :—	m : f	s :-.d¹	s.d¹ : d¹.t	d¹ : s.,f	m : r	d :—
O be	just,	O be	true, Be	kind and tender	hearted, and	mer- ry	too.

$$
\left\{\begin{array}{|l|l|l|l|l|l|}
\text{d} :\text{r} & \text{m} :\!\!— & \text{m} :\text{f} & \text{s} :\!\!-.\text{d}^1 & \text{s.d}^1 :\text{d}^1.\text{t} & \text{d}^1 :\text{s.,f} \mid \text{m} :\text{r} \mid \text{d} :\!\!—
\end{array}\right\|
$$

69. BINFIELD HEATH. (S. M. 78, S. S. 103, 127.) KEY C. M. 112.

$$
\begin{array}{l}
\left\{\begin{array}{|l|l|l|l|l|}
:\text{s} & \text{s} :\text{m} :\text{f} & \text{s} :\text{f} :\text{m} & \text{f} :\text{m} :\text{r} & \text{d} :\!\!— :\text{m} & \text{r} :\text{r} :\text{r} \\
:\text{m} & \text{m} :\text{d} :\text{r} & \text{m} :\text{r} :\text{d} & \text{r} :\text{d} :\text{t}_1 & \text{d} :\!\!— :\text{d} & \text{t}_1 :\text{t}_1 :\text{t}_1
\end{array}\right.
\end{array}
$$

$$
\begin{array}{l}
\left\{\begin{array}{|l|l|l|l|l|}
\text{r} :\text{t} :\text{l} & \text{l} :\text{t} :\text{l} & \text{s} :\!\!— :\text{s} & \text{s} :\text{m} :\text{s} & \text{d}^1 :\text{s} :\text{m} \\
\text{t}_1 :\text{r} :\text{d} & \text{d} :\text{r} :\text{d} & \text{t}_1 :\!\!— :\text{r} & \text{m} :\text{d} :\text{r} & \text{m} :\text{m} :\text{d}
\end{array}\right.
\end{array}
$$

$$
\begin{array}{l}
\left\{\begin{array}{|l|l|l|l|l|}
\text{f} :\text{m} :\text{r} & \text{d} :\!\!— :\text{d} & \text{l} :\text{l} :\text{s} & \text{s} :\text{f} :\text{m} & \text{f} :\text{m} :\text{r} \\
\text{r} :\text{d} :\text{t}_1 & \text{d} :\!\!— :\text{d} & \text{f} :\text{f} :\text{m} & \text{m} :\text{r} :\text{d} & \text{r} :\text{d} :\text{t}_1
\end{array}\right.
\end{array}
$$

```
{| d  :— :d  | d¹ :t :l  | s  :m :d  | d¹ :t :l  | s  :— :s  |
{| d  :— :d  | m  :s :f  | m  :d :d  | m  :s :f  | m  :— :m  |

{| m¹ :m¹ :r¹ | d¹ :t :d¹ | r¹ :s :t  | d  :—     ||
{| s  :s  :f  | m  :f :m  | r  :f :f  | m  :—     ||
```

70.   OAKHILL.   (S. M. 106, S. S. 117, 114, 130.)   KEY F or G. M. 80.

```
                                                              s.
{| :d¹.t | l  :f |m :r | m :d |l₁ :-.t₁ | d :d |d.r :m.f | s  :— |m :d¹.t
{| :m.r  | d :l₁ |d :t₁| d :s₁|l₁ :s₁   | d :d |d :d     | t₁ :— |d :m.r

                                                    P.
{| l  .s.f |m :r | m :d |l₁ :d | t₁.d :r |s₁ :t | d  :— |— :s.f
{| d  :l₁  |d :t₁| d :s₁|l₁ :f₁| s₁ :f₁  |m₁ :f₁| m₁ :— |— :m.r

                                                D. S.
{| m :s |l :t | d¹ :s |m :s.f | m :s |l :t | d¹ :— |t  ||
{| d :m |f :r | m :m  |d :m.r | d :m |f :r | m  :— |r  ||
```

71.   LIVERPOOL CHANT.   (S. M. 42, S. S. 42.)   KEY A.   M. 66.

```
{| d.d       :d.d  | m   :t₁  | d.d   :—     | r    :—  | m    :s.s  | f.f   :m
{| Blessed  are the| poor in  | spirit,      | For      | their's is the| kingdom of
{| m₁.m₁ : m₁.m₁   | s₁  :r₁  | m₁.m₁ :—     | s₁ :t₁   | d    :m.m  | r.r   :d

{| r.r :—      | r.r    :r   | t₁  :l₁  | s₁  :—   | d  :—  | l₁ :r  | d  :t₁
{| Heaven.     | Blessed are | they that| mourn,   | For    | they   | shall be
{| t₁.t₁ :—    | s₁.s₁ :s₁   | s₁ :tu₂  | s₁ :—    | s₁ :—  | f₁ :l₁ | s₁ :f₁

{| d.d  :d  | d.d    :—.  | m   :t₁  | d  :—   | r  :—  | m  :s.,s  | f.f :m
{| comforted.| Blessed    | are the  | meek,    | For    | they shall in-| herit the
{| m₁.m₁ :m₁ | m₁.m₁ :—.  | s₁  :r₁  | m₁ :—   | s₁ :t₁ | d :m.,m   | r.r :d

{| r  :—  | r,r,r     :r,r,r   | r.,r :r  | t₁  :l₁.l₁ | s₁.s₁ :s₁  | d :—
{| earth. | Blessed are they which do| hunger and| thirst after| righteousness,| For
{| t₁ :—  | s₁₄s₁s₁  :s₁₄s₁₄s₁ | s₁.,s₁ :s₁| s₁ :tu₂.tu₂| s₁.s₁ :s₁ | s₁ :—

{| l₁ :r  | d :t₁    | d.d  :—  | d.d  :—  | m  :t₁  | d.d :d   | r :—
{| they   | shall be | filled.  | Blessed  | are the  | merci- ful,| For
{| f₁ :l₁ | s₁ :f₁   | m₁.m₁ :— | m₁.m₁ :— | s₁ :r₁  | m₁.m₁ :m₁| s₁ :t₁

{| m.,m :s  | f  :m  | r.r :—   | r.r :r.r | t₁ :l₁  | s₁ :—  | d :—
{| they shall ob-| tain | mercy.  | Blessed are the| pure in | heart,  | For
{| d.,d :m  | r  :d  | t₁.t₁ :—  | s₁.s₁ :s₁.s₁| s₁ :tu₂ | s₁ :—  | s₁ :—
```

l_1 : r	d : t_1	d :—	d.d :—.	m : t_1	d : d.d	: r
they shall	see	God.	Blessed	are the	peace- makers,	For
f_1 : l_1	s_1 : f_1	m_1 :—	$m_1.m_1$:—.	s_1 : r_1	m_1 : $m_1.m_1$	: s_1

r : r.r	m.,m : s	f.f : m	r :—	r_er_er : r_er_er	r.r : r.r
they shall be	called the	children of	God.	Blessed are they which are	perse- cuted
s_1 : $t_1.t_1$	d.,d : m	r.r : d	t_1 :—	$s_{1e}s_{1e}s_1$: $s_{1e}s_{1e}s_1$	$s_1.s_1$: $s_1.s_1$

r :—	$t_1.t_1$: l_1	s_1 :—	d :—	l_1 : r.r	d.d : t_1	d.d :—
for	righteous- ness	sake,	For	their's is the	kingdom of	Heaven.
s_1 :—	$s_1.s_1$: tu_2	s_1 :—	s_1 :—	f_1 : $l_1.l_1$	$s_1.s_1$: f_1	$m_1.m_1$:—

d_ed_ed : d.d	d : d.d	d : d.d	m.m : t_1	d : r.r
Blessed are ye when	men shall re-	vile you, and	perse- cute	you, and shall
$m_{1e}m_{1e}m_1$: $m_1.m_1$	m_1 : $m_1.m_1$	m_1 : $m_1.m_1$	$s_1.s_1$: r_1	m_1 : $s_1.s_1$

r.,r : r_er_er	r_er_er : r.r	m.,m : s	f : m	r :—.r	r.,r : r.r
say all manner of	evil a- gainst you	falsely, for	my	sake. Re-	joice and be ex-
$s_1.,s_1$: $s_{1e}s_{1e}s_1$	$t_{1e}t_{1e}t_1$: $t_1.t_1$	d.,d : m	r : d	t_1 :—.s_1	$s_1.,s_1$: $s_1.s_1$

t_1 : l_1	s_1 :—.d	d :—.d	l_1 : r	d : t_1	d.d :— ‖
ceed- ing	glad, For	great is	your re-	ward in	Heaven.
s_1 : tu_2	s_1 :—.s_1	s_1 :—.s_1	f_1 : l_1	s_1 : f_1	$m_1.m_1$:— ‖

SECTION VIII.

OF TRANSITION AND THE NOTES TU AND FI, AND OF CHROMATIC NOTES.

1. Sometimes, in the course of a tune, the notes are so ordered as to direct the ear to A NEW GOVERNING or key NOTE, diverting the mind, for the time, from considering the original DOH as the principal note of rest and close. The music is then said to have passed into a new key, and the notes exchange the "characters" (or mental effects) which they possessed as members of the old key, for those which are proper to their position in the new key. This is called TRANSITION, and is effected by an alteration in one or more of the notes.

"Modulation" is another name commonly given to this magical change of musical intention and effect—which, at the call of some single new note, characteristically heard as it enters the music, causes all the other sounds to acknowledge a new ruler and sovereign; and, suddenly assuming the new offices he requires, to minister in their places around him. *Modulation* means, more properly, singing *in* "*mode*," which, of course, includes the singing which passes into various modes, but is also applicable to a correct performance in one mode. See Mr. Graham's article "Music" in the Cyclopædia Britannica, and on the whole subject, M. Jeu de Berneval's "Music Simplified," page 107 and onward.

H

s^1 —· d^1
    t
f^1
m^1—l

r^1—· s

d^1—f
t —· m

l — r

s — d
    t_1
f ⟋
m—· l_1

r — s_1

d —f_1
t_1 — m_1

l_1 — r_1

s_1 —d_1

2. The note most frequently chosen to become a new governing (or key) note is SOH—the fifth of the common mode. The transition of music into the key of SOH is indicated to the ear by the introduction of a new note instead of the FAH of the original key. This note is a tonule below SOH. If SOH, having for the time become the key note, is now called DOH, the new note would of course be called TE, and the other notes would change their names, with their "characters," ME becoming LAH, RAY becoming SOH, DOH becoming FAH, &c., as at the side—where the italic letters show the key of SOH. But when it is desired simply to indicate the new note alone, and to distinguish it from the TE of the original key, it is named TU.

In introducing the subject of transition to young people, the object would be first, to make them feel and recognise by the ear the change of musical effect and intention among the notes—next, to set them enquiring what has caused this change—then, suggesting the supposition of SOH being treated as a key note (for this, the most common transition, should be first introduced to them) to help them to discover what change would be required for framing a key upon it, keeping the tonules in their right places—and last, to show that this is just the change which does take place, and which gives to the music the new intention and feeling of which we speak. The teacher might open the subject as follows:

"Listen to me while I sing to you a tune (MELCOMBE). If you are thoughtful and attentive, I think I can make you understand a beautiful thing in music. I will "figure" the first line and you shall tell me what note that is on which the figure eight falls, and describe its "character." it on the modulator, and we will all sing it * To help you I will tell you that the tune together. begins on SOH. Listen again * Yes, the "eight" "You said that the TU made SOH sound as was SOH—the *grand* or *clear* note. What is the though it had been changed into DOH. Let us difference between SOH and DOH? Which gives suppose that this is really the case—that SOH has the greater sense of *repose?* Which is the stronger been taken for the key note instead of the former resting note? (DOH, see page 20.) Now notice DOH;—what difference will it make? First, tell the "character" of the note which falls to the me, if SOH is called DOH—what will LAH be syllable eight in the second line, which I will called? (Ray.) Let us draw the old key on the now sing. * Was that SOH? Listen again while I black board, (keeping the half spaces for the sing both lines and you compare the two "eights." tonules), and as you name the notes of the new * What was the difference between them? Yes, key I will write them at the side (as above). just the kind of difference there is between SOH What will TE be called ?—DOH¹?—RAY¹?—ME¹? and DOH. And yet the second "eight" was —FAH¹? Ah! you have no place for FAH in exactly the same *sound* as the first:—how came your new key. It will not do for TE, for then you it to have so different a "character" (mental would have a Tone, instead of a Tonule, between effect)? What made it so much more a note of your TE and DOH¹. So you must leave out the rest and conclusiveness? old FAH and make a new note for TE, and that is "Let us take the modulator, and you shall the "difference it makes" when you take SOH solfa the two lines you have heard as I point to for the key note. Now, is not that new note just them. (The teacher points, while the pupils sing, the note we found in the tune we were singing, but gives the FAH of the original key where the and which we called TU? Whenever you meet TU occurs.) Was that as before? Try it, how- with TU, then, you will know that the tune is ever, in that way again. * Did the SOH become changing its key; it has gone into the SOH KEY. "conclusive" then? Did it sound at all differ- Such a change of key is called TRANSITION." It ently from the other SOH? (No.) Then we want will be better, if the pupils can bear so much, to some new note instead of FAH to make the SOH teach the next two propositions before you proceed change its character. Can any one remember the with the above tune or any other exercises. sound of it as I gave it at first? * I will give it The tune ST. ANN'S would enable the teacher again, and call it TU. It is a little higher than to compare the TE DOH of both keys. The FAH. It is a tonule below SOH. I will mark student of the mathematics of musical science will perceive that other changes of note, besides that of FAH to TU, must take place in the "transition" of a good voice into the SOH key. If any one will place the figures 9, 8, 5, 9, 8, 9, 5, in their proper places, as given in page 40, (under "Proximate Measurement of the Mode,") between the several notes of the two keys above, he will see that there is a difference of one degree between the LAH of the old key and the RAY of the new with which it should correspond. But as RAY is,

according to Col. Thompson's interesting theory, a *variable* note, it can easily accommodate itself to the LAH, taking its flatter position if necessary. Such minute distinctions a good voice will produce naturally, even though the ear can recognise them only in the general smoothness of effect.

The key of SOH is sometimes called the KEY OF THE DOMINANT, and TU is called the "sharp fourth."

3. The note FAH—the fourth in the common mode—is also very frequently taken by "transition" as a key note. The whole "intention" of the music is diverted to FAH as its new centre, and the tune is said to have passed into the FAH KEY. This transition is indicated to the ear by the introduction of a new note instead of the TE of the original key. This note is a *tone* (a great tone, see page 40) below DOH, and a *tonule* above LAH. It is the FAH of the new key, but is called FI when it is wished to distinguish it from the FAH of the previous key. The FAH key is represented, in the diagram at the side, by the left hand column.

This point may be introduced to the notice of young people by attracting their attention at once to FI itself, the distinguishing note of the new key. The last proposition might also be introduced in a similar manner.

"Listen while I "figure" you a short phrase. The first four notes I will point on the modulator as I sing the figures, but the fifth you must notice well, for I shall not point to it, and I shall ask you to tell me where it is, and what note it sounds like. (The teacher "figures" some such phrase as this :d | t₁ :s₁ | d : ʄʋ₁ | l₁ :s₁ | f₁ or, as it should be written :d | t₁ :s₁ |ᵈ⌄₁ :ʄ₁ | ʍ₁ : ʋ₁ |∂₁) Listen again • Where is that "five"? It is not TE. (Singing to figures, first d | t₁ :s₁ | d :t₁ and pointing to the TE, and immediately after figuring d | t₁ :s₁ | d :ʄʋ) There is a great difference. Is it lower or higher than TE? It is lower, but still a tonule above LAH. We will put this dot on the modulator to stand for it. Now listen again, and tell me what is the "character" of this new nôte. Which of the notes you already know is it most like? (The pupils cannot hesitate to answer "FAH.") Yes, it is the FAH of a new key, but we will call it FI, to distinguish it from the FAH of the first key. If this new note is FAH in the new key, what must LAH, a tonule below it, become? (ME.) What does SOH become? (RAY.) What does FAH become? (DOH.) Yes, whenever you hear FI coming into the music, you may know that the tune has elected FAH to be its new DOH or key note. It has gone into THE FAH KEY.

"You say that FAH has become DOH, but does it take the "character" of DOH, and *sound* like a

strong, *resting*, and governing note? Listen again and tell me. • How did the "eight" sound?—Like FAH—the *desolate* and *leaning* note it was? • No, it has taken the proper "character" of DOH. If then I solfa thus :d | t₁ :s₁ | d :f₁ | l₁ :s₁ | f₁ do the last three notes sound right? Does LAH seem the *weeping* note and FAH the *desolate* as before? (No.) Try yourselves. • How would you rather solfa it? (| m :r | d according to the real—though changed—"characters" of the notes.) Yes, that will be much better, but you will be obliged, for the sake of the "old notation," as I will afterwards explain to you, to solfa in the imperfect manner I first showed you."

The key of FAH is sometimes called the KEY OF THE SUBDOMINANT, and FI is called "the flat seventh."

Other kinds of "transition" will be described in the next section.

4. In simple music the tune is seldom carried, by transition, more than one remove from the original key, and soon returns to it. The "return" from the SOH key must be made by a transition which has the same effect as passing into

d¹—f	
t	m
l	r
s —d¹	
	t
f	
m	l
r	s
d — f	
t,	m
l,	r
s,—d	

a FAH key, and the "return" from the FAH key has the same effect as transition into a SOH key. A study of the diagram at the side will show that each key is the FAH (subdominant) key to its own SOH (dominant) key, and the SOH key to its own FAH key. The first FAH which occurs (whether in the air or any other "part" of a tune) after TU has been heard, and the first TE after FI, are respectively the signals of a "return" to the old key.

"Listen once more, while I figure to you the tune MELCOMBE again. When I come to the third line—just after the transition into the SOH KEY—notice carefully what is the effect of figures "three" and "eight." * (They sound like FAH.) Yes, but are they only the common FAH? Listen again. (Sings the 6, 7, 8, of the second line, followed by the third line.) It is the FAH of transition: it is the same thing as FI, though you do not call it so. It tells you that the tune has gone back again into the first key. I think it has a very solemn and awe-inspiring effect in this tune. Let us solfa the tune together, taking care to give proper effect to the "characteristic" or distinguishing notes TU and FAH (FI). * Remember always to notice, in the same way, the first TE (TU) which occurs after a FI."

In lengthened pieces of music the tune sometimes passes from key to key till it is several removes from the original key, and then returns through the same keys till it reaches the original key again. And sometimes, though rarely, it passes *immediately* into a distant key.

MODULATOR.
f¹
m¹
r¹
d¹
te
[i—
lah
soh
—tu,
fah
me
ray
doh
t,
[—
l,
s,
—t₂
f,
m,
r,
d,

5. The notes TU and FI produce on the mind the effects proper respectively to TE and FAH, but somewhat softened.

"It is clear that the whole artifice of these two modulations," says M. Jeu de Berneval, "depends on the *properties* of the *subdominant* (FAH) and of the *sensible* (TE) which exchange their respective offices," i. e. give FAH when the ear expected TE, and TE when the ear expected FAH.

TU and FI must now be inserted on the modulator, given on page 5, as at the side.

6. Occasionally, in the course of a tune, a note is introduced which is somewhat less than half a tone higher or lower than some given note of the mode. It is called a CHROMATIC note, and the interval between it and the note of the mode, from which it springs, is called a CHROMATIC PART-TONE. When a note is *raised* a chromatic part-tone the diphthong oi is given to the syllable which represents it; thus FAH becomes FOI, and RAY becomes ROY. When a note is *lowered* a chromatic part-tone the diphthong ow is given to the syllable; thus TE becomes TOW, ME MOW, &c. Such notes give a *colouring* to the music, as the name (*chroma*) indicates, but do not produce the effect of transition.

The chromatic semi-tone (*half*-tone), as it is sometimes incorrectly called, is described as that part of a tone which is left when a tonule (of the mode) has been taken from it. If so it must sometimes contain three degrees of the "scale of fifty-three" given on page 40, and at other times four degrees—as it may be taken from the greater or the smaller tone. There is some difficulty in distinguishing these chromatic notes, in the old notation, from the characteristic notes of transition—but they may generally be marked as following immediately the notes from which they spring; thus FOI generally follows FAH, TOW TE, &c. It is usual, in elementary works, to treat this interval as the foundation of a scale or mode—called the "chromatic scale," in which each tone of the common mode is divided into a chromatic interval and a tonule. In one form of this "scale" the chromatic note leaves the large interval above it, and in the other below. But the fact is that these chromatic notes are only *occasional variations* from the common mode. Why then puzzle us with a whole "scale" of them? "*No piece of music,*" says Dr. Bryce, "*is ever composed in the chromatic scale.*" Then how can it be called a scale?

The musical *effect* of the chromatic notes should be shown by the teacher in examples from the exercises which follow. It will soon appear that the "character" of *foi* is very distinct from that of *tu*.

Another minute interval, spoken of in musical works, it will be sufficient to mention. It is described as that which is left of a tone when a chromatic part-tone has been taken from each end, or that which is left of a tonule when a chromatic part-tone has been taken from it, so that it must be equal to one degree and sometimes two, on the "scale of fifty-three," page 40. It is called the DIESIS, and sometimes most unreasonably the "enharmonic *semitone.*" This too is made into a *scale!*

The proposition which follows may be omitted by those who do not proceed beyond this—the third "stage"—of this book.

7. In transition the music should pass out of the old key through some note which is convertible into a note of corresponding pitch in the new key. Thus we may pass into the SOH KEY through the note ME, which is convertible into the LAH of the new key, or through SOH convertible into DOH, as well as through others. But if we were to pass directly from FAH, which cannot form part of the new key, to TU, the note which "distinguishes" it, the note TU would then seem to spring, as a *chromatic* note, from FAH, and would not suggest to the mind the formation of a new key. For the same reason we could not produce the proper effect of transition by passing into the FAH KEY from TE.

The "convertible" note, from which transition is taken, should be indicated, in solfaing, by pronouncing the syllabic name it bears in the old key together with that which it takes in the new. Thus ME converted into LAH of the new key would be pronounced M'LAH—DOH converted into SOH, D'SOH, and so with the rest. The mention of the first syllabic name gives help to the ear (by association) *in striking* the note, and the sliding into the new syllable prepares the ear for the interval by which we *leave* the note, and makes us feel our place in the new key. In writing, this convertible (and preparatory) note may have the initial letter of its syllabic name as a member of the old key placed, in small size, before and above the initial of its syllable in the new key, thus—ᵐl ᵈs ˢr &c. The second and third lines of MELCOMBE, for instance, would be thus written— :s | d¹ :t | l :s | ᵈd :t₁ | d :¹m | m :f | s :m | r :—.m | f and BRUNSWICK would appear thus :d | d :m :f | s :— :ᵈs | f :— :m | r :— :m | l₁ :t₁ :d | d.,r :m :r | d :— :— | : : :ᵈf | m :s.f :m &c.

When one "part," in a piece of music, enters a new key, the other "parts,'' which are heard at the same time, enter the same key, and should be written accordingly. For the distinguishing note, (TU, FI, &c.) occurring in any one part, changes the "character" and "intention" of the whole music for the time, and brings it into the new key.

Miss Glover indicates transition to the right on the modulator (transition into the SOH KEY) by giving the vowel u to the first note of the new key, and transition to the left (which must be into the FAH KEY) by means of the vowel i used in the same way. The plan here adopted will be found very much more easy in practice, as it does not destroy the power of syllabic association by changing the vowel—and gives the interval in both keys.

In the former edition of this work the SOH KEY was printed in italics, and the FAH KEY in other distinct type. This plan may sometimes be convenient, but it is not necessary where the convertible note is so distinctly given, and in cases of " continued" transition could not be carried out.

The method of denoting transition given in this last (seventh) proposition, is evidently far more philosophical and true to nature than that which marks nothing of the new key but the TU or FI, and compels us to solfa its other notes with wrong syllables, associating the LAH " character" with ME, the FAH "character" with DOH, &c. But, as the old, and universally received, notation gives no sign by which the convertible note, which *prepares* the transition, may be recognised, (merely placing a mark on the " distinguishing" note) and as the method of taking transition above indicated requires some attention and thought from the pupil, we have been compelled to accommodate both the old notation and ordinary learners by adopting, to some extent, the imperfect method. Those, however, who have tried the better plan, and have used it as a guide in the study of difficult music, would be very unwilling to lay it aside. It is indeed essential to all those who would carry our method of solfaing into the higher branches of music. The imperfect method of expressing transition will therefore be used to the end of the present " stage," the " Strawberry Girl" being the only exception. It will be found sufficient for common purposes. But the perfect method, except in some cases of merely passing transition, will be used in the last stage. A little practice will make it very easy, and it will well reward diligent use.

For the convertible or " doubtful" note and " chord" see Mr. Hickson's " Rudiments of the Science of Harmony," and Dr. Crotch's "Elements of Musical Composition." Transition taken without the intermediate " doubtful chord" Dr. Crotch calls " sudden" transition, in distinction from the ordinary transition which he calls " gradual." It is very rare. Mr. Mainzer, in his " Musical Grammar," pages 121, 122, 123, gives some remarkable examples of transition. The subject will be further illustrated in the next section.

MELCOMBE, 72. The teacher will pattern this with care, and from the modulator, that the position and proper sound of *tu* may be rightly understood by his pupils. The effect of the " returning" *fah*, as mentioned above, should also be clearly shown. This is a tune of surpassing beauty and pathetic power. It might be used in singing classes to the words attached to it. The word " rises," having an accent contrary to the music, will require that its first syllable should be sung with some force of voice, and its second promptly but very lightly.

TYTHERTON, 73. This fine bold tune, with its admirable " replies" of the third to the first and the fourth to the second lines, enters the SOH KEY at the close of its second line, and continues

there to the close of the third. At the opening of the fourth it is regarded as having returned to the original key, but does not declare this decisively for want of the " returning" *fah*. It is, nevertheless, diverted, as though from the original key, into the FAH KEY for a moment, (by the *fi* in the second,) till the accented FAH of the cadence and the TE which follows in the "second" make a perfect and undoubted close on the original key note.

ST. ANNS, 74. The second is altered. Notice how well suited this tune is to express the sweetest and most grateful emotions of the Christian heart. The third line of each verse, except the last, in hymn 45, will require the rising expression of grateful hope which that line of the tune is so adapted to give. The third line of the last verse should be sung softly.

PLAISTOW, 75. This music, so soft and gentle, yet full of life and feeling, should not be sung, at least to these words, slower than at the rate marked. The contrast brought out, in the opening, of the " clear" and " calm" notes ME and SOH, with the more *emotional* effects of FAH and RAY, will at once strike the student. The genius of Handel appears in his producing marked effects by the simplest means. He knew the power which dwelt in every note, and how and when to use it. Let justice be done by the singer to the bold, bright, and elegant close, especially at the end of Song 112.

O, England, my home' is in thee',
THE LAND' OF THE BIBLE IS MINE.

EDGEWARE, 76. Notice the solemn effect of TU as it enters the " second." It is " the softened effect of TE" at a low pitch. Observe also the dream-like music of the fourth line. Let the whole be sung lightly and with most tender regard to accent. Mr. Hickson has set very suitable words to this tune. See the " Harmonious Blackbird" in his " Singing Master," the words for which are also printed in a separate book price 1d. Let not the " returning" FAH in the " second" of the third line escape remark.

MORTON MILLS, 77. In Song 136, the old man's answer should open more softly than the young man's questions, rising in confidence however on the closing line. But the last answer should be made more bold, urgent, and conclusive, thus—

" I am cheer'ful, young man'," father William replied,
" Let the cause' thy atten'tion engage',
In the days of my youth I remembered my God,
And He HATH NOT FORGOTTEN MY AGE."

BEETHOVEN, 78. Give prompt and tasteful effect to the touching appeal of higher FAH on the third and fourth syllables of the last line especially in connection with the words, "O SAVE US FOR THY MERCY'S SAKE."

BRUNSWICK, 79. Notice, in the second line, the false effect with which the syllables must be used in this method of solfaing "transition" passages, as noticed in page 51. The Bass, in this case, will be even more *easily* solfaed by use of the better method mentioned above. Mark how *fi* throws a subdued and worshipful awe into the music, aptly expressive of the solemn words. Let the second and sixth syllables of the third line be struck with bold and forceful accent, and let the short notes appended to each by the slur be given very distinctly but very lightly. The TE of the sixth syllable reminds us very tastefully of our return to the first key. The words may be marked for expression thus—

To Father, SON, and *Holy* Ghost,
One God whom we adore,
BE GLO'RY AS IT WAS', IS NOW,
AND SHALL' BE EVER MORE.

SERENITY, 81. This tune beautifully exhibits the qualities of FAH and TE. Its rhythm is very elegant, and should be executed with much precision and taste. Precision is specially needed on the second syllable of the last line. It is well adapted to such hymns as those which begin thus—"Did Christ o'er sinners weep?" "Is this the kind return?" or, "Art thou a child of tears?" It is a good exercise, not only of taste but also of serious thought, for the pupils to select hymns to suit the expression and character of particular tunes, and to chose a fitting tune for any hymn, the full beauty and power of which they have been made to feel.

PERSEVERANCE, 82. Be careful to master the complex rhythm of the "air" with the "second" which twice occurs in the last line but one.

ALMA, 83. The rhythm is difficult, but it will well repay most careful execution. Attend to the medium accents, and see that you do not sing the high notes at the opening of the last line laggingly or heavily—as sleepy, tasteless singers do, who feel not the delicate beauty of the tune. Execute gently but perfectly the FAH of the third line in the "second." It softly restores the key. When first struck it forms a dissonance with LAH is held firmly till its consonance with LAH is heard, and then "resolves" itself on ME.

TRENT BRIDGE. 84. Notice the exceeding boldness of DOH in the first and second lines. Observe, in the next part of the tune, the joyous eloquence of FAH, RAY, TE, and LAH (all the "emotional" notes) increased by a triplet rhythm; and mark, in the last line but one, the brilliance of SOH brought out by the contrast of FAH, RAY, TE, and LAH, which characterise the preceding

phrase, and increased by its high pitch. The tune is adapted to some song of buoyant and triumphing gladness.

FONTHILL, 86. The tune opens with a cheerful boldness—softens on LAH and ME in the second line—appeals to us by LAH and FAH, in the third line—and rises to a bright and joyous close by the help of TE and RAY contrasted with LAH. It is well suited to express the fresh, changeful, and gushing emotions of SONG 159.

CLIFTON GROVE, 87. A good exercise in time. It abounds in pretty triplets, and has a pathetic phrase which is well introduced.

DELABORDE, 88. To observe the *medium* accents throughout this tune, especially on the high notes, is very difficult, but it is necessary to do so if we would give to the tune all its own dreamy and luxurious sweetness, and yield ourselves to its charm, and hear it

" Untwisting all the chains that tie
The hidden soul of harmony."

The teacher will pattern clearly the chromatic ROI and FOI. It may be noticed how different is the musical effect of FOI and TU, though identical in pitch. If TU had been, in the last line, instead of FOI, or, in other words, if the note had not been immediately preceded by FAH, the TE which follows, being in the SOH KEY (by virtue of the TU), would have been converted into ME, and would have had the *softer* "character" which belongs to that note—but preceded by FOI, it must be felt by all that TE loses none of its own *piercing* effect.

PORTLAND, 89. This tune may be sung to the hymn which begins—"Jesus, my all, to heaven is gone."

THE STRAWBERRY GIRL, 90. The better method of solfaing transition passages is also much the easier for this tune. Let the "convertible" or "preparatory" notes be carefully shown and patterned on the modulator.

DR. BOYCE'S CHANT, 91. This exquisite chant would be more perfectly solfaed thus—

d |r   :f |m   : —

r |ᵐl₁.t₁ :d |d   :t₁ |d   : —

d₃ |ˢr   :f |m   : —

ᵐl.,s |f   :m |r   : — |d   : —

The changes of key should be traced on the modulator. They are very beautiful, and suited to aid the expression of this penitential psalm. Do not fear the dissonance DOH RAY. Hold the DOH firmly.

72.   MELCOMBE, L. M.   KEY F.   M. 50.

:s	s :f	m :r	d :l	s :s	d¹ :t	l :s
See	how be-	neath the	moon- beam's	smile, Yon	lit- tle	bil- low
Thus	Man, the	sport' of	bliss' and	care', Ris-	es on	Time's e-
:m	m :r	d :t₁	d :f	m :m	m :r	d :t₁

s :tu₁	s :m	m :f	s :m	r :-.m	f :f
heaves its	breast, And	foams' and	spark'- les	for a-	while', And
vent- ful	sea: *And*	*hav-* *ing*	*swelled a*	*mo- ment*	*there,* Thus
t₁ :l₁	t₁ :d	d :l₁	t₁ :d	t₁ :-.d	r :r

m :r	s :f	m :r	d ‖
mur- m'ring	then sub-	sides to	rest.
melts in-	to e-	ter- ni-	ty.
d :t₁	d :l₁	d :t₁	d ‖

73.   TYTHERTON, S. M.   (S. M. 63, S. S. 70.)   KEY E.   M. 66.

:d	m :s	d¹ :l	s :f	m :d.r	m :tu₁	s :s	r¹ :d¹
:d	d :r	m :f	m :r	d :d.t₁	d :d	t₁ :t₁	s₁ :l₁

t :s	s :tu₁	s :m	d¹ :m	f :r	d ‖
t₁ :d	l₁ :l₁	t₁ :d	d :fi	l₁ :t₁	d ‖

74.   ST. ANNS, C. M.   (S. M. 61, S. S. 45, 72.)   KEY D.   M. 66.

:s	m :l	s :d¹	d¹ :t	d¹ :s	d¹ :s	l :tu₁	s :t
:m	d :f	m :d	m :r	m :m	m :t₁	d :d	t₁ :r

d¹ :l	r¹ :t	d¹ :l	t :s	l :d¹	r¹ :t	d¹ ‖
m :f	f :r	m :tu₁	s :m	f :m	f :r	m ‖

75.   PLAISTOW. 8s.   (S. M. 76, S. S. 112, 113.)   KEY E.   M. 112.

:s	s :m :f	s :m :f	s :— :l	f :r :m	f :r :m
:m	m :d :r	m :d :r	m :— :f	r :t₁ :d	r :t₁ :d

f :— :s	m :r :d	s :f :m	r :— :d¹	t :l :s
r :— :t₁	d :t₁ :d	m :r :d	t₁ :— :r	r :d :t₁

$$\left\{\begin{array}{l} \text{r} \quad :\text{s} \quad :tu_{\text{1}} \mid \text{s} \quad :— \quad :\text{s} \mid \text{s} \quad :\text{m} \quad :\text{f} \mid \text{s} \quad :\text{m} \quad :\text{f} \mid \text{s} \quad :— \quad :\text{l} \\ \text{t}_\text{1} \quad :\text{t}_\text{1} \quad :\text{d} \mid \text{t}_\text{1} \quad :— \quad :\text{m} \mid \text{m} \quad :\text{d} \quad :\text{r} \mid \text{m} \quad :\text{d} \quad :\text{r} \mid \text{m} \quad :— \quad :\text{f} \end{array}\right.$$

$$\left\{\begin{array}{l} \text{f} \quad :\text{r} \quad :\text{m} \mid \text{f} \quad :\text{r} \quad :\text{m} \mid \text{f} \quad :— \quad :\text{r} \mid \text{m} \quad :\text{f} \quad :\text{s} \mid \text{l} \quad :\text{s} \quad :\text{m} \\ \text{r} \quad :\text{t}_\text{1} \quad :\text{d} \mid \text{r} \quad :\text{t}_\text{1} \quad :\text{d} \mid \text{r} \quad :— \quad :\text{t}_\text{1} \mid \text{d} \quad :\text{r} \quad :\text{m} \mid \text{f} \quad :\text{m} \quad :\text{d} \end{array}\right.$$

$$\left\{\begin{array}{l} \text{r} \quad :— \quad :\text{t} \mid \text{d}^\text{1} \quad :\text{s} \quad :\text{l} \mid \text{m} \quad :\text{f} \quad :\text{r} \mid \text{d} \quad :— \quad \| \\ \text{t}_\text{1} \quad :— \quad :\text{r} \mid \text{d} \quad :\text{d} \quad :\text{d} \mid \text{d} \quad :\text{r} \quad :\text{t}_\text{1} \mid \text{d} \quad :— \quad \| \end{array}\right.$$

76.   EDGEWARE.   (s. M. 116, s. s. 108, 120.)   KEY E.   M. 66.

$$\left\{\begin{array}{l} \text{d} \quad :\text{m} \quad \text{,r} \quad :\text{s} \mid \underline{\text{f.m}} \quad :\text{r.d} \quad \text{,r} \quad :\text{s} \mid \text{m} \quad :\text{l.d} \quad \text{,t}_\text{1} \quad :\text{s.t}_\text{1} \mid \text{l}_\text{1} \quad :tu_\text{1} \quad \text{,s} \quad :— \\ \text{d} \quad :\text{d} \quad \text{,d} \quad :\text{t}_\text{1} \mid \text{d} \quad :\text{d} \quad \text{,d} \quad :\text{t}_\text{1} \mid \text{d} \quad :tu_\text{2} \quad \text{,s}_\text{1} \quad :\text{s}_\text{1} \mid tu_\text{2} \quad :\text{d} \quad \text{,t}_\text{1} \quad :— \end{array}\right.$$

$$\left\{\begin{array}{l} \text{s} \quad :\text{d}^\text{1}.\text{s} \quad \text{,l} \quad :\text{s} \mid \text{m.s} \quad :\text{d}^\text{1}.\text{t} \quad \text{,l} \quad :\text{s} \mid \underline{\text{m.s}} \quad :\text{d}^\text{1}.\text{t} \quad \text{,t.l} \quad :\text{l.s} \mid \text{s.f} \quad :\text{m,f.s} \quad \text{,r} \quad :— \\ \text{m} \quad :\text{m} \quad \text{,f} \quad :\text{m} \mid \underline{\text{d.m}} \quad :\underline{\text{m.s}} \quad \text{,f} \quad :\text{m} \mid \underline{\text{d.m}} \quad :\underline{\text{m.s}} \quad \text{,s.f} \quad :\underline{\text{f.m}} \mid \underline{\text{m.r}} :\text{d.r} \quad \text{,t}_\text{1} \quad :— \end{array}\right.$$

$$\left\{\begin{array}{l} \text{s} \quad :\text{d} \quad \text{,m.r} :\text{d} \mid \underline{\text{s.m}} \quad :\text{r.d} \quad \text{,r.t}_\text{1} \quad :\text{d} \mid \text{s} \quad :\underline{\text{d.r}} \quad \text{,l}_\text{1}.\text{f} \quad :\underline{\text{m.r}} \mid \text{m} \quad :\text{r} \quad \text{,d} \quad :— \| \\ \text{d} \quad :\text{d} \quad \text{,t}_\text{1} \quad :\text{d} \mid \text{s}_\text{1} \quad :\underline{\text{f}_\text{1}.\text{m}_\text{1}} \quad \text{,f}_\text{1} \quad :\text{m}_\text{1} \mid \text{d} \quad :\text{d} \quad \text{,d} \quad :\text{d} \mid \text{d} \quad :\text{t}_\text{1} \quad \text{,d} \quad :— \end{array}\right.$$

77.   MORTON MILLS.   (s. M. 126, s. s. 15, 136.)   KEY C.   M. 112.

$$\left\{\begin{array}{l} :\text{s} \mid \text{d}^\text{1} \quad :\text{t} \quad :\text{d}^\text{1} \quad \text{,m}^\text{1} :\text{r}^\text{1} :\text{d}^\text{1} \mid \text{f}^\text{1} \quad :\text{l} \quad :\text{l} \quad \text{,l} \quad :— \quad :\text{l} \mid \text{s} \quad :— :\text{s.s} \quad \text{,s} \quad :\text{d}^\text{1} :\text{m}^\text{1} \\ \cdot\text{m} \mid \text{m} \quad :\text{m} :\text{m} \quad \text{,s} \quad :\text{f} \quad :\text{m} \mid \text{f} \quad :\text{f} \quad :\text{f} \quad \text{,f} \quad :— :\text{d} \mid \text{d} \quad :— :\text{m.m} \quad \text{,m} \quad :\text{s} \quad :\text{d}^\text{1} \end{array}\right.$$

$$\left\{\begin{array}{l} \text{r}^\text{1} \quad :— :— \quad \text{,—} \quad :— \quad :\text{s.s} \mid \text{m}^\text{1} \quad :\text{r}^\text{1} :\text{d}^\text{1} \quad \text{,d}^\text{1} \quad :\text{t} \quad :\text{l} \mid \text{s} \quad :\text{t} \quad :\text{r}^\text{1} \quad \text{,r}^\text{1} \quad :— \quad :\text{r}^\text{1} \\ \underline{\text{d}^\text{1}} \quad :— :— \quad \text{,t} \quad :— \quad :\text{s.s} \mid \text{s} \quad :\text{f} \quad :\text{m} \quad \text{,l} \quad :\text{s} \quad :tu_\text{1} \mid \text{s} \quad :\text{s} \quad :\text{s} \quad \text{,s} \quad :— \quad :\text{s} \end{array}\right.$$

$$\left\{\begin{array}{l} \text{s}^\text{1} \quad :\text{r}^\text{1} :\text{t} \quad \text{,m}^\text{1} :\text{r}^\text{1} :tu_\text{1} \mid \text{s} \quad :— :— \quad \text{,—} \quad :— \quad :\text{s} \mid \text{d}^\text{1} \quad :\text{t} \quad :\text{d}^\text{1} \quad \text{,m}^\text{1} :\text{r}^\text{1} :\text{d}^\text{1} \\ \text{s} \quad :\text{s} :\text{s} \quad \text{,r} \quad :\text{r} \quad :\text{d} \mid \text{t}_\text{1} \quad :— :— \quad \text{,—} \quad :— \quad :\text{m} \mid \text{m} \quad :\text{m} :\text{m} \quad \text{,s} \quad :\text{f} \quad :\text{m} \end{array}\right.$$

$$\left\{\begin{array}{l} \text{f}^\text{1} \quad :\text{l} \quad :\text{l} \quad \text{,l} \quad :— :\text{l} \mid \text{s} \quad :— :\text{s.s} \quad \text{,s} \quad :\text{d}^\text{1} :\text{m}^\text{1} \mid \text{r}^\text{1} \quad :— :— \quad \text{,—} \quad :— \quad :\text{s.s} \\ \text{f} \quad :\text{f} \quad :\text{f} \quad \text{,f} \quad :— :\text{f} \mid \text{d} \quad :— :\text{m.m} \quad \text{,m} \quad :\text{s} \quad :\text{d}^\text{1} \mid \underline{\text{d}^\text{1}} \quad :— :— \quad \text{,t} \quad :— \quad :\text{s.s} \end{array}\right.$$

$$\left\{\begin{array}{l} \text{l} \quad :\text{t} \quad :\text{d}^\text{1} \quad \text{,r}^\text{1} :\text{m}^\text{1} :\text{f}^\text{1} \mid \text{m}^\text{1} :\text{r}^\text{1} :\text{d}^\text{1} \quad \text{,t} \quad :— \quad :\text{l.l} \mid \text{s} \quad :\text{d}^\text{1} :\text{m}^\text{1} \quad \text{,s}^\text{1} :-.\text{f}^\text{1} :\text{t} \\ \text{d} \quad :\text{r} \quad :\text{m} \quad \text{,f} \quad :\text{s} \quad :\text{l} \mid \text{s} \quad :\text{f} \quad :\text{m} \quad \text{,r} \quad :— \quad :\text{d.d} \mid \text{d} \quad :\text{d} \quad :\text{d} \quad \text{,t}_\text{1} \quad :\text{r} \quad :\text{f} \end{array}\right.$$

$$\left\{\begin{array}{l} \text{d}^\text{1} \quad :— :— \quad \text{,—} \quad :— \quad \| \\ \text{m} \quad :— :— \quad \text{,—} \quad :— \quad \| \end{array}\right.$$

I

78.   BEETHOVEN.   (S. M. 46, S. S. 56, 97.)   KEY B flat.   M. 80.

```
{ |s₁  :d  :t₁ |d   :—  :r  |s₁ :-.l₁ :t₁ |d  :—  :  |d  :t₁ :l₁
{ |m₁ :m₁ :f₁ |m₁ :s₁ :s₁ |s₁ :—  :f₁ |m₁ :—  :  |l₁ :s₁ :tu₂

{ |r   :—  :t₁ |t₁.l₁ :s₁ :tu₂ |s₁ :—  :s₁ |s₁ :—  :d  |d  :-.t₁ :l₁
{ |s₁  :—  :s₁ |m₁ :r₁ :d₁ |t₂ :—  :f₁ |m₁ :—  :m₁ |m₁ :-.r₁ :d₁

{ |s₁ :m :d |l₁ :—:d |d :t₁ :f |f :m :d |d :r :t₁ |d :—: ‖
{ |d₁ :—:d₁ |d₁ :—:m₁ |m₁ :r₁ :s₁ |s₁ :—:m₁ |m₁ :f₁ :r₁ |m₁ :—: ‖
```

79.   BRUNSWICK, C. M.   (S. M. 2, S. S. 30.)   KEY F.   M. 80.

```
{ :d |d :m :f |s :—:d¹ |fʲ :—:l |s :—:l |r :m :f |f.,s:l :s
{ :d |d :—:r |m :—:l |s :—:f |m :—:d |fʲ :—:l₁ |r :d :fʲ

{ |f :—:—  | :  :f |m ʲ:s.f :m |m :r :d |d¹ :t.l :s.f |m :r :m
{ |l₁ :—:— | :  :d |d :r :d |d :t₁ :d |d :—:r |d :t₁ :s₁

{ |l₁ :t₁ :d |d.,r :m :r |d :—:— | : ‖
{ |f₁ :—:m₁ |l₁ :s₁ :f₁ |m₁ :—:— | : ‖
```

80.   SONNING.   (S. M. 109, S. S. 119.)   KEY B flat.   M. 96.

```
{ :s₁ |s₁ :d.r |m :m |m :-.f |m :m |m :m |m.r :d.r
{ :s₁ |m₁ :m₁.s₁ |d :d |d :-.r |d :s₁ |s₁ :s₁ |s₁.f₁ :m₁.f₁

{ |m :—  |d :d |s₁ :d.r |m :m |m :-.f |m :m |s :s |s.f :m.r
{ |s₁ :—  |m₁ :m₁ |m₁ :m₁.s₁ |d :d |d :-.r |d :d |m :m |m.r :d.r

                 F.
{ |d :—  |— :s₁ |s₁ :t₁.d |r :r |r :-.m |r :r |m :d |r :s₁
{ |d :—  |— :s₁ |s₁ :s₁.l₁ |t₁ :t₁ |t₁ :-.d |t₁ :t₁ |d :d |t₁ :s₁

{ |s₁ :-.l₁ |s₁ :s₁ |s₁ :t₁.d |r :r |r :-.m |r :r |m :d |r :s₁
{ |r₁ :-.f₁ |m₁ :s₁ |s₁ :s₁.l₁ |t₁ :t₁ |t₁ :-.d |t₁ :t₁ |d :d |t₁ :s₁

          r                     D. C.
{ |f :— |f :— |m.r :d.t₁ |l₁ ‖
{ |s₁ :— |— :— | : | ‖
```

81.   SERENITY, S. M.   KEY A.   M. 66.

$$
\left\{
\begin{array}{l}
:m \\
:d
\end{array}
\right.
\begin{array}{|l|}
\underline{m} :r :m \\
\underline{d} :t_1 :d
\end{array}
\begin{array}{|l|}
f :— :t_1 \\
\underline{l_1} :s_1 :f_1
\end{array}
\begin{array}{|l|}
d :— :d \\
m_1 :— :m_1
\end{array}
\begin{array}{|l|}
t_{1,,}d :r :s \\
s_{1,,}l_1 :t_1 :t_1
\end{array}
\begin{array}{|l|}
s :— :tu_1 \\
l_1 :— :l_1
\end{array}
$$

$$
\left\{
\begin{array}{|l|}
s :— :s \\
t_1 :— :m
\end{array}
\begin{array}{|l|}
s :f :m \\
r :— :d
\end{array}
\begin{array}{|l|}
\underline{m} :r :d \\
t_1 :— :l_1
\end{array}
\begin{array}{|l|}
\underline{d} :t_1 :l_1 \\
s_1 :— :tu_2
\end{array}
\begin{array}{|l|}
s_1 :— :d.,t_1 \\
s_1 :— :s_1
\end{array}
$$

$$
\left\{
\begin{array}{|l|}
l_1 :-.t_1 :d.r \\
\underline{f_1} :-.r_1 :m_1.f_1
\end{array}
\begin{array}{|l|}
m :— :m.r \\
s_1 :— :f_1
\end{array}
\begin{array}{|l|}
d :— \\
m_1 :—
\end{array}
\right\|
$$

82.   PERSEVERANCE.   (S. M. 98, S. S. 144.)   KEY B flat.   M. 112.
D. C.

$$
\left\{
\begin{array}{|l|}
s_1 :d |t_1 :d \\
m_1 :m_1 |f_1 :m_1
\end{array}
\begin{array}{|l|}
r :m |t_1 :— \\
r_1 :d_1 |s_1 :—
\end{array}
\begin{array}{|l|}
d :— |r :— \\
m_1, :— |f_1 :—
\end{array}
\begin{array}{|l|}
m :d |d : \\
s_1 :m_1 |m_1 :
\end{array}
$$

$$
\left\{
\begin{array}{|l|}
m :s |s :\underline{f.m} \\
d :m |m :r.d
\end{array}
\begin{array}{|l|}
f :f |f :— \\
r :d |t_1 :—
\end{array}
\begin{array}{|l|}
f :-.m |r :d \\
r :-.d |t_1 :l_1
\end{array}
\begin{array}{|l|}
t_1 :r |s_1 : \\
s_1 :tu_2 |s_1 :
\end{array}
$$

$$
\left\{
\begin{array}{|l|}
s :\underline{l.s} |f :m \\
s_1 :-.d |t_1 :d
\end{array}
\begin{array}{|l|}
r.m :f.r |d.t_1 :l_1.s_1 \\
f_1 :-.f_1 |s_1 :f_1
\end{array}
\begin{array}{|l|}
d :— |r :— \\
m_1 :— |f_1 :—
\end{array}
\begin{array}{|l|}
m :d |d :— \\
s_1 :m_1 |m_1 :—
\end{array}
\right\|
$$

83.   ALMA. 8.7.   KEY D.   M. 80.

$$
\left\{
\begin{array}{|l|}
s :-.m |d :— \\
d :— |d :—
\end{array}
\begin{array}{|l|}
l :— |s :— \\
t_1 :— |d :—
\end{array}
\begin{array}{|l|}
f :-.m |f.s :l.t \\
d :— |'d :—
\end{array}
\begin{array}{|l|}
d^1 :— |s :— \\
d :— |t_1 :—
\end{array}
$$

$$
\left\{
\begin{array}{|l|}
m :— |m :— \\
d :— |t_1 :—
\end{array}
\begin{array}{|l|}
f :l |d^1 :l \\
l_1 :— |l_1 :—
\end{array}
\begin{array}{|l|}
tu_1 :— |tu_1 :— \\
r :— |d :—
\end{array}
\begin{array}{|l|}
s :— |— : \\
t_1 :— |— :
\end{array}
$$

$$
\left\{
\begin{array}{|l|}
d^1 :— |t :l \\
m :— |f :—
\end{array}
\begin{array}{|l|}
s :— |m :— \\
m :— |d :—
\end{array}
\begin{array}{|l|}
d^1 :— |t :l \\
m :— |f :—
\end{array}
\begin{array}{|l|}
s :— |m :— \\
m :— |d :—
\end{array}
$$

$$
\left\{
\begin{array}{|l|}
s :m^1 |m^1 :d^1 \\
m :— |m :—
\end{array}
\begin{array}{|l|}
d^1 :l |l :f \\
f :— |r :—
\end{array}
\begin{array}{|l|}
m :— |r :— \\
d :— |t_1 :—
\end{array}
\begin{array}{|l|}
d :— |— :— \\
d :— |— :—
\end{array}
\right\|
$$

84.   TRENT BRIDGE. (S. M. 102, S. S. 152, 130, 87.) KEY C. M. 66, two
swings to each measure.

$$
\left\{
\begin{array}{l}
:d \\
:d
\end{array}
\right.
\begin{array}{|l|}
d :— :d^1 |t :— :l \\
d :— :m |f :— :f
\end{array}
\begin{array}{|l|}
s :—:f |m :—:s \\
m :— :r |d :—:m
\end{array}
\begin{array}{|l|}
f :—:m |r :— :d \\
r :—:d |t_1 :— :d
\end{array}
$$

D. C.
{ |d¹ :— :— ι— :— :s | d¹ :— :r¹ ιm¹ :— :f¹ | r¹ :t :d¹ ιl :— :s
{ |m :— :— ι— :— :m | m :— :f ιs :— :l | s :f :m ιf :— :f

{ |d¹ :— :t ιl :— :s | s :— :— ι— :— :r¹ | s¹ :— :m¹ ιd¹ :-.r¹ :m¹
{ |m :— :s ιf :— :m | r :— :— ι— :— :f | m :— :s ιs :— :s

{ |f¹ :— :r¹ ιt :— :t | d¹ :— :m ιr :— :t | d¹ :— :— ι— :— ‖
{ |s :— :f ιr :— :f | m :— :d ιt₁ :— :r | m :— :— ι— :— ‖

85.   LULLABY.   (S. M. 92, S. S. 134, 121.)   KEY C.   M. 80.

{ |d¹ :— :m¹ | s¹ :m¹ :d¹ | l :-.t :d¹ | s :— :m | s :l :t
{ |m :— :s | s :— :m | f :— :f | m :— :d | m :f :r

{ |d¹ :— :r¹ | m¹ :r¹ :d¹ | r¹ :— :s | d¹ :— :m¹ | s¹ :m¹ :d¹
{ |m :— :s | d¹ :t :l | t :— :s.f | m :— :s | s :— :m

{ |l :-.t :d¹ | s :— :m | s :-.l :t | d¹ :— :r¹ιm¹ιf¹ | m¹ :— :r¹
{ |f :— :f | m :— :d | m :-.f :r | m :— :f.s.l | s :— :f

{ |d¹ :— :— | d¹.r¹ :m¹ :— | r¹.t :s :— | d¹.l :f :— | s.m :d :—
{ |m :— :— | m.f :s :— | f.r :m :— | f.f :f :— | m.d :d :—

R.
{ |t :r¹ :f¹ | m¹ :d¹ :l | s :l :t | d¹ :— :— ‖
{ |r :— :t₁ | d :— :f | m :f :r | m :— :— ‖

86.   FONTHILL.   (S. M. 90, S. S. 159, 124.)   KEY E.   M. 80,
                                                    Beating twice in a measure.

{ :s | d¹ :— :s ιm :f :s | d¹ :— :s ιm :f :s | l :s :f ιm :r :d
{ :m | m :— :m ιd :r :m | m :— :m ιd :r :m | f :m :r ιd :t₁ :d

{ |r :— :— ι— :— :s | l :f :s ιl :— :s | f :m :f ιs :— :s
{ |t₁ :— :— ι— :— :d | d :— :d ιd :— :m | r :d :r ιm :— :m

{ |l :-.t :d¹ ιt :-.d¹ :r¹ | d¹ :— :— ι— :— ‖
{ |f :— :m ιf :-.m :r | m :— :— ι— :— ‖

87. CLIFTON GROVE. (s. m. 72, s. s. 85, 111.)   KEY C.   m. 160.

```
{ : s  | d¹ :— : d¹ ι d¹ :— : s | l  :— : s ιs :— : s | d¹ :— : d¹ ιr¹ : d¹ : r¹
{ : m  | m  :— : m ιm :— : m | f  :— : m ιm :— : m | m : s : d¹ ιt :— : t

{ |m¹ :— : d¹ ι d¹ :— : m¹ | f¹ :— : f¹ ιm¹ :— : m¹ | r¹ : m¹ : d¹ ιt :— : l.s
{ |d¹ :— : d¹ ι d¹ :— : fι | l  :— : l ιs :— : s | f : s : m ιr :— : f.m

{ |l  : s : f ιm : f : s | l :— : s ιs :— : l.t | d¹ :— : s ι d¹ :— : s
{ |f  : m : r ιd : r : m | f :— : m ιm :— : f | m :— : m ιm :— : m

{ |l  :— : s ιs :— : s | d¹ :— : d¹ ιr¹ :—.m¹ : f¹ | m¹ :— : d¹ ι d¹ :— : r¹.m¹
{ |f  :— : m ιm :— : m | m : s : d¹ ιt :—.d¹ : r¹ | d¹ :— : s ιm :— : s

{ |f¹ :— : f¹ ιm¹ :— : m¹ | r¹ : m¹ : d¹ ιt :— : l.s | l : s : f ιm : f : s
{ |l  :— : l ιs :— : s | f : s : m ιr :— : f.m | f : m : r ιd : r : m

{ |l  :— : s ιs :— ‖
{ |f  :— : m ιm :— ‖
```

88. DELABORDE. 8.7.   KEY E.   m. 66.

m : f ιf : s	l : s ιs : m	s : f ιf : m	m :— ιr :
Peace	be	to	this	ha-	bi-	ta-	tion!
Peace	that	speaks	the	heaven-	ly	giv-	er;
d : r ιr : m	f : m ιm : d	m : r ιr : d	d :— ιt₁ :

m : f ιf : s	l : s ιs : d¹	t : d¹ ιl : d¹	l :— ιs :
Peace	to	all	that	dwell	there-	in!
Peace	to	world-	ly	minds	un-	known;
d : r ιr : m	f : m ιm : d	r : m ιf : foi	foi :— ιs :

f : m ιr : l	s : f ιm : d¹	l : t ι d¹ : r¹	d¹ :— ιt :
Peace	the	ear-	nest	of	sal-	va-	tion!
Peace	di-	vine	that	lasts	for	ev-	er;
r : d ιt₁ : f	m : r ιd : m	f : r ιm : f	m :— ιr :

s : f ιr¹ : f	f : m ι d¹ : m	m : r ιl : s	f :— ιm :
Peace	the	fruit	of	par-	don'd	sin!
Peace	that	comes	from	God	a-	lone;
t₁ :— ιt₁ :—	d :— ιd :—	d : t₁ ιf : m	r :— ιd :

m : f ι foi : s	t : l ιs : f	m : d¹ ι d¹ : t	t :— ι d¹ : ‖
Peace	the	fruit	of	par-	don'd	sin.
Peace	that	comes	from	God	a-	lone.
d : r ιroi : m	r : f ιm : r	d : m ιm : r	r :— ιd : ‖

89.   PORTLAND, P. L. M.   KEY B flat.   M. 66.

{ | d :m₁ :s₁ | d :— :r | m :r :d | r :— :r | m :— :r
  | m₁ :m₁ :f₁ | m₁ :— :f₁ | s₁ :f₁ :m₁ | f₁ :— :f₁ | m₁ :d :t₁

R.
{ | r :d :t₁ | l₁ :— :r | t₁ :— :r | s :— :r | m :d :t₁
  | t₁ :l₁ :s₁ | s₁ :— :tu₂ | s₁ :— :d | t₁ :— :t₁ | d :— :s₁

{ | l₁ :— :r | s₁ :— :s₁ | r :— :m | s :f :m | r :d :m
  | f₁ :— :foi₁ | s₁ :— :s₁ | t₁ :— :d | t₁ :l₁ :s₁ | f₁ :m₁ :s₁

{ | m :r :s₁ | s :— :d | s :f :m | m.r :d :t₁ | d :— :— ‖
  | s₁ :— :f₁ | m₁ :— :m₁ | m₁ :f₁ :s₁ | s₁.f₁ :m₁ :r₁ | d₁ :— :— ‖

90. THE STRAWBERRY GIRL. (S. M. 93, S. S. 158.) KEY B flat. M. 80, two
                                                    swings in each measure.

S.
{ (:s₁ | d :—:t₁ ı d :—:r | m :—:m ı m :—:f.m | r :—:r ı r :—:m.r
  (:m₁ | m₁:—:r₁ ı m₁:—:f₁ | s₁ :—:s₁ ı s₁:—:s₁ | f₁ :—:f₁ ı f₁ :—:s₁.f₁

{ | d :—:— ı—:—:s₁ | d :—:t₁ ı d :—:r | m :—:m ı m :—:f.m
  | m₁:—:— ı—:—:m₁ | m₁:—:r₁ ı m₁:—:f₁ | s₁ :—:s₁ ı s₁ :—:s₁

P.
{ | r :—:r ı r :—:m.r | d :—:— ı—:—:s₁ | m :—:m ı m :—:r.m
  | f₁ :—:f₁ ı f₁ :—:s₁.f₁ | m₁:—:— ı—:—:m₁ | s₁ :—:s₁ ı d :—:fı

{ | f :—:f ı f :—:s.f | m :—:m ı m :—:f.m | r :—:— ı—:—:s₁
  | l₁ :—:l₁ ı l₁ :—:t₁ | d :—:d ı d :—:r.d | t₁ :—:— ı—:—:m₁

{ | m :—:m ı m :—:r.m | f :—:f ı f :—:s.f | m :—:m ı m :—:f.m
  | s₁ :—:s₁ ı d :—:fı | l₁ :—:l₁ ı l₁ :—:t₁ | d :—:d ı d :—:r.d

{ | r :—:— ı—:—:ˢd | t₁ :l₁ :s₁ ı s₁ :l₁ :t₁ | d :—:d₁ ı d₁ :—:d
  | t₁ :—:— ı—:—:ᵗm₁ | r₁ :m₁:f₁ ı f₁ :m₁:r₁ | m₁ :—:d₁ ı d₁ :—:m₁

{ | t₁ :l₁ :s₁ ı s₁ :l₁ :t₁ | d :—:— ı—:—:d | t₁ :l₁ :s₁ ı s₁ :l₁ :t₁
  | r₁ :m₁:f₁ ı f₁ :m₁:r₁ | m₁:—:— ı—:—:m₁ | r₁ :m₁:f₁ ı f₁ :m₁:r₁

D. S.

{ | d :— :d₁ | d₁ :— :l | s :f :m | r :m :r | d₁ :— :— | — :— :ᵈs₁ ||
{ | m₁ :— :d₁ | d₁ :— :f | m :r :d₁ | t₂ :— :t₂ | d₁ :— :— | — :— :¹m₁ ||

91.   DR. BOYCE'S CHANT.   KEY F.   M. 50.

{ | .d | d.d | :d | r :f | m :—.r | r.r :r | m.tu₁ :s | s :tu₁
  | Have | mercy up- | on | me, O | God, Ac- | cording to | thy | lov- ing
  | .d | d.d | :d | d :t₁ | d :—.t₁ | t₁.t₁ :t₁ | d.l₁ :t₁ | l₁ :d

{ | s.s | :—.s | s.s | :s.s | s,s,s | :s.s | s :fʲ | l.l :— | l :—.s
  | kindness. Ac- | | cording | to the | multitude | of thy | ten- der | mercies, | Blot
  | t₁.t₁ | :—.t₁ | t₁.t₁ | :t₁.t₁ | t₁,t₁,t₁ | :t₁.t₁ | d :m | f.f :— | f :—.m

{ | f :m | r :— | d.d :— | d :—.d | d,d,d | :d.d | r :f
  | out my | trans- | gressions, | Wash me | throughly from | mine in- | i- qui-
  | r :d | d :t₁ | d.d :— | d :—.d | d,d,d | :d.d | d :t₁

{ | m :— | r :— | m.tu₁ :s | s :tu₁ | s :— | :s,s,s | s.s :—
  | ty, | And | cleanse me | from my | sin, | For I ac- | knowledge
  | d :— | t₁ :— | d.l₁ :t₁ | l₁ :d | t₁ :— | :t₁,t₁,t₁ | t₁.t₁ :—

{ | s :fʲ | l :—.l,l | l :—.s | f.f :m | r :— | d :— | :d.d
  | my trans- | gressions, And my | sin is | ever be- | fore | me. | Against
  | d :m | f :—.f,f | f :—.m | r.r :d | d :t₁ | d :— | :d.d

{ | d :— | d :d.d | r :f | m.m :—,r | r :r | m.tu₁ :s | s :tu₁
  | Thee, | Thee only, | have I | sinned, And | done this | evil in | thy
  | d :— | d :d.d | d :t₁ | d.d :—,t₁ | t₁ :t₁ | d.l₁ :t₁ | l₁ :d

{ | s :—.s | s :s,s,s | s,s :s | s :fʲ | l :—. | l :—.s
  | sight, That | Thou mightest be | justi- fied | when thou | speakest, | And be
  | t₁ :—.t₁ | t₁ :t₁,t₁,t₁ | d,d :d | d :m | f :—. | f :—.m

{ | f :m | r :— | d.d :— | d.d :d | r :f | m :—.r | r.r :r
  | clear when | thou | judgest. | Hide thy face | from my | sins, And | blot out all
  | r :d | d :t₁ | d.d :— | d.d :d | d :t₁ | d :—.t₁ | t₁.t₁ :t₁

{ | m.tu₁ :s | s :tu₁ | s :—,s | s.s :s.s | s :— | s :fʲ | l :—.l,l
  | mine in- | i- qui- | ties. Cre- | ate in me a | clean | heart, O | God, And re-
  | d.l₁ :t₁ | l₁ :d | t₁ :—,t₁ | t₁.t₁ :t₁.t₁ | t₁ :— | d :m | f :—.f f

{ | l.l :l.s | f :m.m | r :— | d :— | d.d :d.d | d :— | r :f
  | new a right | spi- rit with- | in | me. | Cast me not a- | way | from thy
  | f.f :f.m | r :d.d | d :t₁ | d :— | d.d :d.d | d :— | d :t₁

{ | m.m :—,r | r :r.r | m.tu₁ :s | s :tu₁ | s.s :—,s | s.s,s :s.s
  | presence, And | take not thy | Ho- ly | Spi- rit | from me. Re- | store unto me th
  | d.d :—,t₁ | t₁ :t₁.t₁ | d.l₁ :t₁ | l₁ :d | t₁.t₁ :—,t₁ | t₁.t₁,t₁ :t₁.t₁

s :-.s	s :fi	l.l :-.l,l	l :-.s	f :m	r :—	d.d :—
joy of	thy sal-	vation, And up-	hold me	with thy	free	spirit.
t₁ :-.t₁	d :m	f.f :-.f,f	f :-.m	r :d	d :t₁	d.d :—

d :d.d	d :d	r.r :f	m :-.r	r.r,r :r.r	m.tu₁ :s
Then will I	teach trans-	gressors thy	ways, And	sinners shall be con-	ver- ted
d :d.d	d :d	d.d :t₁	d :-.t₁	t₁.t₁,t₁ :t₁.t	d.l₁ :t₁

s :tu₁	s :-.s	s :s.s	s :fi	l :l.l	l :-.s
un- to	thee. O	LORD, OPEN	THOU MY	LIPS, AND MY	MOUTH SHALL
l₁ :d	t₁ :-.t₁	t₁ :t₁.t₁	d :m	f :f.f	f :-.m

f: :m	r :r	d :—
SHOW	FORTH THY	PRAISE.
r :d	d :t₁	d :—

SECTION IX.

OF "MINOR TUNES," THE LAH KEY, AND THE NOTES NE, BAH, NI, AND NU.

1. *a.* In some tunes—chiefly those which are intended to express a mournful
sentiment—the note LAH is found to predominate. It is necessarily heard both
at the beginning and at the end of such tunes; and assumes the importance of a
governing or key note, but without changing, (as SOH and FAH do when they
become key notes by "transition") its own musical effect. It still leaves on the
mind the impression of "sorrowful suspense." See Section vi. 1 and 2.

b. Modern musicians, in order to give to LAH a closer resemblance to the
ordinary key note, and to direct the ear to it more decisively as the note on
which the tune closes, as well as to increase the general effect of such tunes,
occasionally introduce a new note, which we shall call NE, a tonule below LAH.
This note bears the same relation to LAH which TE bears to DOH. Musicians
also find it necessary sometimes, especially in ascending passages when designing
to use NE instead of SOH, to introduce another new note which they then use
instead of FAH. It is a tone below NE, or a chromatic part-tone above FAH.
We call it BAH. It is very seldom used in ordinary music.

c. Tunes of this kind are commonly called Minor tunes from their having the
interval called a minor (smaller) third immediately above their predominating
note LAH—(LAH, DOH), and in distinction from other tunes which have a major
(larger) third above their predominating note DOH. They may be said to be in
the LAH KEY. It is advisable to take their pitch by means of DOH, as in other
tunes. The signature should therefore be written in this form, "LAH KEY.
DOH IS A."

The phrase LAH KEY is to be distinguished from such phrases as "KEY A," "KEY C," &c., in that it does not indicate pitch, but only a certain "character" of tune—and from the phrases "SOH KEY" and "FAH KEY" in that it indicates no necessary change in the position of the notes and no change in their character or mental effects, but simply a predominance of LAH, *approaching* to that of DOH in other cases.

The musical facts which are here ascribed simply to the *Common Mode* used in a peculiar manner, and admitting occasional variations—are usually supposed to be founded on an entirely new Mode or Scale, and that of a very remarkable structure.

This *new* scale is described as having its "semitones" (*tonules*) between its second and third, and fifth and sixth notes. (If you reckon from LAH₁ to LAH, in the common mode, you will find the tonules thus placed.) But the scale, it is said, only retains this form in *descending*, for in *ascending* the sixth and seventh are sharpened (making our *occasional* BAH and NE) so as to place the "semitones" (tonules) between the second and third, and seventh and eighth. This is, in fact, two scales; and some teachers of the pianoforte have gone so far, Dr. Mainzer tells us, with this "illogical system," as to make their pupils play, with the right hand ascending the scale—BAH and NE, at the same time that the left hand descending produced the sounds FAH and SOH! He justly remarks that "the simultaneous union of notes so opposite, producing an effect so discordant, is more calculated to destroy than awaken the musical sentiments of the pupil." Let us examine facts and authorities on this subject.

First, then, it appears that *the common mode, even without any new note* (ne or bah), but simply allowing LAH to predominate and to be heard at the opening and at the close of a tune (as described above, prop. 1, a,) *is quite sufficient to produce a true "minor" tune*—and that *many fine melodies, manifestly minor, are formed on this model*, using the ordinary notes of the Common Mode (from LAH, to LAH) both ascending and descending, and not requiring the aid of any accidental note. Mr. Hickson gives the following illustration of the "minor scale;" it is simply part of the Common Mode commencing and closing with LAH. DOH IS C. |l :t |d¹ :r¹

Far from home and

| m¹ :f¹ | m¹ :r¹ | d¹ :— | t :—.l | l :—

from my kind- red, far   far a- way.

The well known minor melody, ST. BRIDES, 92, contains no note but those which are found in the Common Mode. It is so also with that most elegant minor melody, WIRKSWORTH. DOH IS B FLAT.   :l₁ | m.r :d :t₁ |l₁ :— :m | s.f :m :r | m :— :d | t₁.l₁:m :d | r.d :t₁ :t₁ | m.r:d :t₁ | l₁ :—   No one can doubt that

K

these are minor tunes, nor hesitate to allow that they are formed on the Common Mode, and are simply distinguished by their making LAH, the proper mournful note—predominate. Accordingly we find Dr. Crotch describing his "ancient diatonic minor key" (which corresponds with our Common Mode when you reckon from LAH to LAH¹) as "the scale of the ancient Greek music, and found in the oldest national tunes, in psalms and cathedral music"—Dr. Bryce speaking of this as the "proper" formula of minor tunes, in which are written "multitudes of exquisite melodies, especially among the ancient national music of different countries," (pages 4 and 26)—and Dr. Mainzer maintaining that this is the only true and the only *agreeable* arrangement of notes for such tunes. By fact, then, and by competent authority—the COMMON MODE with LAH predominating is declared sufficient to produce a true minor tune. But still, it may be argued, are not BAH and NE, the "sharp sixth and seventh" (reckoning from LAH, as though it were the key note) *always used*, in tunes of this kind, (instead of FAH and SOH) *when the music ascends?* Are they not, therefore, *essential* at least to *every* minor passage in which the music *ascends* from its sixth or seventh note? Must we not necessarily suppose a distinct scale in which these essential notes may find a place? We deny the proposition and the conclusion falls, for—

Secondly, it appears that *the new notes* BAH and NE ("the sharp sixth and seventh") *are not essential even in ascending passages*, and that *the use of them is entirely arbitrary*. Nothing can prove this more clearly than the great discrepancy and disagreement among the best authorities on this subject. If there had been any fixed usage, long established by the requirement of good ears and the example of the best composers, such opposite statements of fact could not have existed. In reference to BAH (the "sharp sixth") we find Dr. Callcott describing this note as "accidental," but rendered necessary for the sake of avoiding what he calls "the harsh chromatic interval," FAH NE, "from F natural to G sharp"—while M. Galin and M. Jeu de Berneval refer to this very interval, as "a constitutive interval of the minor mode," full of "melancholy," "replete with anguish and tears," and speak indignantly of those who would "cancel" the very interval which is most "characteristic" of the "minor mode." (See Music Simplified, pp. 199 and 224.) Is it not evident, from this, that the use of BAH is arbitrary—by some approved, by others disapproved? In reference to NE, Dr. Callcott declares that it is an "essential" part of the "minor scale" in *ascending*, but not to be used in *descending*. But M. Galin and M. Jeu (pages 134, 224) speak of NE as "invariable" and essential both in ascending and in descending, and M. Jeu gives examples of its use in descending. Schneider, in his "Elements of Harmony," maintains the same opinion. Marpurg, "one of the most influential theorists, who flourished during the latter half of the last century," (Mainzer 77) declares that "this custom" (of using BAH and NE) by no means changes the essential nature of the tonality, (key or mode, reckoning from LAH to LAH[1]) and the two sharps which are prefixed to the sixth and seventh degree are *purely accidental.*" Dr. Crotch says distinctly, of both BAH and NE, "*these alterations are only occasional.*" Dr. Bryce ascribes the introduction of these notes to modern musicians, who prefer harmony to melody, (p. 26.) Dr. Mainzer says that there are a very large number of compositions "in which the leading note (NE) does not appear at all in the minor keys, and this is the case with many composers of the fifteenth, sixteenth, and seventeenth centuries." He then adduces examples, such as the following, from Gabrielis. DOH IS O. | d¹ :— | — :t | t :l

Eg.   o   ln
ı m :s | l :— , the following from Palestrina,

e-   o.
DO IS F. | l₁ :— | d :-.t | l.s :l | — :— ,
Ku-   ri-   e.
and the following from the anthem of Morale's "Lamentabatur Jacob," DOH IS O. | d :—
| t₁ :l₁ | d :t₁.l₁ | l₁.s₁.f₁ :s₁ | l₁ :— , and also shows how, in the eighteenth century, along with professedly improved harmonies, NE was introduced as an *occasional* note but not *essential*—Marcello, for example, introducing the following passage immediately after one in which NE had occurred, DOH IS B FLAT.   :l₁ | l₁ :s₁.f₁ | s₁
se   pul-
:s₁ | l₁ :—   Dr. Mainzer, who is a high authority on subjects of musical taste, and none the less so because he has laboured generously to make music the property of the people, thus concludes—" Let any one sing the above scales one after the other, (four varieties of the so-called " minor scale") and assuredly he will not be long in discovering which of the four is the most agreeable and natural, and most in the character of the minor Tonality (key). It is evident that the scales with leading notes (NE), instead of being pleasing, are disagreeable to the ear, and impracticable to the voice. The *absence* of the leading note (NE) on the contrary often gives to the melody *something majestic and solemn.* The Gregorian Chant, so remarkable for melodious beauties, affords many proofs of this, and also the popular melodies of different countries, especially those of Ireland and Scotland, so much admired by the greatest musicians." Surely here is example and testimony enough to prove these notes—whether good or bad—at least non-essential and arbitrary.

One question yet remains. Should not the scale on which minor tunes are framed be still treated as a distinct one, and something more than the Common Mode used in a peculiar manner? To which we answer—Yes, *if it is distinct,* but, if otherwise, why multiply difficulties and conceal the truth? But *it clearly is not, in any particular, distinct.* First, in reference to the "character" or musical effect of the notes—the most important particular of all—the notes of the so-called Minor Scale correspond precisely with those of the Common Mode reckoning from LAH to LAH[1]. Not a single note of the Common Mode changes its character when used in a Minor Tune. LAH is still the *sorrowful,* TE the *piercing,* FAH the *awe-inspiring* note, &c., as before. Next, in reference to the exact intervals between the notes—they are precisely the same as those of the Common Mode (from LAH to LAH[1]) with only this peculiarity, that the *graver* part *position* of the "variable note" RAY is *ordinarily used* in tunes of this character, whereas it is only *occasionally used* in other tunes. (See pages 40, 51.) Premising that from DOH to DOH[1] is commonly called by musicians a major key (beginning with a major, or greater, third DOH ME,) and that a minor key beginning on a note in the position of our LAH would be called its *relative minor,* let us quote the following testimonies to the last point. Colonel Thompson says—"The change to the relative (or as it would *more properly be called, the synonymous*) minor reduces itself to avoiding the acute second of the old key (r') and using only the grave (r')." (See Westminster Review, April, 1832.) Dr. Crotch says—" Some authors make it" (the first note of the principal minor key) "the same as the note LAH of the relative major key, viz. A in the key of C, a minor tone" (smaller tone—of eight degrees) " above O (SOH). In that case all the *natural* notes excepting D (LAY) correspond with those of the major key of C." (See Crotch's "Elements" —Tuning, &c.) Turning to his illustrative plates we find the scale of minor tunes requiring the smaller tone (eight degrees) between DOH RAY, and the larger tone (nine degrees) between RAY ME, while other tunes usually require a larger tone between DOH RAY and a smaller one between RAY ME. In fact the variable note assumes its *grave* position. But it sometimes does the same in the Common Mode. Is this then a peculiarity sufficient to establish a new scale? Moreover, is it not natural to suppose that the *Common Mode,* which, beginning either on DOH or LAH₁, and omitting or excluding FAH and TE, is found to be essentially the *musical scale of all nations,* must hold a peculiar accordance with the ear and the sympathies of the human race? and is it not proper, therefore, to consider this as *the one scale* and everything else that cannot establish a dist and independent character as but a modification or a peculiar use of it? It is certain that great detriment must be done to the mind of our pupils and great hindrance given to their progress, if we first delay them to study and practise *our theory* of a new and self-contradictory Minor Scale, and then leave them to discover that, in *music itself*, instead of the artificial difficulties they have so laboriously mastered, there is only to be found *the Common Mode—so used as to produce a peculiar effect, and the merely occasional, non-essential, introduction of a new note!*

The subject might be introduced to children very easily and naturally thus—" What kind of note is LAH?—what is its effect on our minds? (It is the sorrowful note). Then suppose I were to sing you a tune that begun with LAH and ended with LAH and had several LAHs in the middle of it—what sort of a tune would that be? (A sorrowful tune). You might call it a LAH TUNE. Listen while I point on the modulator and sing you such a tune. (Sings one of the examples above or part of one of the exercises). Is it not sorrowful? Sometimes you will find a new note introduced into these LAH tunes instead of SOH. It is a tonule below LAH; we call it NE. Listen to it. (Sings a tune with NE). Now try whether you can produce the new note. (Points a short phrase including NE, while the pupils sing). Another new note is sometimes used in place of FAH, but so seldom that I need not puzzle you much with it. It is a tone below NE—a chromatic part tone above FAH. We call it BAH. Let us write both the new notes in their places on the modulator. We can practise them as they occur in our tunes. Where is BAH? Where is NE?"

The tune "Martyrs," as now commonly writ-

ten, may be used for illustration of BAH and NE from the modulator or black board. DOH IS G.

:l₁ | d :l₁ | m :d | t₁ :l₁ | m :m | s :m
| bah. ne :l | m :m | s :r | m :d | t₁
:l₁ | m :s | bah :r.m | bah :m | l₁
(See "Free Church Psalmody"). Let the pupils also try this melody with the original notes FAH SOH instead of BAH NE. Several English Ballad Tunes, in the minor key, close thus | ne :bah :ne || l :— . The following old melodies may also be used in illustration. It would be well if they were suited with better words than the heathenish ones to which much fine music is now prostituted. DOH IS B FLAT. *Quickly.*

:m₁ | l₁ :— :l₁ | ne₁ :— : m₁ | d :—
:d | t₁ :— :r | d :— :l₁ | l₁ :—
: ne₁ | l₁ :— :— :— :— D. C. d.r | m
:— :m | m :— :d | r :— :r | r :—
:t₁ | d :— :l₁ | r :— :d | d :—
:— | t₁ :— :m₁ | l₁ :— :l₁ | ne₁ :bah₁
:m₁ | d :— :d | t₁ :— :r | d :-.t₁
:l₁ | l₁ :— :ne₁ | l₁ :— :— :— :—

DOH IS F. *Boldly.* :m | l :ne
| l :m | f :m.r m :-.m | f :m | r
:d | s :s₁ | d :—. D.C. .m | l :-.ne
| l :-.t | d¹ :t | d¹ :— | d.r :m.f | s
:s | r.m :f.s | l :l | l :— | s :—
| f :— | m :— | d¹.t :l.ne | l :r | m
:m | l₁ :—

The careful practise of minor melodies will greatly improve both the ear and the voice.

---

2. Sometimes in the course of a tune the music takes the "minor" character, introducing the new note NE, and returns again to the ordinary use of the Common Mode. Occasionally too the music passes into the "minor" of the SOH KEY, making a new note, a tonule below ME, which (to distinguish it from NE of the original key) we call NU; and, not unfrequently, it enters the "minor" of the FAH KEY, originating another note, a tonule below RAY (r), which we call NI. The modulator at the side will illustrate these changes.

s	d¹	f
	t	m
ʄi—f		
m	l	r
	ne	
r	s	d
		t₁—tu₁
d	f	
t₁	m	l₁
		n₁—nu₁
	l₁	r	s₁
ŋi₁—n₁		
	s₁	d	f₁

The teacher will explain these new notes of TRANSITION as they occur in the exercises. Transition into what is called "the minor of the same tonic," or that in which DOH becomes LAH, (transition into the key of ME flat or MOW) should the teacher meet with it, may be written thus dl rt, &c. or, retaining the syllables of the original key, the additional notes may be treated as chromatic. Thus DOH of the new key becomes MOW, FAH

LOW, and SOH TOW, as any one may perceive by drawing the two keys side by side, and bearing in mind the difference between the tonule and the chromatic part-tone.

ST. BRIDES, 92. Let the teacher point out the

"characters" of LAH, ME, and TE, when he gives the first pattern, and let the chord of DOH be carefully and firmly taken before the pupil attempts the tune.

WINCHFIELD, 93. The last verse of song 135 should be sung with a full and cheerful voice.

GEORGIA, 94. Be careful that the time is perfectly kept, and let the "minor" passage be so accurately and thoroughly taught that *every member* of the class shall sing it as familiarly as the rest of the tune. Else it becomes "a tune with a hitch."

COSSACK'S LAMENT, 95. This exquisite tune may be sung to the hymn which begins "Sweet the moments, rich in blessing," or to other appropriate words of the same metre.

COTTINGHAM, 96. The hymn beginning "Lord we come before thee now" will suit this tune. The transition into the minor of the FAH key should be tastefully patterned.

FARNWORTH, 98. This exceedingly beautiful tune requires most minute attention to time and accent.

IRISH AIR, 99. Execute carefully the complex rhythm of Air and Second occurring in several places. Let the tune and *the pauses* be well watched.

PLEYEL, 100. Another most elegant and tasteful melody, requiring minute attention to *time* and *pause*.

SEVILLE, 101. An exercise in time.

PATRIOT, 102. A fine enthusiastic German Melody, requiring delicate performance both in reference to time and accent. The continuance of a note, from a soft pulse into a stronger pulse, as is the case with LAH and SOH in the second line, is called SYNCOPATION. See "Music Simplified," p. 31.

---

92. ST. BRIDES, S. M.   LAH KEY, DO IS C.   M. 50.

```
{ :l | m :l.t | d¹ :t  | l :d¹ | s :d¹.r¹ | m¹ :r¹ | d¹ :m¹ | r¹ :d¹
{ :d | d :d.r | m :r   | d :m  | m :m.f   | s :f   | m :m   | ne :l

{ t :l  | s :f   | m :m¹ | l :r¹ | d¹ :t  | l ||
{ m :f  | t₁ :r  | d :m  | f :r  | m :ne  | l ||
```

---

93. WINCHFIELD. (s. m. 122, s. s. 135, 110.) LAH KEY, DO IS B flat. M. 80.

```
{ :m₁     | l₁ :-.l₁ ı t₁.d :r.t₁ | d :-.r ı d :m   | r :d ı t₁.d :r.t₁
{ :m₁.r₁  | d₁ :-.d₁ ı r₁.m₁ :f₁.r₁ | m₁ :-.f₁ ı m₁ :s₁ | f₁ :m₁ ı r₁.m₁ :f₁.r₁

{ d :— ı— :m    | r :-.d ı t₁ :r  | d :-.t₁ ı l₁ :d  | t₁ :l₁ ı l₁ :ne₁
{ m₁ :— ı— :s₁  | f₁ :-.m₁ ı r₁ :f₁ | m₁ :-.r₁ ı d₁ :m₁ | r₁ :d₁ ı d₁ :t₂

{ l₁ :— ı— ||
{ d₁ :— ı— ||
```

---

94. GEORGIA.   (s. m. 121, s. s. 164.)   KEY G.   M. 120.

```
{ s :— ı m :-.f  | s :— ı d :—   | r.m :f.s ı f :m  | r :— ı— :—
{ m :— ı d :-.r  | m :— ı d :—   | s₁ :— ı t₁ :d    | t₁ :— ı— :—

{ m.f :s.l ı s :s  | d¹ :— ı s :—  | m.r :d.r ı m :r  | d :— ı— :—
{ d.r :m.f ı m :m  | m :— ı d :—   | s₁ :— ı— :f₁     | m₁ :— ı— :—
```

{ |m.r :m.f ı m :m | r :— ı d :— | f :m ı r :d | t₁ :— ı— :—
{ |d.t₁ :d.r ı d :l₁ | l₁ :ne₁ ıl₁ :— | r :d ı t₁ :l₁ | ne₁ :— ı— :—

                                                              D. C.
{ |l.ne :l.t ı l :t | d¹ :— ı l :— | t.l :s.l ı t :l | s :— ı— :— ‖
{ |d.t₁ :d.r ı d :t₁ | l₁ :— ı tu₂ :— | s₁.l₁ :t₁.d ı r :d | t₁ :— ı— :— ‖

95.   COSSACK'S LAMENT. 8.7.   LAH KEY, DO IS C.   M. 50.

{ |l :l | l.d¹ :t.l | ne :ne | ne.t :l.ne | l :l | l.d¹ :t.l | m¹ :ne
{ |d :d | d.m :r.d | t₁ :t₁ | t₁.r :d.t₁ | d :d | d.m :r.d | d :t₁

{ |l :— | d¹ :d¹ | d¹.m¹ :r¹.d¹ | t :t | t.r¹ :d¹.t | l :. | l.d¹ :t.l
{ |d :— | m :m | m.s :f.m | r :r | r.f :m.r | d :d | d.m :r.d

{ |m¹ :ne | l :— ‖
{ |d :t₁ | d :— ‖

96.   COTTINGHAM. 7s.   KEY A.   M. 96.

{ |m :— :r | d :— :t₁ | d :— :r | m :— : | s :— :f
{ |s₁ :— :f₁ | m₁ :— :f₁ | m₁ :s₁ :t₁ | d :— : | m :— :r

{ |m :— :r | d :— :t₁ | d :— : | r :— :m | f :— :f
{ |d :s₁ :f₁ | m₁ :— :r₁ | m₁ :— : | f₁ :— :s₁ | l₁ :— :l₁

{ |m :r :ŋi₁ | r :— : | f :— :m | l :— :s | f :m :r
{ |s₁ :f₁ :m₁ | f₁ :— : | l₁ :— :s₁ | f₁ :— :m₁ | f₁ :s₁ :f₁

{ |d :— ‖
{ |m₁ :— ‖

97.   WINDSOR, C. M.   LAH KEY, DO IS C.   M. 50.

{ :l | l :t | d :t | l :l | ne :d | m¹ :r¹ | d¹ :t | d¹ :d¹
{ :d | d :r | m :r | d :d | t₁ :m | s :f | m :r | m :m

{ |m¹ :r¹ | d¹ :t | l :t.l | ne :d¹ | t :l | l :ne | l ‖
{ |d :r | m :r | d :r | m :m | m :f | m :r | d ‖

98.   FARNWORTH, S. M.   KEY A.   M. 80.

```
{ :d  | m  :r  :m.f,s | s.f :m  :r | d  :— :d | r.,d :t₁ :d | r.,m :f  :m
{ :m₁ | s₁ :— :s₁    | s₁.l₁:s₁ :f₁ | m₁:— :m₁ | f₁.,m₁:r₁ :m₁ | f₁.,s₁:l₁ :d

{ | m  :r  :r  | m  :r  :d | s  :—.f :m | f.,s :f  :m | m  :r  :r·
{ | d  :t₁ :t₁ | d  :t₁ :d | s₁ :t₁ :d | r  :— :d   | d  :t₁ :s₁

{ | m.,f :m.r :d.s | s.f :m  :r | d  :—  ‖
{ | s₁.,l₁:s₁.f₁:m₁ | m₁.f₁:s₁ :f₁ | m₁ :—  ‖
```

99.   IRISH AIR.   (s. m. 58, s. s. 116, 46.)   KEY F.   M. 80.

```
{ :d | s :—.l :s :m | l :—.t :d¹ :—.l | s :m :r :—.m | d :— ı :s
{ :d | m :—.f :m :d | f :—.r :m :—.f | m :d :d :t₁ | d :— ı :f

{ | d¹ :—.t :d¹ :r¹ | d¹ :t :l :s | l :—.s :d¹ :m | s :— ı :s
{ | m :—.r :m :f   | m :s :f :m  | f :—.m :d :d | t₁ :— ı :f

{ | d¹ :—.t :d¹ :r¹ | d¹ :t :l :s | l :s :f :m | l :— ı :t
{ | m :—.r :m :f   | m :s :f :m  | f :m :r :d | f :— ı :r

{ | d¹ :—.t :l :s | l :—.t :d :.l | s :—.m :r :—.m | d :— ı— ‖
{ | m :—.s :f :m | f :—.r :m :.f | m :d :d :t₁ | d :— ı— ‖
```

100.   PLEYEL.   (s. m. 105, s. s. 160, 117.)   KEY F.   M. 80.

```
{ :s | s :—.d¹ :s :—.m | s.f :f.m :r :.r | d :r :m.d :s.m | m :r ı :.s
{ :m | m :—.m :m :—.d | m.r :r.d :t₁ :.t₁ | d :t₁ :d :d | d :t₁ ı :.m

{ | s :—.d¹ :s :—.m | s.f :f.m :r :.f | m.d¹ :l.f :m :r | d :— ı :.m
{ | m :—.m :m :—.d | r :d :t₁ :.r | d :—.l₁ :s₁ :f₁ | m₁ :— ı :.d

{ | r :—.m :f :—.l | s :—.m :d :.m | r :—.m :f :—.l | l :s ı :.s
{ | t₁ :—.d :r :—.t₁ | d :—.d :d :.d | t₁ :—.d :r :—.f | f :m ı :.m

{ | d¹ :—.s :m :—.s | s.f :f.m :r :.f | m.d¹ :l.f :m :r | d :— ı— ‖
{ | m :—.m :d :—.d | t₁ :d :s₁ :.r | d :—.l₁ :s₁ :f₁ | m₁ :— ı— ‖
```

101. SEVILLE. (s. m. 95, s. s. 165, 51.) KEY A. M. 138.

$$\left\{ \begin{array}{l} .s_1 \mid s_1.d \quad :t_1 \quad :-.d \mid r.,r \quad :m,r.d \quad :d.t_1 \mid l_1 \quad :-.s_1 :l_1.t_1 \mid d \quad :- \quad : .s_1 \\ .m_1 \mid m_1.m_1 :f_1 \quad :-.m_1 \mid s_1.,s_1 :s_1,f_1.m_1 :m_1.s_1 \mid f_1 \quad :-.m_1 :f_1.r_1 \mid m_1 \quad :- \quad : .m_1 \end{array} \right.$$

$$\left\{ \begin{array}{l} s_1.d \quad :t_1 \quad :-.d \mid r.,r \quad :m,r.d \quad :d.t_1 \mid l_1 \quad :-.s_1 :l_1.t_1 \mid d \quad :- \quad : .d \\ m_1.m_1 :f_1 \quad :-.m_1 \mid s_1.,s_1 :s_1,f_1.m_1 :m_1.s_1 \mid f_1 \quad :-.m_1 :f_1.r_1 \mid m_1 \quad :- \quad : .m_1 \end{array} \right.$$

$$\left\{ \begin{array}{l} d.,r \quad :m.s \quad :f.m \mid r.d \quad :m \quad :f \mid s \quad :- \quad : .s_1 \mid d.,r \quad :m.s \quad :f.m \\ m_1.,f_1 :s_1.d :t_1.d \mid s_1.d :d \quad :d \mid t_1 \quad :- \quad : .f_1 \mid m_1.,f_1 :s_1.d :t_1.d \end{array} \right.$$

$$\left\{ \begin{array}{l} r.d \quad :m \quad :r \mid d \quad :- \quad : . \\ s_1.d :d \quad :t_1 \mid d \quad :- \quad : . \end{array} \right. \Big\|$$

102. PATRIOT. (s. m. 96, s. s. 147.) KEY C. M. 160.

$$\left\{ \begin{array}{l} .s :l.t \mid d^1 \quad :-.m \mid s.f \quad :m.r \mid d \quad :- \quad | \quad :d^1. \mid d^1.,l :l \quad |- \quad :d^1 \\ .m :f.r \mid m \quad :-.d \mid m.r \quad :d.t_1 \mid d \quad :- \quad | \quad :s \mid l.,f :f \quad |- \quad :l \end{array} \right.$$

$$\left\{ \begin{array}{l} d^1.,s :s \quad |- \quad :d^1 \mid t_1 \quad :-.t_1 \mid d^1 \quad :-.d^1 \mid r^1 \quad :-.t \mid s \quad :s \mid d^1 \quad :-.d^1 \mid r^1 \quad :-.r^1 \\ s,m :m \quad |- \quad :m \mid f \quad :-.f \mid m \quad :-.m \mid r \quad :-.r \mid r \quad :f \mid m \quad :-.m \mid s \quad :-.s \end{array} \right.$$

$$\left\{ \begin{array}{l} m^1 \quad :-.d \mid s \quad :s \mid m^1 :-.r^1 \mid f^1.m^1 :r^1.d^1 \mid l \quad :- \quad | \quad .l :d^1.l \mid s.d^1 :d^1.m^1 \mid m^1.r^1 :d^1.t \\ d^1 \quad :-.s \mid m \quad :m \mid s \quad :-.f \mid l.s \quad :f.m \mid f \quad :- \quad | \quad .f :l.f \mid m \quad :m.s \mid s.f \quad :m.r \end{array} \right.$$

D. S. and F.

$$\left\{ \begin{array}{l} d^1 \quad :- \quad | \quad . \\ m \quad :- \quad | \quad . \end{array} \right. \Big\|$$

EXAMINATION OF PUPILS ON THE THIRD STAGE.

SECTION VII.

1. What is the general character common to TE and RAY, and how are they distinguished, in this respect? How do you distinguish the "independence" of RAY and LAH?

2. How do you distinguish TE and RAY from FAH and LAH in respect to their emotional effect? By what names are TE and RAY called?

3. What is the character which these notes, quickly sung, help to give to the tune in which they are placed?

• Give illustrations of RAY.

• I will give you DOH, and you shall strike the lower RAY.

• I will figure a tune, and you shall tell me which numbers fall on RAY.

• Give illustrations of TE from the exercises.

• Strike the upper TE to my DOH.

* While I figure a tune, notice which numbers fall on TE, and tell me.

4. What are the best consonances with RAY?—with TE?

What is Col. Thompson's theory concerning these notes? In what cases is the grave form of RAY (r') naturally used by the voice?

If the scale is divided into fifty-three degrees—how many degrees are there in each tonule?—how many in the greater tone?—how many in the smaller tone? Where are the smaller tones?—where the greater?

Wherein appears the imperfection of "keyed instruments"?

5. Which notes are most used at the close of a line, in music?—which are next in frequency?—and which are least used in this position? Give examples of FAH at the close of a line—of TE.

Describe the character of each line of music in BATTISHILL. What notes does the tune specially illustrate?

Where, in FAIRFIELD, do you notice that reply of line to line which consists chiefly of rhythmical resemblance?

Write your own description of the manner of "reply" in ST. CLAIR, and CHARMOUTH, describing also the general character of each tune.

What is the general character of the tune SOLOMON, and what its special points of beauty?

Where do you notice the rhythmical resemblance of lines in CALLCOTT, and what is the character of the melody?

Mention anything remarkable in the tunes HANOVER, VALLIS VALE, and KETTERING.

Describe the responses of SAMSON, and WELLS.

What points are worthy of observation and study in BINFIELD HEATH, and OAKHILL?

In what manner should the rhythm of a chant be first practised, and what are the advantages of a rhythmical division of the reciting note?

* Follow my "pointing" in a "voluntary," including *skips* on RAY and TE, as well as on the other notes.

* Pitch (striking C¹ from memory) and solfa from the book, any of the exercises I may choose from those you have learnt in this section.

* Be prepared to "figure," without mistake, at least two-thirds of them.

* Be prepared to "point," on the modulator, from memory, a similar number.

* Write, from memory, any five or six of them.

SECTION VIII.

1. To what is the ear directed in "transition"? and what is noticeable in it *besides* the introduction of a new note?

2. To what note, as a new governing note, is the ear most commonly directed in transition?

What is the new note which distinguishes the key of SOH? where is it placed? and what note of the old key does it supersede?

What does ME become when the music changes to the SOH KEY? What does RAY become?—DOH? Do they change only in name?

* Draw a modulator representing two keys, the right hand one being the SOH KEY to the other.

* Give illustrations of transition into the SOH KEY.

* I will figure a tune, and you shall tell me which number falls on TU.

3. What other note does transition frequently choose as the new key note?

What is the new and "distinguishing" note of the FAH KEY? What is its position? and what note does it displace?

Into what note does the FAH KEY convert SOH?—LAH?—ME?—RAY? &c.

* Draw a modulator representing two keys, the left hand one being the FAH KEY to the other.

* Give illustrations of this transition.

* I will figure a tune, and you shall tell me which number falls on FI.

4. What is the signal of a "return" from the SOH KEY?—from the FAH KEY? Give examples of both.

5. What are the mental effects of TU and FI?

6. What is the interval of a "chromatic part-tone"?

How do you name a note which is raised a chromatic part-tone? How do you distinguish one which is lowered by the same interval? How do you distinguish FOI from TU? See note on "Delaborde."

What is the interval of the DIESIS?

7. Why is it necessary that transition should be taken from a "convertible" note or one common to both keys?

How should the convertible note be solfaed?

What is the effect of transition in one "part," of a piece of music, on the other "parts"?

Describe the "transition" and the "return" in MELCOMBE.

Describe the general character, the "replies" and the "transitions" of TYTHERTON.

What feelings is ST. ANNS best suited to express?

What are the points of contrast illustrated in PLAISTOW, and what is the character of its close?

What do you admire in EDGEWARE and BEETHOVEN?

Explain the "transition," and the "return" of BRUNSWICK. What is the character of FI? Write out the words from memory and mark them for expression.

Mention the points of beauty in SERENITY, ALMA, TRENT BRIDGE, FONTHILL, &c.

Describe the transitions in DR. BOYCE'S CHANT.

* Follow my "pointing" in a "voluntary," including TU, FI, FOI, &c.

* Be prepared to pitch, without a tuning fork, and to solfa from the book any of the exercises I may choose from those you have learnt in this section.

* Be prepared to "figure," at least, two-thirds of them.

* Be prepared to point on the modulator, from memory, a similar number.

* Write from memory any five or six of them.

SECTION IX.

1. *a.* In what respects does LAH predominate in certain tunes? In what respects does it *not* resemble a new key note?

b. What new notes do modern musicians introduce into such tunes, and with what design? What note does NE resemble in its effect?

c. By what name are LAH tunes generally known, and why were they so called?

What is the common theory of "minor" tunes?

What is the first *fact* elicited in reference to the *real nature* of these tunes? By what examples and authorities is it supported?

What is the second fact, and by what argument, illustration, and authority is it supported?

By what points of argument is the "LAH KEY" proved to be not essentially distinct from the "DOH KEY," but only a peculiar mode of using it? What is the one peculiarity of interval?

2. What are the three kinds of transition introduced by the LAH KEY, and what are their distinguishing notes?

* Sing me a "minor" phrase without NE—with NE.

* I will "figure" part of a tune, and you shall tell me which numbers fall on NE—NI.

* Follow my pointing in a "voluntary," including NE and NI.

* Be prepared to pitch, without an instrument, and solfa from the book any of the exercises I may choose from those you have learnt in this section.

* Be prepared to "figure," without mistake, at least two-thirds of them.

* Be prepared to point on the modulator, from memory, any that I may name.

* Write, from memory, any four of them.

What is meant by syncopation?

FOURTH STAGE.

SECTION X.

OF MELODY—ITS NATURE—ITS STYLES—ITS STRUCTURE. OF COPYING BY EAR, AND OF COMPOSITION.

1.   The proper succession of single musical sounds is called MELODY.

Some study of melody is absolutely essential to the good singer. "Although it is not necessary," says Mr. Charles Dawson, in the preface to his Analysis of Musical Composition, "that every performer should be a composer, it is certain that he who thoroughly understands, so as to be enabled to *scan,* the piece he has to perform, will execute it with much more *taste* and *feeling* than he who depends merely on various signs and marks [to tell him] when and where to give particular emphasis or expression: it is therefore desirable that *every* performer should be acquainted with the construction of the piece he has to execute, in order to give it due effect."

The composer is an artist, who, possessed of all the appliances of music, knows well how to group its pleasant sounds and arrange them in becoming procession. His aim in doing this, if he be a true artist, is to excite in the mind, as his music comes before it, ideas great and good and beautiful.

L

But the composer can seldom be also his own performer. He must be content to send forth his thoughts in symbol, and to declare the emotions which inspired him by means of mechanical notation. He draws the bold outline and groups effectively the figures, but the light and the shade, the distance and the colour, the warmth and the life of the picture he must leave another artist to supply.

That other artist is *the singer*, or, in instrumental music, the performer. He, well skilled in the language with which music addresses the soul, is not only able to execute the high note or the low, but knows how to use the *loud* and the *soft*, the abrupt expression or the swell of sound, the retarded movement or that which is quick and impassioned, and to introduce those nameless beauties of utterance which give to music a spirit, a feeling, and a living power. The singer must enter into sympathy with the composer's mind;

he must take a full survey of the piece; he must catch the intention of its author and feel the sentiment which inspired him, and then, but not till then, he may know how to clothe the whole with the witching charms of song.

In the "hints and criticisms on tunes," in the preceding sections of this book, the study of melody has been kept in view. The pupil has been taught "how to observe" the chief points of beauty, and has been led on to admire and enjoy by sympathy with his teacher's manifested feelings. This section will lead him to a fuller knowledge of the subject and to larger enjoyment of the feasts of music. Those who wish to study melody thoroughly with a view to composition will be interested by "Hamilton's Catechism on Musical Ideas," "Callcott's Grammar," and Reicha's great "Treatise on Melody". But a habit of analyzing the melodies of the best masters will be more instructive than all.

2. It is important that the singer should learn to distinguish the STYLE and general character of a melody, that he may know how to sing it in a corresponding spirit and manner. The different styles of melody may be named thus—

a. THE DIGNIFIED MELODY. This melody is distinguished by the marked use of the notes DOH, ME, and SOH, (See SEC. v. 4,) and usually moves slowly and in the BINARY MEASURE, (See SEC. iii. 4,) but occasionally the bold notes may be so employed as to give a noble majesty even to the Trinary Measure, as in the well-known tune WAREHAM; and HANOVER, 60. The OLD HUNDREDTH, 25; LUTHER'S HYMN, 46; STEPHENS, 43; and ST. CLAIR, 51, are examples of this style. The following exercises may also be considered as belonging to this class, though they partake largely of the qualities of the next;—Ex. 27, 29, 45, 49, 56, 72.

b. THE EMOTIONAL MELODY. This melody introduces largely and emphatically the notes LAH, FAH, RAY, TE, according to their peculiar effects. (Compare SEC. vi. 2, 3, with SEC. vii. 2.) It moves somewhat slowly, and frequently uses the TRINARY MEASURE. (See SEC. iii. 5.) The tunes WEIMAR, 35; SOLOMON, 55; KETTERING, 62; PROSPECT, 20; OAKHILL, 70; and especially IRISH AIR, will furnish illustrations of this style.

c. THE ELEGANT MELODY. These terms are used to describe a melody which is not decidedly either "dignified" or "emotional," and equally removed from the next style to be mentioned. The largest number of tunes belong to this class. It uses every kind of note in its own manner, and not unfrequently employs the lighter measures—the QUATERNARY and the SENARY. (See SEC. iii. 6, 7.) MOZART, 23; SWALLOW, 24; TROUBADOUR, 34; ITALIAN HYMN, 37; FAIRFIELD, 50; CROSSCOMBE, 54; VALLIS VALE, 61; and NORWOOD, 64, are examples.

d. THE CONVERSATIONAL MELODY. This style of melody is usually rapid. It frequently repeats the same note in succession, and it adopts simple and flowing sequences. The Quaternary and Senary Measures are admirably suited to its purposes of light and rapid utterance. The following exercises are good specimens of this style. WINTER SONG, 16; JESSE, 21; THE SLUGGARD, 30; WOODLEIGH, 44; and BINFIELD HEATH, 69.

This classification nearly corresponds with the "Aria di portamento"—"Aria cantabile"—"Aria di mezzo caratere"—and the "Aria parlante" of the Italians. (See Hogarth's History of the Musical Drama.) The pupil should answer such questions as these. What is the "style" of Ex. 13, 15, 17, 19, 31, 32, 39, 41, 42, 65, and 67? What other examples do you know of the Dignified Melody?—of the Emotional?—of the Elegant?— of the Conversational?

3. The student should next observe the parts into which a melody is divisible.

a. It may be easily noticed that, at short distances throughout a tune, there constantly occur certain places of rest for the mind, which, like the points where the stops are placed in ordinary language, divide the musical sense into distinct portions, containing ideas more or less complete. HANOVER, 60—one of the very finest specimens of melody we have (See p. 42)—will show how a good tune naturally divides itself into distinct melodial members. The marks ∧ ☐ or ○ are placed over the last note of each member. Let the learner sing to the figures 1, 2, 3, 4, 5; or 1, 2, 3, 4, 5, 6, each member separately, and notice how distinct it is, and yet how beautifully related to the rest.

:s₁ |d :d :r |m̂ :— :s |d :r :t₁ |d̄ :— :r |m :r :d |t̂₁ :— :d |r :d.t₁ :l₁ |s̄₁ :—
:t₁ |d :r :m|d̂ :l₁ :f |m :r :d |s̄ :— :s₁|l₁ :t₁ :d |r̂ :s₁ :m |l₁ :r   :t₁ |d̄ :—

The closing notes of each melodial member are called a CADENCE. The cadence is considered more or less "perfect" according to the kind of note which falls on *its last strong pulse.* Thus DOH, SOH, and ME, will suggest, according to their characters, (See SEC. v. 2) the more perfect close; and RAY and TE (See SEC. vii. 5) the less perfect. FAH and LAH would indicate a cadence less perfect still. The cadences of HANOVER occur in the following order—ME, DOH; TE, SOH; DOH, SOH; RAY, DOH; affording a delightful variety of closes. The fifth and seventh cadences are still further varied by the addition of supplemental notes on the weaker part of the measure.

b. The smallest of the portions into which Melody divides itself is called a PHRASE. It contains some simple melodial "design," and seldom occupies more than two measures. The notes :s₁ | d :d :r | m :— form the first phrase of HANOVER. The mark ∧ is used to show the close of a phrase.

c. Two or more phrases combine to form a SECTION. The section contains some complete musical idea, and is closed by a more conclusive cadence than that of the phrase. The closing phrase of a SECTION may be called the cadence-phrase. This mark ☐ is used to denote the close of a section, as in the tune HANOVER above. The close of a SECTION implies that of its cadence-phrase, and it was, therefore, unnecessary to repeat the sign ∧ .

d. Several sections united form a PERIOD, in which the musical sense is yet more fully developed. The PERIOD usually closes with a cadence, which from its nature and position in the tune, is yet more decided than that of the simple section. That section which bears the cadence of the PERIOD is called the cadence-section. The close of a PERIOD is indicated by the mark ○, which also

implies the close of a section and a phrase. The tune HANOVER, above, mani-
festly divides itself into two distinct PERIODS, each containing two SECTIONS,
each of which are formed by two PHRASES. These points will be more fully
illustrated under the next proposition.

4. The mutual relationship of the several members of a melody will now
claim attention.

a. The various members—the Phrases, Sections, and Periods—of every good
melody are observed to obey some symmetrical arrangement, in respect to the
number of Measures contained in each; and there is sometimes a correspondence
between particular measures in the manner in which their notes are apportioned.
This SYMMETRY OF RHYTHM may be easily illustrated by examples.

CALLCOTT, 56, (See page 41) is composed of two Periods, each containing
two Sections, each of which have two Phrases—all of equal length. The
quickened movement of the notes falls on corresponding measures in the opening
Section of each Period, and again in the Cadence-section of each Period. Let
the pupil verify this by "figuring" the tune.

$$:d \mid d \ :r \mid \hat{m} \ :s \mid s.f \ :m.r \mid \overset{\square}{m} \ :s \mid f \ :m \mid d^1.t \ :l.s \mid f \ :m \mid \overset{O}{r}$$

$$:m \mid m \ :f \mid \hat{s} \ :s \mid f.m \ :l.s \mid \overset{\square}{t} \ :t \mid d^1 \ :r^1 \mid \overset{\wedge}{m^1}.d^1 :s.l \mid m \ :r \mid \overset{O}{d}$$

FAIRFIELD, 50, (See p. 41) contains four Periods, the first, second, and fourth
of which are the same. The third Period is an elegant though distant variation
of the first, but sufficiently reminds the ear of the first by its similar distribution
of notes on the cadence-section. Moreover, it will be noticed that the first
Phrase of each alternate SECTION is so brief, and contains so small a musical
design, as scarcely to need distinction. The symmetrical order of the tune is
then as follows :—

$$:s \mid d^1 \ :s \mid \hat{l} \ :t \mid d^1 \ :t.l \mid s \ :f \mid \hat{m} \ :s.f \mid m \ :r \mid \overset{O}{d} \quad \text{D. C. and F.}$$

$$:d^1 \mid t \ :d^1 \mid \overset{\wedge}{r^1} \ :t \mid d^1 \ :r^1 \mid m^1 :d^1 \mid \hat{t} \ :r^1.d^1 \mid t \ :l \mid \overset{O}{s} \quad \text{D. C.}$$

BURNETT, 67, will afford an illustration in the Trinary Measure. It has, like
the last tune, two Periods, of two Sections each, and in every alternate Section
the Phrases are of unequal length. Moreover, the small Phrases have suppli-
mental notes to their simple Cadence, and the Cadence-sections of each Period
are alike.

$$:s_1 \mid d \ :— \ :r \mid \hat{m} :— \ :d \mid t_1 \ :r \ :f \mid m :— \ :d \mid \overset{\wedge}{l_1} :r \ :d \mid t_1 \ :l_1 \ :s_1 \mid \overset{O}{d} :—$$

$$:d \mid t_1 \ :-.l_1 \ :s_1 \mid \hat{d} :— \ :d \mid r \ :t_1 \ :s_1 \mid d :— \ :d \mid \overset{\wedge}{l_1} :r \ :d \mid t_1 \ :-.l_1 :s_1 \mid \overset{O}{d} :—$$

ST. CLAIR, 51, (See p. 41) and TYTHERTON, 73, will show a somewhat different
arrangement of members, though still symmetrical. Only the third line has a
full Phrase. Study also the well-known tune IRISH. ST. CLAIR may be divided
thus :—

$$:d^1 \mid \hat{s} \ :l \mid r \ :s \mid \overset{\square}{m} \ :s \mid \hat{l}.t \ :d^1 \mid t \ :l \mid \overset{O}{s}$$

$$s \mid t \ :t \mid \overset{\wedge}{d^1} :d^1 \mid l \ :r^1 \mid \overset{\square}{t} \ :r^1 \mid \overset{\wedge}{m^1} :d^1 \mid r^1 \ :t \mid \overset{O}{d^1}$$

MOZART, 23, contains three Periods, of which the third is the same as the first. Let the student compare its various members. He will notice that some of the Phrases almost subdivide themselves into yet smaller melodial designs.

|m :— :— ıf :m :f |s :— :d¹ ıd̂¹ :— :— |d :— :— ır :d :r |m :f :m ır :— :—

|m :— :— ıf :m :f |s :— :d¹ ıd̂¹ :— :— |m :— :— ır :d :r |d :—:—ı—:— F.

:s |s :— :f ır :m :f |s :— :m ıd̂ :— :s |s :— :f ır :m :f |s :—:m ıd :—

:s |l :— :f ıd¹:—:l |s :— :m ıd̂¹ :—: |s :l :s ıs :f :m|m :—:—:ır :— D. C.

The WINTER SONG, 16, in which the second Phrase of each Cadence-section blends almost inseparably with that which precedes it, may be divided thus :—

:s, | d :d :d ıd̂ :— :d | r :r :r ır :— :r | m :r :d ıd :t, :d | r :— :s, ıs, :—

:s, | d :d :d ıd̂ :— :d | r :r :r ır :— :f | m :f :m ır :d :r | d :— :d ıd :—

PROSPECT, 20, is constructed thus :—

|m :m :m ıf̂ :— :f |s :f :m ır :m :f |s :d :f ım :— :r |d̂ :— D. C. and F.

:s |s :m :s ıd̂¹ :— :s |s :m :s ıs :— :s |l :— :s ıf :— :m |m :—:— ır :— D. C.

LAUSANNE, 31, with its "repeats," is divided by Mr. Dawson into four "Sentences" or *Sections*, of two Phrases each, the first Phrase being | m :-.f ıs :s |1 :1 ıs :— but according to Hamilton, (Catechism of Counterpoint Melody and Composition, page 58) this short member contains two Phrases, and the whole should be divided into four *Periods* of two Sections each. Let the pupil decide which is the proper division.

The pupil should answer the questions proposed at the end of this "stage" of the book.

b. The corresponding parts of a good Melody are observed to hold a certain relationship of musical expression, the one to the other. One member will remind the ear of some preceding member in such a manner as, by that means, to heighten its own effect. When one Phrase or Section is viewed as suggesting all the variations and "replies" which follow, it is called the SUBJECT, or *Theme*. These various "responses" of Melody, when well arranged, form the SYMMETRY OF MUSICAL EXPRESSION.

WELLS, 65, (See p. 42) affords a beautiful illustration of this topic. Let the pupil sing it, line by line, to the figures. This he should always do when wishing to compare the whole effect of one member of a Melody with that of another, for the solfa syllables would rather distract his attention to the special effect of particular notes, while the figures greatly assist him in marking "the symmetry of rhythm."

|s :m :f |ŝ :— :d¹ |r¹ :d¹ :t |d̂¹ :—:— |l :d¹ :l |ŝ :— :m |s :f :m |r :—:—

|s :m :f |ŝ :— :d¹ |r¹ :d¹ :t |d̂¹ :—:— |l :d¹ :l |ŝ :— :m |l :-.s :f.m|r :—:—

|r¹:— :t |d̂¹:— :s |m¹:r¹ :d¹|d̂¹ :— :t |d¹:t :l |ŝ :— :m |f :— :r |d :—:—

It is easy to observe how the second Phrase answers to the first. The one may be called the "consequent," the other the "antecedent." In the same manner, the whole of the second *Section* gives a beautiful variation and a response to the first—the first Phrase of the one having its antecedent in the first Phrase of the other, and the Cadence-phrase of the one replying to that of the other. With corresponding symmetry the second *Period* answers to the first, being indeed but slightly varied from it; and the third Period, though varied widely, still keeps the first in mind, and produces its brilliant and beautiful effect by the help of an implied contrast, as it passes along, with each member of the preceding Periods.

Next, let the student, after noticing, for instance, the beautiful reply of the second *Section* to the first—turn off his mind, for a moment, to some tune entirely foreign to this—then suddenly returning, let him strike at once the second Section alone, and ask himself—Is it so beautiful as it was? The ready answer will be 'No,' for it has lost its antecedent, and it is evident, now, that the memory of the antecedent accompanies the consequent, and, in a good Melody, heightens its effect.

The first Phrase of this tune, like that of HANOVER, may be said to be the SUBJECT or *Theme* of all the rest.

For the purpose of expressing and comparing the development of musical ideas in different tunes, it may be found convenient to represent the first *complete idea*, or the first *Section*, by *a*, and the next, which is ordinarily a reply to it, by *b*. If the Sections which follow exhibit a new and progressive development, they may be represented by *c, d, e*, &c.; but if they seem to look back and reply to *a*, or *b*, let them be represented thus—a^2, b^2, a^3, b^3, &c. The musical relation of the Sections in WELLS, might be expressed as follows—*a b ; a b² ; a² b²*.

LUTHER's HYMN, 46, unfolds its majestic melody in a different manner. It has three Periods, of which the first two are alike;—the third is lengthened and contains three Sections. The melodial replies may be thus exhibited—*a b ; a b ; a² a³ b*. Let the pupil verify this assertion, as well as those which follow, by himself, "figuring" the tunes and listening to their replies. Such an exercise will cultivate and greatly improve his perception and enjoyment of the beauties of Melody.

HANOVER, CALLCOTT, ST. CLAIR, OLD HUNDREDTH, BATTISHILL, and ALMA, have replies according to the following formula—*a b ; a² b²*.

MOZART has the two Sections of its second Period so varied that, while their relation to the original theme is readily perceived, they do not refer distinctly to either of the preceding Sections, but rather carry the mind forward in an entirely new development. Its replies may therefore be thus expressed—*a b ; c d ; a b*. There are Sections in LAUSANNE, 31; OLD BASING, 32; FAIRFIELD, 50; CROSSCOMBE, 45; OAKHILL, 70, and SWALLOW, 24, which tempt us to indicate them in a similar manner.

CHARMOUTH, 52, seems to develope itself entirely by *direct progression*, thus— *a b ; c d*. And PATRIOT, 102, may have its musical relationships thus described —*a b ; c d ; e a²*.

SERENITY, 81, and FARNWORTH, 98, present their responses in a yet different order, thus—$a\,b$; $b^2\,a^2$; or, as some may prefer to express it, thus—$a\,b$: $c\,a^2$.

VALLIS VALE, 61—$a\,b$; $a\,b$; $a^2\,b^2$; $a^2\,b^3$.

ITALIAN HYMN, 37—$a\,b$; $a\,b^2$; $a^2\,b^3$; $a\,b^2$.

IRISH AIR, 99—$a\,b$; $a^2\,b^2$; $a^2\,b^3$; $a^3\,b$.

PLEYEL, 100—$a\,b$; $a\,b^2$; $a^2\,a^3$; $a^4\,b^2$.

BINFIELD HEATH, 69—$a\,b$; $a^2\,b^2$; $b^3\,b^4$.

BURNETT, 67, and COSSACK'S LAMENT, 95—$a\,b$; $a^2\,b$.

PORTLAND, 89, like LUTHER'S HYMN, has an *extended Period* of three Sections. It seems to reply thus—$a\,b\,b^2$; $c\,c^2$.

ENDLESS PRAISES, 19, has a Period which is rhythmically *contracted*. It is arranged—$a\,b$; $a^2\,b^2$; $a^3\,b^3$.

The pupil, having thoroughly examined for himself and disputed or attested all these assertions, will find a new world of beauty opened to him in music, and will be the better prepared, by the improvement of his *perceptive* faculty, for the exercises of "musical reporting" and *musical construction*, which follow. He should not be contented, however, until he has fully satisfied the teacher's demands in such exercises as the following. "Find a tune which has a similar musical relation between its members to that of *Wells—Callcott—Mozart—Serenity*, &c." "Write the formula which expresses the symmetry of musical expression in Exercises 27, 28, 29, 39, 45, 55, 62, 72, 75, 77, 85, 86, 87, &c." He should also examine some of the notes on pages 41 and 42.

Col. Thompson very beautifully traces the connection of these various phrases, sections, and periods—the greater and lesser "waves of melody"—with the general subject of rhythm. "Whoever has been rocked in a boat upon what, in plain prose, may be called the "ocean waves," will have been conscious that besides the petty furrows which lifted its head and stern alternately in a time approaching to the vibrations of a church pendulum, there was a larger swell of which the others were but inconsiderable parts, and even a mightier still, of which this second was but a limb and portion. Something like this appears to be the nature of the undulations of musical notes. There is a great swell and a little one, and both of them contribute to the general effect. The examination may therefore on this principle be conducted in two directions;—first, to enquire what quantity of minor undulations may be within the compass of a bar (or "measure")—and secondly, to ask whether bars themselves may not be fractions of greater undulations, and whether out of these again may not be constituted undulations of higher orders in succession, to an extent that can only be measured by the skill of the performer, and probably also by the cultivated sensitiveness of the hearer. Any person who will attend critically to the execution of superior instrumental performers, will be surprised to find to what an extent this species of "linked sweetness" may be traced, and how large a number of bars may be formed into a connected whole, by means of the relations of what is here termed accent."—See Westminster Review, October, 1832.

5. The pupil will now be prepared to cultivate his power of musical perception still further, by learning to mark the proper qualities and relationships of notes, as they fall on the ear—and that so quickly and truly as to enable him to express the music either on paper, or by naming the notes, without further help. This exercise is called COPYING BY EAR, and may be pursued as follows.

a. Let the teacher first remind his pupils of the *general* rule, that tunes begin on DOH, ME, or SOH, and tell them that their success in "copying by ear" will depend on their skill in recognising the first two or three notes. Let him give them a certain sound for the key note and allow them to strike the chord, and then let him "figure" the opening phrase of some simple tune, requiring the pupils immediately to name the notes. If they err, let them take the chord again, and again try. In correcting mistakes, the teacher will often have to remind his pupils of the qualities of notes and of various points of melodial beauty, which they may have neglected to perceive. In the same manner the teacher may proceed with the opening phrases of other tunes—giving the chord, singing with the figures, and requiring the pupils to name the notes.

b. The teacher may now give only the key note, while the pupils take the chord *mentally.* He may figure, moreover, a whole section, requiring the pupils to name the notes; or he may figure some short tune throughout several times, giving the pupils an opportunity to write the notes on their "solfa music paper" and to correct them. The Chants in SEC. xiii. will be useful for this purpose. When these exercises have been frequently tried and with success—

c. The learner should try to recognise the notes of a tune without having the key note given. For this purpose he should first copy by ear, from the teacher's figuring, the opening Phrases of Melodies which, like Exercises 15, 20, 27, 32, 34, 37, 49, 52, 55, &c., have their principal notes contained between the key note and its replicate. These Melodies are called by some of the old writers *Authentic Melodies.* The teacher might first select, for his figuring, tunes which the pupils have heard before, and afterwards those with which they were not familiar. Of the latter he should first try those which begin with the notes DOH TE, or SOH FAH ME, or ME FAH DOH SOH₁, or ME SOH.

d. The learner should proceed in the same manner with the opening Phrase of Melodies, which, like Exercises 13, 16, 17, 25, 28, 45, 50, 60, &c., have their principal notes contained between SOH and its replicate. These are called *Plagal Melodies.*

The pupil may now learn to copy the whole of a Melody in this way.

This exercise of copying by ear without having the key note is often difficult and uncertain, especially if only the air is heard, for the key may remain undecided through several measures. Thus in HARTS, if the listener were to take the first and second notes to be DOH, the third FAH, &c., he might continue, without finding his mistake, till he came to FAH in the second section. If in WINTER SONG he were to make the same mistake, he would not be corrected till he came to FAH at the opening of the last section. A little practice, however, would teach that few tunes begin with the interval DOH FAH. Again, if a listener were to suppose CHORLTON PLACE to begin on SOH, he might continue in his error until the TE at the close of the second section decided the key for him. But, on the other hand, tunes which begin with the notes DOH TE, like OLD HUNDREDTH, or SOH FAH ME, like MELCOMBE and GLOVER, or SOH ME, like BATTISHILL and SWALLOW, or ME FAH, like LAUSANNE and ITALIAN HYMN, or DOH¹ SOH like Ex. 18, are not easily mistaken.

6. "To invent and write down melodies is a very useful exercise for the musical student; for, though he may not have the ambition to become a composer, the practice will conduce greatly to his facility in reading and comprehending the music of others." (See Mainzer's Grammar.) The following cuorse of progressive exercises will assist the learner.

Exercises of this kind are very attractive. It is always pleasant to create and to construct. And a pupil cannot become thoroughly acquainted with the beauties of melodial rhythm and reply until he has himself tried the composer's work. The effort will compel him to *observe* the best models more carefully than he had hitherto done, for he will now observe for a purpose. It will also bring him into some sort of sympathy with the composer's mind. It is surprising how much better we understand an art as soon as we have fairly set our hands to work at it. It is worth our while to learn a little of drawing and colouring, (provided it be upon good principles) even though we should gain no other advantage than the increased facility of comprehending and enjoying the works of the great masters, which must be the result.

Composition is usually treated in connection with harmony as well as melody, and the pupil is required to construct phrases on certain *chords.* Thus Dr. Mainzer gives exercises on the tonic chord (DOH ME SOH)—then on the same with the addition of the dominant chord (SOH TE RAY)—and further exercises with the addition of the subdominant chord (FAH, LAH, DOH[1]). What is this, as far as melody alone is concerned, but saying—"First make a tune on three of the notes of the scale, next construct one with five, and then with all seven"?—and why these limitations? Mr. Dawson, who gives however some good hints on the subject, fixes, in the earlier exercises, a certain chord for each bar, and soon after like Dr.

Mainzer, by the help of "passing notes," transgresses his limitation very freely. Mr. Hamilton adopts a far more simple and natural method. The symmetry of musical "replies," in the structure of melody, is but lightly dwelt upon in these and other elementary works, but the reader will have perceived that it is an absolutely essential element of every good melody.

a. To construct a melody of a given Rhythmical form, and from a given Theme. Suppose the Rhythmical structure to be that which corresponds with the "common metre" of poetry—such an exercise might be set forth to the eye of the pupil in the following manner:—

:s₁ | d :r | m :d | : | ^ : | ^ : | : | O
: | : | ^ : | : | □ . | ^ : | : | O

The "subject" given above is a note more than the opening phrase of LANCASTER, 17. Two other beautiful tunes open with the same theme, but take a different cadence-phrase to the first section, and produce melodies of a very different character. They are as follows:— .

TIVERTON s₁ | d :r | m :d |l₁ :t | d :m | r :s₁.d | t₁ :l₁ | s₁ :r |d.t₁ :l₁.s₁ | d :r.m | f :m | r :d | s₁ :l₁.f | m :r | d ST. JAMES s₁ | d :r | m :d | r :f | m :m | l₁ :t₁ | d :l₁ | s₁ :r | m :d | f :m |l₁ :r | t₁ :s₁ | d :m | f :r | d The learner need not hope to produce very soon such exquisite melodies as these. Let him, however, make two or three more variations according to the formula, and be content, at first, with the lamest and humblest production. The following exercises, with illustrations, actually written by learners like himself, will perhaps be more encouraging.

Ex. 2. Develope the following theme according to the rhythmical structure stated.

| d :— | m :t₁ | d :— | :— | : | : | □ :
| :— | : | ^ : | :— | : | : | O :

Learners have produced from this the following melodies, which are given, not as models, but as illustrations. | d :— | m :t₁ | d :— | m :— | f.s :l |s :tu₁ | s :— | f :— | m :l | s :— | s :— | l.t :d¹ | d¹ :t | d¹ :— and | d :— | m :t₁ | d :— | l₁ :— | t₁ :d | r :d | t₁ :— | s :— | m :d | r :— | m :— | d :f | m :r | d :— For a *model*, see LIVERPOOL CHANT, 71.

Ex. 3. :s | f :m | r :f | m : | ^ : | : | O
: | : | ^ : | : | □ . | ^ : | : | O

This was treated by a learner thus— :s | f :m | r :f | m :s | d¹ :l |s :tu₁ | s :s | f :m | r :f | s :f | m :s | m¹ :r¹ | d¹ :t | d¹ and thus— :s | f :m | r :f | m :d | r :m | f :m | r :r | m :f |s :l | s :f | m :l | s :f | m :r | d but by Samuel Wesley (in the "Psalmist," 305,) thus— :s | f :m | r :f | m :t₁ | d :m | r :d |t₁ :s | f :m | r :d | r :m | f :m | m :r | d :t₁ | d

M

Ex. 4.   :d | r :t₁ | l̂₁ :s₁ | l₁ :t₁ | d̄ : | ∧ : | : |⁰

: | : | ∧ : | : | ⁰ : | ∧ : | : |⁰

Developed by a learner thus—   :d | r :t₁ | l₁ :s₁ | l₁ :t₁ | d :l₁ | r :d
| t₁ :l₁ | s₁ :s₁ | d :r | m :d | f :m | r :s | m :d | l₁ :t₁ | d   and
thus—   :d | r :t₁ | l₁ :s₁ | l₁ :t₁. | d :r | m :s | f :m | r :d
| r :t₁ | l₁ :s₁ | l₁ :t₁ | d :m | s :f | m :r | d   but, in an old
Gregorian Melody (Psalmist, 236,) thus—   :d | r :t₁ | l₁ :s₁ | l₁ :t₁
| d :l | s :d | f :m | r :r | f :m | f :r | d :t₁ | d :m | l₁ :f
| m :r | d

Ex. 5.   :s | m :s :d¹ | l :r¹ :t | d :— : | ∧ : : | : : | :

: | : : | ∧ : : | : : | ⁰ : : | ∧ : : | : : | :

Given, in exercises, thus—   :s | m :s :d¹ | l :r¹ :t | d¹ :— :s | l :s :f
| m :r :d | s :— :s | m :s :f | m :s :d¹ | l :r¹ :t | d¹ :— :m¹
| f¹ :r¹ :t | s :m :r | d :—   and thus—   :s | m :s :d¹ | l :r¹ :t
| d :— :m | m :m :s | l :s ·:tu₁ | s :— :r | f :l :r¹ | d¹ :t :s
| l :r¹ :d¹ | t :— :s | s :s :f | m :m :r | d :—   and thus—   :s
| m :s :d¹ | l :r¹ :t | d¹ :— :m¹ | m¹ :d¹ :m¹ | r¹ :t :l | s :— :s
| m :f :s | m :r :d | r :s :tu₁ | s :— :f | m :s :d¹ | l :r¹ :t
| d¹ :—   but by Samuel Wesley, (Psalmist, 101,) with a fine transition in the
third line, thus—   :s | m :s :d¹ | l :r¹ :t | d¹ :— :m¹ | r¹ :t :s
| l :d¹ :tu₁ | s :— :ˢr | f :m :r | d :— :d | m :r :d | t₁ :— :ˢd¹
| t :l :s | l.f :m :r | d :—

Ex. 6.   :s | l :t :d¹ | r¹ :l :t | d :—   to be developed in three
other sections (lines) of the same structure, as thus—   :s | l :t :d¹ | r¹ :l
:t | d¹ :— :m | f :m :f | s :f :m | r :— :s | s :f :m | m :r :d
| s :— :s | l :t :d¹ | r¹ :l :t | d¹ :—   or thus—   :s | l :t :d¹
| r¹ :l :t | d¹ :— :m¹ | r¹ :t :s | d¹ :t :l | s :— :s | l :t :d¹ | r¹
:l :t | d¹ :— :m¹ | f¹ :s¹ :l¹ | s¹ :m¹ :r¹ | d¹ :— &c. Samuel Wesley
(Psalmist, 296,) developes the same theme thus—   :s | l :t :d¹ | r¹ :l :t
| d¹ :— :d¹ | d¹ :r¹ :t | l :s :tu₁ | s :— :t | d¹ :t :l | t :d¹ :r¹
| d¹ :— :m¹ | r¹ :t :d¹ | s :m :r | d :—

The teacher will easily multiply exercises of this kind. It will be interesting
to compare the different manners in which the theme is developed by different
pupils.

   b. *To construct, from a given theme, several melodies, of different Rhythmical
structures, and of different "melodial replies."*
   Ex. 7. From the following theme | d :s | f :l | s :f | m :—   con-
struct a melody, having four sections of equal length, and another having also
four sections, but the second and fourth of which are contracted thus—

| : | ∧ : | ⁰ | Let the first reply thus— *a, b, c, d,* and the second thus—
a, b, a², b². This has produced the following melodies from learners— | d :s
| f :l | s :f | m :— | d.r :m | f :m.r | d :m | r :— | s :s | d¹ :t

|s :l.t | d¹ :— | r¹ :d¹.t |l :f | s :m | d :— and | d :s | f :l
|s :f | m :— | f :m | r :d | r :— | m :r | d :m | f :m | r :—
|s :f | m :r | d :—

Ex. 8. Take the phrase :d | m :d | s and construct upon it a
Long Metre tune, containing four sections of four measures each; a tune of six
lines, the first four of which contain six syllables and the last two eight; and a
chant of the same structure as Dr. Boyce's and the Liverpool Chant; as thus—
:d | m :d | s :s | l :t | d¹ :m¹ | r¹ :d¹ | t :d¹ | r¹.d¹ :t.l | s :m¹
| r¹ :d¹ | t :d¹ | r¹ :d¹ | t :s | m :d | s :d¹ | m¹ :r¹ | d¹ and
:d | m :d | s :f | m :s | l :s | l :t | d¹ :d¹ | m¹ :r¹ | m¹ :d¹
| t :m | f :m | r :s | d :d | m :d | s :m | s :f | m :m | f :m
| r :d | s :m | d and DOH | m :d | s :— SOH | f :m | r :d | r :—
DOH | l₁ ·:r | t₁ :— SOH | l :f | m :r | d :—

When exercises like these have been frequently practised, and the pupil is able
to construct melodies less clumsy than some of the illustrations above, he may
proceed—

c. *To invent a theme and to construct a melody upon it according to a given
model of rhythmical arrangement and musical reply, and in a given "style."*

Ex. 9. Construct a melody in the "elegant" or "middle" style, having three
periods, each formed according to the following structure—

 : | : : ı :̂ . | : : ı :□ : | : : ı ,:̂ : | : : ı : ○

and with replies, arranged thus— *a b; c d; a² b²;* thus— :s | s :l :s | s
:f :m | s :l :s | s :— :s | d¹ :t :d¹ | r¹ :d¹ :t | d¹ :t :l | s
:— :m | m :f :m | m :r :d | m :f :m | m :— :d | r :m :f | f
:m :r | m :r :r | r :— :s | s :l :s | s :f :m | s :l :s | s :—
:s | s :l :t | d¹ :s :m | f :m :r | d Is this correct? See the note
on Mozart, page 78.

Ex. 10. The same with this structure for each period.

 : | : ı :̂ | . ı :□ | : ı :̂ | : ı :○

Ex. 11. Write an "emotional" melody, of two periods, having the same
symmetry in Rhythm and Musical Expression with Solomon 55, but from a
different theme, and using the Plagal division of the Common Mode (the notes
between SOH₁ and SOH), instead of the Authentic. What notes should be
employed in prominent positions, to fill a melody with emotion? See page 74.
Something more, however, is required than the mere presence of certain notes—
their symmetrical and expressive arrangement.

:d | t₁ :l₁ | t₁ :—.d | r :—.d | t₁ :d | t₁ :l₁ | l₁ :s₁ | l₁
:d | r :m | f :—.m | f :—.m | r :m | d :l₁ | l₁ :s₁ | l₁

Ex. 12. Compose a similar melody in the same style, using the "authentic"
division of the scale.

Ex. 13. Compose two melodies, one in the Quaternary and the other in the
Senary Measures, with any arrangement of phrases, periods, sections, and replies,
you may prefer—but both in the Conversational Style. The pupils may search
for good themes in the works of great composers. Something more than the

theme of the following was taken from Handel—　　:s₁ | d :d :d ır :r :r
|m :— :r ıd :— :s₁ | d :r :d ıt₁ :l₁ :t₁ | d :r :d ıt₁ :— :d
|m :m :m ıf :f :f | s :— :f ım :— :s₁ | d :r :d ıt₁ :l₁ :t₁
|d :r :d ıt₁ :— :s₁ | d :d :s₁ ıd :d :s₁ | d :— :r ım :— :m
|s :f :m ır :d :m | s :f :m ır :— :s₁ | d :d :s₁ ıd :d :s₁
|d :— :r ım :— :s | d¹ :t :l ıs :f :m | m :— :— ır :— :—
|d :— :— ı— :—

d. To construct a melody which shall be adapted to express the sentiment of certain words which are given.

In introducing this kind of exercise, the teacher should take an example and "work it out" on the black board *with* his pupils, showing them each step of thought he takes, asking their advice or criticism, and encouraging them to help him. A few examples, thus dealt with, will enable the pupils to work alone. The examples chosen should be various and decided in character, such, for instance, as the words by Mrs. Hemans, "Oh! call my brother back to me, I cannot play alone"—or those by Mrs. Howitt, "How pleasant the life of a bird must be, Flitting about in each leafy tree"—or Cowper's "John Gilpin was a citizen, Of credit and renown," &c.

The first question proposed to the pupils should be—What general style of melody is suited to these words?—the Conversational? or the Emotional? or (as for the first mentioned example) a union of both styles?

Next it should be asked—What Measure will best correspond with the style chosen and the character of the words? Shall it be the Binary—for a bold or solemn expression? or the Trinary—for something soft or pleading? or shall it be the Binary intermingled with a sort of Trinary movement, as in the IRISH AIR? &c. &c.

These points being settled—what Rhythmical arrangement do the lines require? and what symmetry of reply will best suit the responses of thought? Shall it be a direct development, thus, *a, b; c, d;* or an alternate one, thus, *a b; a² b²,* &c. &c.

Again—Which notes of the scale does your style or the expression of particular words require to be well "brought out" and contrasted? The bold notes DOH ME SOH? or the more emotional LAH TE? &c. Do you wish them to be produced with brilliancy, or with a softer and more shaded expression? If with brilliancy, let the chosen note stand high in the division of the scale you use. If you wish its expression to be more shaded, pitch your key so that the effective note may fall on the lower part of the voice's compass. Thus, if you wish the note LAH to produce its peculiar effect with something of brilliancy, let your Melody be Plagal, and use the higher LAH for this purpose—if you simply desire for it a distinct and marked effect, make the Melody Authentic, the LAH standing at a lower pitch—and if you would have it more soft and solemn, use again a Plagal Melody, but the lower LAH.

When these things have been fairly discussed and clearly decided, it will remain for the class to try who can invent the most suitable theme. The invention must, of course, be a mental process. When each in turn has produced his theme, let the best be chosen, and then the development of the melody may be discussed line by line, by teacher and pupils together, and their joint production, as it appears on the black board, will, at least, be the fruit of much healthy and delightful mental effort.

Many of the melodies given in illustration above have much of clumsiness and inaccuracy, which should be marked and avoided. It was sufficient merit for them—to exhibit the kind of effort that was required, without discouraging competition by any marked excellence of their own.

Exercises in composition shackled by so many conditions as those given above, may not be the most gratifying to a young aspirant, but they will compel him to study the powers of particular notes and rhythmical combinations far more closely and usefully than any course less strict could have done, and they will thus prepare the diligent pupil for higher endeavours. Let him remember that that which is to the *learner* a matter of strenuous observation, careful process, and often unsatisfactory endeavour, becomes to the *practised man* a thing of intuition—a facile accomplishment. Let him not despise that toil of thought which alone can win for him refinement, facility, and power. On the other hand, let it not be supposed, that every one who can

make a little melody is at once a Composer. "To compose good melodies," says Mr. Hickson, (Singing Master, p. 94) "it is not sufficient to string musical phrases together, however scientifically. Good music must be written upon the same principle as good poetry. The heart must be made to speak. Poetry that consists of words or phrases, that appeals to no kindred feeling, or that awakens no strong emotion, is always of an inferior character; and so it is with music. A good composer will give himself up to the inspiration of his feelings. If writing music to words expressive of affliction, he will endeavour to feel like one afflicted. If the words be expressive of triumph, he will endeavour to call up in his mind the emotions of joy and exultation. According to his ability to do this, (and it is an art to be acquired) will be his power of producing works such as are commonly ascribed to genius alone. The passions will always find utterance; but the passionless cannot express the language of the passions."

SECTION XI.

OF THE DIFFERENT KINDS OF VOICES; OF SINGING IN PARTS; AND OF ENUNCIATION.

1. The voice of one individual differs from that of others in quality, in power, and in pitch. This difference is occasioned by peculiarities in the substance, strength, and form of the different vocal organs.

Those who would study this subject should examine the extended treatise on it in Müller's Physiology, Book iv. Sec. 3, or the admirable statement in the article "Larynx" of the Penny Cyclopædia, and, in addition, the lucid and most interesting paper by Sir Charles Bell in the "Philosophical Transactions," for the year 1832.

The chief instrument of voice is the Larynx, which we may feel, (with the hand outside) as a little lump, in the upper part of our throats, moving with almost every utterance of voice. It is a small tube placed at the top of the Trachea or wind-pipe. Its walls are of cartilage or gristle. Its upper opening is protected by a little valve, called the Epiglottis, which falls down upon it in every act of swallowing, and at the lower opening are two elastic membranes, one depending from

each side, which can be stretched to any degree of tension required, and can be made to meet each other through their whole length or through any part of it. Various muscles, attached to the walls of the Larynx, in obedience to nervous action and the mind's will, regulate these movements.

These elastic membranes, sometimes called the Vocal Chords, are the source of voice. During ordinary breathing they rest, relaxed, against the walls of the Larynx, but, in the production of voice, they are brought into such a position as to vibrate freely in the air as it ascends from the lungs, (much like the tongue of any reed-instrument)—and this vibration makes the breath vocal.

The PITCH of a note depends on the degree of *tension* given to the vocal membranes, and on the *length* of the parts which are left free to vibrate, just as in the harp, violin, and guitar. It is also affected by the *force* of the air-current, as is common in reed-instruments. It may be noticed that the Larynx rises for the production of high notes, to adapt the column of air above it to the pitch of the vibrating tongue, as is necessary in regulating the length of the various reed-organ-pipes. Hence in females and boys, whose voices are naturally higher than those of men, the Larynx is placed *higher in the throat,* and is also smaller, so as to make the vibrating membranes *shorter.* When a voice "*breaks,*" the Larynx gradually takes a lower place in the throat and also enlarges in size, so that the voice necessarily becomes deeper. Müller states that the vocal membrane in the male is half as long again as in the female—as three to one. To produce a given note, (say D below the staff) the male voice, especially if a Bass, would require strong tension of the vocal membranes, but the female voice would produce the same note with very little tension because its vocal membranes are shorter.

The TIMBRE, or *Quality* of a note—see p. 18— (which is so different in different individuals) depends on the quality and resonance of the fleshy material of which the organ is composed, much as the sounds of a musical box differ according to the substance on which the box may be placed, and as the 'timbre' of a violin is said to depend on the form and quality of the wood as well as on the nature of its strings. The quality of voice is also much affected by the form of the air passages above the Larynx. Thus we are sometimes able to imitate the voice of others not only in reference to its peculiarities of pitch and inflection, by movements of the larynx, but even in its 'timbre,' by certain conformations of the mouth.

The general STRENGTH of a voice appears to depend upon the vibrating power of the vocal membranes, the size of the organ, and the capacity of the chest. We know how easily a slight inflammation or other affection of the mucous membrane lining the larynx weakens the voice. The voices of old persons are made tremulous by the loss of nervous and muscular power.

The special FORCE or *loudness* given to an accented note may be occasioned, Müller thinks, by relaxing the tension of the vocal membranes while we increase the force of the air-current. Sir Chas. Bell speaks of the back of the mouth and the veil of the palate (the soft palate) as playing a most important part in giving the delicate impulses of accent.

Good MODULATION or correct *tune* requires a *mental* effort. "Man," says Müller, "like the singing bird, learns unconsciously the different internal changes in the state of the Larynx, and the different muscular actions necessary for each note. Sounds accidentally uttered, and the muscular actions which accompany them, become

associated in the sensorium, and afterwards readily excite each other when a melody is to be imitated." Correct tune, therefore, depends upon the skill with which the sound is perceived and its "idea" retained, and upon the accuracy with which the mind can *command* and *combine* the various muscular movements necessary for its production. Hence it may easily be understood how the voice will *flatten,* when, from inattention or weariness, the singer does not give prompt and firm tension to the proper muscles of the Larynx or Chest. The *loud* singer is especially liable to this, because, as noticed above, his notes are made to depend less upon the easily governed tension of the vocal chords, and more upon the regulated force of air from the chest—the muscles of which are sooner wearied and less easily commanded with accuracy. Hence, the importance of cultivating a *medium force of voice,* such as is consistent with the *easy* action of the lungs.

The FALSETTO voice, in men, is produced, as Müller shows, by the vibration of the thin borders only of the vocal membranes, while, for the natural voice, they vibrate in their whole breadth. At a certain high degree of tension, the falsetto only can be produced. There is a more moderate tension of the membranes at which a soft breath will produce the falsetto, and a stronger breath the natural voice. And at a still lower degree of tension, the natural voice only can be produced.

The term REGISTER is used to denote "a certain number of sounds in a voice, which differ in quality or timbre from another number of sounds in the same voice." The *lower* register usually contains about five, and the *upper* about eight notes of the voice. Most of the Italian authorities distinguish a *third* register in the *highest* sounds of the voice. We follow Dr. Bennati—as kindly quoted to us by Mr. Graham. This change of register is probably occasioned by some difference in the *manner* in which the notes are produced. It may be that the lower notes are successively produced by somewhat relaxed membranes, which are shortened as the notes rise, and that notes of the higher register are produced mainly by the tension of the membranes without any shortening of the chords. If so, there will be a note or two, at the junction of the registers, which may be produced on either principle, and an uncultivated voice may not decide with sufficient promptitude which principle is to be used, or on which note the new register should begin. This would account for the great difficulty, which many have, in making the notes of one register follow smoothly with those of the other. Such persons require considerable practice and care to "*blend*" the registers. They should be instructed to keep the notes of the lower register down in strength or force, while they seek to strengthen those of the higher one.

2. THE VOICES OF WOMEN AND CHILDREN are, on an average, about eight notes higher than those of men. They are very various in character, but may be conveniently classified according to their "*compass*" or the extent of notes which they can reach on the *standard scale*. See p. 10.

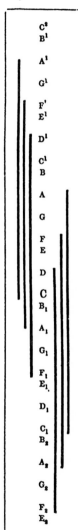

a. The First Soprano Voice has its *extremest* compass from E^2 (above the staff) down to B_1 (below the staff). Its *easy* compass is from A^1 down to C. "It is weak in the lower sounds, but light and brilliant (if well developed) in the higher ones above B. The organ has not much muscular strength, and cannot easily give effect to sustained sounds," but is very flexible.

b. The Second Soprano Voice reaches, in its extreme compass, from C^2 down to G_1. Its easy compass is from F^1 down to A_1. "It is generally full and round in its quality, and flexible. The organ is of a stronger muscular construction."

c. The Contra-Alto Voice sometimes reaches from B^1 flat down to E_1. Its easy compass is from D^1 to F_1. "Its organ is" large and "of a very strong muscular construction. It is not very flexible. The upper sounds are harsh or weak. It is, however, sometimes full from D^1 down to G. It is most powerful from G to G_1."

3. THE VOICES OF MEN are classified as follows.

a. The Tenor Voice is of two sorts. "The first is that very delicate light and rare voice for which the 'alto' part is written in some of our tune books. Like the first soprano voice, among females, it is not adapted to sustained sounds. Its compass is about a tone higher than that of the common tenor voice." The stronger tenor voice has for its extreme compass from B flat down to B_2 flat (in the bass cleff). Its easy compass is from A down to C_1. "It is full, round, and capable of sustaining and expanding sounds with firmness. Great care should be taken not to force the higher sounds. They should be sustained firmly though lightly, and without making use of *falsetto*—a quality of voice dissonant and unpleasant, and which ought never to exist in a well-cultivated voice."

b. The Baritone Voice has its extreme compass from G down to F_2 sharp (below the bass cleff). Its easy compass is from F down to A_2. "It partakes in some degree of the quality of both Bass and Tenor. It is more soft and flexible than the former. From the ease with which it takes the notes D E F, (treble cleff) it may sometimes be mistaken for the Tenor. But from the different position of the organ in the throat, these sounds, instead of being full, will be of a hollow quality—being the extreme sounds of the Baritone,

whilst they are in the middle and fullest part of the Tenor.   If the voice is at all
strained on this part, instead of gaining the soft and full Baritone quality, it will
become an imperfect mixture of the Baritone and Tenor.'

    c.   The Bass Voice reaches its extreme sounds in E (on the lowest line of the
treble cleff) and E, (below the bass cleff).   Its easy compass is from D down to
F,.   "It is naturally of a hard and inflexible quality, but very full and powerful
in sustaining sounds."

    Those who understand the old notation will like to see the following diagram.

STANDARD SCALE.   COMPASS OF VOICES.

The statement of the extreme compass of voices
and the remarks included between inverted commas are either condensed or extracted from the
"Art of Singing," by D. Crevelli, a work which is
"the result of study and experience, for nearly
thirty years" of a gentleman, who is spoken of by
the Athenæum as "the most successful vocal
teacher in England."

    It should be noticed that boys' voices, especially
for some time before they begin to break, are of a
different timbre from those of girls, are heavier
and less flexible.   They should, as much as possible, be employed in singing "seconds."

    The voices of women and children are com-
monly called "Treble Voices."   The highest
female voice is often called simply "Soprano,"
and the second voice is then called "Mezzo
Soprano."   The 'part' adapted to the Second
Soprano or Contra-alto is sometimes called the
"*Seconds*," but that term is occasionally used in
reference to the Tenor!   The "Alto" is a very
high man's voice, reaching very nearly to the
lowest of women's voices, which is called, on that
account, the Contra-alto.   But the two voices
differ greatly in character—the one being light
and flexible, the other not so.

    Every pupil should mark the extent of his own
voice on the scale above given at the side of the

page.   It would be well if the voice of every
pupil were periodically examined and its compass
and condition registered.   Thus, instead of the
simple entry, p. 21, a fuller statement, with remarks, might be given, as thus—

ADMIT [*William Flower*]
TO THE ADVANCED SINGING CLASS
VOICE [*First Soprano*]
Extreme Compass [C^2 to B₁]
Easy Compass [A^1 to c]
Registers separate at [F or G but are well
    blended.]

[He should try to sing softly and clearly. He should
study expression, and throw his feelings into the
words.   A soul for music is better than a voice for
music.]
                 [A. MATTHEWS,] *Teacher.*
[*March* 2, 1848.]

    The pupils need scarcely be warned against the
common foolishness of boasting "how *high* they
can sing."   Let them remember that God has
made their voices differently, that it is the honour
of some to sing the lower parts for which their
voices were made, as it is of others to sing the
higher parts—and that the *medium* sounds of
every voice are not only its easiest, but its *very
best.*

    4.   Vocal music is commonly so written that several melodies may be sung
together—each melody being adapted, in its compass, to one particular voice.
The leading (or most striking) melody is almost invariably, and very properly,
that which is sung by the highest voice.   Each of these concurring melodies is
called a "part":—the highest is called the "Air."

    Those who sing in parts should seek to *attune* their voices one to the other,
and to maintain the several parts with an *equal volume* of voice, so that one part

may not overpower the others. Each singer should also take care to sing the part proper to his own voice.

We have music "in two parts" written for Soprano and Contra-alto voices, or for Tenor and Bass, (like the exercises in this book) or for Soprano and Bass,—music "in three parts" written "for three equal voices" (that is, for three female or for three male voices) or for Soprano, Contra-alto, and Baritone, (like "School Music") or for Soprano, Tenor, and Bass, &c.—music "in four parts" for Soprano, Contra-alto, Tenor, and Bass, &c. (like most Psalm tunes)—also music in five, six, and eight parts.

There is no harmony more perfect than the "concord of sweet voices." "All musicians knew," says Col. Thompson, "that by practising together, and, as it were, mutually rubbing down each other's asperities and defects, a quartett of performers on instruments of the viol kind arrived at a perfection of execution in point of harmony, or what is popularly called "being in tune," which nothing could excel, and no known thing, *except a quartett of singers*, equal. In short, there was no doubt that by following the directions of the ear as to what was most harmonious, and each labouring to accommodate the other with this common object in view, they did practically break in upon the thing so much sought for under the title of correct harmony. • • • But nobody could tell what it was they did." The Colonel then shows that the thing they did was—to sing or play notes which were mathematically correct according to the scale which the human ear requires—to free themselves from the temperament of keyed instruments—and to observe that double form of TE and RAY which he calls "the duplicity of the dissonances." (See Sec. vii. p. 39, 40.) Let the singer make full use of the advantage he thus possesses.

The "balancing" of parts is important. For a congregation containing every kind of voice, music in four parts, Soprano, Contra-alto, Tenor, and Bass, is most appropriate. The Second So-

prano and the Baritone voices, in such music, would have to join with the parts above or below according to convenience. But in the Sabbath School, where the immense preponderance of voice is that of females and children, to divide the voice of the male teachers into Bass and Tenor would make them, out of all proportion weak. A far better distribution and more equal volume of voice is obtained by using music written for three parts—two for the voices of females and children, and one (of medium compass), for the united voices of the men—as in "School Music." A similar proportion is desirable for boys' schools with a master, but the parts should be so written that the two upper melodies may be harmonious when the Bass is absent. In girls' schools music in two parts is desirable.

After these explanations, it is scarcely necessary to warn the pupil against the too common but absurd practice of females attempting to sing the Tenor, or that of males sullying, with their Tenor or Baritone voices, the purity and brightness of the "Air." If men are obliged to *pitch* the air of a tune, let them do so; but let them leave the females to *sing* it, while they return to the part which is proper to their own voices.

In "*Leading*" a tune it is advisable first to let all the school or congregation distinctly hear the key note. If necessary, the first note or two (not more), may be sung by the Leader in the "Air." The leader should then take his own part. He will find himself able to keep up the *pitch* or the *rate of movement* much better by means of a *firm bass* or a *clear tenor*, both well accented—than by singing the air however loudly or however angrily. When a "clerk" or "precentor" *will* sing the "air," it takes the spirit from the female voices: but if, perchance, for a line, he leaves them to themselves, they seem to rise with new vigour, sweetness, and brilliancy.

5. A good enunciation of words is most important to the singer. He cannot use that accent and inflection on each word which so much help us to distinguish the words of the *speaker*, however badly uttered. It is, therefore, the more necessary for the singer, if he would be 'intelligible and edifying,' to use an articulation strong, distinct, and correct.

Care should be taken to make the *vowel* sounds most *clear* and *accurate*, and to deliver the *consonants* both *quickly* and *forcibly*.

For this purpose, the words should be read aloud by the teacher, so as to show the feeling and proper expression belonging to them, and to exhibit a "pattern" of good utterance. This the class should imitate, in one voice, taking the teacher's pattern line by line. The practice of reading together in a loud whisper will be found very conducive to the end sought.

N

It will sometimes be convenient to shorten a note when it falls on an ill-sounding syllable, and sometimes to throw the sound of a final consonant on to the following word.

The teacher who wishes to pursue the subject of enunciation should study "The Philosophy of the Human Voice"—Sec. iii. iv. v.—an incomparable work by Dr. Rush of America, in connection with "Müller's Physiology"—Book iv. Sec. iii. Cap. 3—and Sir Chas. Bell's article mentioned above. A compendious and valuable exhibition of principles is also given in Mr. Cull's articles, "Voice" and "Stammering," in the Penny Cyclopædia.

The following tunes, written for various voices, will illustrate many points in this section. The admirable stirring song by the Rev. H. M. Gunn will attract attention. Exercises 105, 107, are called CANONS. The marks D. S. and S. will guide the singer. In the "Round" precisely the same melody is heard in the different parts;—in the "Canon" the melody is imitated by the successive voices, in its "sequence," but at a lower pitch. The "convertible" notes of transition must be carefully traced on the Modulator. When understood they are easily performed. In Ex. 105, the melody of the first "part" is imitated by the second "part," in the subdominant key—starting from F'DOH, and repeated by the third "part" in the lower replicates. The FAH KEY is indicated

by a peculiar type. In Ex. 107 the melody of the first voices is taken up by the second set of voices in the dominant (or soh) key—starting from R'SOH, and again by the third set of voices in the lower replicates. The SOH KEY is printed in italics.

The noble song, "God speed the right," is inserted by the permission of Mr. Hickson, whose works contain several of a similar kind, among which, "When the might with the right and the truth shall be," deserves special mention. The teacher with the help of black board and solfa-music-paper (p. 15) will have no difficulty in introducing any new tunes to common use in his school.

AZOTUS is inserted by permission of the proprietors of the "Psalmist." The very beautiful hymn by Josiah Conder should be a favourite in every social circle.

If there were much occasion for printing, in this notation, the parts for Tenor and Bass voices, it would be found convenient to prefix the words "Tenor" or "Bass" to the part, and then to print it as though it were a replicate higher. The constant use of the figures below the notes would thus be avoided.

103.   HOME, SWEET HOME.   KEY G.   M. 112.
(For two female voices and one male voice.)

$$\left\{\begin{array}{l}\text{s} :\!-\; '\!-\; :\!-\; |\text{f} :\!-\; |\text{r} :\!-\; |\text{d} :\!-\; |\text{r} :\!-\; |\text{m} :\!-\; |\text{ :s}\\ \text{Home!}\qquad\qquad\text{Home!}\qquad\text{Sweet, sweet home,}\qquad\text{There's}\\ \text{m} :\!-\; |\!-\; :\!-\; |\text{r} :\!-\; |\text{t}_1 :\!-\; |\text{d} :\!-\; |\text{t}_1 :\!-\; |\text{d} :\!-\; |\text{ :m}\\ \text{d}_1 :\!-\; |\!-\; :\!-\; |\text{s}_2 :\!-\; |\text{f}_2 :\!-\; |\text{m}_2 :\!-\; |\text{s}_2 :\!-\; |\text{d}_1 :\!-\; |\text{ :d}_1\end{array}\right.$$

$$\left\{\begin{array}{l}\text{d}^1 :\!-.\text{t} |\text{l} :\!-.\text{s} |\text{s} :\!-\; |\text{m} :\text{s} |\text{s} :\text{l} |\text{f} :\text{r} |\text{d} :\!-\; |\!-\; \|\\ \text{no place like home,}\qquad\text{There's no place like home.}\\ \text{m} :\!-.\text{s} |\text{f} :\!-.\text{m} |\text{m} :\!-\; |\text{d} :\text{m} |\text{m} :\text{f} |\text{r} :\text{t}_1 |\text{d} :\!-\; |\!-\;\\ \text{d}_1 :\!-\; |\text{d}_1 :\!-.\text{d}_1 |\text{d}_1 :\!-\; |\!-\; :\text{d}_1 |\text{s}_2 :\!-\; |\text{s}_2 :\text{s}_2 |\text{d}_2 :\!-\; |\!-\;\end{array}\right.$$

104. THE MARTYRS.   KEY B flat.   M. 96.

(For two female voices and one male voice.)

$$\left\{\begin{array}{l}\text{s}_1 :\!-.\text{s}_1 |\text{s}_1 :\!-.\text{m}_1 |\text{s}_1 :\!-.\text{l}_1 |\text{d} :\!-\; |\text{l}_1 :\!-.\text{l}_1 |\text{l}_1 :\!-.\text{s}_1 |\text{l}_1 :\!-.\text{t}_1 |\text{d} :\!-\;\\ \text{Chil-dren of the pi-ous dead,}\qquad\text{Who for conscience no-bly bled;}\\ \text{m}_1 :\!-.\text{m}_1 |\text{m}_1 :\!-.\text{d}_1 |\text{m}_1 :\!-.\text{f}_1 |\text{m}_1 :\!-\; |\text{f}_1 :\!-.\text{f}_1 |\text{f}_1 :\!-.\text{m}_1 |\text{f}_1 :\!-.\text{f}_1 |\text{m}_1 :\!-\;\\ \text{d}_2 :\!-.\text{d}_2 |\text{d}_2 :\!-.\text{d}_2 |\text{d}_2 :\!-.\text{d}_2 |\text{d}_2 :\!-\; |\text{f}_2 :\!-.\text{f}_2 |\text{f}_2 :\!-.\text{d}_2 |\text{f}_2 :\!-.\text{s}_2 |\text{d}_2 :\!-\;\end{array}\right.$$

$$\left\{\begin{array}{l}\text{m} :\!-.\text{f} |\text{r} :\!-.\text{m} |\text{d} :\!-.\text{r} |\text{m} :\!-\; |\text{d} :\!-.\text{l}_1 |\text{l}_1 :\!-.\text{s}_1 |\text{s}_1 :\!-\; |\!-\; :\\ \text{By the blood those martyrs shed,}\qquad\text{Guard their ho-ly cause.}\\ \text{s}_1 :\!-.\text{l}_1 |\text{f}_1 :\!-.\text{s}_1 |\text{m}_1 :\!-.\text{f}_1 |\text{s}_1 :\!-\; |\text{m}_1 :\!-.\text{f}_1 |\text{f}_1 :\!-.\text{m}_1 |\text{m}_1 :\!-\; |\!-\; :\\ \text{d}_1 :\!-.\text{d}_1 |\text{s}_2 :\!-.\text{s}_2 |\text{d}_2 :\!-.\text{d}_2 |\text{d}_2 :\!-\; |\text{d}_2 :\!-.\text{f}_2 |\text{f}_2 :\!-.\text{d}_2 |\text{d}_2 :\!-\; |\!-\; :\end{array}\right.$$

$$\left\{\begin{array}{l}\text{m} :\!-.\text{m} |\text{m} :\!-.\text{r} |\text{m} :\!-.\text{f} |\text{s} :\text{m} |\text{r} :\!-.\text{r} |\text{r} :\!-.\text{d} |\text{r} :\!-.\text{m} |\text{f} :\!-.\text{l}\\ \text{Their's the cause of truth and right,}\qquad\text{Their's the fight of faith to fight,}\\ \text{s}_1 :\!-.\text{s}_1 |\text{s}_1 :\!-.\text{f}_1 |\text{m}_1 :\!-.\text{r}_1 |\text{d}_1 :\!-\; |\text{f}_1 :\!-.\text{f}_1 |\text{f}_1 :\!-.\text{m}_1 |\text{r}_1 :\!-.\text{d}_1 |\text{t}_2 :\\ \text{d}_2 :\!-.\text{d}_1 |\text{d}_1 :\!-.\text{t}_2 |\text{d}_1 :\!-.\text{t}_2 |\text{d}_1 :\text{ } |\text{s}_2 :\!-.\text{s}_1 |\text{s}_2 :\!-.\text{s}_2 |\text{s}_2 :\!-.\text{s}_2 |\text{s}_2 :\end{array}\right.$$

$$\left\{\begin{array}{l}\text{s} :\!-.\text{m} |\text{r} :\!-.\text{m} |\text{d} :\!-.\text{r} |\text{m} :\!-.\text{r} |\text{d} :\!-.\text{l}_1 |\text{l}_1 :\!-.\text{s}_1 |\text{s}_1 :\!-\; |\!-\; : \|\\ \text{Their's the souls of ear-nest might,}\qquad\text{And the great ap-plause.}\\ \text{m}_1 :\!-.\text{s}_1 |\text{f}_1 :\!-.\text{s}_1 |\text{m}_1 :\!-.\text{f}_1 |\text{s}_1 : |\text{m}_1 :\!-.\text{f}_1 |\text{f}_1 :\!-.\text{m}_1 |\text{m}_1 :\!-\; |\!-\; :\\ \text{d}_1 :\!-.\text{d}_1 |\text{s}_2 :\!-.\text{s}_2 |\text{d}_2 :\!-.\text{d}_2 |\text{d}_2 : |\text{d}_2 :\!-.\text{f}_2 |\text{f}_2 :\!-.\text{d}_2 |\text{d}_2 :\!-\; |\!-\; :\end{array}\right.$$

2 Thorny was their path below,
Path of torture, fire and foe,
Sighs of grief and tears of woe
    Were their common lot.
Still undaunted on they went,
Up to heaven their prayer was sent,
They on crowns of glory bent,
    All their pains forgot.

3 Shall the fathers stand alone?
Is their noble courage gone?
Is their mantle fall'n on none?
    Are such men no more?

No! the truth shall yet prevail,
Strong in souls that never quail;
Sons, arise, you will not fail,
    In the trying hour.

4 From the lofty seats above,
Sires are bending eyes of love;
They your fight of faith approve,
    And on you look down.
See the martyrs, prophets there,
There apostles, angels are;
See the King of kings prepare
    Your immortal crown.
    H. M. GUNN.

105.   GLORIA.   *(A Canon for three voices.)*   KEY B flat.   M. 66.

s.

d	:s	f	:m	r	:f	m	:s	d	:—	r	:r	d	:t₁
Glo-	ri-	a	in	ex-	cel-	sis	De-	o		et	in	ter-	ra
	:	fᵈ₁	:ₛ₁	f₁	:ₘₘ₁	t₁	:f₁	mₘ₁	:ₛ₁	ᵈ₁	:—	t₁	:t₁
		Glo-	ri-	a	in	ex-	cel-	sis	De-	o		et	in
	:		:		:	d₁	:s₁	f₁	:m₁	r₁	:f₁	m₁	:s₁
						Glo-	ri-	a	in	ex-	cel-	sis	De-

DAL SEGNO.

d	:—		:		:	d	:s
pax						Glo-	ri-
ᵈ₁	:t₂	ᵈ₁	:—		:		:
ter-	ra	pax					
d₁	:—	r₁	:r₁	d₁	:t₂	d₁	:—
o		et	in	ter-	ra	pax.	

105.   GLORIA IN EXCELSIS.   KEY B flat.   M. 50.

(More correctly written.)

s.

d	:s	f	:ᵐt₁	l₁	:d	t₁	:r	s₁	:s₁	l₁	:l₁	ˢd	:t₁
	:	f₁	:ᵈs₁	f₁	:m₁	r₁	:f₁	m₁	:s₁	d₁	:d₁	ʳs₁	:s₁
	:		:		:	ᵈs₂	:r₁	d₁	:t₂	l₂	:d₁	ᵗm₁	:s₁

D. C.

d	:—		:		:	d	:s
f₁	:m₁	f₁	:—		:		:
d₁	:d₁	r₁	:r₁	d₁	:t₂	d₁	:—

106.   HARRINGTON, C. M.   KEY E.   M. 66.

(For two female voices and one male voice.)

:s	dˡ :t	:l	s	:—f :m	f	:s	:l	l	:s	:s	ˢd :t₁	:d
:m	s :f	:m	r	:— :d	d	:m	:f	f	:m	:r	ʳs₁ :f₁	:m₁
:d₁	m₁ :r₁	:d₁	t₂	:s₂ :d₁	l₂	:s₂	:f₂	d₁	:—	:t₂	ᵗm₂ :r₂	:d₂

l₁.r :d	:t₁	d	:— :s₁	ᵈs :f	:m	m	:r	:d	r.,m :f	:m
f₁	:m₁ :r₁.m₁.f₁	f₁	:m₁ :m₁	ˡm :r	:d	d	:t₁	:s₁.d	t₁.,d :r	:d
f₂	:s₂ :—	d₂	:— :d₂	ᵈs₂ :—	:d₁	s₁	:f₁	:m₁	r₁ :t₂	:d₁

l	:— :s	dˡ :t	:dˡ	r.m,f :m	:r	d	:—
d	:— :d	f	:— :m	l₁.,r :d	:t₁	d	:—
f₁	:— :m₁	r₁ :s₂	:d₁	f₁	:s₁ :s₂	d₁	:—

107. NON NOBIS. *(A Canon for three voices.)* KEY C. M. 96.

s :—	l :t	d¹ :—.d¹	s. t :t	l :—	s :—		:r¹
Non	no- bis,	dom- i-	ne, non	no-	bis.		Sed
:	rs₁ :—	l₁ :t₁	d :—.d	t₁ :t₁	l₁ :—	s₁ :—	:—
	Non	no- bis,	dom- i-	ne, non	no-	bis,	
:	:	:	s₁ :—	l₁ :t₁	d :—.d	t₁ :t₁	t₁ :t₁
			Non	no- bis,	dom- i-	ne	non,

m¹.m¹ :d¹	s¹ :—	s¹ :f¹	m¹ :—.m¹	r¹ :—	:l	t.t :s
nomi- ne	tu-	o da	glo- ri-	am.	Sed	nomi- ne
:r	m.m :d	s :—	s :f	m :—.m	r :—	:l₁
Sed	nomi- ne	tu-	o da	glo- ri-	am.	Sed
l₁ :—	s₁ :—	:r	m.m :d	s :—	s :f	m :—.m
no-	bis,	Sed	nomi- ne	tu	o da	glo- ri-

DAL SEGNO.

r¹ :—	r¹ :d¹	t :—.t	l :—	s :—	l :t	d¹ :—.d¹
tu-	o da	glo- ri-	am.	Non	no- bis	dom- i-
t₁.t₁ :s₁	r :—	r :d	t₁ :—.t₁	l₁ :—	s₁ :—	l₁ :t₁
nomi- ne-	tu-	o da	glo- ri-	am.	Non	no- bis
r :—	:l₁	t₁.t₁ :s₁	r₁ :—	r :d	t₁ :—.t₁	l₁ :—
am.	Sed	nomi- ne	tu-	o da	glo- ri-	am.

---

108. GOD SPEED THE RIGHT. KEY D. M. 66.

(For two female and two male voices.

s :s	d¹ :—.s	m :m	s :m	m :—	r :—.r	m :—	:
s :s	d¹ :—.s	m :m	s :m	d :—	t₁ :—.t₁	d :—	:
Now to	heaven our	prayers as-	cend- ing,	God	speed the	right!	
s₁ :s₁	d :—.s₁	m₁ :m₁	s₁ :m₁	s₁ :—	s₁ :—.s₁	s₁ :—	:
s₁ :s₁	d :—.s₁	m₁ :m₁	s₁ :m₁	d₁ :—	s₂ :—.s₂	d₁ :—	;

s :s	d¹ :—.s	m :m	s :m	m :—	r :—.r	m :—	:
s :s	d¹ :—.s	m :m	s :m	d :—	t₁ :—.t₁	d :—	:
In a	no- ble	cause con-	tend- ing,	God	speed the	right!	
s₁ :s₁	d :—.s₁	m₁ :m₁	s₁ :m₁	s₁ :—	s₁ :—.s₁	s₁ :—	:
s₁ :s₁	d :—.s₁	m₁ :m₁	s₁ :m₁	d₁ :—	s₂ :—.s₂	d₁ :—	:

d¹ :t	l :s	l :s	f :m	r :m	f :r	s :f	m :r
m :s	f :m	f :m	r :d	t₁ :d	r :t₁	m :r	d :t₁
Be their	zeal in	heaven re-	cord- ed,	With suc-	cess on	earth re-	ward- ed,
d :d	d :d	d :d	d :d	s₁ :s₁	s₁ :s₁	m₁ :f₁	s₁ :s₁
d₁ :d₁	d₁ :d₁	d₁ :d₁	d₁ :d₁	s₂ :s₂	s₂ :s₂	s₂ :s₂	s₁ :f₁

```
{ d¹ :— │ r¹   :-.r¹ │ m¹ :— │— :   │ s :— │ s  :-.s │ d :— │— :
  d  :— │ s    :-.s   │ s  :— │— :   │ s :— │ s  :-.s │ d :— │— :
  God    speed   the   right!          God     speed  the  right!
  s₁ :— │ s₁   :-.s₁  │ d  :— │— :   │ s₁ :— │ s₁ :-.s₁│ d₁ :— │— :
  m₁ :— │ r₁   :-.r₁  │ d₁ :— │— :   │ s₁ :— │ s₁ :-.s₁│ d₁ :— │— :
```

Now to heaven our prayers ascending,
    God speed the right!
In a noble cause contending,
    God speed the right!
Be their zeal in heaven recorded,
With success on earth rewarded,
    God speed the right!

Be that prayer again repeated,
    God speed the right!
Ne'er despairing though defeated,
    God speed the right!
Like the good and great in story,
If they fail they fail with glory,
    God speed the right!

Patient, firm, and persevering,
    God speed the right!
Ne'er the event, nor danger fearing,
    God speed the right!
Pains nor toils, nor trials heeding,
And in Heaven's own time succeeding,
    God speed the right!

Still their onward course pursuing,
    God speed the right!
Every foe, at length, subduing,
    God speed the right!
Truth! Thy cause, whate'er delay it,
There's no power on earth can stay it.
    God speed the right!
            W. H. HICKSON.

109.   AZOTUS.   KEY A.   M. 66.

(For two female and two male voices.)

```
{ s  :s │ l :l │ f :f │ r :— │ m :m │ f  :f  │ r :r │ t₁ :—
  d  :d │ d :d │ r :r │ t₁ :— │ d :d │ d  :d  │ l₁ :l₁│ s₁ :—
  Where- so- ever  two or  three     Meet, a  chris- tian com- pa- ny;
  m₁ :m₁│ f₁:f₁│ l₁:l₁│ s₁ :— │ s₁ :s₁│ l₁ :l₁│ f₁ :f₁│ r₁ :—
  d₁ :d₁│ f₂:f₂│ f₂:f₂│ s₂ :— │ d₁ :d₁│ f₂ :f₂│ f₂ :f₂│ s₂ :—
```

```
{ s₁ :l₁ │ t₁ :d │ r :m │ f :— │ m :m │ r :r │ d :—
  s₁ :l₁ │ t₁ :d │ r₁:m₁│ f₁ :— │ s₁ :l₁│ l₁ :s₁,f₁│ m₁ :—
  Grant us, Lord, to  meet with Thee!  Gra- cious Sa- viour hear!
  s₂ :l₂ │ t₂ :d₁│ r₁:m₁│ f₁ :— │ d₁ :d₁│ d₁ :t₂│ d₁ :—
  s₂ :l₂ │ t₂ :d₁│ t₂:d₁│ r₁ :— │ d₁ :l₂│ f₂ :s₂│ d₂ :—
```

1 Wheresoever two or three
    Meet, a Christian company,
    Grant us, Lord, to meet with Thee;
        Gracious Saviour, hear!

2 When with friends beloved we stray,
    Talking down the closing day,
    Saviour! meet us in the way;
        Gracious Saviour, hear!

3 When, amid the gloom of night,
    Storms arise and perils fright,
    Let thy voice our hearts delight;
        Gracious Saviour, hear!

4 In the festive hour, refine
    Earthly love to joy divine:
    Turn the water into wine;
        Gracious Saviour, hear!

5 In the time of lonely grief,
    Let thy presence bring relief;
    Then shall longest nights grow brief;
        Gracious Saviour, hear!

6 When the world and life recede,
    Saviour! in our hour of need,
    Then be visible indeed;
        Gracious Saviour, hear!

SECTION XII.

OF HARMONY AND COUNTERPOINT.

1. Two or more melodies, so suited to each other that they may be agreeably heard at the same time, form HARMONY, and the art of attaching to a given melody one or more others, which shall accompany it harmoniously, and heighten its effect, is called COUNTERPOINT.

"The ancients," says Col. Thompson, quoting Euclid and other Greek writers, "by *Harmony* meant only *being in tune.* But the moderns have appropriated the term to the combination of such sounds as are agreeable when heard *simultaneously;* while they use *Melody* for the arrangement of such sounds as are agreeable when heard in *succession.* The same scale of sounds which enables us to produce harmony produces melody. The difference between the sounds uttered, in the attempt to sing, by a person who has not a musical ear and one who has, is that the sounds of the first are not in the intervals of the scale which produce Harmony, and those of the other are. The reason why the intervals, that produce Harmony, produce also Melody, seems to be, that *Melody is retrospective Harmony,* or depends on a perception of harmonical relation to sounds that have preceded. • • • The connection between Harmony and Melody is nowhere so apparent as in the *arpeggio* passages so common in music for the guitar and stringed instruments in general. For these arpeggios are in fact chords, spread out by the notes being sounded in succession instead of together, as the means of obviating the want of *sostenuto* tone inherent in the instrument. • • • The same connection which exists in the most striking degree among the notes of an arpeggio, exists in a certain degree among all others. The memory of the sounds that have preceded *lingers in the ear,* and requires to be accommodated, as far as possible, by meeting with harmonious combinations in those which follow." (See "Instructions to my Daughter, for playing on the Enharmonic Guitar," or "Westminster Review," April, 1832.)

The term Counterpoint "is derived from the ancient *points* or notes which were placed *counter* or opposite to each other on the staff."

2. Harmony, in two parts, is formed by the following combinations of notes.

a. The *same* note occurring in both parts, called the UNISON, and *Replicate* notes, which are said to be at the interval of an OCTAVE, as DOH DOH¹; ME₁ ME, &c.

b. Those notes which have between them the interval of a *tone* and a *tonule,* called the interval of a MINOR (or smaller) THIRD, (including three notes) such as, TE₁ RAY; RAY FAH; ME SOH; LAH DOH¹.

c. Those which have between them the interval of *two tones,* called the MAJOR (or greater) THIRD, such as, DOH ME; FAH LAH; SOH TE.

d. Those which have between them the interval of *three tones* and a *tonule,* called a FIFTH, (including five notes) such as, DOH SOH; RAY LAH; ME TE; FAH DOH¹.

e. The same notes which compose the major and minor *thirds,* when one of them is raised or lowered (an octave) to its replicate, thus, TE₂ RAY; FAH RAY¹; ME SOH; DOH LAH, and ME DOH¹; LAH FAH¹; TE₁ SOH.

Consonances are said to be *inverted* when the note which was the lower becomes the higher of the two; thus, TE₁ RAY inverted would be RAY TE, and ME SOH inverted would be SOH ME¹. Consonances are said to be *dispersed* when the lower note falls or the higher note rises an octave. Thus DOH ME dispersed would be DOH ME¹, and RAY FAH dispersed would be RAY₁ FAH, &c.

f. The notes which form the interval of a FIFTH when *dispersed*, thus, DOH SOH¹; RAY₁ LAH; ME TE¹; FAH₁ DOH¹, &c. The *inversion* of this consonance (SOH₁ DOH; LAH RAY¹; TE₁ ME; and DOH FAH,) is not approved in two-part harmony, though it adds greatly to the beauty of harmony in three or more parts.

g. Notes which do not sound agreeably together, called DISSONANCES, are occasionally introduced, by the skilful composer, to highten the effect of the consonance which follows. The most common dissonances are those in which FAH or TE form one note.

The pupil should now be exercised in finding and writing down all the simple consonances to any given note. He will then produce a table like the following.

The consonances

of DOH *are*	{ d l / l₁ d	m d¹ / d m	s¹ / d	d¹ / f
of RAY *are*	{ f r¹ / r f	r t / t₁ r	l / r	r¹ / s
of ME *are*	{ s m / m s₁	m d¹ / d m	t / m	m / l₁
of FAH *are*	{ f r¹ / r f	l f / f l₁	d¹ / f	
of SOH *are*	{ s m / m s₁	t s / s t₁	r¹ / s	s / d
of LAH *are*	{ d¹ l / l d	l f / f l₁	m¹ / l	l / r
of TE *are*	{ r t / t₁ r	t s¹ / s t	t / m	

There might have been added to the above list such combinations as TU₁ LAH; FI SOH, &c.; but these should be studied in connection with the "better method of denoting transition," which gives them their real characters TE RAY; FAH RAY, &c. The new intervals formed by *chromatic* notes and by *ne* may be judged by the general rules above given. NE LAH would be a third and consonant, NE DOH¹ a "tritone" and dissonant, &c. &c.

When the notes which form the interval of a *third* are inverted, they form the interval of a *sixth*. The major thirds become minor sixths, (having two tonules) and the minor thirds become major sixths, (having only one tonule.) Let the pupil trace this on the modulator. Thirds and sixths are the commonest intervals in two-part harmony.

When the interval of a *fifth* is inverted it be-

comes a *fourth*, and is called a *perfect fourth* to distinguish it from the *Tritone* FAH TE, which is larger by about a tonule, and is dissonant. It is this interval of the *perfect fourth* which is disallowed in two-part harmony, though welcomed in harmony of three or more parts. A few transgressions of this rule may be found in the previous exercises. While positive discords are allowed, why should fourths be *absolutely* banished. When the exercises are accompanied by the Bass from "School Music," not even the critic will reckon these fourths a defect.

It has been stated before (page   , that consonances are reckoned *perfect* in proportion as the notes of which they are composed most nearly resemble each other in effect. Hence the *Unison*, the *Octave*, and the *Fifth* are called *perfect* consonances, and the *Third* and *Sixth*, though more agreable, are called *imperfect* consonances.

Dr. Bryce (p. 78) shows that the resemblance between any two notes depends on the frequency with which the vibrations causing them end together. The most perfect resemblance is that of a note and its octave, the latter requiring exactly two vibrations of the sonorous body for every one required by the former. In the consonance of the fifth there is a coincidence of endings at *every other* vibration of the lower note—the upper note having exactly three vibrations to every two of the lower one. In the consonance of the major third the coincidence is still less frequent. It is at every *fourth* vibration of the lower note, the higher one having exactly five vibrations in the same time. The consonance of the minor third gives a coincidence at every *fifth* vibration of the lower note, the higher note having exactly six vibrations in the same time.

The dissonant interval of a *Tone* only gives a

coincidence at every *eighth* vibration of the lower note, the higher note having nine vibrations in the same time. The *Tonule* has coincidence of vibrations at every *fifteenth* of the lower note, the higher one giving sixteen in the same time. But notice—the *perfect fourth* gives a coincidence at every *third* vibration of the lower note, the higher one having four in exactly the same time. Why, then, should it be reckoned less consonant than those above mentioned? It is more "perfect" than the thirds, and has less "sameness" than the fifth. Will the following theory of Dr. Bryce's explain this?

"In all objects of taste, the combination of a certain degree of uniformity with a certain degree of variety gives pleasure. Too much uniformity is tiresome and stiff; too much variety is disorderly and unmeaning. This principle holds good in music as well as in the other fine arts; and on it depends the effect of the notes which form a "chord."* The first and eighth (d and d¹) heard simultaneously are pleasing; but they are so much alike that their effect is the same. The first and fifth (d and s), with or without the eighth, form a striking and pleasing harmony, but one which does not bear frequent repetition; so that even this combination seems to have too much uniformity. But the coincidences of the first and third (d and m) are neither so frequent as to weary the ear with too great uniformity, nor so rare as to distract it by too great variety;—the notes are so like that their resemblance cannot miss being perceived, and yet so unlike that their distinctness cannot fail to be felt;—they neither offend by dissonance nor weary by monotony. The consequence is that this combination is more frequently used than any other, and bears more repetition. (See note on GREGORIAN CHANT, p. 23.) But the pleasing effect of this union of uniformity and variety is greatly increased by sounding the fifth along with the key note and third, because there is thus introduced both more uniformity and more variety."

3. The MENTAL EFFECT of the different consonances depends partly on the sense of sameness or of pleasing variety produced by the coincidence of any two notes standing at the given interval, (see note above) but it is chiefly influenced by the position which the two notes hold in reference to the key note—the governing note—of the tune. Thus, among the minor thirds, the effect, on the mind, of TE, RAY would be very different indeed from that of LAH, DOH.

Any one may prove this by trying the experiment mentioned, SEC. vi. 4, and asking some other person to describe his mental impressions from the two consonances. (See also note, SEC. v. 1.) The difference of effect is just that which might be expected from the combination of the "piercing" with the "rousing" note being changed (by "establishing," in the ear, a new key), into a combination of the "sorrowful" with the "strong" note. The simple names by which we have called the notes would have reminded us that the first consonance should be one of "urgent desire," and that the other should give the impression of "determined sadness." In connection with the "mental effect of consonances,' refer to Sec. vi. 4.

The effect of different harmonies accompanying the same melody may be studied by the pupils in the following exercise, which is taken, by permission, from Messrs. Turle and Taylor's admirable collection of exercises and tunes, entitled "The Singing Book," published by Bogue, Fleet Street. In the second variation the tune is made to pass, by its change of harmony, into the minor key—in the next into the key of the dominant—and, in the fourth, into the key of the subdominant.

AN AIR VARIOUSLY HARMONIZED. KEY C.

d¹ :t	l :s	d¹ :r¹	m¹ :m¹	f¹ :r¹	r¹.d¹ :t	l :r¹
As the	tints of	morn or	even- ing,	Give the	scene its	diff'- rent
m :s	f :m	s :t	d¹ :s	l :t.d¹	l :s	s :tu,

t :—	s :d¹	d¹ :t	s :m¹	r¹ :—	d¹ :d¹	t :d¹
hue,	So does	va- ried	har- mo-	ny,	Clothe the	strain in
s :—	m :l.s	tu, :s.f	m :d	s :—	m :m	s :m

d¹ :t	d¹ :—	d¹ :t	l :s	d¹ :r¹	m¹ :m¹	f¹ :r¹
co- lours	new.	As the	tints of	morn or	even- ing,	Give the
l :s.f	m :—	l :ne	l :t	d¹ :l	ne :m	r :t

o

```
{ |r¹.d¹ :t | l  :r¹ | t  :—  | s  :d¹ | d¹ :t   | s  :m¹ | r¹ :—    |
  |scene its | diff-rent| huc, | So docs| va- ried| har- mo-| ny,     |
{ |l    :ne | l  :r  | m  :—  | m  :m  | r  :m.f | m  :d  | s  :soi  |

{ |d¹ :d¹ | t  :d¹ | d¹ :t   | d¹ :—   ‖ d¹ :t  | l  :s | d¹ :r¹ |
  |Clothe the| strain in| co- lours| new.    ‖ As  the| tints of| morn or|
{ |l  :l  | ne :l  | m  :ne | l  :—   ‖ tu₁ :s | d¹ :t | s  :t  |

{ |m¹ :m¹ | f¹ :r¹ | r¹.d¹ :t | l  :r¹ | t  :—  | s  :d¹ | d¹ :t   |
  |even- ing,| Give the| scene its| diff- rent| hue,  | So does| va- ried|
{ |d¹ :d¹ | f  :f  | foi :s  | r  :tu₁| s  :—  | d.r :m| tu₁ :s  |

{ |s  :m¹ | r¹ :—  | d¹ :d¹ | t  :d¹  | d¹ :t   | d¹ :—  ‖ d¹ :t  |
  |har- mo-| ny,   | Clothe the| strain in| co- lours| new.  ‖ As  the|
{ |m  :d¹ | d¹ :t | l  :tu₁| s  :m   | r  :s   | m  :—  ‖ d  :r.m|

{ |l  :s  | d¹ :r¹ | m¹ :m¹ | f¹ :r¹  | r¹.d¹ :t | l  :r¹ | t  :—  |
  |tints of| morn or| even- ing,| Give the| scene its| diff- rent| hue, |
{ |f  :m  | l  :s  | s.f'i :d'.'i| l  :f'i| l  :s   | s  :tu₁| s  :—  |

{ |s  :d¹ | d¹ :t  | s  :m¹ | r¹ :—   | d¹ :d¹  | t  :d¹ | d¹ :t   |
  |So docs| va- ried| har- mo-| ny,    | Clothe the| strain in| co- lours|
{ |m  :d  | r  :r  | m  :d¹ | d¹ :f'i | f'i :l  | s.f :m.l| f.l :s.f|

{ |d¹ :—  ‖
  |ncw.   ‖
{ |m  :—  ‖
```

4. In composing two part harmony, or in adding to a given melody another which shall accompany it, the attention of the learner will be directed to three points;—first, to the use of such consonances as are agreeable in themselves according to the rules above given—next, to the selection from them, of such as shall be most agreeable or effective in reference to one another and to the general *progression* of the music—and, then, to the fashioning of the second melody, so that it may be in itself agreeable. In reference chiefly to the second of these points—"the succession of consonances"—the following hints will be found useful.

a. When the two parts ascend or descend together they are said to move in *similar motion.* When the notes ascend in one part and descend in another, they are said to be in *contrary motion.* When one part continues or repeats a note, while the other ascends or descends, they are said to be in *oblique motion.*

b. When two fifths or two octaves occur together, unless it be in simple repetition of previous notes, the effect is not esteemed agreeable. Thus the following successions of consonances would be disallowed:—

CONSECUTIVE FIFTHS.				CONSECUTIVE OCTAVES.		
d :r	m :s	d :t₁	l₁ :s₁	d¹ :r¹	m¹ :t	d¹
f₁ :s₁	l₁ :d	f₁ :m₁	r₁ :d₁	d :r	m :t₁	d

But the following consecutives would be allowed:—

d¹ :d¹	l :l	l :l	s :s	s :s	m :m	m :m	d :d	d :—
d :d	r :r	l₁ :l₁	d :d	s₁ :s₁	l₁ :l₁	m₁:m₁	f₁ :f₁	d₁ :—

The pupil should be able to name the interval of each consonance.

c. When the two parts pass from any interval to an unison, a fifth or an octave, *by similar motion,* the progression is not esteemed agreeable, and is seldom approved by musicians.

Hence the following consecutives are allowed :—

s :f	l :s	s :d	s :l	d¹ :t	m :f	d¹ :s
m :f	r :s	d :d	m :r	d :m	d :f₁	m₁:s₁

But the following are disallowed :—

s :r	l :d	s :d¹	d¹ :m	m :d	t :s¹
m :r	r :d	m :f	d :l₁	d :d₁	m :s

Let the pupil name the intervals and trace the application of the rule.

d. The thirds and their inversions, the sixths, are the intervals most frequently used, but it is seldom that more than three or four of the same interval are allowed in succession.

e. The two parts should be kept distinct, each having an easy, flowing melody of its own. Hence it is well to avoid the unison (or doubling of the same note), and all movements which may produce a confused effect, or cause one part to overlap the other. The note TE especially should not be doubled, lest, followed as it usually is by DOH, consecutive unisons, or consecutive octaves, should be produced.

f. When one part holds a note while the other moves *obliquely* to it, the first note of the oblique movement should be a perfect consonance according to the above rules, but the others may ! e dissonances, (i. e. *seconds,* dr; rm; mf, &c.; their inversions the *sevenths,* ,nd their dispersions the *ninths,* and the *tritone* or imperfect fourth tf) provided they are both preceded and followed by notes which stand next to them in the scale. Such notes are called *passing* discords. Let the pupil name the dissonant intervals in the following example :—

d¹ :ṫ	l :ṫ	d¹ :s	l :t	d¹ :—	l.r¹ :d¹.ṫ	d¹ :—
d :—	f :—	m :—	r :—	d :—	r :—	d :—

g. Every dissonance should be immediately followed by a perfect consonance. It is then said to be *resolved.* If FAH is one note of the dissonance, it is usually but not invariably followed by ME in the same part. TE₁ in similar circumstances, is followed by DOH, LAH by SOH, and RAY commonly by DOH. See SEC. v. 2; SEC. vi. 1; and SEC. vii. 1. Dissonances are also more allowable when the dissonant note was heard in an immediately preceding *consonance.* They are then said to be *prepared.* "Preparation" is not considered so necessary for FAH and TE as for any of the other notes when dissonant. See the notes on BED-

FORD, PASCAL, and ST. JAMES, p. 30, 31; and those on EX. 53, VALLIS VALE, and OAKHILL, p. 41, 42.

h. It should be observed that transgressions of these rules become more *noticeable* when they occur on the accented part of a measure. Dissonances are however occasionally found in this position. Two fifths or two octaves occurring on the strong pulses of consecutive measures would be disapproved.

i. The dissonances become more allowable in proportion as the notes of which they are composed are more distant. (See SEC. vi. 4.) It is on this principle that the "Pedal Basses," in organ music, are allowed. They consist of DOH or SOH (the *Tonic* or the *Dominant*,) at a low replicate, held continuously through several measures, whatever be the notes above.

The Editor is indebted, for many observations in this section, to the very admirable and *sensible* little work, entitled "Hamilton's Catechism of Counterpoint Melody, &c." and to Dr. Goss's "Introduction to Harmony and Thorough Bass," which, with its course of exercises for the pupil, forms the most practicable guide to those who would pursue the subject in connection with keyed instruments and on the principle of "temperament." "Music Simplified,' by M. Jeu de Berneval, contains many most ingenious and valuable suggestions on Harmony. Mr. Graham's "Theory and Practice of Musical Composition," and the well-known works of Dr. Callcott and Dr. Crotch are necessary to one who would thoroughly master the subject. Weber's great work on Composition is now translated into English, but it is voluminous, and, like all that are built upon keyed instruments and temperament, very puzzling and unattractive to the learner. There is great need that some one should arise, combining the talents of Mr. Graham, Col. Thompson, and Dr. Bryce, who will give us a truly "Rational Introduction" to Harmony—which should be founded exclusively on the experience of correct singers, whose voices have not been spoilt by the piano, and of correct players on "untempered" instruments, like the violin—and which should first declare the great laws of musical taste and beauty, and then trace their application in every detail. The popular diffusion of such philosophy of music as this elementary work contains, must contribute to so delightful and desirable an end.

Does not Dr. Bryce's theory, (that well proportioned uniformity and variety—likeness fitly blended with dissimilarity—forms an important element of Harmonic Beauty,) find new illustrations in the rules above? The ready exclusion of fifths and octaves (the most "perfect" of the consonances technically, and those which have the greatest *sameness of effect*,) especially when any new element of *sameness* is introduced, as that of their consecutive *repetition* or of their being approached by *similar* motion, seems to be founded on the same principle.

The fifths and octaves mentioned at *c* are called, with very insufficient reason, *hidden* fifths and octaves. Mr. Hickson, in his "Rudiments of Harmony," says that these intervals are allowed "when the upper part does not move by *skips*, but from one *degree* to another," and, in a note, he gives a rule, of which this is the result—that the fifths — d s — sr¹ — fd¹ may be approached by similar motion, but not — rl — mt — lm¹. He allows the use of consecutive octaves when no notes are heard between them, as those commonly played with the left hand on the piano.

Mr. Hickson illustrates the importance of progression by easy intervals, as mentioned at *c*, by the following examples. In the first the accompanying harmony would be scarcely bearable, even on an instrument, on account of its extreme and sudden skips; in the second it is adapted to the voice.

| KEY B | d | :r | m | :f | m | :r | d | :— |
| | l₁ | :r₁ | d | :l₁ | d₁ | :t₁ | m₁ | :— |

| KEY B | d | :r | m | :f | m | :r | d | :— |
| | m₁ | :s₁ | d | :l₁ | s₁ | :f₁ | m₁ | :— |

"The same progression of harmonies," he says, "that may be easily performed upon the organ or piano, and which may seem satisfactory, will often appear forced and unnatural when sung by voices. Hence it has often happened that clever writers of organ and piano-forte music have utterly failed when writing glee and choral music."

5. The pupils should be practised, for some time, in analyzing the previous exercises. They might "parse" the harmony thus—BEDFORD, 27; DOH SOH a fifth; DOH ME a major third; DOH DOH unison; FAH LAH major third; * * * FAH SOH dissonance; FAH resolved on ME; ME upper DOH¹ a minor sixth, &c.

They should next familiarise themselves with the simple consonances of every note in the scale, and be able to name the consonances of RAY—of ME—of SOH, &c.

The teacher might then give his class some simple phrase, like that above, to be harmonized. The production of each member might be written, the next day, on the black board, and sung and criticised by the class. Gradually more difficult passages of melody may be given to be harmonized, until the pupils are able to add an accompanying melody to any simple tune.

6. Harmony in three or more parts is produced when each of the notes sounding together forms a consonant interval with *each* of the others. In addition to the intervals (octaves, fifths, thirds, and sixths), allowed in two part harmony, fourths (s d¹ — t, m — d f — l r¹ — r s — m l, which are inversions of the fifths—see above 2. *f.*)—are also esteemed consonant. Such combinations of notes are called CONSONANT CHORDS. A combination of three such notes is called a TRIAD.

a. Consonant triads can be formed on each note of the Common Mode except TE. Those which have the major third (as d m — f l — s t) below are called *Major Triads.* Those which have the minor third (as l, d — r f — m s) below are called *Minor Triads.*

MAJOR TRIADS.

Chord of Doh or the Tonic	{	SOH ME DOH	Chord of Fah or the Subdominant	{	DOH¹ LAH FAH	Chord of Soh or the Dominant	{	RAY¹ TE SOH

MINOR TRIADS.

Chord of LAH	{	ME DOH LAH,	Chord of RAY	{	LAH FAH RAY	Chord of ME	{	TE SOH ME

b. When the notes of a consonant triad are inverted, in any manner, the triad remains harmonious; and, as its general character and musical effect is not greatly altered, it still retains its original name. Thus—

TRIADS OF DOH	{	s m d	d¹ s m	m¹ d¹ s	TRIADS OF LAH	{	m d l,	l m d	d¹ l m	TRIADS OF SOH	{	r¹ t s	s¹ r¹ t	t s r

c. Consonant chords, containing more than three notes, can only be formed by doubling, in unison or replicate, one of the notes of a triad. Thus—

CHORDS OF FAH	{	f¹ d l f	l f f d	d¹ f d l,	CHORDS OF RAY	{	r¹ l f r	l¹ r¹ f f	l f r l,	CHORDS OF ME	{	m¹ t s m	t¹ m¹ t s	s m m t,

d. Dissonant intervals may be introduced, by the skilful musician, not unfrequently. They are more allowable when one of the dissonant notes is "prepared" and "resolved" as mentioned above (4. *g.*). A chord containing a dissonant interval is called a *Dissonant Chord.* Of these chords the triad on TE (TE, RAY FAH containing the tritone), is the least dissonant in its effect. The triad on NE (NE, TE, RAY) is of a similar kind.

e. The rules given above for the progression of simple consonances apply also to the progression of Chords. The prohibitions of consecutives are confined to consecutives between the same "parts." The following examples of the resolution of Dissonant Chords should be studied. Let the pupil name the dissonances and show their resolution.

$$
\begin{array}{ccccccc}
\mathrm{f^1}\!\!\searrow_{\mathrm{m^1}} & 1\!\!\searrow_{\mathrm{s}} & 1\!\!\searrow_{\mathrm{s}} & \mathrm{r-r} & \mathrm{r}\;\;\mathrm{f}\!\!\searrow_{\mathrm{m}} & 1\;\;\mathrm{f}\!\!\searrow_{\mathrm{m}} \\
\mathrm{r^1}\!\!\searrow_{\mathrm{d^1}} & \mathrm{f}\!\!\searrow_{\mathrm{m}} & \mathrm{r}\!\!\nearrow^{\mathrm{m}} & \mathrm{d}\!\!\searrow_{\mathrm{t_1}} & \mathrm{d}\!\!\searrow_{\mathrm{t_1}}\!\!\nearrow^{\mathrm{d}} & \mathrm{r}\;\;\mathrm{r}\!\!\searrow_{\mathrm{d}} \\
\mathrm{t}\!\!\nearrow^{\mathrm{d}} & \mathrm{r}\!\!\nearrow_{\mathrm{d}} & \mathrm{t_1}\!\!\nearrow^{\mathrm{d}} & \mathrm{l_1}\!\!\searrow_{\mathrm{s_1}} & \mathrm{l_1}\!\!\nearrow^{}\!\!\searrow\mathrm{s_1-s_1} & \mathrm{d}\!\!\searrow\mathrm{t_1}\!\!\nearrow^{\mathrm{d}} \\
\mathrm{s-s} & \mathrm{t_1}\!\!\nearrow & \mathrm{s_1-s_1} & \mathrm{f_1}\!\!\nearrow^{} & \mathrm{f_1}\!\!\nearrow^{} & \mathrm{f_1}\;\;\mathrm{s_1}\;\;\mathrm{s_1}
\end{array}
$$

The teacher should encourage his pupils to find out, for themselves, what notes are, according to the sixth proposition above, consonant with a given note and with one another. They will thus *discover* the triads. They may afterwards be taught to classify them as above.

The minor triads are chiefly used in minor tunes. If we considered the Minor as a distinct scale from the Common Mode, we should call the first of the minor chords the Minor Tonic Chord, the second the Minor Subdominant Chord, and the third the Minor Dominant Chord. They are so named in some books.

Some persons reckon TE RAY FAH among the consonant triads, calling it the "Chord of the diminished fifth," the "neutral triad," &c.

The first of the dissonant chords "resolved" at *e* above is called the "Dominant Seventh." It is the Dominant (or Soh) Chord, with the Seventh note above the dominant added. The second dissonant chord is called by Dr. Crotch the "Leading Seventh." It is the chord of the Leading Note (TE) with the seventh note above it added. The third is, for similar reasons, called the "Added Ninth," and the rest are illustrations of the "Added Sixth"—the sixth note above added to the Chord of FAH. For an account of Chromatic Dissonant Chords the student is commended to Dr. Crotch and other authorities.

7. The musical effect of the different chords may be exhibited by causing a class to sing them, first in *rapid* unison as a melody, (See note on "quick succession," p. 19) and then in parts. It will be seen that each minor triad has two notes in common with a corresponding major triad. In the following exercise the related triads are placed together.

EXERCISE ON THE CONSONANT CHORDS.   (*For three voices.*)   KEY B.

$$
\begin{array}{l}
\left\{\begin{array}{l}
\mathrm{d:m:s\,|\,d:m:s}\;\;|\;\mathrm{s}:-:-\,|-:\;\;\;|\;\mathrm{l_1:d:m\,|\,l_1:d:m}\;|\;\mathrm{m}:-:-\,|-:\\
\mathrm{d:m:s\,|\,d:m:s}\;\;|\;\mathrm{m}:-:-\,|-:\;\;\;|\;\mathrm{l_1:d:m\,|\,l_1:d:m}\;|\;\mathrm{d}:-:-\,|-:\\
\mathrm{d:m:s\,|\,d:m:s}\;\;|\;\mathrm{d}:-:-\,|-:\;\;\;|\;\mathrm{l_1:d:m\,|\,l_1:d:m}\;|\;\mathrm{l_1}:-:-\,|-:
\end{array}\right.\\[2em]
\left\{\begin{array}{l}
\mathrm{s_1:t_1:r\,|\,s_1:t_1:r}\;|\;\mathrm{r}:-:-\,|-:-:\;\;|\;\mathrm{m_1:s_1:t_1\,|\,m_1:s_1:t_1}\;|\;\mathrm{t_1}:-:-\,|-:-:\\
\mathrm{s_1:t_1:r\,|\,s_1:t_1:r}\;|\;\mathrm{t_1}:-:-\,|-:-:\;|\;\mathrm{m_1:s_1:t_1\,|\,m_1:s_1:t_1}\;|\;\mathrm{s_1}:-:-\,|-:-:\\
\mathrm{s_1:t_1:r\,|\,s_1:t_1:r}\;|\;\mathrm{s_1}:-:-\,|-:-:\;|\;\mathrm{m_1:s_1:t_1\,|\,m_1:s_1:t_1}\;|\;\mathrm{m_1}:-:-\,|-:-:
\end{array}\right.\\[2em]
\left\{\begin{array}{l}
\mathrm{f_1:l_1:d\,|\,f_1:l_1:d}\;|\;\mathrm{d}:-:-\,|-:-:\;|\;\mathrm{r_1:f_1:l_1\,|\,r_1:f_1:l_1}\;|\;\mathrm{l_1}:-:-\,|-:-:\\
\mathrm{f_1:l_1:d\,|\,f_1:l_1:d}\;|\;\mathrm{l_1}:-:-\,|-:-:\;|\;\mathrm{r_1:f_1:l_1\,|\,r_1:f_1:l_1}\;|\;\mathrm{f_1}:-:-\,|-:-:\\
\mathrm{f_1:l_1:d\,|\,f_1:l_1:d}\;|\;\mathrm{f_1}:-:-\,|-:-:\;|\;\mathrm{r_1:f_1:l_1\,|\,r_1:f_1:l_1}\;|\;\mathrm{r_1}:-:-\,|-:-:
\end{array}\right.\\[2em]
\left\{\begin{array}{l}
\mathrm{s_1}:-:-\,|-:-:-:-\,\|\\
\mathrm{m_1}:-:-\,|-:-:-:-\,\|\\
\mathrm{d_1}:-:-\,|-:-:-:\,\|
\end{array}\right.
\end{array}
$$

In a similar manner each of the dissonant chords, above given, may be sung, first in quick succession of notes, and then in chord followed by the chord into which it is resolved.

The pupils should again be practised in " parsing" the consonances of the three-part or four-part exercises. Thus—HARRINGTON, 106.   " Chord of DOH." " Chord of DOH—first inversion."   " Chord of TE—second inversion, the FAH resolved in next chord."   " Chord of LAH—second inversion."   " Chord of SOH —second inversion."   " Discord of the dominant seventh, TE omitted, FAH resolved in next chord," or " Chord of SOH, with dissonant FAH resolved, &c."

The teacher may again give his class melodies to be harmonized, advancing from the simplest phrases to more difficult airs. These he will require to be harmonized sometimes in three, sometimes in four, and sometimes in five or six parts.

A little practice would enable the pupil to re-cognise by ear and to name the chords which are struck on an instrument. This would lead to the " copying by ear" of harmony as well as melody. It would cultivate the power of "making music in the mind," and even give some facility in transferring musical ideas—both of melody and harmony—to paper without requiring them first to be sung or played. It was by " mental com-position" that the great works of Beethoven and Mozart were elaborated and fully written, before even a single note of their mighty music had been heard—except within the walls of that wondrous temple, the composer's own mind.

If any one is filled with ambition to become a composer of music, let him remember the words of Mr. Graham. " Genius, and observation, and a careful study of the best models, are really the only things which can ever make a good poet, or a good painter, or a good composer of music. * * * In the works of the greatest composers are found many passages of excellent effect, though pro-hibited by the rules of the theorists. * * * The student ought never to give up his reason and his judgment to any theoretical authorities. * * * He ought to keep in view that, in music, nothing is out of rule except what offends the ear, the taste, and the judgment; but that he must not attempt to imitate the freedom and bold effects of the greatest masters, until he has acquired great knowledge and command of his materials."

SECTION XIII.

OF THE CHANT AND THE PRACTICE OF CHANTING.

1. The chant is the most ancient and the most simple kind of tune. Its only essential elements are a single note, of indefinite length, to which any number of words may be sung, followed by one or more other notes of measured length adapted to the closing syllables. The first part is called the RECITING or *Declaiming* NOTE. The second is called the CADENCE or *Terminal*. In the following example the Reciting note is printed in Capital letters.

EXAMPLE 1.   A Gregorian Tone.   KEY A.

DOH	r :d	DOH	l₁ :d	r :d
Beautiful for situ-	a- tion.	The joy of the whole earth	is Mount	Zi- on.

a. The Cadence or Terminal may be of various lengths, sometimes filling on y one measure, and sometimes two, three, or even four. It is usually in the Binary Measure, but occasionally in the Trinary.

  b. The Reciting Note is sometimes introduced by two or three distinct notes, called the *Reciting Preface.* Such a preface seems not unnatural to the voice in commencing a recitation, especially if the opening words are unemphatic. In some chants the Reciting Note is closed by a single separate note, called the *Reciting Affix* or Grace Note, which should serve to lead the ear to the measured cadence which follows.

  c. In the following examples the mark ‖ is used to separate the words of the Reciting note from those of the cadence. The mark | signifies, as in music, that the syllable following has the stronger accent; and · shows the place of the weaker. The horizontal mark — indicates the continuance of a word. The syllables of the Reciting Preface are followed by | , the recitation opening with an accented syllable.

EXAMPLE 2.   Ancient "Tone," having a preface and one-measure terminals.   KEY F.

d   r   ME | m :—   ME | r : d
By the | rivers of Babylon there we sat down, yea, we ‖ wept ·— When we remembered ‖ Zi- · on

EXAMPLE 3.   Ancient Tone, having one three-measure terminal.   KEY F.

⎰ d   r   ME | r   : m   ME | r : d | r : m | r : d
⎱ Beau-ti- | ful for situ-   ‖ a   · tion. The joy of the whole‖ earth · — | is · Mount | Zi- · on,
  On   the | sides of the north, ‖Great · King. God is known in her‖ pala- · ces | for · a | re- · fuge.
           the city of the

EXAMPLE 4.   Ancient Tone, having a trinary terminal.   KEY G.

⎰ d   r   RAY | f : m | r   : m   RAY | m   :r : d | t₁ :r
⎱ I   was | glad when they ‖ said · unt' | me   · — Let us go into the ‖ house · of · the | Lord ·—
  Our | feet shall stand ‖ in   · thy | gates ·—   O Je-   ‖ ru-   · — · sa- | lem ·—

  d. The most usual structure of the modern chant is that in which the first Phrase is a Reciting note (without a preface), followed by a two-measure Terminal, and the second a Reciting note followed by a three-measure Terminal. One section thus formed is called a *Single Chant.* Two such sections make a *Double Chant.* The GREGORIAN, 15, and the NORWICH, 48, Chants are *single.* The LIVERPOOL CHANT, 71, and DR. BOYCE's, 91, are double.

  e. The following is a double chant with a Reciting Affix or Grace Note. When the last syllable or syllables are *cut off* for the Grace Note, Dr. Gauntlett places an apostrophe before them. When the last syllable is *slurred* to the Grace Note he puts the apostrophe after.

EXAMPLE 5.   Dr. Gauntlett.   KEY G.

⎰ DOH   r | m   : s | s   : m   ME | r : d | r : m | m : r
⎨ I will sing 'un-‖to   · the | Lord · — For He hath ‖tri- · umphed | glo- · rious | ly · —
⎩ The Lord is my' ‖strength · and | song · — And he is become‖my · sal-   va- · — | tion · —

⎰ DOH   r | m   : s | s : m   ME | r   : d | d : l₁ | d :—
⎨ The   horse' ‖and · his | ri- · der Hath he   ‖ thrown · in- | to · the | sea · —
⎩ He is my God and I   My Father's
  will prepare him ' an ‖hab- · i-   ta- · tion; God and I ‖ will   · ex-   alt · — | Him · —

These remarks are intended to exhibit the essential structure of the chant and its various modifications. The beautiful examples of nature's own wild melody, which are used in illustration, may be found, with many others, in Dr. Gauntlett's small tract, entitled "Organ Harmonies for the Ancient Church Tones," published by Burns. The fifth example is from Dr. Gauntlett's "Three Hundred and Seventy-three Chants." (Houlston and Stoneman). The prefaces to these works and to Dr. Gauntlett's "Bible Psalms, &c." contain admirable explanations of the chant by a man of high musical taste and genius. Mr. Oakley's "Laudes Diurnae," and the early numbers of the "Parish Choir," are worth studying. Reference should also be made to the very valuable treatise by the Rev. J. A. Latrobe, entitled, "The Music of the Church." The best complete arrangement of the Book of Psalms for chanting is "The Songs of Zion," (B. L. Green, London) by John Brown, Esq., with an elegant preface by the Rev. E. Conder—a work of long and earnest labour and of purest taste. If it had provided for that Rhythmical Division of the Reciting Note, of which we shall presently speak, it would have left nothing further to be desired. It far surpasses other arrangements in bringing out the full and appropriate expression of the sense.

The practice of Chanting has fallen much into disuse, partly on account of the supposed difficulty of the performance, but chiefly because of the abuses to which it has been subject. Nor can we wonder at the disgust of the devout man, who does not know what chanting really is, and has never tasted the spiritual delight of singing the Psalms of the Ancient People in "the words which the Holy Ghost teacheth"—when he sees, in some churches and cathedrals, the antics of unregenerate choristers, and hears their indecent gabbling of sacred words. But let him remember that *that* is not the "singing of Psalms" which, in the House of God, at the Family Worship, and in the lonely Closet, we delight in. Ours is the song which ministers to worship, but cannot hinder it. We hold the music wholly subordinate to the sense. The music is of the simplest and easiest kind. Our whole attention is given to the just expression of the words.

Much misunderstanding has arisen from the idea that the Reciting Note, commonly written as a "semibreve" in the old notation, is always of the same length, however many or however few the words which are sung to it, and that, of necessity, the words must sometimes be indecently hurried. The careless haste of many organists has helped to maintain this delusion. But all the authorities on this subject combine to show that the Reciting Note may be of any length or brevity we please, and that the Recitation, however long it may be, should be delivered with dignity and distinctness,

and seldom with greater rapidity than we use in ordinary speech. Common sense supports this opinion, and reminds us that it is better that the organ should be silent, if the Organist cannot, while he plays, devoutly sing the Chant.

It should be remembered that the Hebrew Poetry is not disposed, like ours, in lines of equal length and measured rhythm, but that the lines are of irregular length and the correspondence between them rather that of thought than language. The figurative expression of one line is heightened by another poetical image in the next. Or one line answers the question of the preceding one, or exhibits to it some beautiful contrast of thought. Dr. Lowth (See his noble essay on "Hebrew Poetry") calls this response of line to line Parallelism. It is the sublime and beautiful principle which governs the earliest poetry of most nations, and no refinements of metre or rhyme will permit the true Lyric Poet entirely to lay it aside. Dr. Gauntlett mentions the 114th Psalm as "an exemplification of this alternateness, and perfect symmetry, in idea, expression, and form." The second line is the echo—the answering thought—to the first. "So also the second verse perfects the idea of the first verse, the fourth verse that of the third, the sixth continues the enquiry of the fifth, the eighth explains the reason of the admonition announced in the seventh. And all these characteristics are conveyed with *a rapidity of thought and force of expression, which no human genius can give to the bonds of metre*, whether that metre be the rhythm of music or that of language." Compare any of the Psalms with the best metrical versions of them by Dr. Watts and others, and it will soon be felt how much superior the original is, both in majesty of thought, and in that abrupt language of emotion which has power to touch the heart. How ought we to welcome, then, that simplest form of musical expression, nearest to the music of ancient days, which enables us to sing the Psalms of David just as they burst forth from his own heart—if not in his very words, yet with the same changeful manner of language, and in the same tide of thought and emotion !

The Psalms, moreover, were meant to be sung. Their full power to subdue or to elevate the feelings is not known till we sing them. Who can *read* without something of weariness the ever-recurring chorus of the 136th Psalm—"For his mercy endureth for ever"? But in the majestic flow of song the wondrous thought seems to expand, and the mind rises in holy fervour at each repetition. Why should we only *read*, with comparative coldness, that which the ancient saints were wont to *recite* in the natural and becoming tones of Gratitude and Joy? Why should we not make, as they did, the "statutes of the Lord *our song* in the house of our pilgrimage"?

P

There is something in the delayed and pleasant utterance of song which at once impresses the words on the mind and endears them to the memory. Why are verses of hymns so much more quoted on the bed of sickness than *texts?* Because the mind has been made to dwell frequently and delightedly, with sweet music, upon their words.

Nor are these the songs of the ancient church alone. They are the types of devout emotion in all ages. The outward dispensation is changed, but the human heart, with its stirrings of hope and fear, love and joy, still remains the same. The doctrinal *knowledge* of the Psalmists was limited indeed, but the rich and varied *experience* they so truthfully pourtray is fully akin to our own. We feel them brethren of the one family, members of the one church. Their penitence, their prayer, the *song* of their pilgrimage, is ours. We own the fellowship of saints when we prolong their strains. It is sweet to comfort ourselves with the inspired song which solaced David's deep distress, and to rejoice in the same words of gladness with which his soul was lifted up. It is delightful to recite again that beautiful chain of Psalms (cxv to cxviii), which our Saviour chanted with his disciples before he "went to the Mount of Olives." And it is instructive to notice that, while the deeper perceptions and the loftier aspirations of the Apostles' days required new "hymns and spiritual songs," yet the "Psalms" are always mentioned first, as still the most familiar and the best used, and it is doubtless the Old Psalms to which reference is thus distinctively made.

But the Psalms, each with its delicate chain of emotions, require to be better understood, and more powerfully felt by the people before they are fit to sing them. Christians will need to be better read in the glorious "comments" of Calvin and Hengstenberg, and in the natural workings of the devout heart—the best comment of all. It should be remembered also that the Psalms were written in the boldest style of ancient poetry, and must be understood and used accordingly. Psalms, which were primarily written for special occasions, or contain references to particular places and persons, were inserted in the Canon of Sacred Song, and used in the Temple Service as well as in private worship, long after the special occasion or the particular person had passed away. That which was once real and actual becomes to another age an instructive parable, a poem of life, and perhaps the figurative representation of higher realities. The christian will not, therefore, depart from the ancient use of the Psalms when he makes new and delightful appropriations of their high poetic meaning. This must be the case, for instance, when the words "Zion," "altar," "tabernacles," "harp," &c., occur. It is thus we use that beautiful image of holy happy fellowship in "the Valley of Baca," (Ps. 84). Thus too the song is appropriated that welcomed the ark to Jerusalem, (Ps. 24). The Jews of after generations continued to sing it, acknowledging the Lord as King of his chosen people, and the christian recites it now to welcome "the Lord of Hosts" to his spiritual Zion—to yield him the throne of his own heart. "Lift up your heads, O ye gates, and be ye lift up ye everlasting doors!" has become the chorus of joy and triumph to all generations. After the same manner, also, have the saints in all times gained strength from that *memorial Psalm*, (Ps. 46) which tells of Hezekiah's faith and Sennacherib's overthrow—appropriating, with joy, the words—"God is our refuge and strength, a very present help in trouble"—and sympathizing in the triumphant expression—"Come, behold the works of the Lord! what desolations he hath made in the earth!"

Even in the worship of dissenters this delightful practice of singing the Psalms has begun to be revived. In some places, where what is called "the long prayer" is divided into two parts, a penitential or some other Psalm is sung by the people between them. In other places the service opens with a Psalm, sung by all the people "entering into His courts with praise"—which is followed by the first division of prayer, and the worship proceeds as usual. Wherever the people are willing to be instructed, this simple psalmody may be introduced with great pleasure and spiritual advantage. It gives variety to the service without excluding any other engagement. Its memorial character gives it a new hold upon our feelings, and brings us into nearer fellowship with the church of all ages. It is wholly a gain to the devotions of the People.

2. Musical recitation, in connection with solemn and dignified subjects, should be delivered with a distinct Rhythm, having regularly recurring accents at equal distances of time.

The words which are to be sung to the Reciting Note of a Chant should previously be divided according to the pleasantest and most expressive rhythm of which they are capable. The marks to indicate the stronger and weaker accents may correspond with those used above in dividing the syllables of the cadence. The rate of movement should correspond with that of the cadence.

This method of recitation will enable a congregation to sing with one voice and with correct expressive accent. It will also permit them to "take breath" in a regular easy manner, and to recite a whole Psalm without the slightest haste or confusion.

The following example will illustrate the method. It is given both in the Old and the New Notation. The Reciting Note is divided and rhythmically marked to correspond with the words below. Let it be remembered that in both notations, and also in the division of words, the "bar" | shows that the note or syllable following it has the stronger accent. The old notation has nothing to indicate the secondary accent.

ROBINSON'S CHANT. (Sch. Mus. 37. Sch. Songs 37.)   KEY E.

The Reciting Note rhythmically divided to suit the words.

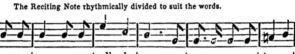

| s :s . s | s :s. s | d¹ :l | s :—.m | m., m : m. m | tu₁ : s |
| He ˙was de | spised˙and re ‖ jected˙of | men˙— A | man of ˙ sorrows ‖ and˙ac- |

s : tu₁ | s :— | :s. s | s ₄s ₄s:s . s | f :m | l | :s ₄s ₄s |
quainted˙ with | grief˙ — | ˙And we | hid as ˙ it ˙were our ‖ fa ˙ces | from him˙ He was de-‖

s :—.s | r :m | r˙ :r | d :—‖
spised ˙ — And ‖ we ˙ es | teemed˙him | not˙ —

Let not the pupil fall into the too common error of singing each note of the recitation as though it were "staccato," with one heavy accent. But let the whole be sung lightly and tastefully.

It will be noticed that the reciting notes are made of different lengths according as the fitting expression of the words seem to require. The first reciting note above fills two measures or "bars," but when applied to the words of the next verse—" | Surely · he hath ‖ borne · our | griefs, &c." it would only be half as long. It might be extended to three or four measures if the words required it.

If we make the rhythm continuous from line to line, it is sometimes necessary to shorten the closing note of the previous phrase for the opening of the new reciting note. See the opening of the second and fourth lines above. When the music or the sense require it, a short pause may be made, as at the opening of the third phrase. The lengthening of a syllable through *half* the following "pulse" or beat will be marked, as at the close of the last reciting note. This method

affords, it will be seen, a delightful variety of rhythmic expression, the *triplet* "pulse" intermingling with the *dual* and the *extended*. Each reciting note above gives a different distribution of notes in the measure.

In dividing the words for the first recitation above, it was thought that the *person* should be emphasized as well as the *act*. Therefore "He" is accented—but in the fourth reciting note, where the same words occur again, the sense requiring a heightened expression of the word "despised," and the person having already been indicated, the rhythmical distribution is altered.

The *appropriate, easy*, and *uniform* delivery of the Reciting Note has been the chief difficulty of chanting. When the Psalms were sung by a small choir, it was easy for the Choir Master to train his singers to his own particular method of dividing and delivering each particular Psalm; but when it was desired that a whole congregation should unite in the exercise, it became necessary that there should be some notation to indicate the manner of delivery to the eye, and so to secure uniformity of utterance. It is clearly required, for congregational worship, that the people should lift up their voice as one man, and that their bold united recitation should be markedly expressive of the sense. It was one great step to vindicate our true declamation against that scandalous gabble which has brought such discredit on the Chant itself, and produced the impression of its unfitness for popular use. (See Latrobe, p. 268). Dr. Gauntlett, after giving two examples of recitation, (and they are, different from most of his own, *rhythmically* divided) says, " This accentuation of the text is adopted from Barnard's work (published in 1641, illustrating the mode of singing then in use), and is another exemplification of the *true* and *clear* declamation of the Prose Psalms, so contradistinguished from the hurry and gabble in which the chant of the English Church has been supposed by some to consist." (See " Singing Class Manual," p. 37.)

A deliberate expressive Recitation being then allowed us, how shall we secure its uniformity? In connection with efforts to introduce chanting into sabbath schools, and by noticing the recitation of some expressive chanters, we were led to adopt the plan (in " Hymns and Chants for Sunday Schools,") of marking, by a stroke above, the syllables on which the sense seemed to require an accent or swell of the voice—thus,

He was despised and re | jected · of | men
A man of sorrows-| and · ac | quainted · with | grief
And we hid as it were our | fa · ces | from him
He was despised and | we · es | teem'd · him | not.

This was found to be a help, but it was not sufficient to keep the singers together without the " pattern" of the living voice; there was also a confusion between 'accent' and 'swell,' and, the recitation not having a natural and flowing rhythm, it was still difficult to manage the breath. The reciting note was not easy and was not liked. Only a few sang it, and they had to wait for one another at the end. The majority only joined in the cadence! Dr. Gauntlett introduces a comma, where there is long recitation, " to break the speed, and to keep the congregation in unity." "At this comma," he says, " let each singer say '*one*' to himself silently, and then go on." But this plan also leaves much indefinite, and is far from securing an expressive, dignified, and uniform declamation.

The method now proposed seems, when once suggested, so easy a deduction from well-known and acknowledged principles of Elocution and Oratorical Declamation that it cannot claim to be called a discovery; and it is so true to nature that many will perceive that they have adopted it in their own practice unwittingly. The Editor's first attempt to make a Sunday School recite

rhythmically (a 'pattern' being given for each line, accompanied by the regular 'beating of time'), was most surprising and delightful in its effect. The children understood it quickly. There was something natural in it which took a ready hold on both the ear and the mind. It was the thing so long sought for—an appropriate, easy, and *united* recitation. All sang the reciting note now, as well as the cadence. There was no hurry and confusion, no waiting at the end, and no difficulty in taking breath. Its application to Congregational use has now been tried for some time with complete success. See the " Psalms arranged in proper Rhythm for Chanting," published by Ward and Co.

Mr. Joshua Steel was the first to describe that Rhythm which there is in all *good* speaking. See his " Essay towards establishing the Melody and Measure of Speech," A. D. 1775, and his " Prosodia Rationalis," 1779. Dr. Rush, the most acute observer of the speaking voice, fully acknowledges and approves Mr. Steel's views. (Philos. of the Voice, p. 364.) Dr. Barber, whose Lectures in this country have done much to diffuse Rational Views of Elocution, illustrates more at large the principles of Measure as applied to good speaking. See also Chapman's Rhythmical Grammar, and' the close of the article "Oratory," in the Penny Cyclopædia. Some elementary works on Elocution make use of this principle only in its application to poetry. But the authorities above quoted and common experience show that well-delivered prose has its Rhythm also. The difference is this, that Poetic Rhythm contains, in each measure, a regulated number of syllables, while Prose Rhythm allows the utmost irregularity and variety in this respect, only requiring that accents should recur at equal intervals of time. Even in the ordinary conversation of an elegant speaker, this rhythm may be noticed. It is still more observable in reading aloud; and the effective public speaker invariably exhibits it. It is this that enables him to send his voice distinctly to a distance, that gives him an easy command of his breath in every utterance, and adds a charm to his sentences.

If Measured Rhythm, then, be an important element of Oratorical declamation, must it not be a *necessary* element of that declamation which is Musical? For Rhythm is one of the first essentials of music. It seems very strange that any attempt should have been made to perform a musical declamation without it. Let us return to that which is natural, then, and deliver rhythmically the reciting note of the chant.

Some persons object to this, that *Recitative* is an acknowledged style of music without any imposed fixed rhythm. Yes, we answer, but it is not on that account *without rhythm*. The time and the rhythm are left to the taste and feeling of the accomplished singer, and if the words are expressive of uncontrolled passion or sudden excitement the rhythm would *naturally* be irregular, for any sudden excitement deranges the beating of the pulse and other instinctive muscular motions from which our first idea and sense of rhythm proceed. But the words of the chant relate only to dignified excitement and to holy passion. They carry with them the dignity of poetic feeling, and should therefore be recited with no loose and troubled rhythm. Others, finding that the notation in which the ancient chants were first written, contains no *marks* of accent, suppose that the ancients *sung* without accent or with *any* accent. This notion of "intoning," as they call it, is utterly unnatural and unsensible. Equally wild is the notion of leaving each singer in a congregation to give his own accent and make his own division. When that is the case, there is always an unmeaning pause at the end of the Reciting Note, to let the lagging singers come up, and then a sudden rush into the cadence. There cannot be dignified consentaneous utterance.

It may be well to mention here the practice of alternate or Antiphonal chanting. This was no doubt the ancient mode, and the structure of Hebrew poetry is well adapted to it. It was the only way then known by which musical variety could be gained from the different qualities of voices. The bold voices of Moses and the men of Israel raised the song of triumph on the borders of the Red Sea, and, at the turn of every verse, the thrilling voices of the women poured in the lofty chorus. In social life, the husband sang to the wife and the wife answered in song. But since the discovery of Harmony and Counterpoint, this variety and sympathy of voices may be manifested far more delightfully in a united and *blended* expression. This practice, like that of dancing, with which David sometimes accompanied his song, is suited to a simpler state of society than that in which we live, and its object is now accomplished in a better way. See an able defence of it in "Parish Choir," vol. i. p. 162. Its chief attraction lies in the holy rivalry of praise, which it implies, between one side of a congregation and the other. A similar rivalry we have often enjoyed in the striving of the different "parts," in harmony, when the heart of the people is full.

3. The learner should confine his attention at first to the art of correct and easy recitation. He should take a Psalm marked for chanting, and simply recite it on some one note which may be easy to his voice. If accustomed to "beating time," he should do so now, taking care that the hand *falls* at every perpendicular stroke, and *rises* at each dot. He will then see that some words must be sung much more rapidly than others. Thus, in the line, "He | maketh me to · lie ‖ down in · green | pastures," of the Psalm below, the words "maketh me to" must be pronounced so rapidly as to occupy no more time than the word "lie," which follows in the soft beat. And, in the line, "He | leadeth me in th' · paths of | righteous · ness ‖ for · his | name's · — | sake," the words "leadeth me in the" must be sung very lightly and quickly, occupying only one beat, and the word "righteousness" will have to be delivered in a more deliberate manner. There is thus given to some words—as "lie," "righteousness," &c., in this Psalm—that delicate expression of "quantity," which adds so much to the beauty of speech. (See Rush on the Voice, p. 133.) Let the learner carefully study the recitations of the twenty-third Psalm, and then let him sing it to the "Gregorian Chant." ("School Music," 94.)

PSALM XXIII.—*Rhythmically arranged for Chanting.*

The | Lord · — ‖ is · my | Shepherd;
| I · — ‖ shall · — | not · — | want.
He | maketh me to · lie ‖ down in · green | pastures;
He | leadeth · me be ‖ side · the | still · — | waters.
| He · — re ‖ storeth · my | soul:
He | leadeth me in the · paths of | righteous · ness ‖ for · his | name's · —
    | sake.

· Yea though I | walk through the · valley of the ‖ shadow · of | death,
| I · — will ‖ fear · — | no · — | evil;
| For · — ‖ Thou · art | with me;
Thy | rod and · thy ‖ staff · they | com · fort | me.
· Thou pre | parest a · table be | fore me · in the ‖ presence · of mine | enemies:
· Thou an | ointest my · head with | oil · my ‖ cup · — | run · neth | over.
· Surely | goodness and · mercy shall | follow me · all the ‖ days of · my | life
And | I will · dwell in the ‖ house · of the | Lord · for | ever.

In teaching children to chant, the subject may be introduced in the following manner. "I wish you to look into your books ("Psalms arranged for Chanting,") at the twenty-third Psalm, while I *sing and beat time.* (Sings two lines to the Gregorian Chant.) Did you notice anything in the book every time that I beat down with my foot? * Yes, the upright mark. Was there anything where you would suppose my foot went up in beating time? * Yes, the dot. Now listen once more and try to find out what the mark along the line of letters means? * Yes, a continuance. Once more listen and look into your books. * Now, you shall sing those two lines by yourselves. Will you want another pattern? * The next line is more difficult. Which will take the longest to sing?—the words "maketh me to" or the word "liv"? Both take the same time. "Maketh me to," you see, must all be sung in the down-beat, and "lie" alone in the up-beat. Let us sing those words by themselves. I will give you a pattern. (Sings "He | maketh me to · lie," beating time). * Now take my pattern for the whole line. * Who can tell me whether the word "maketh" or the word "leadeth" must be pronounced quickest? The word "leadeth" has a whole beat. It must be more gently pronounced. It reminds us of the "still waters" which follow. Now, let us sing the whole line. * Now, from the beginning. * " In this way let the teacher proceed with the utmost care at first, correcting mistakes by criticism and renewed "pattern," never singing with his pupils, and very often taking a reciting note separately and confining attention to it until it is perfectly executed. If the chant is a new one, it should be taught separately from the words by pattern and figuring. Let him remember that when the rhythm is once clearly learnt, nothing could be more easily remembered. If it has been arranged in accordance with the proper sense and expression of the words, it will naturally and forcibly fix itself in the mind and ear. Hence it is that when a Congregation has heard a Psalm well sung, in the manner here described, a few times, they will fall into the proper rhythm, without any conscious effort. A

large portion of the Congregation, however, must take great pains to perfect themselves in a separate practice, before they are able thus to lead the rest.

In selecting chants, care should be taken to choose those which are adapted to the character of the words; and sometimes it may be well to take a new chant, in the course of a Psalm, when the strain of emotion changes, as it often does, from sadness to hope, from affecting supplications to loudest expressions of joy. When this is done, the new chant should be in the same key as the first, or in that of its fourth (FAH) or fifth (SOH). It is also important to select such chants as have their reciting notes at a medium pitch—in each "part." The "Gregorian" is a perfect model in this respect. The following examples and exercises will be useful in illustration.

Examples 6, 7, 8. The harmonies may be found in Gauntlett's "Church Tones." Mr. Oakley directs that the "preface" should be sung by the leader alone! Mr. Gauntlett says it should be used to the first line only, except on festival days, when it may be used to every line !! It was most likely invented as an ease to the voice, when the Recitation commences on the lighter part of the measure, and so may be used or not according to the singer's convenience. The "examples" may be sung antiphonally, if not sung in "parts."

PURCELL, 110, and EXETER, 111. The Tenor and Bass are here written an octave higher than their true pitch for convenience. When this is the case, the parts should be distinctly marked as belonging to Male Voices, and therefore an octave lower. The singer will easily distinguish where the horizontal line — lengthens the preceding syllable a whole beat, as after "fault," &c.; and only half a beat, as after "able," "power," &c., in Ex. 110. Give full and leisurely expression to the word "dominion." In the first and the last lines of this exercise, as in many other cases, it will improve the expression to let the recitation increase in loudness towards the end, giving full emphasis to the words "able" and "power." It keeps up the spirit of the recitation, and may be made a general rule.

EXAMPLE 6.   *Eighth Gregorian Tone.*   KEY G.

s l DOH | r :d   DOH | t₁ :d | l₁ :s₁

When the | Lord turn'd a · gain the cap | tivi · ty of ‖ Zi · on
        | We were · like ‖ them · that | dream · —
Then was-our | mouth · filled with ‖ laugh · ter
        | And · our ‖ tongue · with | sing · ing
  Then said | they a · mong the ‖ hea · then
        The | Lord hath · done ‖ great · things | for · them
    The — | Lord hath · done | great · things ‖ for · us
        | Where · of ‖ we · are | glad · —
  Turn a | gain our · cap | tivi · ty O ‖ Lord · —
        | As · the ‖ streams · in the | south · —
  They that | sow · in ‖ tears · —
        | Shall · — ‖ reap · in | joy · —
  He that | goeth · forth and ‖ weep · eth
        | Bear · ing ‖ pre · cious | seed · —
    Shall — | doubtless · come a | gain · with re ‖ joic · ing
        | Bringing · his ‖ sheaves · — | with · him

EXAMPLE 7.   *An Ancient Tone.*   KEY D.

d m SOH | l :s | f :m   ME | f :m | r :d

Oh — | praise th' · Lord ‖ all · ye | na · tions
        | Praise · him ‖ all · ye | peo · ple
For his | merciful · kindness is ‖ great · to | ward · us
        · And the | truth of the · Lord en ‖ dureth · for | ev · er
Praise — | — · — ‖ ye · the | Lord · —
        | Praise · — ‖ ye · the | Lord · —

EXAMPLE 8.   *Peregrine Tone.*   KEY F.

ME ‖ m :r | f :m | r :d   RAY ‖ r :l₁ | d :d | t₁ :l₁

The | Lord · — ‖ bless · thee and | keep · — | — · thee
The | Lord · make his ‖ face · — | shine · up | on · thee
The | Lord lift · up his ‖ coun · te | nance · up·| on · thee
        | And · — ‖ give · — | thee · — | peace · —

110.   PURCELL'S CHANT.   KEY G.

Air	ME	r :d	r :—		SOH	f :m	r :r	d :—
Second	DOH	s₁ :l₁	t₁ :—		DOH	d :d	d :t₁	d :—
Tenor	SOH	s	s :—		SOH	l :s	s :s.f	m :—
Bass	DOH	t₁ :l₁	s₁ :—		ME₁	f₁ :d₂	s₁ :s₁	d₂ :—

| Now unto · him that is | able · — to ‖ keep you · from | falling
| And · to pre ‖ sent · you | fault · — | less
  Be | fore the · presence ‖ of · his | glory
| With · ex ‖ ceed · — | ing · — | joy
· To the | only · wise ‖ God · our | Saviour
  Be | glory and · majesty do | mini · on and | power · — both ‖ now · and
  | ever · A | men.

111.   EXETER.   KEY B flat.

Air	ME	r	:d	t₁	:—	DOH	t₁	:l₁	s₁	:f₁	m₁	:—
Second	SOH₁	f₁	:s₁	s₁	:—	SOH₁	s₁	:f₁	m₁	:r₁	m₁	:—
Tenor	DOH	l₁	:m	r	:—	ME	r	:d.r	d	:t₁	d	:—
Bass	DOH₁	r₁	:m₁.f₁	s₁	:—	ME₁f₁	s₁	:l₁.t₁	d	:s₁	d₁	:—

DOH	r	:m	f	:—	RAY	m	:l₁	s₁	:t₁	d	:—
SOH₁	f₁	:s₁	f₁	:—	SOH₁	s₁	:f₁	m₁	:s₁.f₁	m₁	:-
ME	r	:d	d	:—	TE₁	d	:d	d	:r	d	:—
DOH	t₁	:tow₁	l₁	:—	SOH₁	d	:f₁	s₁	:s₁	d₁	:—

PSALM XXIV.

The | earth · is the | Lord's · and the ‖ fulness · there | of
The | world · and ‖ they · that | dwell · there | in
· For he hath | founded · it up ‖ on · the | seas
| And · es ‖ tablished · it up | on · the | floods

| Who · shall as | cend in · to the ‖ hill · of the | Lord
Or | who · shall ‖ stand · in his | ho · ly | place
| He that hath · clean | hands · and a ‖ pure · — | heart
Who | hath not · lifted up his | soul · unto ‖ vani · ty nor | sworn · de | ceit
  fully

| He shall re · ceive the | blessing · — ‖ from · the | Lord
And | righteousness · from the ‖ God · of | his · sal | vation
| This is the gene · ration of ‖ them · that | seek him
That | seek · thy ‖ face · O | God · of | Jacob

| Lift up your · heads ‖ O · ye | gates
And | be ye lift · up ye ‖ e · ver | last · ing | doors
| And · the ‖ King · of | glo · ry
| Shall · — ‖ — · — | come · — | in

| Who is · this || King · of | glory
The | Lord · strong and | mighty · — th' || Lord · — | mighty · in | battle
| Lift up your · heads || O · ye | gates
Even | lift them · up ye || e · ver | last · ing | doors

| And · the || King · of | glory
| Shall · — || — · — | come · — | in
| Who is · this || King · of | glory
The | Lord of · hosts || he · is the | King · of | glory

4. When the pupils have been thoroughly familiarized with a few good examples, they should be exercised in copying the Psalms for chanting, and marking the rhythmical division as above. If a whole class were to take the same Psalm for division, they might find great improvement in comparing their exercises. Some would exhibit greater refinement of ear, and some a more delicate perception of the sense of the words than the others. Some, out of a too severe regard for the sense, would present a rugged rhythm, while others, for the sake of a smooth cadence, might betray a neglect of just expression. No one can tell, without trial, how valuable an exercise of mind this is.

SECTION XIV.

OF THE ANTHEM AND THE HYMN TUNE, AND OF CONGREGATIONAL SINGING.

1. An Anthem is a tune which is specially adapted to give musical expression to particular words. The words are usually selected from prose or poetry of a sacred character. Every appliance of music is allowable in the Anthem, which can heighten the effect of the chosen words on the mind of the hearer. Impressive words may be repeated with varying harmony. Passages may be sung by two or three voices alone, and then repeated or replied to, with thrilling power, by the full chorus of all. Even the style of the music may be made to change with the sentiment of the words—sometimes taking the bold Binary Measure, and sometimes the gentler Trinary—sometimes moving rapidly and sometimes with more stately tread—now subdued, "a soft and solemn breathing sound"— and now bursting forth in some loud acclaim of triumph or of joy.

Some simpler tunes of the Anthem kind, like the Sanctus given below, may be used in congregations, as soon as the mass of the people are sufficiently acquainted with music to sing them *with real devotion,* and without distracting atten- tion to the mere sound. Thus used, they might become a great gain to the people of God, supplying a new expressive vehicle of gratitude, joy, and praise. But in how few places, at present, can they thus be sung! For the "service of

Q

song" and the *duty of praise* has been well nigh forgotten in "the house of the Lord." And to have Anthems sung by a choir, for show, is one of the most fearful desecrations of God's worship that could be invented. It is true that, in the assemblies of the early church, individuals occasionally arose, and recited in simple strains some spiritual song for the edification of the silent and listening people. But these were devout men, moved by the Holy Ghost, and they carried the heart of the people with them in their inspired fervour; and when our choirs are composed of the choicest and most heavenly-minded members of our churches, and they can arise and sing Anthems, with simple truthful hearts, so as to elevate our minds and fill us with devout emotion, then shall we too rejoice in such delightful "means of grace." But even then we should more commonly prefer those simpler strains in which every soul and voice could join with one accord.

2. The Hymn Tune is adapted, in its structure, to the metre of particular hymns, but as it is used for all the verses of the same hymn, and commonly for several hymns of similar character, its music can only have a *general adaptation* to the sense and spirit of the words. Everything therefore which, like "the repeat," belongs to the musical enforcement of particular words, must be excluded from the Hymn Tune, and the force of voice with which the tune is sung, as well as, to some extent, the rate of movement, should be suggested by the feelings of the singer in accordance with the different words he utters.

The Hymn Tune, moreover, being adapted to the voice of a Congregation, it is important that its leading melody should be of a striking character, so as to be easily remembered, and that the tune should contain no passages of rapid or difficult execution.

The duty of giving united vocal expression to the feelings of the christian heart has often, in the history of the christian church, like other duties, fallen into neglect for a season. In times of spiritual decay the songs of Zion have become a cold performance of the few, and not the free voice uprising from every heart. The music may have been refined, but its soul of gratitude and praise and joy was gone. In times of spiritual revival, however, the revived people have ever resumed the work of vocal praise to themselves. They, at once, feel it to be the natural expression of God's love in the heart, and the means, in return, of inspiring elevated thought and renewed grace. How much did Luther's Reformation— how much did that of Whitfield and Wesley, owe to the soul-stirring power of a revived Psalmody! The devout President Edwards thus describes the true use and advantage of sacred song in the revivals of his own church. "The goings of God were seen in his sanctuary; God's day was a delight, and his tabernacles were amiable. Our public assemblies were then beautiful; the congregation was alive in God's service. Our public praises were then greatly enlivened. God was then served in our psalmody, in some measure, "in the beauty of holiness." It has been observable that there has been scarce any part of divine worship *wherein good men amongst us have had grace so drawn forth, and their hearts so lifted up in the ways of God, as in singing his praises.* Our congregation excelled all that ever I knew in the external part of the duty before, the men generally carrying regularly and well three parts of the music, and the women a part by themselves; but now they were wont to sing with unusual elevation of heart and voice, which made the duty pleasant indeed."

Many efforts have been made of late to revive this duty and make it a delight. Among them should be mentioned the publication of the "Psalmist," and, more recently, of the Rev. J. J. Waite's small collection of choice tunes, (called Hallelujah) with the noble Essays prefixed to it. But Mr. Waite's lectures and practical illustrations, in various parts of the country, have done more than anything else for this great cause. A devout and ardent man thus going forth to revive, enlighten, and purify the praises of the church, performs a blessed and a glorious work. "The Service of Song in the House of the Lord," a sermon by the Rev. T. Binney, full of beautiful scriptural statements, and written in the spirit of high and sacred poetry, forms a noble contribution to the same cause. But before a complete reformation of Psalmody is effected, there must be a long, quiet, steady work of preparation done in schools and families. Musical skill must become a common thing. Right principles of taste in the application of music to sacred subjects must be generally acknowledged. The high and holy purposes of Psalmody must be widely appreciated. And there must be, moreover, a rich diffusion of *spiritual happiness*—of "joy and peace in believing"—by the grace of God. Let schools and families, by teaching and by prayer, seek this, and the church of the next generation will sing God's praises aright—*with one heart and one voice.* Who will set their hands to so hopeful a work? This book is sent to help them. Much, however, may be done immediately. If any are inclined to promote a Psalmody reformation in the congregation with which they are connected, let us recommend them to begin by persuading to their duty, with patience, forbearance, and love, the pious people—the members of the church. The reformation is vain unless founded on highest principles, and urged on by holy motives. The following practical hints may be useful.

1. Secure the use of *one* hymn book, so cheap that the poor may possess it, and that in large type. Let copies be given to those who cannot buy, and let the pew-openers be provided with copies, which they shall put into the hands of strangers. This, of itself, will improve the congregational singing, and will render unnecessary that very heavy and distracting practice of "lining out" the hymns. *One* cheap Tune Book also should be fixed upon for exclusive use. All must give up some favourite tunes for the sake of unity. And the choice of tunes in every service, prayer meeting, and bible class, should be under one management.

2. Persuade the most pious and influential persons of the congregation to meet with the rest, after the week evening service, for the purpose of preparing themselves in voice and heart for the "service of song" on the sabbath following. On such occasions lectures and lessons in vocal music may be given. The humblest and most elementary means will be sanctified by the greatness of the people's aim and the earnestness of their feeling. Every week-night Bible Class should spend ten or fifteen minutes in music practice. The day and Sunday schools might practice, though not exclusively, the same tunes; and the family worship of every house might familiarize the songs of the sanctuary. To produce any permanent effect, minister, elders, and people must make up their minds to give, for at least two winters, very large, steadfast, and devout attention to this important subject.

3. Let no one presume to the office of leading the Praises of God's People who cannot "sing with the spirit and with the understanding also." The same reasons, which make true piety necessary for the Prayer-Leader and the Minister, render it essential to the Leader of Sacred Song and to the member of a choir. Ungodly choirs will not be endured for a moment when once the christian people are awake to their solemn responsibility in this respect.

4. Take care that the tunes selected are adapted to their high purpose, and really fitted to aid the people of God in "the noblest and most sacred of all earthly employments." The following passage from Mr. Waite's Essay deserves careful study. "An examination of the best models of the psalm tune will confirm the principle we have laid down, that general and not special adaptation is their essential property. Look, for example, at the Old Hundredth, Hanover, St. Anns, and all our best tunes. * * * The authors of these unexceptionably fine compositions well understood the nature of their task. They knew that the psalm tune should be of a grave and sacred character; that its melodies should be sweet, its harmonies rich and varied, and that its principal excellence would consist in its adaptation to all the verses of a hymn or psalm. They could not have been guilty of the absurdity of writing a solo in a psalm tune. To them it would have appeared supremely ridiculous to silence a whole congregation at a given line in each verse, while two or three persons were singing a trio or duet. To construct a psalm tune so as to compel a repeat of the whole or part of certain lines in every verse, would have been, in their estimation, an outrage upon common sense, and an insult to the understanding of the people for whom it is written. To direct a given line in every verse to be sung piano, and another given line to be sung forte, without any regard to the sense and meaning of the line, would in their judgment have been a disgrace even to a child. To have inserted a Fugue in either of the lines of a psalm tune, would have been to necessitate such frequent and egregious absurdities as would to them have seemed nothing less than a desecration of the house of God. How comes it to pass that many of our modern tunes contain all these monstrous incongruities? The reason is obvious; their authors have never studied the matter. Many of them are, doubtless, men of considerable musical talent and knowledge, but then they have never studied the nature and design of this species of sacred music. * * * Here has been their mistake; they have taken the first verse of a hymn or psalm and composed their tunes to that. Overlooking the essential principle of the psalm tune, they have tried to give the best expression to the meaning of that particular verse. In this perhaps they may have succeeded; but the special fitness of their tunes for the words of the first verse has necessarily rendered them, to a greater or less degree, inappropriate to those of other verses."

To a similar effect are the following quotations from Latrobe's "Music of the Church." The first is against rapid movements. "The voice of the multitude is harsh, diverse, and unbending in management—the voice of a practised singer, on the other hand, is, by natural power and exercise, perfectly at the possessor's command—it is the smooth and ready consequence of the intention, the very echo of the will. Thus, when a note is sounded, it is not, upon the moment, taken up by every one who professes to sing in the great congregation. Some portion of time is lost, too minute perhaps in its duration to obtain even a name, but sufficiently long to throw back the unwieldy tone, and in a rapid movement, leave it to follow up as it may a clumsy inarticulate and breathless chase." The next refers to the fugue style of tunes. "When the treble is left to perform singly, and the bass has its pauses and places of conjunction to mark, the mind of the singer is too much engrossed to feel the benefit of a spiritual exercise, and the people at large are utterly precluded from a cordial participation. They are continually at fault. They can understand neither when to sing nor when to be silent. The Bass is ever obtruding itself upon the Treble, and the Treble poaching into the domains of the Bass. And thus the compositions, professing to be congregational, are, in effect, choral, and confined to the few persons who dignify themselves by the name of 'the singers!'" The next is against the slow and heavy style in which good tunes are often sung. "The Hundredth Psalm is indeed a beautiful tune—but such is the style of its common performance, that it is not easy to discover the peculiar charm which has enabled it to work its way into popularity. Instead of being presented to the people one regular and flowing melody, it is generally sung with such deliberation, that the breath is more than expended upon each word, and instead of a mutual connection and dependence, the notes stand apart and disunited. * * To understand the beauty of a tune is impossible when it is thus leisurely dissected, limb by limb; beside that, necessarily, the energy and life, of which it is so capable, and which are its chief recommendations to the popular ear, are entirely lost. Let the character of a tune be properly considered, and its time determined, and we shall readily acknowledge, that full and deliberate harmony is perfectly consistent with vigour and sprightliness." Mr. Waite's "Hallelujah" would form a perfect model of the Hymn Tune Book, if there were added to it a goodly number of those lighter and more cheerful tunes which the majority of our Hymns require.

3. It will be useful to divide Hymn Tunes into three classes, in accordance with the different character of the hymns to which they may be adapted. The first class will include those of a BOLD and *Lively* character—the second those which, without a very marked expression, are FLOWING and *Pleasant*—and the third, those which have a GRAND and *Solemn* expression. The second class, which may be subdivided into the "Emotional," and the simply "Elegant" melody of our former more scientific classification (p. 74), is that which will be most required by the hymns in common use. The first and last classes both belong to the "Dignified" melody mentioned before, and many tunes which will suit a "grand" and "solemn" hymn, when sung slowly, become at once "bold" and "lively" when sung quickly. If, therefore, it were possible to use a congregation to sing a tune in both styles, several, like "Stephens," "Old Hundredth," &c., would have to be marked as belonging to the first as well as to the third class.

Every Leader should form a list of the Tunes, which the Congregation have in use, arranged, under the different metres, according to this classification. It will very greatly facilitate his quick selection of appropriate tunes. If such a list of tunes were entered into a ruled book, like the "Class Attendance Book" of Sunday Schools, he could easily mark how often each tune was used. These provisions would guide his choice much more usefully than the taste and suggestion of the moment.

Taking the Bible Psalms, which were specially provided for public worship by Divine Authority, as our guide in reference to the range of subjects, and the style of sentiment which may be profitably introduced in the songs of Religious Assemblies, we find a wide scope and a delightful variety. Sometimes our song is Didactic, describing Truths in which we glory; sometimes Historical, recounting wondrous deeds of Grace; and sometimes Lyrical, speaking all the voices of

Christian experience, and pouring forth our own emotions, or those of others with which we sympathize and which we desire to possess. Sometimes we speak to our fellow-men of redeeming love, ("Let him that heareth say, Come") and sometimes address our song direct to the Eternal Throne. But in all the spirit of Praise is heard—Praise to the Lord most high. The following admirable description of the proper purpose of Psalmody is taken from Mr. Binney's sermon mentioned above.

"The 'Service of Song in the House of the Lord' may include not only *direct praise*, to which some think hymns should be confined, but all the exercises and emotions of the heart. The varied vicissitudes of the inward life may find fitting expression here;—the works and ways of God—the wonders of his universe—the mysteries and felicities of his Providential administration;—the great facts of our spiritual redemption—the advent of the Lord—his life, and death;—the previous delineations of prophetic song;—the subsequent discoveries of apostolic light, revealing the invisible, and foretelling the future;—all that faith realizes of the existent, all that hope desires and expects of the foretold; these things, and such as these, may all find, in the Psalmody of the church, some forms of appropriate united utterance. We are to sing, not merely *directly* to praise God, but to "edify" and "admonish," impress and excite each other and ourselves. Not merely *because* we feel, but that we *may* feel; not merely to present adoration, but to profess truth—and so to profess it, that we may show we "glory" in it—that "the word of Christ dwells in us richly"—and that, by repeated and exultant avowal, its impression on ourselves, and its permanency among men, may be respectively deepened and secured."

This variety in the subjects and style of hymns necessitates a great variety in the character of the tunes. While therefore tunes of a frivolous and secular style should be utterly excluded, we should not, on the other hand, confine ourselves exclusively to those of a grave and solemn effect.

Great objection is taken against tunes, like that called "Prospect," which, though far from frivolous themselves, were originally written for frivolous words. Much deference should be shown to the feelings of those who have painful associations of vanity in connection with these tunes, and in many cases they should be entirely excluded on this account, however well suited they may be in themselves to express religious emotion, and however much we may desire to use them. But the great lack of soft, tasteful, and lively tunes, free from repetitions, fugues, 'runs,' and 'shakes,' and otherwise adapted to the voice of a multitude, forms a strong excuse for such adaptations; and in music for children, where the necessity for beautiful and striking melodies is still more apparent, it is an amply sufficient excuse. Similar remarks will apply to the adaptations from the great masters, such as "Samson," "Solomon," &c. The number of pure original Hymns Tunes, *with good melodies*, is exceedingly small. In this respect, the inordinate love of Harmony and the Organ has done great harm to the taste of our musical men. We find, for instance, the following tune, which has no *melodial unity* whatever, quoted as a model in a recent work of an able music teacher. Key n flat. :d | d :l₁ | s₁ :m | r :t₁ | d :— | :d | r :m | r.t₁ :l₁ | s₁ :— | :d | l₁ :r | t₁ :m | d :f | r :— | :r | m :f | m :r | d :— The first two lines are good, but the third line bears no relation to them. It does not heighten their effect by further development or by skilful contrast. It is the intrusion of a foreign and discordant thought. The former lines, changing into this, are like a gentleman suddenly assuming the gait and look of a clown. See remarks on the "Symmetry of Rhythm," and the "Symmetry of Musical Expression," pages 76, 77, 78 of this book.

4. The duty of a Leader of Singing in a congregation is—to provide, by practice meetings as well as by private exhortation, instruction, and encouragement, that there be a sufficient number of persons able to sustain the several "parts" in any tune that is sung—to keep such tunes as the people can sing in frequent use—to select the tunes for each service, in accordance with the sentiment of the appointed hymns—to have his own mind deeply imbued beforehand with the spirit of each hymn—in "starting" the tune, to pitch distinctly the key note, giving time for each person to take, either in a soft voice or mentally, the first note of his own part, and then to "lead" the tune by singing, after the first note or two, the part proper to his own voice, with good accent and heart-born expression.

The office of him who leads the praises of the sanctuary is a high and honourable one. It re- | quires a correct ear, a moderate voice, and a soul full of spiritual sympathies. A plain singer, whose heart is engaged with the subject of the hymn, and who gives free expression to his own fervour, will lead not only the voices, but also the hearts of the people, while the self-conscious man, with his fine voice and mechanical delivery, can neither awaken among them the sympathy of song, nor the pulse of responsive emotion.

In the manner of leading above indicated a firm Bass voice will be quite as useful as a Tenor. It is naturally a *stronger* voice. The Bass "part" also usually marks the accent with greater decision. And the Bass Singer has less temptation to spoil the pure and brilliant "air" by pouring on to it the deadening sound of a man's voice.

At present, however, it is not common, in England, for a whole congregation to sing in parts. The members of a choir may take their proper parts, and here and there in the congregation an occasional Bass, or Tenor, or Alto may be heard singing a part of his own making, to the distraction of his own thoughts and those of others, and to the confusion of all true harmony. It were better that all voices should join to sing the "Air," in unison, than thus make discord. But alas! even this refuge is denied us. For many voices *cannot* sing the Air. It is too high for them. Our tune books were prepared for choirs, and the "air" is properly adapted to the pitch and compass of the highest voices—the Sopranoes. But the Contra-altoes and Basses—forming at least one third of the vocal power of a congregation—cannot possibly sing in that compass without extreme fatigue. (See p. 87, 88.) Many of them are therefore silent. Others try to sing, and so flatten the "air," making its lower notes (if it has a full compass), quite distressing to the Sopranoes—insomuch that they cry out for an organ to keep up the pitch. Others again sing their sorry voluntaries in the manner above referred to. Thus our tunes are *made* for part-singing, but are *used* in a motley manner, which is neither the full, rugged, but often grand, unison, nor the united movement of many voices, each sustaining the part easiest to itself, and vying one with the other in the ardour of sacred song.

" But why not," it may be said, "alter the tunes and adapt them to the old and simple plan of unison singing? It is certainly the easiest! It requires neither tune book, nor teacher, nor effort! Every one can join in a simple Air!" There is much of good sense in this proposal. The practice is the common one in musical but non-evangelical Germany. The " Parish Choir," already quoted, publishes a series of Hymn Tunes, to be sung in unison, with accompanying Harmonies, to be played by the Organ or sung by the choir. The harmonized tunes which followed the Reformation of the sixteenth century, had the principal melody written in the Tenor cleff,

and intended to be sung by the body of the people, male and female, while the other parts were sung by the more musical. But the following considerations will, it is hoped, satisfy any serious, earnest labourer in this cause that such a return to the simple practice of ruder ages should not be the goal of his efforts.

1. To bring back the few among our people, who have perceived the advantages and realized the delights of Harmony, to the practice of heavy unison would be a far more difficult enterprise than that of teaching the many to sing their proper parts. There is a charm in that variety in unity, that wondrous blending of voices from a whole congregation as the voice of many, but yet the voice of one, which no people who have enjoyed it, even to a small degree, can willingly loose; and this very charm, felt powerfully even by the uncultivated ear, will act as a stimulus to those whom we would encourage to simple though higher acquirements. It is, too, an incomparably more pleasant work to persuade men to advance than to ask them to retrograde.

2. As musical knowledge is greatly increasing in the land, and as such acquaintance with its simple elements as is sufficient to qualify for taking a part in a plain Hymn Tune is already widely spread, it were a shame for us to use the noble powers of Harmony for our own recreation at home, and not bring them to the service of the sanctuary. An evangelized people are always a willing people. They will strive to improve, that they may "serve God with their best." They will not be content that their tribute of song should be of an inferior kind to that which is so common in the land.

3. To adapt our tunes properly to unison singing would sadly confine the "compass" of our sacred melodies. They must not rise higher than the note which the lowest voices—Bass and Contra-alto—can easily sing, and they must not go lower than is agreeable to the highest voices—Tenor and Soprano. A reference to page 87, will show that from c_1 to D, or from c to D^1 is the extreme compass which such melodies could take. How would this cramp the genius of the composer and the expressive power of the tune! And yet as soon as these limits are transgressed, and the melody delays upon the higher notes about D or ascends above it, so soon do the lower voices (Bass and Contra-alto), which are the strongest in structure, and therefore the most powerful in unison singing, begin to flatten and drag down the whole by reason of the strain to which they are subject.

4. The union of male and female voices in one part tends to overpower and discourage the latter. One loud, out-singing Tenor will easily hide the beauty and sweetness of a hundred female voices. It was partly as a relief from this that the

Ancients had recourse to the Alternate Singing mentioned in the last section. But in Part Singing, no voice dominates over the others;—each contributes to adorn and encourage the rest.

5. We ought not to neglect a discovery, like that of Harmony, which God has permitted to enrich the world in these later ages. Its finest application is to large masses of the human voice, and its noblest employment in the service of God. The invention of Harmony was simply the discovery of that for which God had already provided the materials and prepared the effect in the very nature of things. It was welcomed, at once, by pre-existing adaptations to its purpose in the relation of musical vibrations, in the varieties of the human voice, and the natural requirements of Taste. It would not be difficult to show that, to every general assembly, (composed of both sexes and various ages in the usual proportion) God has given a natural adaptation of voice and ear to singing in *four* parts. The wonderful variety of voices, alone considered, would allow an indefinite number of melodies to be sung together; but the ear limits the number, for it requires that there should not be much "doubling" of notes in a chord, and no "interlacing" or confusion of one concurrent melody with another; and to fulfil these conditions well, not more than two melodies for the male and two for the female voices can be allowed. Thus we have arranged for us, first, the higher voices of Woman raising the sweet clear melody of the "air;" next, her lower voices, rendering a soft and close accompaniment; then the higher voices of Man, enriching the music with a mellow and expressive sound; and last, his lower voices, supplying the strong bold Bass on which this moving pillar of Harmony is sustained. An art thus approved by nature should not be rejected from the highest service to which it can be applied. It suits the instincts of the human heart. It suits the worship of God. This cordial fellowship of various sounds, this rich confluence of melodious streams, is most becoming to the assembly of saints. It speaks of holy rivalry and blending sympathies.

While we seek thus to promote improvement, let us have forbearance towards those who do not join in the endeavour. Let us never take a critical ear and a fastidious taste to the sanctuary. In the congregational practice and in the singing class we can criticise; but in the house of God we are assembled to worship. God bears with the rude voices of our brethren in Christ: why should they disturb us? We would not silence our neighbour's ill-trained voice, for it speaks the music of his heart, though there be little of music in its sound. We can overlook a thousand musical enormities so that our fellow-worshippers are earnest in praising God. Let us therefore be content, in reference to some, if we can persuade

them to "sing more softly," reminding all that God is best pleased with the most "comely" offering of praise we can render.

In reference to men singing the "air," (or women meddling with the Tenor or with the Alto in the higher octave) Mr. Hickson says, "The highest part will always predominate over every other, and therefore none of the notes given to the second, third, or fourth voices should rise above the first, unless it be intended that the melody of their part should, for the time, take the lead. In most collections of Psalm Tunes, harmonized for four voices, the parts are so written that the Tenor and Counter *appear* above the air; but the air, in these collections, is intended to be sung by Treble voices, and the other parts by the voices of men, in which case the air would still be the uppermost part. Ignorance of this rule is one of the reasons why congregational singing often produces an unpleasing effect, especially when there is not a majority of female singers in the church or chapel. A Clerk leads the air, while the Tenor and Counter-tenor voices sing their parts a third and fifth above him. Hence the air has the grumbling effect of a Bass, while the Inversion of the chord, contrary to the design of the composer, sometimes produces consecutive fifths and octaves." The Counter-tenor part is now often sung, as it should be, in the lower octave by the lower female and boys' voices.

Some say that they cannot take a "part" with so much spiritual enjoyment as when they sing the air. If they were as *familiar* with the part most convenient to the compass of their own voice, as they are with the air, they would have *greater* spiritual enjoyment in using it. Many have given the needful attention and effort, and have delightfully verified this remark.

Some persons recommend that the congregation should sing in unison, but that there should be an Organ to play the harmony, and that this harmony should be changed with each verse according to its character and expression. Never let us permit the voice of God's people in solemn worship to be used as a foil to display an organist's skill.

In reference to the use of Organs, the "Parish Choir" says: "We are inclined to suppose that in almost every case where a decided objection is felt against the use of the Organ, it is owing to the player rather than to the instrument. There are many organists, though the number is happily decreasing, who lose sight of the fact that their instrument is intended not simply to be played upon but to accompany; not only to exhibit its or their powers, but to aid the voices and elevate the devotions of others." We knew one organist, an enthusiastic lover and a master of his instrument, who was wont to place his hymn book before him (the tune book lying open on the floor)—to keep the voices from the gallery in his ear—and so to pour out his own voice and heart, with the harmony of his noble instrument, in the song of praise. He now unites in the harmonies of Heaven. Oh! that there were many such! Miss Glover makes the following important remark: "I suspect an erroneous notion often prevails respecting the powers of the organ, which hinders the cultivation of congregational singing. Is it not frequently regarded as an instrument calculated to teach, or at least to lead psalmody? The inability of the Organ, generally speaking, *to express the accent* in musical feet, renders it, in my opinion, a bewildering guide to novices, when it attempts to lead them; and it seems to me, to be too unwieldy an instrument to serve well as an accompaniment to an unskilful choir. I freely acknowledge its utility in prompting the pitch and air of a tune before the psalm is sung; and its power of drowning bad voices while the psalm is being sung; but does not this latter quality tend *to conceal the articulation of words*, and to encourage indolence with respect to the cultivation of the human voice?" Mr. Binney's opinion,

expressed in the latter part of the following quotation, is that with which we most heartily concur. "There is nothing wrong in principle, indeed, in the use of an Organ, employed with simplicity, as a mere substratum, guide, and support for the volume of voice rising from the people; or, for filling the place with suggestive intonations, with hallowed, soothing, preparatory utterances of penitential, grateful, adorative symphonies, as the congregation is assembling. There is nothing wrong in this. There is much that may be useful. [Would not a serious silence be a more comely preparation?] *But we do not want it.* We neither advocate nor need the *instrumental* accompaniment, if the grand *human and spiritual organ*, composed of hundreds of minds and hearts, with its fulness of power, and niceties of modulation and varieties of pipes, and *its conscious life, intelligence, and love*, will only send forth what is in it."

Let the leader be reminded that, if the people's voices *flatten*, it arises from one of four causes—from lazy singing—from loud singing—from low voices, trying to take high parts—or from general

---

112.   SANCTUS.   By Dr. Camidge.   *Air and Second Treble.*   KEY E.

d :— :d	r :— :r	m :— :m	l :t :d¹	d¹ :t :
Ho- ly,	Ho- ly,	Ho- ly,	Lord God of	Hosts;
s₁ :— :s₁	t₁ :— :t₁	d :— ·d	d :f :m	m :r :

d¹ :— :s.,f	m :— :s	d¹ :t ·l	s :s :	s :l :s
Heaven and	earth are	full of	thy glo- ry.	Glo- ry
m :— :r	d :— :r	m :r :r.d	t₁ :t₁ :	m :f :m

With spirit.

f.,l :s :f	m :— :s	l.r¹ :d¹ :t	d¹ :— :— ‖
be to	Thee, O	Lord most	high.
r.,f :m :r	d :— :d	d.f :m :r.m,f	d :— :—

---

113.   CARMEL.   *Air and Second Treble.*   KEY G.

m :d ıs :r	m :r ıd :m	s :s ıs :f.m	r :— ı— :
Meet and right it	is to sing, In	ev'- ry time and	place;
d :d ır :t₁	d :d.t₁ ıs₁ :d	d :r ıd :d	t₁ :— ı— :

m :d ıs :r	m :r ıd :m	s :s ıs :f.m	r :— ı— :
Glo- ry to our	God and King, The	God of Truth and	Grace.
d :d ır :t₁	d :d.t₁ ıs₁ :d	d :r ıd :d	t₁ :— ı—

m :r ım :l	s :f ım :—	f :l ıs :f	m :r ım :—
Join we then with	sweet ac- cord,	All in one thanks-	giv- ing join:
d :t₁ ıd :d	r :t₁ ıd :—	d :d ıd :d.t₁	d :t₁ ıd :—

want of vocal cultivation—all which causes he can remove, by private expostulation or public instruction. If the *time* lags, let him, singing the Bass if possible, slightly anticipate the people, with some decision and clearness, on each *accented* note. There is a moment, however brief, between one note and the next, at which he may thus "prompt" the time, and if the voice which strikes forward, at that moment, be recognised as the Leader's voice, a large congregation may gradually be pushed on into a much faster pace. If the music moves too quickly, let him hang with a heavy delaying sound on the *unaccented* part of the measure, and the desired effect will soon be produced. The voice of a congregation is a weighty thing. It must be studied, and to some extent humoured.

Let new tunes be, at first, very frequently used, till the people know them thoroughly. Do not seek a great variety of tunes. One hundred is quite as many as most congregations can keep in good familiar use. As musical skill becomes more general, we may use a larger number, and especially among those which are adapted to "Pecu-

liar Metres," and which give so much variety, life, and beauty to our psalmody.

THE EXERCISES which follow are, some of them, difficult, but they will give fine cultivation to the voice, and supply a feast of harmony when Male and Female Singing Classes are together. The learner is referred to the many excellent collections of Anthems and Hymn Tunes printed in the Old Notation, which the appendix to this book will quickly enable him to understand. Few things could contribute to the easy spread of true congregational psalmody so much as the publication of a Hymn Tune Book, and a Book of truly Congregational Anthems, in our simpler notation. The tunes might be printed in two parts, one for men, and the other for women and children. The exercises below are thus divided. It will be seen that the Tenor and Bass are given an octave above their proper pitch for convenience of writing. By the help of the "Black Board," the "Solfa Music Paper," and the practice of "Dictation," (See p. 15) copies of tunes may be easily placed in the hands of a class.

SANCTUS. By Dr. Camidge. *Tenor and Bass.* KEY E.

(musical notation in tonic sol-fa)

CARMEL. *Tenor and Bass.* KEY G.

(musical notation in tonic sol-fa)

```
{ |s  :r  |m :f  |m :m  |r  :r  |m :f  |m :r  |d :— |— :  ||
  | Ho- ly, Ho- ly,  Ho- ly, Lord! E- ter- nal praise be  thine!
  |r  :t, |d :r  |r :d  |t, :t, |d :d  |d :t, |s, :— |— :  ||
```

114.   ST. ALBANS.   *Air and Second Treble.*   KEY D.

```
{ | :m |l  :s  |f :'m |r .— |m :t  |d¹ :t |l :ne |l :— |— :m
  |    Oh|won- der past ex- |pres- sion! Chas- tened and bruised for |me,   Strick-
  | :d |d  :m |r :d  |d :t, |d :r  |m :f |m :m |m :— |— :d
```

```
{ |l  :s  |f :m  |r .— |m :t  |d¹ :t |l :ne |l :— |— :t
  |en for my trans- |gres- sion, The |Lord, my God, I see;    My
  |d  :m  |r :d  |d :t, |d :r  |m :f |m :m |m :— |— :s
```

```
{ |d¹ :s |l  :t |d¹ :— |d¹ :s |l  :s |f :f |m :— |— :d¹
  |grief and shame en- |dur- ing, He |poured his soul to |death;   My
  |s  :m |f :f  |m :f |m :m |f :m |m :r |ɱ, :— |— :tu,
```

```
{ |t :r¹ |d¹ :t |l :— |t :m  |f :m |r :r |d :— |—  ||
  |end- less life se- |cur- ing, When |he re- signed his |breath.
  |s :s |s.tu, :s |s :tu, |s :d |r :d |d :t, |d :— |—  ||
```

115.   A LA TRINITA.   *Air and Second Treble.*   KEY F.

```
{ |d  :r  |m :r.d |f :m.r |m :m  |r :m.f |m :r.d |r.f :m.r
  |Sweet the |mo- ments rich in |bles- sing, Which be- fore the |cross I
  |s, :s,.t, |d :t,.d |d :d.t, |d :d |t, :d |d :t,.d |t,.d :d.t,
```

```
{ |d :— |s :s.l |f :f  |s.f :m.r |m :m  |r.d :f.r |m :f.m
  |spend; Life and health and |peace pos- sess- ing, From the sin- ner's
  |s, :— |m :m |r :r |r :d.t, |d :d |t,.l, :l,.t, |d :d
```

```
{ |r.d :f.r |d :— |s :s.l |fd :r.m |f.m :r.t, |df :r |d :r.m
  |dy- ing friend! Here I'll sit for ev- er view- ing, Mer- cy's
  |t,.l, :l,.t, |s, :— |m :m.d |rl, :l,.d |r.d :l,.s, |sd :t, |s, :t,.d
```

```
{ |f :m  |r.d :f.r |d :— |s :s.l |fd :r.m |f.m :r.t, |df :r
  |streams in |streams of |blood;  Pre- cious drops my soul be- dew- ing,
  |d :d |t,.l, :l,.t, |s, :— |m :m.d |rl, :l,.d |r.d :l,.s, |sd :t,
```

```
{ |d :r.m |f :m |r.d :f.r |d :—  ||
  |Plead and claim my |peace with God.
  |s, :t,.d |d :d |t,.l, :l,.t, |s, :—  ||
```

116.   GREGORIAN CHANT.   (Tallis.)   *Air and Second Treble.*   KEY F.

```
{ |ME |m :r |m :— |ME |r :d |r :r |m :—
  |DOH |d :t, |d :— |DOH |t, :l, |t, :t, |d :—
```

s	:s	ıs	:s	s	:s	ıs	:s	s	:l	ıs	:s.f	m	:—	ı—	: ‖
Ho-	ly,	Ho-	ly,	Ho-	ly,	Lord!	E-	ter-	nal	praise	be	thine!			
t₁	:s₁	ıd	:t₁	d	:d₁	ıs₁	:s₁	d	:f₁	ıs₁	:s₁	d₁	:—	ı—	: ‖

ST. ALBANS.   *Tenor and Bass.*   KEY D.

:s	l	:d¹	ıd¹.t:s	l	:s	ıs	:soi	l	:t	ıd¹	:t	d¹	:—	ı—	:s
	Oh	won- der	past ex-	pres-		sion!	Chas-	tened and bruised for	me,						Strick-
:d	f	:d	ır	:m	f	:s	ıd	:t₁	l₁	:r	ım	:m	l₁	:—	ı—	:d

l	:d¹	ıd¹.t:s	l	:s	ıs	:soi	l	:t	ıd¹ :t	d¹	:—	ı—	:r¹
en	for	my trans-	gres-		sion,	The	Lord, my God, I	see;				My
f	:d	ır	:m	f	:s	ıd	:t₁	l₁	:r	ım :m	l₁	:—	ı—	:s.f

d¹	:d¹	ıd¹	:s	s	:l	ıs	:d¹	d¹	:d¹ ıl	:l	l	:—	ı—	:l
grief and shame en-	dur-		ing,	He	poured his soul to	death;				My
m	:d	ıf.m	:r	d	:f₁	ıd	:d	f	:d ır	:r	l₁	:—	ı—	:r

t	:t	ıd¹	:r¹	m¹	:r¹	ır¹	:s	s	:s	ıl	:s	s	:—	ı— ‖
end- less life se-	cur-		ing,	When	he	re- signed his	breath.			
s	:s₁	ıl₁	:t₁	d	:r	ıs₁	:d	t₁	:d	ıf₁	:s₁	d	:—	ı— ‖

A LA TRINITA.   *Tenor and Bass.*   KEY F.

m	:m.s	s	:s	l	:s	s	:s	s	:s.l	s	:s.m	s.l	:s
Sweet the	mo- ments	rich in	bles- sing,	Which be-	fore the	cross I
d	:d.s₁	d	:s₁.d	f₁	:d.s₁	d	:d	s₁	:d.f₁	d	:s₁.l₁	s₁.f₁	:d.s₁

m	:—	d¹	:d¹	l	:l	t	:s	s	:s	s.m	:f.s	s	:l.s
spend;	Life and	health and	peace pos-	sess- ing,	From the	sin- ner's
d	:—	d	:d.l₁	r	:r	s₁	:d.s₁	d	:d	s₁.l₁	:r₁.s₁	d	:f₁.d

s.m	:f.s	m	:—	d¹	:d¹	lm	:f.s	l.s	:f.r	m]	:s	m	:s
dy- ing	friend!	Here I'll	sit for	ev- er	view- ing,	Mer- cy's
s₁.l₁	:r₁.s₁	d	:—	d	:d.l₁	rl₁	:f₁.m₁	r₁.m₁	:f₁.s₁	df₁	:s₁	d	:s₁.d

l	:s	s.m	:f.s	m	:—	d¹	:d¹	lm	:f.s	l.s	:f.r	m]	:s
streams in	streams of	blood;	Pre- cious	drops my	soul be-	dew- ing,
f₁	:d	s₁.l₁	:r₁.s₁	d	:—	d	:d.l₁	rl₁	:f₁.m₁	r₁.m₁	:f₁.s₁	df₁	:s₁

m	:s	l	:s	s.m	:f.s	m	:— ‖
Plead and	claim my	peace with	God.
d	:s₁.d	f₁	:d	s₁.l₁	:r₁.s₁	d	:— ‖

GREGORIAN CHANT.   (Psalm 23, p. 109.)   *Tenor and Bass.*   KEY F.

SOH	s	:s	s	:—	SOH	s	:m	s	:s	s	:—
DOH	d	:s₁	d	:—	DOH	s₁	:l₁	s₁	:s₁	d	:—

117.   ST. PANCRAS.   *Air and Second Treble.*   KEY F.

:d	s :— :d¹ ·	t :l : s	f : s : f.m	m : r : m
Des-	cend	from heaven, im-	mor- tal	Dove; Stoop
:d	r :t₁ :d	r :— : m	l₁ :r :d	d :t₁ :d

f :l : d¹	s : f.m :r.d	d.,r : m : r	d :— : m	l :— : t
down	and take us	on thy	wings; And	mount an॰
d :— :l₁	d :— : s₁	d :— : t₁	d :— :d	m :— : r

d¹ :—.t :l	ne :l : f	m :— : t	d¹ :— : m	l :— : d.,r
bear us	far a-	bove The	reach of	these in-
d :—.r : m	r :d : d	t₁ :— : r	d :— :d	d :— :d

m :— : r	d :— ‖
fe- rior	things.
d :— : t₁	d :—

118.   BURFORD.   *First and Second Treble.*   LAH KEY, DOH IS C.

:l	l :— :t	d¹ :— : r¹	m¹ : r¹ :d¹	t :— :ne	l :— : t
Thee	we a-	dore, E-	ter- nal	name, And	hum- bl
:d	m :— : m	l :— :l	l :ne :l	m :— : m	m :— : n॰

d¹ :— : r¹	m¹ :— : m¹	r¹ :d¹ : t	d¹ :— : r¹	m¹ : r¹ :d¹
own to	Thee, How	fee- ble	is our	mor- tal
l :— :l	ne :— : s	f : s : f	m :— : s	s : soi :l

t :— :ne	l :t : d¹	t :l :ne	l :— ‖
frame,	What dy- ing	worms are	we!
ne :— : m	m : r :d	f : m : m	m :—

119.   ANTHEM.   By Farrant.   *First and Second Treble.*   KEY F.

d :—	d :—.r	m : r	d : f	r :—	: r	m l₁.t₁ : d	d : t₁
Lord,	for thy	ten- der	mer- cies'	sake,	lay	not our sins	to our
s₁ :—	l₁ :—.t₁	d : t₁	l₁ :—.d	t₁ :—	: t₁	d f₁ : m₁	s₁ : s₁.f₁
						not our sins to our	

d :—	d s : f	m :—	r : d	r.m : f	m : r	d : m.m	r : d
charge;	But for-	give	that is	past, and	give us	grace to a-	mend our
m₁ :—	d s₁ :l₁.t₁	d :—	t₁ :l₁	t₁ : d	d :l₁	l₁ : d.d	t₁ : l₁
charge;							

r : t₁	d :—	d :—.r	m : f	m :—	m :—.f	s : m	l :—
sin- ful	lives,—	to de-	cline from	sin,	and in-	cline to	vir-
l₁ : s₁.f₁	m₁ :—	s₁ : s₁	d : d	d :—	d : d	d : d	d :—

s :—	— :—	:	: d	s : s	f : m.r	m : m	d :—
tue,			that	we may	walk with a	per- fect	heart,
t₁ :—	:	: s₁	d : d	t₁ : l₁.s₁	l₁ : t₁	d :—	:
		that we	may walk with a per- fect	heart,			

ST. PANCRAS. *Tenor and Bass.* KEY F.

: s	s :— : m	s :t :d¹	l :s :s	s :— :s
Des-	cend from	heaven, im-	mor- tal	Dove; Stoop
: d	t₁ :— :l₁	s₁ :f :m	r :t₁ :d	s₁ :— :d

f :— :f	m :l.s :f.m	s.,l :s :f	m :— :m	m :— :m
down and	take us	on thy	wings; And	mount and
l₁ :— :f₁	d :— :d	m₁.,f₁:s₁ :s₁	d :— :l₁	d :— :ne₁

l :-.ne :l	m :— :l	m :— :m	m :— :s	l :— :s.,l
bear us	far a-	bove The	reach of	these in-
l₁ :-.t₁ :d	t₁ :l₁ :l₁	ne₁ :— :ne₁	l₁ :— :d	f₁ :— :m₁.,f₁

s :— :f	m :— ‖
fe- rior	things.
s₁ :— :s₁	d :— ‖

BURFORD. (Purcell.) *Tenor and Bass.* LAH KEY, DOH IS C.

: l	l :— :ne	m¹ :— :r¹	·d¹ :t :l	ne :— :t	d¹ :— :t
Thee	we a-	dore, E-	ter- nal	name, And	hum- bly
: l₁	d :— :m	l :s :f	m :— :l₁	m :— :m	d :— :m

m¹ :— :r¹.d¹	t :— :d¹	l :s :s	s :— :t	m¹ :— :m¹
own to	Thee, How	fee- ble	is our	mor- tal
l :s :f	m :— :d	f :m :r	d :— :s	d¹ :t :l

m¹ :— :t	l :ne :l	t :d¹ :t	d¹ :— ‖
frame, What	dy- ing	worms are	we!
m :— :r	d :t₁ :l₁	r :m :m	l₁ :— ‖

ANTHEM. *Tenor and Bass.* KEY F.

m :—	m :-.s	s :s	m :l	s :—	:s	sd :d	r :r.r
Lord,	for thy	ten- der	mer- cies'	sake,	lay	not our	sins to our
d :—	l₁ :-.s₁	d :s₁	l₁ :f₁	s₁ :—	:s₁	df₁ :l₁	s₁ :s₁.s₁

d :—	¹m :f	s :—	s :m	s :l	s :f	m :s.s	s :m
charge;	But for-	give	that is	past, and	give us	grace to a-	mend our
d₁ :—	¹m :r	d :—	s₁ :l₁	s₁ :f₁	d :r	l₁ :m₁.m₁	s₁ :l₁

f :r	d :—	m :-.f	s :l	s :—	s :-.f	m :m	f :—
sin- ful	lives,—	to de-	cline from	sin,	and in-	cline to	vir-
f₁ :s₁	d₁ :—	d :d	d :l₁	d :—	d :d	d :d	f₁ :—

r :r	m :m	r :m.s	f.m :r.d	r :m	f :f	s :m
tue,— that	we may	walk with a	per- fect	heart—with a	per- fect	heart—that
s₁ :s₁	d :d	t₁ :l₁.s₁	l₁ :l₁	s₁ :f₁.m₁	r₁ :r₁	d₁ :d

— :d	f :f	m :r.r	d :r	t₁ :m	l₁.t₁ :d	t₁ :d	r :t₁
that	we may	walk with a	per- fect	heart be-	fore Thee,	now and	ev- er-
:s₁	l₁ :r₁	s₁ :t₁.t₁	l₁ :l₁	s₁ :s₁	f₁ :m₁.f₁	s₁ :s₁	l₁ :s₁

d :—	:	:	:d	s :s	f :m.r	m :m	d :—
more,			—that	we may	walk with a	per- fect	heart—
m₁ :—	:	:m₁	d :d	t₁ :l₁.s₁	l₁ :t₁	d :—	:
		—that	we	may	walk with a	per- fect	heart.

— :d	f :f	m :r.r	d :r	t₁ :m	l₁.t₁ :d	t₁ :d
—that	we may	walk with a	per- fect	heart be-	fore Thee,	now and
:s₁	l₁ :s₁	s₁ :t₁.t₁	l₁ :l₁	s₁ :s₁	f₁ :m₁.f₁	s₁ :s₁

r :t₁	d :—
ev- er-	more.
l₁ :s₁	s₁ :—

120. ANTHEM. By Tallis. *First and Second Treble.* KEY G.

d :—	— :d	r :—	m :—	— :m	r :d	f :—	m :—
If	ye	love	me,	keep	my com-	mand-	ments,
s₁ :—	:l₁	t₁ :—	d :—	— :d	t₁ :l₁	d :—	d :—

:m	m :m	s :—	f :m	— :r	m :—	:	:
and	I will	pray	the Fa-		ther		
— :—	:	:	:	:l₁	l₁ :l₁	d :—	t₁ :l₁
				and	I	will	pray the Fa-

:r	d :d	f :—	— :m	— :d	m :r	—.d :d	— :t₁
and	he shall	give	you	an-	o-	ther Com-	fort-
— :ne₁	l₁ :l₁	f₁ :f₁	d :—	d :s₁	d :t₁	l₁ :f₁	s₁ :—.s₁
	ther, and	he shall	give	you an-	o-	ther Com-	fort-

d :—	:	:	:	:	:	:d	s :—
er,						that	he
s₁ :—	:	:	d :—	f :—	— :m.m	r :d	d :t₁
er,			that	he		may a- bide with	you for

— :f.f	m :r	d :m	r :—	r :r	— :s₁	r :d	t₁ :l₁
may a-	bide with	you for	e-	ver, even	the	Spi- rit	of
d :—	d :s₁	l₁ :l₁	l₁ :—	t₁ :—	t₁ :—	t₁ :m	—.m :r
e-	ver, with	you for	e-	ver,	even	the Spi-	rit of

s₁ :s	— :d	s.s :f	m :—	r :d	t₁.t₁ :l₁	s₁ :d	— :s₁
truth, even	the	Spirit of	truth,	even the	Spirit of	truth, even	the
—.d :d	:d	— :l₁	d.d :d	t₁ :s	— :d	s.s :f	m :r
truth,	even	the	Spirit of	truth, even	the	Spirit of	truth, even

l₁ :f₁	s₁ :—	s₁ :—	— :—
Spi- rit	of	truth.	
—.d :d	—.d :t₁	d :—	— :—
the Spi-	rit of	truth.	

l : l	s : f.m	r : r	d : s.s	m : f	r : d	d : d
we may	walk with a	per- fect	heart—with a	per- fect	heart be-	fore Thee
f : f	m : r.d	d : t₁	d : s₁.s₁	l₁ : r₁	s₁ : d	f₁ : l₁

r : m	r : r	d : d	m : m	r : m.s	f.m : r.d	r : m
now and	ev- er-	more,—that	we may	walk with a	per- fect	heart—a
s₁ : m₁	f₁ : s₁	d₁ : d₁	d : d	t₁ : l₁.s₁	l₁ : l₁	s₁ : f₁.m₁

f : f	s : m	l : l	s : f.m	r : r	d : s.s	m : f
per- fect	heart,—that	we may	walk with a	per- fect	heart—with a	per- fect
r₁ : r₁	d₁ : d	f : f	m : r.d	d : t₁	d : s₁.s₁	l₁ : r₁

r : d	d : d	r : m	r : r	m :—
heart be-	fore Thee,	now and	ev- er-	more.
s₁ : d	f₁ : l₁	s₁ : m₁	f₁ : s₁	d₁ :—

ANTHEM. (From People's Music Book.) *Tenor and Bass.* KEY G.

m :—	— : d	s :—	s :—	— : s	s : m	l :—	s :—
If	ye	love	me,		keep	my com-	mand-	ments,
d :—	— : l₁	s₁ :—	d :—	— : d	s₁ : l₁	f₁ :—	d :—

— :—	: m	m : m	l :-.s	f :—	m :—	— :—	:
	and	I will	pray the	Fa-	ther,		
— :—	— :—	:	:		l₁ :—	l₁ : l₁	r :-.d
					and	I will	pray the

:	: f	r : r	l :—	s : m	s :—	f.m : d	r : r
		and	he shall	give	you an-	o-	ther	Com- fort-
t₁ :—	l₁ :	: r	l₁ : l₁	d :—	d : s₁	l₁ : l₁	s₁ : s₁
Fa-	ther,	and	he shall	give	you an-	o-	ther	Com- fort-

d :—	s :—	d¹ :—	— : t.t	l : s	f : s	s : m	r : r.r
er,	that	he		may a-	bide with	you for	e-	ver, may a-
d :—	:	d :—	f :—	— : m.m	r : d	t₁ : d	s₁ :—
er,		that	he		may a- bide with	you for	e-

m : l	s : r	m :—	*tu,* :—	s :—	— :	:	:
bide with	you for	e-		ver,			
d : d.d	d : t₁	l₁ : l₁	r :—	s₁ :—	: s	— : d	s.s : f
ver, may a-	bide with	you for	e-	ver,		even	the Spirit of

: s	s : s	m : l	— : s	— : m	s.s : f	m : l	s.s : r
	the	Spi- rit	of truth,	even	the	Spirit of	truth, the	Spirit of
m :—	d : m	-.d : r	d :—	:	: d	— : f₁	d.d : t₁
truth,	the Spi- rit	of	truth,		even	the	Spirit of

m : d	r.r : r	m :—	— :—
truth, the	Spirit of	truth.	
l₁ : l₁	s₁.s₁ : s₁	d :—	— :—
truth, the	Spirit of	truth.	

EXAMINATION OF PUPILS ON THE FOURTH STAGE.

SECTION X.

1. What is Melody? What advantages, for his own enjoyment, and for good execution, will the singer gain by the study of it?

2. What quality of a melody should the singer first ascertain, that he may sing in the proper spirit and manner?

Describe the four "styles" of melody, and mention instances under each.

3. What is meant by a melodial "Cadence"? How do you distinguish the cadences?

What is a Phrase?

What is a Section? What is the "Cadence-phrase"?

What is a Period? What is the "Cadence-section"?

Write the tunes *Hanover*, *Fairfield*, and *Mozart*, and divide them into their melodial members by means of the proper signs.

4. *a.* What are the two points of correspondence between melodial members, which form the "symmetry of rhythm"? Exhibit these points of rhythmical symmetry in *Callcott, Fairfield, Burnett*, and *Winter Song*.

Find tunes, corresponding in rhythmical structure with those just named.

4. *b.* What is the relationship of melodial members which forms the "symmetry of musical expression"? What is meant by the "Subject" or "Theme"?

Why should you "figure" instead of solfa-ing while studying this subject?

Describe this development of musical ideas in *Wells*. By what experiment could you prove that an "antecedent" member heightens the effect of its "consequent"?

Explain the notation by which the "symmetry of musical expression" is represented in this book?

Write the formula which represents the development of musical ideas in Ex. 31, 27, 32, 29, 50, 39, 45, 52, 69, 89, 61, 37, &c. &c.

Give Col. Thompson's view of "the waves of melody."

5. What two things must the pupil learn to observe quickly and correctly, that he may be able to "copy by ear"?

* I will give you a key note and its chord, and you shall copy by ear any simple phrase I may "figure" to you in that key.

* I will give you a key note only, and you shall copy by ear any section of a tune or any short chant I may "figure" to you in that key.

* Copy by ear, without having the key note given, any tunes beginning with DOH TE, SOH

FAH ME, SOH ME, ME FAH, or DOH¹ SOH, and having an Authentic Melody that I may figure to you.

* Copy by ear Plagal melodies commencing as above.

* Copy by ear any other melodies.

5. What are the advantages, to the non-professional singer, of some practice in the art of melodial composition?

* Construct a melody on any given theme, and according to any given form of rhythmical structure, in the manner of the Exercises on pages 81, 82.

* Construct, from a given theme, several melodies, having different forms of Rhythm and of Melodial Reply, in the manner of the Exercises on pages 83, 84.

* Invent a Theme and construct a Melody upon it, which shall obey any conditions of style, rhythm, or reply I may suggest, in the manner of the Exercises on page 83.

What are the four points which should be considered in adapting music to particular words?

* Write a melody for given words—prose or poetical.

SECTION XI.

1. What are the three chief points in which the voice of one individual differs from that of another, and how are these differences occasioned?

Describe the organ of voice.

2. What is the difference between the voices of women and children and those of men?

How, for convenience, are the voices of women classified? Describe generally the different voices.

3. Describe the voices of men.

What is the extreme compass of your own voice?—its easy compass?

4. What do you mean by a "part" in music? Which is usually the leading melody in part-music? To what points should the part-singer specially direct his attention?

How should part-music be "balanced" for a Congregation?—a Sunday School?—a Day School?

In what manner should a tune be led, and what common fault of Leaders should be avoided?

5. Why is a good enunciation so specially important to the singer? How should the vowels be pronounced?—how the consonants?

How will the distinct reading of the Teacher and the simultaneous repetition of the class conduce to good enunciation?

Write from memory "Gloria in Excelsis," in both ways of denoting transition.

What are the points of beauty in Harrington"—in "God speed the right," &c.? What is there remarkable in Ex. 104?

SECTION XII.

1. What is Harmony? What is Counterpoint?

What is the distinction between Melody and Harmony, and the essential relation between them?

2. Illustrate what is meant by the "Unison," and by the intervals of the "Octave"—the "Major Third"—the "Minor Third," and the "Fifth."

Show, by examples, what is meant by the *Inversion* of Intervals, and what by their *Dispersion?*

What are the intervals which form a consonance, whether in their *direct* form—or *inverted*—or *dispersed?* What is the consonant interval which may not be inverted in two-part Harmony?

Write, from memory, a table of the consonances to each note of the scale.

What name do you give to the interval of an inverted Major Third?—an inverted Minor Third?

What interval does a Fifth become when inverted?

From what is the perfect Fourth to be distinguished?

What is the principle on which the resemblance of effect between any two notes of the scale depends?

How is it that the consonances whose notes are the most similar of all in their effects, are not the most agreeable and the most frequently used?

3. What are the two main conditions on which the mental effect of a consonance depends? How can you prove that the relationship of the two notes to the key (their position in the mode), influences the mental effect produced by their consonance as much as their relationship of interval to one another?

4. To what three points should the attention of the learner be directed in first attempting two-part harmony?

a. What is meant by "similar motion"?—"contrary motion"?—"oblique motion"?

b. In what cases are consecutive fifths and octaves allowed and disallowed?

c. What intervals are disallowed when reached by similar motion?

e. What must be avoided to secure a *distinct* and *flowing* melody?

f. Name the dissonances. Explain the rule of "passing discords."

S

g. Explain the "resolution" and "preparation" of Dissonances.

h. What makes a dissonance more "noticeable"?

i. What effect has distance on dissonances?

How is the principle of Uniformity blending with Variety in matters of Taste illustrated by the above rules for the "succession of consonances"?

5. Parse to me, in writing or verbally, the consonances of Ex. 27, 45, 62, 72, 81, 83, 88, 92, 96, 97, 98.

Write a second part to the following (or any similar), portions of melody, and fix the key in which you would have them sung. (1) | d :r | m :r | d (2) | s :f | m :r | d :t₁ | d (3) | m :f | s :m | r :f | m :d (4) :s₁ | d :m | r :t₁ | l₁ :t₁ | d (5) | s :l :s | s.f :m :d | s :l :s | s :— (6) | d.r :m.f | s :s | l.s :f.m | m :r .

Write a second part to any simple Chant or Hymn Tune I may give you.

6. What is the essential condition of a Consonant Chord? What is the additional consonance allowed in three-part Harmony? What is a Triad?

a. Which note of the Common Mode is it that will not bear a perfect consonant triad, and why?

How are the Triads classified? Enumerate them and give their names.

b. How does inversion affect the triads?

c. How are Consonant Chords formed?

d. What is said of the dissonant triad TE₁ RAY FAH?

e. What are the rules for the "progression of Chords"?

Resolve the Dissonant Chords SOH₁ TE₁ RAY FAH; TE₁ RAY FAH LAH; and FAH₁ LAH₁ DOH RAY.

7. How may the musical effect of the different chords be exhibited?

Parse the chords of Ex. 103, 104, 105, 106, 108, 109, 110, 111.

Harmonize the phrases above (5) in three and in four parts. Try also some simple chants and hymn-tunes.

SECTION XIII.

1. What are the two constituent elements of a Chant?

a. What are the different forms of the Terminal?

b. Explain the Reciting Preface. In what cases does it seem most natural to the voice? What is the purpose of the occasional Affix to the Reciting-note?

c. Explain the marks used in dividing words for Chanting.

• Sing to me examples of various ancient "Tones" and Chants.

d. What is the structure of the "Double" and of the "Single Chant"?

What are the abuses and misunderstandings which have brought the practice of Chanting into disrepute?

Explain the characteristics of Hebrew Poetry. Wherein is a plain translation of the Psalms preferable to a metrical version?

Wherein appears the adaptation of the Psalms to be sung?

How do the "experimental" and the "memorial" expressions of the Psalms affect their use in Christian worship?

In what manner may the Psalms be profitably introduced into public worship?

2. In what manner should the Reciting Note of a chant be delivered?

What advantages belong to the Rhythmic method of recitation?

What is the difference between Poetic and Prose rhythm in Elocution? How is the propriety of applying a rhythmic division to the declamation of a chant shown?

What are the arguments for and against Antiphonal Singing?

3. Mention each noticeable point of rhythmical arrangement in the Example, p. 107, and in the 23rd Psalm, p. 109.

* Sing, with perfect accuracy of Rhythm, the 23rd and the 24th Psalms, p. 109, 112; also Ex. 110, and the Examples preceding it.

What is important in reference to the pitch of the Reciting Note of a Chant? p. 110.

4. Make a Rhythmical division of the following Psalms and passages of Scripture, throwing the accent on the emphatic syllables, but retaining also an easy and tasteful Rhythm. Ps. xlvi. lxiii. lxv. xcv. cxxii. Matthew v. 5-12. 2 Cor. xiii. 14. Micah iv. 1-4, 7. Isaiah liv. Mark the "rate of movement" for each, according to the figures of the String-Pendulum or the Metronome, one of which instruments will be almost necessary to your first attempts, and will, at all times, greatly help you in your work.

SECTION XIV.

1. What is the essential characteristic of an Anthem-tune? Mention some of the various appliances of musical expression admissible into the Anthem.

What hinders the profitable use of the truly Congregational Anthem?

2. What is the essential characteristic of the Hymn Tune? What should therefore be excluded from it?

What are the conditions required in a tune to suit a large body of voice?

What was President Edwards' testimony to the power of Psalmody?

Mention four points to be specially observed by those who would improve congregational singing. Describe Mr. Waite's views of "the Psalm Tune."

3. How would you classify Tunes in view of their adaptation to particular Hymns? Mention tunes under each class.

What should be the plan of the Leader's Tune-list?

Mention some of the topics appropriately included in the true "service of song," in addition to that of direct praise.

What is your view of the use of "secular tunes" in religious worship?

4. Enumerate and enforce the duties of a Leader of Congregational Singing.

What are the three essential qualifications of a Leader? Whether is a Bass or Tenor Voice the best for a Leader?

What are the consequences, in the Congregational Singing, of the "Air" being pitched too high for easy Unison, while the people are unprepared for taking their proper "parts"?

What are the points which first commend the practice of Unison Singing to our attention? Mention the five reasons given (p. 118) against the attempt to introduce it in our days.

What should be the compass of unison-tunes?

Show the natural adaptation of four-part music to the capacities and moral requirements of any "general" assembly.

Show the duty of abstaining from criticism and indulgence of fastidious taste in Public Worship. What makes this forbearance easy?

What is your opinion of the use of the Organ in connection with public worship? State its advantages and its prominent disadvantages.

What are the four causes of "flattening" in the voice of a Congregation?

How can the Leader quicken the Time of a tune while a Congregation is singing it? How can he retard the rate of movement?

How should new tunes be introduced to a congregation?

What would be the effect of introducing more Peculiar Metres, as well as Chants and simple Congregational Anthems, into our Services?

Describe the points of beauty or of difficulty in any of the Exercises which you have sung.

APPENDICES:

CONTAINING AN

INTRODUCTION TO THE OLD NOTATION,

SO ARRANGED THAT IT MAY BE COMMENCED AT ANY STAGE OF THE PUPIL'S PROGRESS. THE TEACHER SHOULD TAKE CARE THAT THE PUPIL CAN INTELLIGENTLY ANSWER THE QUESTIONS PREFIXED TO EACH APPENDIX BEFORE HE PROCEEDS.

APPENDIX TO SECTION II.

AIM OF THE OLD NOTATION.—THE STAFF.—DEFECT OF THE OLD NOTATION.—
FIRST EXERCISES.

What is the principal note in every tune? [The Key Note or Governing Note.] Is the Key Note the same sound in one tune that it is in another? [Not the same in pitch. It is sometimes high and sometimes low. But the same in mental effect—always the strong resting note.] How are the notes arranged between any given Key Note and its Replicate? [So that the shorter intervals of pitch—the tonules—shall always come between the third and fourth and the seventh and eighth.] Name the notes of the Common Mode and the intervals between them. Write a Modulator from memory, and be *perfectly familiar* with it.

1. A Musical Notation is a method of representing musical sounds to the eye. The notation now in common use is called the old notation, to distinguish it from that simpler and certainly better one for vocal music, which has been employed in this book.

2. The Old Notation aims to present to the eye a picture of the notes as they move up and down in pitch. For this purpose it provides a ladder of five lines, and four spaces, called the STAFF. [The teacher draws it on the Black-board.]

3. The distance on the staff, from a line to the next space, or from a space to the next line, is called a " degree," and represents the interval between one note and the next in the " Common Mode." The lines and spaces are counted from the lowest one upward.

4. Certain marks are placed on the lines and spaces of the staff to represent the notes—rising and falling, thus— [The teacher draws notes on the staff.] If we want notes to go higher or lower than the staff, it is easy to draw additional lines for them, above or below; these are called Ledger lines. [Teacher draws.]

(1.)   THE STAFF.   (2.)   NOTES ON THE STAFF.

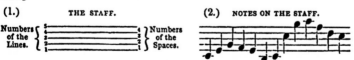

Numbers of the Lines.   Numbers of the Spaces.

5. "There is nothing *in the look* of these notes to show you which is the KEY NOTE (DOH), which is the third note above (ME), &c.; nor is there anything *in the look* of the staff to show where the tones and where the *tonules* come.

"These things were made as plain as possible in your own notation, because they are the most important things in Music. A little pains will enable you to understand them even in the old notation.

6. "To help you, at first, I will make a square note for the key note (DOH), so that you may know it at sight. When you see the key note you will be able to reckon the other notes from it.

"Let us suppose that the key note (DOH) is on the second line, [makes a square note, fig. 3], where must I write RAY? ["in the second space"—the teacher writes it.] Where will ME stand?—SOH?—FAH?—ME?—RAY?—DOH? Now I will give you the sound of DOH, and you shall sing what we have written. [Gives the key note G, and the class sings.]

"Let us have another tune, and its DOH shall be in the second *space*. [Writes it.] Where must I place the lower TE₁,—that which is close under DOH? ["On the second line"]—the lower LAH₁?—the lower SOH₁?—DOH again?—RAY?—ME?—DOH? [The teacher writes as the pupils dictate. See fig. 4.] Now I will give you the sound of DOH, and we will sing what we have written." [Gives A, and class sing.]

(3.)   (4.)

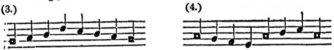

The teacher will easily multiply such exercises as these. Let him use only the smallest intervals except when he rises or falls to DOH.

APPENDIX TO SECTION III.

BARS.—POSITION ON THE STAFF OF DOH, ME, AND SOH.—POSITION OF REPLICATES.—POSITION OF LOWER SOH.—POSITION OF FAH.—POSITION OF THIRDS.—EXERCISES.

How many degrees of accent do you distinguish, and what are they called? [Three; the loud, soft, and medium.] What do you notice concerning the distances between one accent and the next? [They are always equal.] What marks are used to show the accents? [See p. 13.]

1. "The Old Notation has a mark for only one kind of accent;—a stroke across the staff thus—[drawing it as fig. 5]—shows that the note which follows is to have the stronger accent. This stroke is called a BAR.

2. "The *distance* between one Bar (loud pulse) and another, is called a MEASURE. It is sometimes wrongly called a Bar.

3. "Now let us write the first Exercise. We will have DOH in the space below the first line. [Makes the square note.] But the louder accent comes before it, so I will draw a bar. Where should ME be? [RAY on the first line,

ME "in the first space." Writes.] The softer accent comes before ME, but that must be "understood" in the old notation;—we have no distinct mark for it. Where would SOH come? [FAH on the second line, SOH "in the second space." Writes SOH with the bar.] Where shall I write the upper DOH[1]? [—LAH on the third line, TE in the third space, DOH[1] "on the fourth line."] —SOH again? —ME?—DOH? See, I have marked all the bars and a double bar at the end. Now tell me the names of any of these notes we have written—I will ask you dodgingly.

(5.)   (6.)

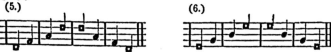

"Let us write the same Exercise—taking the first *line* for the place of our key note. [The teacher proceeds as before, writing fig. 6 by the side of fig. 5.] Hitherto, in finding the solfa names of the notes, you have counted up or down from the square note which represents DOH. Could you not learn to tell the notes *at sight* without counting? Let us try.

4. "In the last figure we drew (fig. 6), DOH was *on a line*. Where were the ME and SOH above? [On the next lines above.] Would that be the case if DOH were on any other line? [Yes.] So that whenever DOH is on a line, the ME and SOH above are also on lines—and the next lines above. Then, need you count, to find them? But in the former figure (fig. 5), DOH was *in a space* Where were the ME and SOH above? [In spaces also—in the *next* spaces.] You perceive then this rule, which, well remembered and carefully tested, will become your main help in singing from the old notation—

"DOH, ME, and SOH *are similarly placed*—i. e. either on adjacent lines or in adjacent spaces.

5. "When the lower DOH was on a line, how was the upper DOH[1] placed? [In a space.] How, when the lower DOH was in a space? [On a line.] If RAY were in a space, how would its upper replicate be placed?—How, if on a line? If SOH were on a line, how would its lower replicate be placed?—How, if SOH were in a space? [The pupil may answer these questions by experiment and counting on the staff.] Then, from this, you may make another general rule, that—

"*Replicates are dissimilarly placed*—i. e. when one is on a line, the other is in a space, and when one is in a space, the other is on a line.

"Now, try by the help of these rules, especially the first, to *name at sight*, as I point to them, the notes of the following Exercises. (Figures 7 and 8.) After that I will give you the key, and you may sing them. The sound must be just twice as long on the *open* notes as on the black ones." [If the rules above have been *found out*, under the teacher's guidance, by the pupils themselves, there will be no difficulty here. If there should be hesitation, let the teacher develope the rules again and show their application in each case, but, on no account, let him permit the pupils to *count* from note to note instead of *seeing* at once what the note is according to the rule. Figures 7 and 8 correspond with Ex. 3 and 4, p. 8—only figure 8 is written in the key of E instead of D.

(7.)

(8.)

The teacher can easily multiply examples of this kind, requiring his pupils to copy them into their own solfa notation.

6. "Now I wish you to notice the position of the lower SOH₁, so as to be able to recognise it at sight. A little observation will enable you to verify this rule, that—

"SOH *is differently placed from the* DOH *above it.* If DOH is on a line, the lower SOH₁ is in the space *next below that space which* DOH *touches ;* if DOH is in a space, SOH is on the line below that which DOH touches. This rule naturally follows from the last.

"Read (without counting), and copy into the solfa notation the following Exercises. Then I will give you the key note (fig. 9, G; fig. 10, A), and you shall sing them."

(9.)

(10.)

The teacher should supply many additional examples till each point is thoroughly mastered.

7. "Next, let us study FAH in its relative positions on the staff. [The teacher draws DOH on any degree of the staff, and requires the pupils to show where the upper and the lower FAH would be placed. They develope the following rule.]

"*Upper* FAH *is differently placed from* DOH. *If* DOH *is on a line, it occupies the space above that which* DOH *touches. If* DOH *is in a space, it occupies the line above that which* DOH *touches.* It has the same position above DOH which SOH has below it.

"*Lower* FAH *is similarly placed to* DOH. *If* DOH *is on a line, it also is on a line, leaving another line between them. If* DOH *is in a space, it occupies the next space, but one, below it.*

"Read, *at sight*, the following Exercises.

(11.)

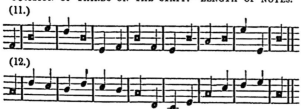

(12.)

8. "These points, clearly understood and made familiar to the eye, will enable you to recognise, even in the dumb signs of the old notation, the position and character of each note as it stands in relation to the key. You will soon discover for yourselves other "rules" which give facility to the art of "reading at sight." The following may be one.

"*Thirds*" (see p. 95) *and successions of thirds are similarly placed*, such as DOH, ME, SOH, TE; RAY, FAH, LAH, DOH¹; TE₁, RAY, FAH, LAH; RAY¹, TE, SOH, ME; DOH¹, LAH, FAH, RAY; TE, SOH, ME, DOH. Read, *at sight*, the following Exercise.

(13.)

Many similar examples may be proposed by the teacher; but it is not recommended that he should propose too many exercises, exclusively illustrating one particular rule, for, in practise, the examples of the various rules will be intermixed, and it is for this the pupil must be prepared. Let the chief attention be given to the first rule.

APPENDIX TO SECTION IV.

LENGTH OF NOTES AND RESTS.—"TIME" SIGNATURES.—CLEFS.

How do you exhibit the *length of notes?* [We exhibit the length of notes—not absolutely, (as—so many seconds to such a note) but relatively, showing pictorially (by help of the regularly recurring accents along the page) what *proportion* of a Measure or of a Beat each note occupies.]

How do you show the pauses in a tune? [5. *h.*] How do you show the *Rate of Movement* in a tune? [By the Metronome—thus fixing the *absolute* length of its notes.] Explain the different Measures. [See SEC. iii.] What is the *Standard Scale?*

1. The Old Notation represents the length of sounds, symbolically, by changes in the form of the notes, as exhibited below.

(1.)

||𝇇|| A BREVE—(a note seldom used.)

○ A SEMIBREVE—half as long as the Breve.

♩ or ⌐ A MINIM—half as long as the Semibreve.

♩ or ⌐ A CROTCHET—half as long as the Minim.

♪ or ⌐ A QUAVER—half as long as the Crotchet.

♫ or ⌐ A SEMIQUAVER—half as long as the Quaver.

♬ or ⌐ A DEMISEMIQUAVER—half as long as the Semiquaver.

♩. ♩. A DOT after a note lengthening it by half. A second Dot would lengthen it three-fourths.

2. The following marks are used to indicate the pauses of the voice. They correspond with the different notes and are called RESTS. Thus the crotchet rest requires the voice to pause just so long as it would take to sing a crotchet in the same tune.

(2.)

I between two lines is a BREVE REST.	⅊ a SEMIQUAVER REST.
‒ under a line is a SEMIBREVE REST.	
‒ upon a line is a MINIM REST.	⅊ a DEMISEMIQUAVER REST.
⌐ a CROTCHET REST.	
⅂ a QUAVER REST.	⌐• or ‒• a DOT, lengthening the Rest by half.

3. Many attempts have been made to fix an *absolute* time to these symbols, and this may have been the original intention, but they now represent only length of sound *relatively to one another*. Thus, if the movement be quick and the semibreve occupy two seconds, the minim will occupy one second, the crotchet half a second, &c.—if the movement be slow, and eight seconds are filled by the semibreve, the minim will fill four, the crotchet two, &c.

4. Neither have these symbols any fixed and uniform relation to the regularly recurring accents—the measure—of a tune. Sometimes one note represents an aliquot part—a "beat"—of the measure, and sometimes another. The same tune which, in one book, is written with a minim to a "beat," is found in another book with a crotchet to a beat, and the crotchet tune *need* not be sung more quickly than that in minims. (See figs. 16 and 18 which follow.) It is, however, sometimes intended that a tune should be sung more or less quickly according as it is written in minims, crotchets, or quavers.

5. The Metronome is the only true standard for the rate of movement. In connection with the Old Notation a swing of the Metronome does not necessarily correspond with an aliquot part of the measure, but with some particular length of note (crotchet, minim, &c.) which is mentioned in the signature. Thus the words " METRONOME, crotchet = 64" placed in the title of a tune, means that one swing of the Metronome when set at 64 corresponds with a crotchet in this tune, whether that crotchet fill an aliquot or only half an aliquot of the measure. The following words are sometimes put into the title of a tune to indicate vaguely the rate of movement—1st, *Grave*, which means very slow, grave, and solemn; 2nd, *Largo*, slow and majestic; 3rd, *Adagio*, leisurely; 4th, *Andante*, easy, flowing; 5th, *Allegro*, very quick.

6. It would be a great advantage if musicians could agree to use one note (the crotchet might be selected for its superior legibility), as the standard representative of an aliquot part of the measure. The nature of the measure and the place of the accents would thus be most easily distinguished. This is the plan adopted in " School Music" where the crotchet represents a beat throughout. Were this the case, the crotchet might be called the " pulse note"—the minim, the "two-pulse note"—the quaver, the " half-pulse note"—the dotted crotchet, the "pulse-and-a-half note," &c.

7. It is usual to place, at the beginning of a tune, certain marks to indicate

7991224151

the "measure," called "time signatures." In our own notation such marks are unnecessary, as the several accents are distinctly marked and the character of the rhythm is visible at once. Even in the Old Notation they are frequently omitted, and the more so, as there is much disagreement about the meaning of some of them.

The mark C placed at the beginning of a staff is said to represent "common time." It is described by one professor as indicating a Measure of two aliquots, ("rhythmical divisions") each represented by a minim or its equivalent in notes or rests, while other professors state that "any movement in which each bar contains the time of a semibreve, whether the measures be divided into two, four, or eight parts, may be marked with the C." This mark is sometimes found with a perpendicular bar drawn through it, and is said to represent "alla-breve time." Some say that the barred C indicates a measure with four aliquots, (the Quaternary) a crotchet to each, while others use it to mark a Measure of two aliquots—the Binary, and others again affirm that the bar simply quickens the movement. (See the Grammars of Callcott, Hullah, Bryce, and Dawson.) It is evident that such indefinite marks can be no sure guide to us. We must listen to a few measures of the music itself before we can tell what the rhythm really is.

The other marks for measure are not so equivocal in their meaning. They are formed by placing two figures, one over the other, at the beginning of the staff. The upper figure shows how many aliquots there are in the measure, and the lower figure shows what note is used for the aliquot. "Two," used as the lower figure, represents the minim or *half* a semibreve; the figure "four" represents the crotchet or fourth of the semibreve; the figure "eight" represents the quaver or eighth of a semibreve. Thus, the figures $\frac{2}{2}$ (and why not add $\frac{2}{4}$) represent the BINARY MEASURE; $\frac{3}{2}, \frac{3}{4}$, and $\frac{3}{8}$, represent different appearances of the TRINARY MEASURE; $\frac{6}{4}$ and $\frac{6}{8}$ represent the SENARY MEASURE; $\frac{9}{4}$ and $\frac{9}{8}$ represent a trinary measure in which each aliquot frequently falls into triplets; and $\frac{12}{4}$ and $\frac{12}{8}$ represent *two* senary measures, or (as they may be called) one quaternary measure, each aliquot of which is frequently divided into triplets. If the plan of making the crotchet the standard aliquot is not adopted, it would be well to use the unmistakeable figures $\frac{4}{2}$ and $\frac{4}{4}$ to represent the QUATERNARY MEASURE, and so avoid the use of such doubtful marks as the plain and the barred C.

The phrase "common time" is used sometimes in reference to the binary and sometimes to the quaternary measures, so very precise is the old notation! The trinary measure is called "triple time." The senary measure is called "compound common time," and the measure represented by $\frac{9}{4}$ and $\frac{9}{8}$ is called "compound triple time."

The word "time" in the ordinary musical language is very equivocal. In the phrases "common time," "triple time," &c., it refers to the orderly recurrence of accents—the *measure*. In the phrases "quick time," "slow time," &c., it means *rate of movement*. And when we are

requested to "keep the time" it is implied that, though we may have been correct in the rate of movement and accurate in the recurrence of accents, we have not given *the exact length to each note*. We use it only in the last sense.

The word RHYTHM is used on page 7, as though it were only a generic term for the different measures, but we found it necessary afterwards (see pages 55, 76 and 107, also page 79) to use it as including not only the regular recurrence of accents, but also the manner in which notes are distributed among them.

T

8. The Old Notation aims to present the notes not only in their *relative* pitch, as compared with the key note, but also in their *absolute* pitch in the scale of sound. As the musical effect of a note, and those qualities which make it to be well remembered and easily executed by the singer, depend on its *relative* more than its absolute pitch, when the key note is once ascertained the singer requires nothing more. It is no advantage to him to have the *absolute* pitch of the other notes constantly shown him. But with the unskilled player on the piano-forte, or other keyed and "tempered" instruments, the case is different. He wants a particular mark in the book for each key of his finger board. He requires, with mechanical precision, the *absolute* pitch.

As the staff of five lines has not compass enough for the different voices and instruments, and it would be inconvenient to enlarge it, certain marks called CLEFS are placed at the beginning of each staff, which decide the pitch of the line on which they stand, and adapt the compass of the staff to that of the voice or instrument for which it is used.

9. A mark, like an H with two strokes joining its upright bars, makes the line which passes between its two strokes to represent the "standard c," (p. 10), the octave (replicate) below that sound which a female or a child would take from the c¹ tuning fork when about to pitch a tune. When placed on the fourth line it adapts the staff to the compass of a tenor voice, and is called the TENOR CLEF. On the third line it suits the staff to the *contra-alto*, or counter-tenor, voice; on the second to the *second soprano*, or mezzo-soprano voice; and on the first to the *first soprano* voice.

Let the teacher write on the black board such exercises as the following, and require his pupils to find the pitch of the key note—(the square form being still retained to distinguish it, and the intervals being measured from it), to explain each sign—and to sing the tune. If the pupil keep the place of the key note in his eye, as he goes along, he will not find the clefs puzzle him.

10. The teacher may take occasion to explain the SLUR, showing that two or more notes are to be sung to one syllable, as on the seventh and eleventh syllables of the next example. (See "School Music," 2, 121.) The dots down the spaces of the staff showing the point *at* which and the point *to* which we are to return in repeating the music. (Sch. Mus. 20, 51.) The DOUBLE BAR, which is placed at the end of a strain of the music, but does not any way affect the measure or the time—the curve with a dot in the centre called a HOLD, which is placed over a note to indicate that it may be prolonged according to the pleasure or feeling of the singer—the BRACE, which joins two or more staves together, and indicates that they are to be sung at the same time, forming only different "parts" in the same music—and the manner in which quavers or semiquavers may be GROUPED, as are the quavers in this example. He may find other opportunities of explaining the curve with a figure 3 in the centre, the TRIPLET mark, which is placed over three notes when they are meant to be sung in the time of two (Sch. Mus. 97, 117)—and the curve, called a TIE, which is placed over two notes, one on each side of a bar, when they are to be sung as one. In the following example the place of the key note is shown, at the beginning of each staff, by a square mark.

(14.) FAIRFIELD. (Ex. 50.) First two lines of the Air and Second Treble, written in C cleffs.

11. A mark, which is said to have been originally made in the shape of a capital G, makes the line on which its lower curve turns to represent the G above the standard C. It is called the G CLEF. It is sometimes found on the first line of the staff, but is commonly used on the second line, in which position it adapts the staff to the *treble voice.*

(15.) SAMSON. (Ex. 63.) First two lines; the Air in the G cleff, and the Second Treble in the C cleff.

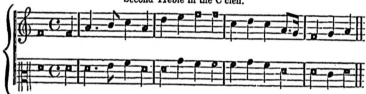

12. A mark, like C turned backwards, followed by a dot on each side of the line on which the C bends, makes that line represent F, below the standard c. It is called the F clef. It is generally placed on the fourth line, and adapts the staff to the compass of a *bass voice,* though sometimes found on the third line, adapting the staff to a baritone voice. If females or children sing, for practise, from the tenor or bass clefs, they should be reminded that they are singing an octave higher than the notes written.

(16.) Two lines of a tune arranged for four voices—Soprano, Contralto, Tenor, and Bass—and written in the proper cleffs.

13. The G clef on the second line, called the treble clef—and the F, clef on the fourth line, called the bass clef, are now used almost exclusively, and the position of the *standard scale* in connection with these clefs should be carefully studied. Let it be noticed that the standard C is found on the leger line *below* the staff of the treble clef, and on the leger line *above* that of the bass.   Thus, by the first clef is represented the notes which females and children sing in pitching a tune from a c^1 tuning fork, and by the second, the notes which a male voice would sing in the same case.

(17.)

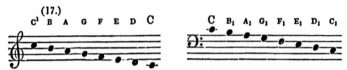

The pupil should now answer such questions as the following :—" On what line or in what space is c^1 in the treble clef?"   " Where is B ?"   " Where is D^1 ?" " Where is F^1 ?"   " Where is D_1 in the bass clef ?—A_2 ?—C_1 ?—G_1 ?" &c.

If the treble and bass clefs were brought together so that the leger line below the one became the leger line above the other, this leger line (used as occasio required) would unite the two into a double staff, giving a complete fixed scal of the notes in use. The same music which is given above (No. 16), in for distinct clefs, if written on this double staff, and in crotchets instead of minim would appear as follows :—

(18.)   The same as figure 16, written on the double staff and in crotchets.

NOTICE TO THE TEACHER. The teacher need not develope the points of this section at once to his pupils. It will be better to give many of these explanations as the need for them arises in practice. The pupils may commence at once solfaing from the Old Notation—using the " School Music," which corresponds with their solfa exercises—the teacher showing them the line or space which belongs to DOH, and encouraging them to keep it " in their eye," as they strive to apply the rules of the last section. The pupils may also be exercised in copying tunes from one clef into another (still making a square note for DOH), and from the old notation (the teacher having pointed out the key note) into the new. Many tunes in "School Music," that are not found among the foregoing solfa exercises, may be useful for this purpose.

It should be noticed that the marks indicating musical expression, mentioned before, (Sec. iv. 8, *b, c, d*) are used in connection with the Old Notation. The Italian words *crescendo* ("increasing" in force of sound) and *diminuendo* ("decreasing") are also used for this purpose, being written over the music. The mark for a repetition of words should also be noticed. See School Music, 6, 7.

APPENDIX TO SECTIONS V, VI, VII.

OF THE NECESSITY FOR "FLATS" AND "SHARPS" IN THE SIGNATURE
OF THE OLD NOTATION TO REPRESENT THE DIFFERENT KEYS.—RULES FOR FINDING
THE KEY NOTE IN THE OLD NOTATION.

What is the structure of the Common Mode or Scale, and where are its tonules placed? [See SEC. ii.] What is the *Standard Scale?* [A scale which has the standard pitch-note C for its key note, is formed, like the Common Mode, with its tonules between the third and fourth and seventh and eighth notes, and has its notes named by the letters of the alphabet C, D, E, F, G, A, B. C¹.

SEC. iv.] What do you mean by a *Key?* [A scale, formed like the Common Mode, which takes a certain note of the Standard Scale named, as its Governing or Key Note.] What is meant by C SHARP, B FLAT, &c.? [Another note, which is about half a tone higher or half a tone lower than the note mentioned. SEC. iv.]

1. The pupil who has been accustomed to solfaing, on "the tonic method" taught in this book, will find it as easy to sing and as easy to read music in one key as in another. In singing, when once the key note is given him, whatever it may be, he finds the other notes of the tune fall naturally into their places, the tonules (or semitones) lying always between ME FAH and TE DOH. In reading music, even from the Old Notation, as soon as the position of DOH on the staff is ascertained, whatever line or space it may occupy, he is familiar with the places of the other notes (by the help of the rules of Appendix to SEC. iii.) and with the relative position of tones and tonules. But what is easy and natural in *music itself*, is difficult and perplexing, especially to the beginner, in the ordinary *notation of music.*

```
 E   d¹
     t
   D/
     l
d¹ C/
t  B   s
l  A   f
       m
s  G/
       r
f  F/
m  E   d
r  D
d  C
```

2. It has already been remarked (p. 138), that the Old Notation aims to express to the eye both the relative and the absolute pitch of each note at the same time. Now, in the different keys, the *relative* pitch of notes is the same in all cases, but the *absolute* pitch is not the same; and *new sounds,* in the scale of *absolute* pitch, have to be found for each new key, on purpose to preserve the *relative* position of its notes unaltered. This will be manifest from the diagram at the side, which represents the standard scale of fixed notes, (or the key of C) and, by the side of it, to the right, a new key which takes its governing note from E. It will be perceived, that, to retain the proper relative position of its notes, the new key is compelled to reject the notes F, G, C, D, and to use four *new sounds* —and, that the new key will have to hold a very different position in the staff and to use four new signs for its new notes. In our own notation we express absolute pitch only in the case

of the key note, and then simply show the relative position of the other notes as compared with that one fixed note. The Old Notation, adapting itself to the demands of keyed and tempered instruments, attempts to express at once the position in pitch and the position in key, and hence its difficulty.

3. When the staff is without any of the marks called flats and sharps at its commencement, it is always understood to contain the notes of the c key—that which we call the "standard scale." This key is commonly called the *natural key*, because it is more natural or easy to the Old *Notation* than any other, though to the *voice* and *ear* any other key is as natural and easy as this.

4. The pupil has already learnt (p. 140), the position of the notes of the standard scale (the "natural" key), in the treble and bass clefs; it is important that he should now notice where the tonules (or semitones) occur, for the staff does not show this, at first sight, as the Modulator did. The distance between a line and the next space cannot be made pictorially smaller in one case than another. Hence the staff cannot pictorially *show* the tonules. They must nevertheless be imagined in their proper places. It must always be *understood*, for instance, that, in the "natural" key on the treble clef, the first line and first space, and the third line and third space, are nearer to one another than the other lines and spaces are. Figure 19 shows (by the dots and the slurs), what would be called, the "natural" places of the tonules in the treble and bass clefs. Let the pupil *observe* them carefully, and point out the places where other tonules must come, above or below those marked; but if he has learnt to solfa on our plan, he need not puzzle himself to *remember* them.

(19.)

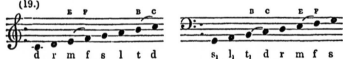

5. Let us now try to represent, on the staff, the key of G, and notice what changes it will require. From the diagram, at the side, it will be seen that the new key requires a new note instead of F, and about half a tone higher. This note is called F SHARP, and a mark is put, at the beginning of the staff, on the place where F would be, to show that throughout that tune, F SHARP must be used instead of F, and that on the treble clef the tonule is to be "understood" between the first space and second line, and not between the first line and first space. Figure 20 will enable the pupil to compare the appearance of the G key with the "natural" key above. The mark for a sharp is placed usually on the place of upper F. It must also be "understood" on the lower F.

(20.)

d r m f s l t d   s₁ l₁ t₁ d r m f s

s	D	d
		t
f	C	╱
m	B	l
r	A	s
d	G	f
t	F.s.m	
l	E	r
s	D	d
f	C	
m	B	
r	A	
d	G	

6. Let it be observed (from the diagram at the side above), that G, which we made our new key note, is the SOH (the fifth above or the fourth below) of the C key, and that the note which required to be sharpened was the FAH of the C key. Now, if we next took the SOH of the G key, or D, for a new key note, what additional note would require to be sharpened? The FAH of the G key, or C. This is evident from the diagram at the side. Then let a "sharp" be placed on C as well as F, and the staff will be adapted to the key of D. (See fig. 21.) Again, if we took the SOH of the D key, or A, for a new key note, what note would have to be sharpened in addition to the other two? The FAH of the former key or G. [The teacher may draw another diagram to illustrate this.] Then let a third sharp be placed on G to adapt the staff to the key of A. (See figure 22.)

(21.)   (22.)

d r m f s l t d   d r m f s l t d

It will be easily perceived that, by taking the SOH of each preceding key for a new key note, a SERIES OF KEYS may be found, each of which will require an additional sharp. The sharps are always placed on the staff in the order of this development—F the first to the left hand, next to it but more to the right C, next G, &c.

7. The signatures of the (so called) sharp keys, thus developed, are given below. Let it be noticed (from the diagrams above) that the last sharp developed, in each case, indicates the TE of the new key, and consequently that the key note, in sharp signatures, is always *the note above the last sharp to the right*.

(23.)

G   D   A   E   B   F

```
d   F   f
t   E   m

l   D   r

s   C   d
    B   t
f/
m   A   l

r   G   s

d   F   f
    E   m

    D   r

    c   d
```

8. Again, let us try to change the "natural" key (key of c) into the key of F, and notice what difference it will make. It is evident, from the diagram at the side, that a new note will be required instead of B, and about half a tone *lower*. This new note is called B FLAT. A mark must then be put in the signature on the place that would belong to B, to signify that throughout that tune B FLAT is to be used instead of B. (See figure 24.)

```
d   B'fl: f
t   A   m

l   G   r

s   F   d
    E   t
f/
m   D   l

r   C   s

d   Bfl: f
    A   m

    G   r

    F   d
```

9. Let it be noticed that F, which was taken above for a new key note, is the FAH (the fourth above or the fifth below) to the former key note c. Suppose we take the FAH of the F key, or B flat, for the next key note, what change will be required? Another new note, instead of E, and about half a tone lower. An additional "flat" must therefore be put in the signature of this key, on the place of E, that the staff may be adapted to the key of B FLAT. (See fig.24.) Thus, by taking the FAH of each preceding key for a new key note, a SERIES OF KEYS is developed, each of which requires an additional "flat" in its signature. The flats are placed, in the signature, according to the order of this development—B the first, E the next to the right, A the next, &c.

10. The signatures of the (so called) flat keys, thus developed, are given below. Let it be noticed (by examination of the diagrams above) that the last flat developed, in each case, becomes the FAH of the new key, and consequently, that the key note, in flat signatures, is always *on the third degree below the last flat to the right*.

(24.)

The pupil may now be practised in finding the proper signatures for each of the exercises in the preceding sections, where the key note was indicated by the square form.

11. By the students of the method of solfaing here developed, the sharps and flats of the signature need not be noticed except for the purpose of finding the

key note. The following simple rules will enable them to see the key note of any tune at once.

a. When the staff is clear of flats or sharps in the signature, it represents the key of C.

b. When there are sharps in the signature, the last sharp (to the right) is on TE.

c. When there are flats in the signature, the last flat (to the right) is on FAH.

TE, "the piercing note," will easily associate in the mind with sharps, and FAH, "the desolate note," with flats. It may also be noticed that, in flat signatures, the last flat to the right *but one* is the key note itself.

The ordinary formula for remembering the keys is as follows :—*One* SHARP in the signature indicates the key of G—*two* sharps the key of D—*three* sharps A—*four* sharps E—*five* sharps B—*six* sharps F SHARP;—*One* FLAT shows the key of F—*two*, B flat—*three*, E flat—*four*, A flat—*five*, D flat.

It is a common opinion among players of the piano-forte that each of the above keys has a peculiar "complexion," as they call it, and produces a peculiar mental impression, apart from and beyond the natural effect of comparative elevation in pitch. (Sec. v. 1.) Some go so far as to give a full but usually indefinite description of these different characteristics. We believe that such distinctions are to be traced in the scales (keys) produced by the piano-forte and organ, but not in those of a violin tuned and played according to the *perfect* intervals of the scale, (see p. 40) or of a well-trained voice true to nature. The following remarks of Colonel Thompson's on this subject are clear and important. "Any difference in the effect of the same music, arranged in different keys, can only arise from some of four causes;—First, a difference in pitch; as for instance, if a violin should produce a marked alteration in the effect of the same tune or air, by screwing up or letting down the strings through a given interval; secondly, an alteration in the quality of tone of a given instrument, by taking the same notes in one part of the instrument instead of another; as the self-same written notes, and at precisely the same pitch, and without any difference in the intervals, may produce a different effect on a guitar from being sounded by stopping near the middle of the thicker strings instead of the top of the thinner; thirdly, a difference in the practical execution of the different keys; as for instance, playing an air on the black keys of a piano-forte, or with a great admixture of them, will give a different fingering from playing it in the key of C or on the white, and this may produce some difference of effect, either directly or through acting on the imagination of the performer; fourthly, an alteration in the degree in which the notes on a fixed instrument severally approximate to the true sounds, when the scale is begun on any particular one for the key note. It may be conceded at once, that the first three causes may, in certain cases, produce a certain degree of effect; but the last is the point to which most importance attaches. And the first question that suggests itself hereon is, *who* are the foremost in asserting the difference of keys? Are they the singers and violinists; or are they the organists and piano-fortists? If they are the latter, then the whole may be suspected to be an innocent partiality, a branch of the *polypus Hagnæ*, for turning the defects of their instrument into beauties. There are some points which want settling also, before issue can fairly be joined. If the key of F is "rich, mild, sober, and contemplative," and G "gay and sprightly;"—when F was G, as it was a hundred years ago, (see articles "Pipe" and "Tuning," Penny Cyclopædia, on the gradual elevation of "concert pitch,") was F "gay and sprightly," or "rich, mild, sober, and contemplative"?!" Temperament then is the cause of the "complexion" of keys. If any one desire to put this question to careful tests, he should first ascertain upon what system the instrument on which he experiments was "tempered," and then compare the amount of flattening or sharpening of intervals in the different keys according to the method described in the article "Tuning," Penny Cyclopædia, page 357. "The fact long practically known to musicians, though not carried into its consequences, of the duplicity of the dissonances (*ray* and *te*, page 40)—and the sharpness and vigour given by making the distinction between the great and small tone in those and other places—are more than sufficient to account for any variety. The comma is about one-third of the smallest simple interval in the scale, which is that between the major and minor thirds, sixths, &c. (chromatic part-tone); and if an engraver were to maintain

U

that rubbing down the prominences of his en- | in their dread of puzzle, is done by the musi-
graving by a third part in one place or in another | cians." (Review of Gardener's Music of Nature,
was a matter of indifference, he would do what, | in the Westminster Review.)

NOTICE TO THE TEACHER. The pupils should now sing the following tunes,
in School Music, (not containing accidentals,) which are not printed among the
Solfa Exercises. Let them begin at the beginning and go on steadily to the
very end, never leaving a tune till it is perfectly and familiarly learnt. The
taste is not to be cultivated nor skill in reading music maintained by singing
only a few "old favourites." There must be constant progress, some stimulus of
novelty, and a sustained exercise of mind.

ADAIR, *Sch. Mus.* 44.—*Song tune.* I'm but a stranger here, *Sch. Songs,* 55.
BAVARIAN, 79.—*Song tune.* . . . I like little pussy, 132.
BLACKSMITH, 81.—*Song tune.* . . As oft in my smithy, 145.
CALAH'S CHANT, 41 . . . . . . Bless the Lord, O my soul, 41.
CANAAN, 68. . . . . Oh! what has Jesus done for me, 67.
CAVERSHAM, 123.—*Old English.* . Be you to others kind and true, 169.
CHEERFULNESS, 88.—*Song tune.* . Away with needless sorrow, 142.
CYPRUS, 111.—*Song tune.* . . . . Turn, turn thy hasty foot aside, 128.
DOXOLOGY, 6. . . . . Glory, honour, praise and power, 6.
EDMESTON, 85. . . . . God entrusts to all, 92.
GERMAN HYMN, 11.—*Pleyel.* . . 'Tis religion that can give, 29.
GRAND CHANT, 39. . . . . God is our refuge and strength, 39.
GREEK AIR, 25. . . . . I think, when I read that sweet story of old, 15.
GLADNESS, 113.—*Song tune.* . . . Behold a little baby boy, 124.
GLORY, 12. . . . . Around the throne of God in heaven, 2.
HOPE, 16.—*Song tune.* . . . . . . How pleasant is the dawn, 12.
INDIAN AIR, 45. . . . . There is a happy land, 71.
LANG SYNE, 103.—*Song tune.* . . A captain forth to battle went, 137.
LEYBURN, 114.—*Old English.* . . Hurrah! hurrah! for England! 146.
MASBURY, 110.—*Old English.* . . We won't give up the bible, 149.
MILAN, 24. . . . . For a season called to part, 5.
MORNING LIGHT, 86.—*Old Eng.* Up in the morning's cheerful light, 139.
MORNINGTON'S CHANT, 38. . . . God be merciful unto us and bless us, 38.
MOSS LANE, 117.—*Old English.* . Little children, love each other, 107.
NATIONAL ANTHEM, 97. . . . . . God bless our native land, 148.
NORWAY, 104.—*Norwegian.* . . . Our fathers were high-minded men, 151.
NORTHGATE, 26. . . . . How glorious is our heavenly King, 11.
OLD ENGLAND, 107.—*Old Eng.* . Hurrah! hurrah! for England! 146.
OLD FRIEND, 77.—*Scottish.* . . . My old friend, he was a good old friend, 12
ORCHARDLEIGH, 100.—*Old Eng.* I'm very glad the spring is come, 155.
PILOT, 48.—*Song tune.* . . . . . Good Daniel would not cease to pray, 51
PORTUGUESE HYMN, 71. . . . . . The spacious firmament on high, 84.
RAINY DAY, 108.—*Song tune.* . . The rain is falling very fast, 141.
RESOLUTION, 91.—*Song tune.* . . Begone dull sloth, 166.
SPANISH CHANT, 29.—*Song tune.* Far, far o'er hill and dale, 163.
TIVERTON, 60. . . . . When daily I kneel down to pray, 78

On commencing a tune, let the teacher ask his class—"What is the key note?" * "How do you know it?" * "What is the first note? * —note two? * —three? * —four? * &c., to the end of the tune. Then, when a pupil has pitched the key note, let the exercise be solfaed, figured, and sung to words.

APPENDIX TO SECTIONS VIII AND IX.

OF "ACCIDENTAL" FLATS AND SHARPS.—RULES FOR RECOGNISING THE NOTES OF TRANSITION TU AND FI, THE DISTINGUISHING NOTES OF MINOR KEYS BAH, NE, NI, AND NU, AND CHROMATIC NOTES.

Of what key is TU the distinguishing note? [The TE of the SOH (dominant) KEY.] What note of the old key does it displace, and what position does it hold in relation to the displaced note? [It displaces FAH, and is about half a tone above it.] Of what key is FI the distinguishing note? [The FAH of the FAH (subdominant) KEY.] What note of the previous key does it displace, and what position does it hold in relation to that note? [It displaces TE, and is about half a tone lower.] What is the use and position of BAH? [It is used, though very seldom, in minor tunes, ascending, instead of FAH, and is about half a tone above it.] What is the use and position of NE? [It is frequently used in minor tunes, ascending, instead of SOH, and is about half a tone above it.] What are NI and NU, and their positions? [NI is the NE, in the minor, of the FAH (subdominant) KEY, and is about half a tone above DOH. NU is the NE, in the minor, of the SOH (dominant) KEY, and is about half a tone above RAY.] What is a chromatic note, and how is it expressed in our solfa notation? [SECTION viii. 6.]

1. All notes which differ from the ordinary notes of the key are distinguished in the Old Notation by flats, sharps, or "naturals," placed immediately before them, and are known by the common name of "accidentals." They are not however truly accidental, for each one has a distinct musical character and a special purpose, as will appear from the previous sections. It is important, then, that the pupil, when he sees the dumb sign of flat or sharp, should be able to discern its meaning, and to tell whether it indicates a transition of the whole music into this or that related key, with such or such a peculiar effect, or merely a chromatic variation without changing the key.

2. The note TU (Sec. viii. 1, 2,) being substituted for FAH of the previous key, and being about half a tone above it, is represented by a note in the place of FAH, with a sharp before it. It is often called the "sharp fourth." See fig. 25, and "School Music," 7, 22, 61, &c.

(25.)

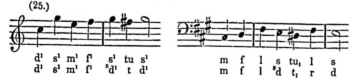

d¹ s¹ m¹ f¹   s¹   tu s¹
d¹ s¹ m¹ f¹   ˢd¹   t   d¹

m   f   l   s   tu, l   s
m   f   l   ˢd t,   r   d

In tunes which have flats in the signature, TU is represented by a note in the place of FAH, with a mark called a "natural" before it, which neutralizes the previous flat, (the last flat to the right is always on FAH) and so answers the purpose of a sharp. See fig. 26, and "School Music," 9, 10, 18, 21, 63, and bass of 89.

(26.)
d f m tu₁ s l tu₁ s
d f ᵐl₁ t₁ d r t₁ d

(27.)
m f r m tu₁ s f m
m f r ᵐl₁ t₁ ᵈs f m

2. The "natural" indicates the removal of some previous flat or sharp, and the restoration of the note before which it is placed to its position in the (so called) "natural" key. It thus sharpens a note previously flat, and flattens a note previously sharp.

3. The power of the "accidental" sharps, flats, or naturals, extends to any notes similarly placed in the after part of the same measure (or bar), even when the sign is not repeated, but no further. Hence the necessity for putting a flat before the returning FAH in fig. 27. It would not have been required if there had been a bar between it and the previous TU. Hence also it was unnecessary to repeat the sharp in "School Music," 7. In "School Music," 93, the "natural" (performing the same office) is *not* repeated before the second TU in each measure.

4. Accidentals are, however, frequently placed before notes where they are not absolutely needed, especially in cases where the composer fears that the singer or player might be in danger of mistake. Thus in "School Music," 25, towards the close of the tune, a "natural" is placed before FAH, though it was already "natural," because TU had just been heard in the bass, and the composer feared lest the ear should lead us to sing TU in the air. See also the "second" of "School Music," 110. In "School Music," 37, the flat is placed on the "returning FAH," even when two bars have intervened between it and the TU. See also "School Music," 42, 80, 83, 89, 124, 125, and the bass of 67. However useful this practice in helping bad players, it is a frequent annoyance to the singer in his early attempts, alarming him by the appearance of difficulty where there is none.

5. The note FI (Sec. viii. 3,) being substituted for TE of the previous key, and being about half a tone below, is indicated by a note in the place of TE, with a flat before it. It is frequently called the "flat seventh." See fig. 28, and "School Music," 2, 4, 18, 31, 72, 93, 108.

(28.) KEY E♭.
d t₁ d d¹ fi l s
d t₁ d ᵈs f m r

(29.) KEY E.
d t₁ d d¹ fi l s
d t₁ d ᵈs f m r

In tunes, which have sharps in the signature, a "natural" effects the same purpose as the flat in other cases. It removes the sharp, (the last sharp to the right is always on TE) and so changes TE into FI. See fig. 29, and "School Music," 36, 57, 68, 70.

6. BAH, being used instead of FAH, and about half a tone above it, is represented, like TU, by a note in the place of FAH, with a sharp, or, in flat keys, a "natural," before it. Some treat it as the same thing as TU. It is commonly called the "sharp sixth (reckoning from LAH,) of the minor key." See fig. 30. There is no example in " School Music."

7. NE, being used instead of SOH, and about half a tone above it, is represented by a note in the place of SOH, with a sharp, or, in keys with three or more flats in the signature, a "natural" before it. It is commonly called the "sharp seventh (reckoning from lower LAH), of the minor key." See fig. 30, and "School Music," 121, 122.

(30.)

l   m   bah ne   l   m   l   l ne bah ne   l

8. NI, being about half a tone above the SOH of its own key, which corresponds with DOH in the original key, is represented by a note in the place of DOH, with sharp or natural before it as the case may require. It is not of infrequent occurrence in minor tunes. See fig. 31, and "School Music," 83, in the "second."

9. NU, being about half a tone above the SOH of its own key, which corresponds with RAY in the original key, is represented by a note in the place of RAY, with sharp or natural before it as the case may require. It is seldom used. See fig. 31. There is no example in " School Music."

(31.)

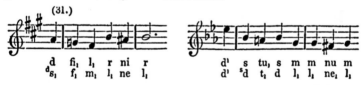

d   fi₁   l₁   r   ni   r   d¹   s   tu₁   s   m   m   nu   m
d s₁   f₁   m₁   l₁   ne   l₁   d¹   s̶d   t₁   d   l₁   l₁   ne₁   l₁

10. Chromatic notes (Sec. viii. 6,) are expressed by the note from which they spring, with a flat, sharp, or "natural" before it. The true chromatic notes (those which produce the chromatic effect), are preceded by the notes from which they spring. See fig. 33, and "School Music," 11, 97, 122, (in bass SOH SOI LAH)—4, 6, 25, 43, 115, (in bass FAH FOI SOH).

(32.)

d   t₁   tow₁   l₁   s   tu₁   f   m   d   doi   r   m   mow   r
s̶d   t₁   tow₁   l₁

11. In consequence of the attempt of the Old Notation to combine the

expression of absolute with relative pitch, (See p. 138, 141) and to mingle, for this purpose, the *symbolic* notation of flats, sharps, and "naturals," with the *pictorial* notation of the staff, several difficulties arise in connection with the subject of this section. For instance:—

How shall we express the note NE in the key of E? The answer is—By putting a sharp on B, which is the SOH of that key. But, is not B SHARP regarded by the learner (and described by many teachers) as the same thing as C NATURAL, and will not this cause a puzzle? Yes, it is the misfortune of the notation to do so. But there are two reasons why C NATURAL would not be correct; first, because it would not indicate the note (SOH), *instead of which* the NE was used (see above 7), and secondly, because the real position of NE is only a *chromatic part-tone* (three degrees, p. 40, 52), above B (SOH), and not a *tonule* (five degrees), as the C NATURAL would make it. Again :—

How shall we express NE in the keys of B and F˙SHARP, or TU in the key of F SHARP, for the note which we would sharpen is already sharpened in the signature? May we use the (so called) "natural" note above? No. Reasons, corresponding to those given in the last case, compel us to invent a new symbol called a *double sharp*. This, placed before the note which would have been SOH, indicates the origin of the NE, and shows more accurately its position. See fig. 34. Again :—

How shall we express a chromatic sharp when the note has been sharpened before in the signature, or a chromatic flat when the note has been flattened before in the signature? For these purposes we shall require, in addition to the double sharp already mentioned, a *double flat.* See fig. 34. These double ♭harps and flats are also needed on other occasions.

(33.)

l₁ ne₁ l₁ d r roi m   s sow f m

12. When the pupil has carefully studied each "accidental," as given above —seeking to appreciate its peculiar mental effect—to know its exact position in relation to the notes of the Common Mode—and to mark the various forms in which it is clothed (if not disguised) by the Old Notation—he should be able to answer for himself the following questions.

When the note that would be TE is lowered, by flat or natural, what does it indicate? FI—the "returning FAH" after a previous TU—or, if TE immediately precede, the chromatic TOW.

When the note that would be SOH is raised, by sharp or natural, what does it indicate? NE—or, if SOH immediately precede, the chromatic SOI.

When the note which would be FAH is raised, by sharp or natural, what does it indicate? TU—the "returning TE" after a previous FI—in minor tunes BAH —or, with FAH preceding, the chromatic FOI.

When the note which would be RAY is raised, by sharp or natural, what does it indicate? NU—or, with RAY preceding, the chromatic ROI.

When the note that would be DOH is raised, by sharp or natural, what does it indicate? NI—or, if DOH precede, the chromatic DOI.

How do you distinguish the chromatic note? By its being immediately preceded by that from which it springs. SOI might be called NE, but when preceded by SOH, it has a different effect on the mind from NE, and therefore should be distinguished. So also with FOI and TU.

When these points have been once thoroughly *understood*, the pupil will find little difficulty in recognising the *ordinary* "accidentals" as he comes upon them. Extraordinary accidentals may still occur, which it is difficult to decipher from the signs of the Old Notation, and, perhaps, difficult to explain on the principles of music.

PLACES
OF THE
ACCIDENTALS.

..— DOH
.
.
.
.— TE

FI —.
.
.
..— LAH
.
.
NE —.
.
..— SOH
.
TU —.
.
.
:.— FAH
.
..— ME
.
NU —.
.
..— RAY
.— r'
.
NI —.
.
..— DOH

The teacher should lead the people to notice, that the sharp used to represent TU is precisely the same which would occur, next in order, in the development of "sharp keys" described in the last section—and that the flat used to make FI is precisely that which would occur, next in order, in the series of "flat keys" there mentioned.

It is interesting to study the precise place of these accidentals in relation to the notes of the Common Mode. The proximate scale of fifty-three degrees (p. 40,) enables us to do so easily. Let the pupil compare the following remarks with the scale at the side.

The position of FI must be reckoned from the level of FAH in the original key, for FAH is its DOH, and it must be the same distance (twenty-two degrees) above FAH that FAH is above its own DOH. This will place it a chromatic flat, of four degrees, below TE. The chromatic note TOW would hold the same position.

The place of NE must be measured from LAH; it bears the same relation to LAH which TE bears to DOH. It is therefore a tonule, or five degrees, below LAH—which makes it a chromatic sharp, of four degrees, above SOH. The chromatic SOI would occupy the same position.

The place of TU must be measured from SOH, for it is the TE of the SOH key, and therefore a tonule, or five degrees, below SOH, and a chromatic sharp above FAH. The chromatic FOI would occupy the same position. BAH, (the sharp sixth of the minor) if it is designed to correspond with LAH, as NE does with TE, must be one degree lower.

The place of NU must be measured from SOH. It is a tonule below the LAH of the SOH key. This will make it a tonule, or five degrees, below ME, or a chromatic sharp, of three degrees, above RAY. The chromatic ROI would hold the same position.

The place of NI must be measured from FAH. It is a tonule below the LAH of the FAH key. The LAH of the FAH key will be (five and nine, or) fourteen degrees below FAH, or one degree below the ordinary RAY, and on the same level with that *grave* form of RAY (r', p. 40,) which is commonly used in minor tunes. See Dr. Crotch quoted page 66. This will make NI a tonule lower than the grave form of RAY, or a chromatic sharp, of three degrees above DOH. The chromatic DOI would hold the same position in minor tunes, and would be a degree higher when the ordinary RAY is used.

This examination will lead us to notice that the symbols used for "flat" and "sharp" represent, in each of the above instances, an interval at least one degree less than half a tone. The interval is sometimes three and sometimes four degrees. It is called a chromatic part-tone. It is also evident that the flats in the signature of keys (being nothing but so many FI s,) and the sharps (being nothing but so many TU s,) have the same meaning. So that, although the *terms* flat and sharp may sometimes be used, especially in connection with tempered instruments, to represent the tonule of five degrees, the *symbols* as found in music always represent the chromatic part-tone of three degrees or four according to the size of the tone from which it is taken. It is a strange proof of the confusion which Temperament and the Old Notation have introduced into the musical understandings of men, that some of the best musicians are still disputing the point whether the flat and sharp represent an interval greater or less than half a tone. On one point however all good musicians are agreed, *that the sharp of a given note and the flat of that a tone above it are not the same sound,* as the piano would teach us. We cannot pass this section without noticing the very *equivocal* import of the signs of the Old Notation. The chief excellence of a language, or of a scientific notation, (those of arithmetic and algebra, for example,) is to give a distinct term or sign for each distinct thing, and not to confuse the learner with several signs for the same thing, or with the same sign for several things. Now, the Old Notation of music is so far removed from this excellence that it requires some other notation, like that we have adopted, before it can be easily interpreted, or made plain to the learner. The notes TU and NE, for instance, which have each their distinct position in reference to the Common Mode, and their distinct recognisable character and mental effect, and which should, therefore, have had their distinct, exclusive, and invariable marks—may be found sometimes on one part of the staff and sometimes on another, sometimes clothed in a sharp, sometimes cloaked in a "natural," and sometimes disguised by a double sharp! On the other hand, the second line of the staff, for instance, which, being distinctly marked to the eye, should have one distinct, exclusive, and uniform meaning, sometimes represents a certain pitch of note, called G, sometimes the pitch, which is a part-tone above G, and sometimes that which is a part-tone below! The same line sometimes carries the governing note of the tune, sometimes the weeping note LAH, sometimes the piercing note TE, &c., and there is nothing in the look of the notes to show this distinction, which is the greatest distinction in music! Again, the symbol "sharp," though it is uniform in indicating a chromatic part-tone above some supposed note, is sometimes employed to distinguish one kind and character of note, and sometimes another, and very often it is used when no new note is to be distinguished at all. The reader will readily discover many other examples of equivocal meanings in the Old Notation.

In connection with the "minor" use of the Common Mode, mention may be made of what are called the "Ancient Modes." The student will

be surprised to find that these "modes" are simply "fragments," as Mr. Graham has expressed it, of the one Common Mode of all nations and ages. As described in the "Parish Choir," page 170, they resolve themselves into the following forms of the Common Mode, the tonules (semi-tones,) always remaining between ME FAH, and TE DOH, and being separated by three tones as you reckon one way, and by two tones as you reckon the other.

AUTHENTIC DORIAN	= r	mf	s	l	td¹	r
PLAGAL DORIAN	= l₁	t₁d	r	mf	s	l
AUTH. PHRYGIAN	= mf	s	l	td¹	r¹	m¹
PLAG. PHRYGIAN	= t₁d	r	mf	s	l	t
AUTH. LYDIAN	= f	s	l	td¹	r	mf
PLAG. LYDIAN	= d	r	mf	s	l	td¹

In a similar manner the MIXO-LYDIAN commences on SOH, its plagal on DOH—the ÆOLIAN begins on LAH, its plagal on ME—the IONIAN on DOH, and its plagal on SOH.

Is it not surprising that these should be treated as distinct modes? Is the arrangement of the tonules (semitones,) different? Some strangely imagine that it is, but any one can see that the tonules are always at the same distance from one another, through all these modes, being separated by three tones reckoning one way, and by two tones reckoning the other way, just as they are in the Common Mode! Is the character and mental effect of the notes changed? No; begin on what note you please, and end where you please in the Common Mode, and DOH will still be the "strong" note, LAH the "piercing" note, LAH the "weeping" note, &c. If they had given us a scale, with its tonules four tones apart one way, and one tone the other, and its notes correspondingly altered in effect, then we should have had a new mode. But these are only different octaves of melody taken from the same scale. They differ only as melodies. Dr. Gauntlett (in Preface to Comprehensive Tune Book,) gives for illustration tunes which lie within the particular compass, and commence or end with the notes above named. No doubt there are tunes distinguished by the peculiar use of certain notes and of a certain campass, as "Scots wha ha" is noted for its use of SOH, and as all "minor tunes" are marked by the predominance of LAH. We may have SOH tunes or RAY tunes as well as LAH tunes. But why make a separate *mode* for each, and give them such grand titles?

NOTICE TO THE TEACHER. The pupil should now be exercised day by day in copying from the Old Notation into the New, and from the New Notation into the Old. This will give the clearest insight into the character of any given piece of music. It would be well if every tune could be copied before it is sung. The pen is a wonderful teacher. The following hints may be useful.

IN COPYING FROM THE OLD NOTATION INTO THE NEW, you must first ask yourself, "Which is the highest "part" in this music?" for that must be written on the highest line in our notation. The clefs *ought* to inform you on this point—the G clef being adapted to the highest voices—the C clef on the second or third line to the second treble or alto (and contra-alto) voices—the C clef on the fourth line to the tenor—and the F clef to the bass. But the "inner parts," the second treble or alto and tenor, are now frequently written with the G clef, and the former is sometimes written on the higher, and sometimes on the lower, part of the staff. Where these variations are made, the names of the "parts" are usually given at the beginning of the book.

You must next ask yourself, "What is the Measure," that you may mark your Solfa Music Paper with the proper accents. The "time signatures," which should assist you, are often very indefinite. But the *upper* figure in the figured time signatures will sometimes be of use, in telling you how many accents there are in the measure. The lower figure is of no use, for it matters not to you whether the minim, the crotchet, or the quaver, is made to represent the aliquot. The safest way of ascertaining the real measure is to sing a phrase or two, and let your ear judge. This done, you will inquire—"What is the pitch of the key note?" The rules given at the close of the last section will easily help you to this. You will write the key in the signature or title.

You will now wish to decipher the solfa name of each note, and its length in relation to the "pulses" or accents of the measure. The first note is usually DOH, ME, or SOH. The length of notes you will easily find when you have noticed what note (crotchet, minim, &c.) is used for the aliquot. If the minim correspond with an aliquot of the measure, a dotted minim will be a pulse-and-a-half note, a crotchet a half-pulse note. If a crotchet is the standard aliquot, a minim will be a two-pulse note, a quaver a half-pulse note, and a dotted quaver a three-quarter-pulse note, &c. See p. 136, 13, 14.

IN COPYING FROM THE NEW NOTATION INTO THE OLD, you will first consider what "part" you are about to copy that you may choose your clef accordingly. The parts for the highest voices are always written highest in our notation, and you will usually find the parts named either in the title of the tune or at the beginning of the book. I would recommend you to use the *proper* clefs, as stated above. See also p. 138, 139.

You will next observe what is mentioned in the title for the pitch of the key note, and put your flats or sharps into the signature accordingly. See p. 143, 144.

"What is the Measure?" will be your next question. This you will *see* at once, by the accent marks. Remember that wherever there is a strong accent you must place, in the Old Notation, a bar: the other accents are not marked in the Old Notation. You are earnestly recommended to take always the crotchet as your standard aliquot, (see p. 136,) and then your "Time Signature" for the binary measure will be "Two, Four"—for the quaternary "Four, Four"—for the trinary "Three, Four"—and for the senary "Six, Four." See p. 137.

You will then, having constant regard to the place of your key note, write the notes of the tune, guided by your previous practice and the rules given p. 133, 134, 135. The rules given p. 147, &c., will guide you when you come to such notes at TU, FI, FOI, NE, &c.

The following tunes from School Music should now be learnt.

X

EXAMINATION OF PUPILS ON THE OLD NOTATION.

SECTION II.

1. What do you mean by the "Old Notation?"
2. What is the aim of the Old Notation?
3. Describe the staff. What is a degree? and how are the degrees named?
4. What is a leger line? How are notes represented?
5. What is the pictorial defect of the staff?

The want of a fixed place for DOH and a correct representation of tonules.

6. Draw a staff; make a square note for DOH on the third line; and write the following notes on the staff d r m f f m r d, d t₁ l₁ s₁ s₁ l₁ t₁ d.

Write the same, taking the third *space* for the place of DOH.

Write the following notes on the staff with DOH on the second line, and then write them with DOH on the second space. d t₁ l₁ t₁ d r m f, s l t d¹ t l t d¹.

SECTION III.

1. How many accents does the Old Notation mark? and how does it do so?
2. Explain the words "bar," "measure."
3. Write the first Solfa Exercise, with the proper bars, making a square note for DOH in the first space. Write it also with DOH on the second line.
4. Keeping the place of DOH in your eye, how would you from that recognise at sight ME or SOH?
5. How do you recognise replicates?

Write the third and fourth Solfa Exercise on the staff, first with DOH in the first space, and then with DOH on the second line.

6. How do you recognise at sight the lower SOH?

Write the following on the staff, making DOH (a square note) on the second line. Then write it with DOH in the third space. | d :s | d :s₁ | s₁ :d | s : | m :d | t₁ :s₁ | d :t₁ | d

7. What are the rules for distinguishing the upper and the lower FAH on the staff?

Write the following on the staff, both with DOH on the third line and with DOH in the second space. | d :m | f :r | d :t₁ | l₁ :d | f₁ :s₁ | d : | d :f | l :s | d :t₁ | h :f₁ | s₁ :s₁ | d

8. How do you recognise "thirds" on the staff?

Repeat a succession of thirds *upwards* from DOH—from RAY—from TE. And downwards from DOH—from RAY—from TE.

Write the following in three different positions on the staff. | d :m | s :t | d¹ :l | f : | t₁ :s₁ | t₁ :r | f :l | s :t₁ | d

SECTION IV.

1. Write from memory the table of symbols representing the length of sounds.
2. Write from memory the table of symbols representing the length of pauses.
3. In what respect do these symbols show the length of time?
4. What relation do these symbols hold to the aliquot parts, or beats, of the measure?
5. Describe two ways in which the rate of movement is indicated.
6. What is the proposal concerning a standard aliquot and the naming of notes?
7. What are the "time signatures" intended to indicate?

Mention the different and contradictory meanings ascribed to the plain and the barred C.

In figured "time signatures," what does the upper figure show?—the lower?

What figures would be put for a Binary Measure with a minim as the aliquot?—with a crotchet as the aliquot?

What figures would represent a Senary Measure with a quaver as the aliquot?—with a crotchet ditto?

What is the signature for a Trinary Measure with a minim? and what with a crotchet as the aliquot?

What is the signature for a Quaternary Measure with a crotchet? and what with a minim for the aliquot?

Put the time signatues to tunes 1, 4, 6, 8, 5, 19, 2, 16, 18, 30, 35, 44, 49, 79, 84, 25, 85, 95, 96, in "School Music."

What are the three meanings of the word Time in musical language? What is the full sense of the word Rhythm?

8. Do the striking and important qualities of a note depend more on its relative, or on its absolute, pitch?

For whose purposes is the notation of absolute pitch chiefly required?

Why are Clefs necessary, and what purpose do they answer?

9. Describe the C clef, and the "parts" to which it adapts the staff in its different positions.

Suppose DOH to be in the second space, what would be its pitch (o! B A G F E or D) if preceded by the C clef on the first line?—on the second line?—on the third line?—on the fourth line?

10. Explain the slur, the tie, the music repeat, the word repeat, p. 141, the double bar, the hold, the brace, the grouping of notes, the triplet, and find examples of each in "School Music."

11. Describe the G clef and its use.

When the G clef is on the second line, where is C1? B? A? F? D? C? D1? F1? A1?

12. Describe the F clef and its use.

When the F clef stands on the fourth line, where is G1? A1? B1? C? E1? D1? C1? A2?

13. Write from memory the standard scale in the G and in the F clefs.

How is the double staff formed?

Write the air of Solfa Exercise 15, in the *tenor*, the *bass*, the *alto*, and the *treble* clefs, first finding in each clef the place of the key note F or F1 or F2

SECTIONS V, VI, VII.

1. Is one key more difficult to sing than another?

Whence arises, then, the perplexity of the beginner in reference to the different keys? [From the awkwardness of the notation.]

2. How many new sounds are required to form the key of E from the standard scale?

Draw, from memory, a diagram like that on page 141, to prove the answer to the last question.

3. Explain what is meant by the "natural key."

4. Where are the tonules in the treble clef, in the natural key?

Draw, from memory, figure 19.

5. Draw, from memory, a diagram like that on page 142, and show, from it, what new note is required for the key of G.

How is the new note distinguished? and how is the staff adapted to the key of G?

Draw, from memory, the key of G on the staff, marking the places of the tonules, as on figure 20.

6. At what interval is G above C? [A fifth—including the extreme notes.]

If the note (SOH), a fifth above any key note, is taken to form a new key, where does that new key require a new note? What note of the old key has to be altered, and how? and into what note of the new key must it thus be changed?

7. Draw, from memory, as figures 21, 22, the keys of G, D, A, E, B, and F SHARP, marking the places of the tonules, and putting the sharps into the signature, in their proper place and order.

8. Show, by a diagram, what change must be made in the "natural" key, to form the key of F.

How is that change represented on the staff?

9. If the note FAH of any key is taken on which to raise a new key, where will the new key require a new note? What note of the old key has to be altered, and how? and into what note of the new key must it thus be changed?

10. Draw, without looking at the book, the five (so-called) flat keys, marking the places of the tonules, and writing the signature accurately.

11. Mention the three simplest rules for finding the key note.

To what cause is the "complexion" of keys to be chiefly attributed?

Write exercises 18, 22, 26, 27, 33, 38, 40, 45, 47, 53, 58, 62, 68, in the Old Notation, in the proper keys and clefs.

SECTIONS VIII, IX.

1. What do you mean by "accidentals," and how are they indicated?

2. How is TU represented on the staff? Write examples.

What is a "natural"?

3. How far does the power of accidentals extend?

4. In what circumstances are unnecessary sharps, flats, and naturals placed before notes?

5. How is FI represented on the staff? Write examples.

6. How does BAH appear on the staff? Write examples.

7. How does NE appear on the staff? Write examples.

8. How does NI appear on the staff? Write examples.

9. How does NU appear on the staff? Write examples.

10. How are Chromatic Notes represented on the staff? Write examples.

11. What is a double Sharp or Flat?

Show cases in which they must be used, and show why the "naturals" of the note above or below would not be correct.

12. When the note that would be TE is lowered by flat or natural, what may it represent?

What does SOH sharpened represent?
What does FAH sharpened represent?
What does RAY sharpened represent?
What does DOH sharpened represent?

NOTICE.—HALLELUJAH CHORUS. We do not despair of hearing this soul-inspiring anthem sung by a whole congregation. Let each pupil write out, into the Solfa Notation, his own "part."

HALLELUJAH CHORUS.

lujah! Hallelujah! Hallelujah! Hallelujah! for the Lord God om-ni - po-tent reign - eth. Hallelujah! Hallelujah! Hallelu-
lujah! Hallelujah! Hallelujah! Hallelujah! Hallelujah! Hallelujah! Hallelujah! Hallelujah! Hal - le-lu-
lujah! Hallelujah! Hallelujah! Hallelujah! Halle-lujah! Hallelujah! Hallelujah! Hal - le - lu - jah! Hallelujah! for the Lord
lujah! Hallelujah! Hallelujah! Hallelujah! Hallelujah! for the Lord
jah! Hallelujah! Halle-lu-jah! Hallelujah! Hallelujah! Halle-lujah! Hallelujah! Hallelujah! Hallelujah! Hallelujah! Hal-lelujah! Hal-
jah! Hallelujah! Halle - lu - jah! Hallelujah! Hallelujah! for the Lord God om - ni - po - tent reign-eth. Hallelujah!
God omni - potent reign - eth. Hallelujah! Hallelujah! Hallelujah! for the Lord God om - ni - po - tent reign-eth. Hal-
God omni - potent reign - eth. Hallelujah! Hallelujah! Hallelujah! Hallelujah! Hallelujah! Hallelujah! Hallelujah! Halle-

3

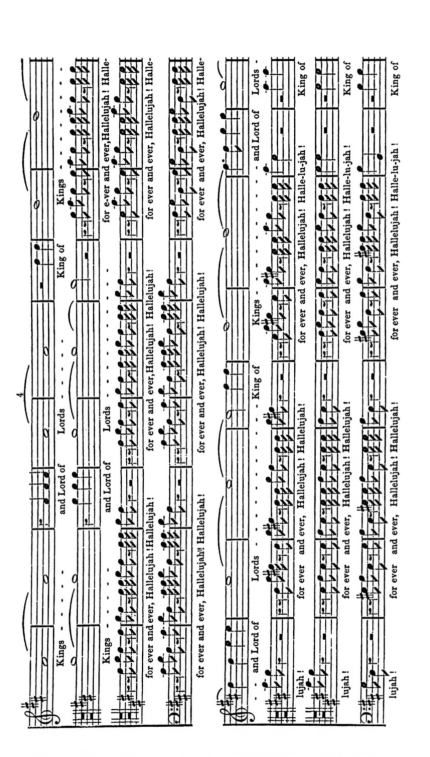

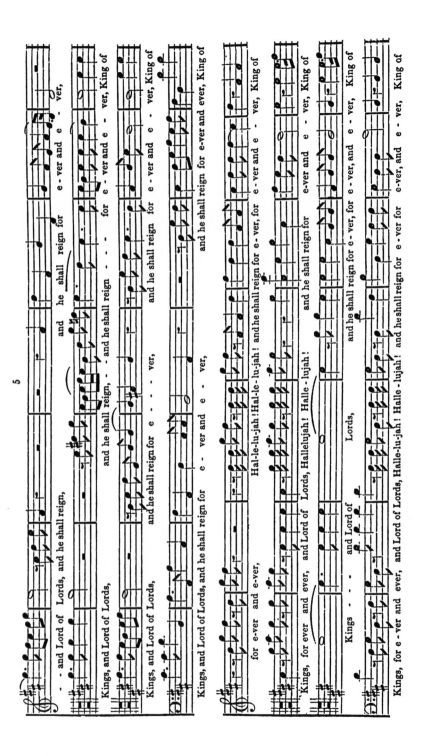

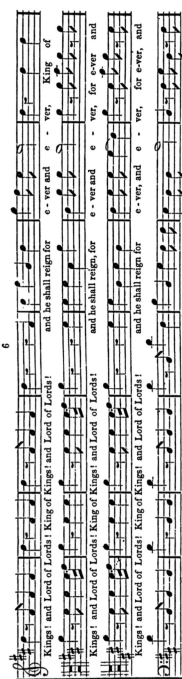

Lightning Source UK Ltd.
Milton Keynes UK
UKOW05f0216290714

235945UK00001B/56/P